ASCENT

CENTER FOR TECHNICAL KNOWLEDGE

Autodesk® Revit® 2018
BIM Management: Template and Family Creation

Learning Guide
Imperial - 1st Edition

AUTODESK.
Authorized Publisher

CONTINUING EDUCATION AIA

ASCENT - Center for Technical Knowledge®
Autodesk® Revit® 2018
BIM Management: Template and Family Creation
Imperial - 1st Edition

Prepared and produced by:

ASCENT Center for Technical Knowledge
630 Peter Jefferson Parkway, Suite 175
Charlottesville, VA 22911

866-527-2368
www.ASCENTed.com

Lead Contributor: Martha Hollowell

ASCENT - Center for Technical Knowledge is a division of Rand Worldwide, Inc., providing custom developed knowledge products and services for leading engineering software applications. ASCENT is focused on specializing in the creation of education programs that incorporate the best of classroom learning and technology-based training offerings.

We welcome any comments you may have regarding this learning guide, or any of our products. To contact us please email: feedback@ASCENTed.com.

Contents

Preface

Building Information Modeling (BIM) is an approach to the entire building life cycle. Autodesk® Revit® for Architecture, MEP, and Structure is a powerful BIM program that supports the ability to coordinate, update, and share design data with team members throughout the design construction and management phases of a building's life. A key component in managing the BIM process is to establish a company foundation for different types of projects by creating standard templates and custom family elements. Having this in place makes the process of any new project flow smoothly and efficiently.

The objective of the *Autodesk® Revit® 2018 BIM Management: Template and Family Creation* learning guide is to enable users who have worked with the software to expand their knowledge in setting up office standards with templates that include annotation styles, preset views, sheets, and schedules, as well as creating custom system, in-place, and component families.

This learning guide contains practices that are specific to each discipline.

Topics Covered

- Create custom templates with annotation styles, title blocks, and custom element types.
- Create schedules, including material takeoff schedules with formula.
- Create custom wall, roof, and floor types as well as MEP system families.
- Set up a component family file with a parametric framework.
- Create family geometry.
- Create family types.
- Modify the visibility of components and incorporate additional family items such as controls, MEP connectors, and nested components.
- Create specific families, including in-place families, profiles, annotations, and parameters.

This learning guide also contains discipline-specific practices for families, including: doors, windows, railings, pipe fittings, light fixtures, gusset plates, and built-up columns.

Note on Software Setup

This learning guide assumes a standard installation of the software using the default preferences during installation. Lectures and practices use the standard software templates and default options for the Content Libraries.

Students and Educators can Access Free Autodesk Software and Resources

Autodesk challenges you to get started with free educational licenses for professional software and creativity apps used by millions of architects, engineers, designers, and hobbyists today. Bring Autodesk software into your classroom, studio, or workshop to learn, teach, and explore real-world design challenges the way professionals do.

Get started today - register at the Autodesk Education Community and download one of the many Autodesk software applications available.

Visit www.autodesk.com/joinedu/

Note: Free products are subject to the terms and conditions of the end-user license and services agreement that accompanies the software. The software is for personal use for education purposes and is not intended for classroom or lab use.

Lead Contributor: Martha Hollowell

Martha incorporates her passion for architecture and education into all her projects, including the learning guides she creates on Autodesk Revit for Architecture, MEP, and Structure. She started working with AutoCAD in the early 1990's, adding AutoCAD Architecture and Autodesk Revit as they came along.

After receiving a B.Sc. in Architecture from the University of Virginia, she worked in the architectural department of the Colonial Williamsburg Foundation and later in private practice, consulting with firms setting up AutoCAD in their offices.

Martha has over 20 years' experience as a trainer and instructional designer. She is skilled in leading individuals and small groups to understand and build on their potential. Martha is trained in Instructional Design and has achieved the Autodesk Certified Instructor (ACI) and Autodesk Certified Professional designations for Revit Architecture.

Martha Hollowell has been the Lead Contributor for *Autodesk Revit BIM Management: Template and Family Creation* since its initial release in 2008.

In this Guide

The following images highlight some of the features that can be found in this Learning Guide.

Practice Files

To download the practice files for this student guide, use the following steps:

1. Type the URL shown below into the address bar of your Internet browser. The URL must be typed **exactly as shown**. If you are using an ASCENT ebook, you can click on the link to download the file.

   Address bar

   `http://www.ASCENTed.com/getfile?id=xxxxxxxx`

   File   Edit   View   Favorites   Tools   Help

2. Press <Enter> to download the .ZIP file that contains the Practice Files.

3. Once the download is complete, unzip the file to a local folder. The unzipped file contains an .EXE file.

4. Double-click on the .EXE file and follow the instructions to automatically install the Practice Files on the C:\ drive of your computer.

   Do not change the location in which the Practice Files folder is installed. Doing so can cause errors when completing the practices in this student guide.

   http://www.ASCENTed.com/getfile?id=xxxxxxxx

   Stay Informed!
   Interested in receiving information about upcoming promotional offers, educational events, invitations to complimentary webcasts, and discounts? If so, please visit:
   www.ASCENTed.com/updates/

   Help us improve our product by completing the following survey:
   www.ASCENTed.com/feedback
   You can also contact us at: feedback@ASCENTed.com

Link to the practice files

Practice Files

The Practice Files page tells you how to download and install the practice files that are provided with this learning guide.

Chapter 1

Getting Started

In this chapter you learn how to start the AutoCAD® software, become familiar with the basic layout of the AutoCAD screen, how to access commands, use your pointing device, and understand the AutoCAD Cartesian workspace. You also learn how to open an existing drawing, view a drawing by zooming and panning, and save your work in the AutoCAD software.

Learning Objectives in this Chapter

- Launch the AutoCAD software and complete a basic initial setup of the drawing environment.
- Identify the basic layout and features of AutoCAD interface including the Ribbon, Drawing Window, and Application Menu.
- Locate commands and launch them using the Ribbon, shortcut menus, Application Menu, and Quick Access Toolbar.
- Locate points in the AutoCAD Cartesian workspace.
- Open and close existing drawings and navigate to file locations.
- Move around a drawing using the mouse, the **Zoom** and **Pan** commands, and the Navigation Bar.
- Save drawings in various formats and set the automatic save options using the **Save** commands.

Learning Objectives for the chapter

Chapters

Each chapter begins with a brief introduction and a list of the chapter's Learning Objectives.

Side notes

Side notes are hints or additional information for the current topic.

Practice Objectives

Instructional Content

Each chapter is split into a series of sections of instructional content on specific topics. These lectures include the descriptions, step-by-step procedures, figures, hints, and information you need to achieve the chapter's Learning Objectives.

Practices

Practices enable you to use the software to perform a hands-on review of a topic.

Some practices require you to use prepared practice files, which can be downloaded from the link found on the Practice Files page.

Chapter Review Questions

Chapter review questions, located at the end of each chapter, enable you to review the key concepts and learning objectives of the chapter.

Command Summary

The Command Summary is located at the end of each chapter. It contains a list of the software commands that are used throughout the chapter, and provides information on where the command is found in the software.

Autodesk Certification Exam Appendixes

This appendix includes a list of the topics and objectives for the Autodesk Certification exams, and the chapter and section in which the relevant content can be found.

Icons in this Learning Guide

The following icons are used to help you quickly and easily find helpful information.

New in 2018	Indicates items that are new in the Autodesk Revit 2018 software.
Enhanced in 2018	Indicates items that have been enhanced in the Autodesk Revit 2018 software.

Practice Files

To download the practice files for this learning guide, use the following steps:

1. Type the URL shown below into the address bar of your Internet browser. The URL must be typed **exactly as shown**. If you are using an ASCENT ebook, you can click on the link to download the file.

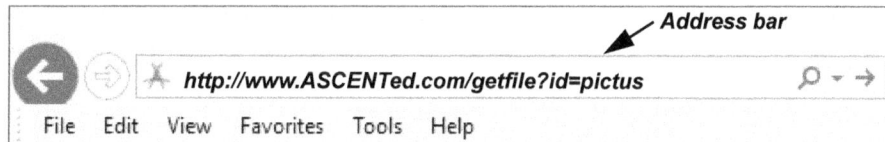

Address bar

http://www.ASCENTed.com/getfile?id=pictus

File   Edit   View   Favorites   Tools   Help

2. Press <Enter> to download the .ZIP file that contains the Practice Files.

3. Once the download is complete, unzip the file to a local folder. The unzipped file contains an .EXE file.

4. Double-click on the .EXE file and follow the instructions to automatically install the Practice Files on the C:\ drive of your computer.

   Do not change the location in which the Practice Files folder is installed. Doing so can cause errors when completing the practices in this learning guide.

http://www.ASCENTed.com/getfile?id=pictus

Stay Informed!

Interested in receiving information about upcoming promotional offers, educational events, invitations to complimentary webcasts, and discounts? If so, please visit:

www.ASCENTed.com/updates/

Help us improve our product by completing the following survey:

www.ASCENTed.com/feedback

You can also contact us at: *feedback@ASCENTed.com*

Creating Custom Templates

Custom templates can save you time and provide consistency in applying office standards when creating similar projects. Templates can include items such as levels, views, sheets, schedules, and annotation types for text, dimensions, and tags. A typical family that is added to templates is a custom title block, which helps you to ensure that sheets are created with the appropriate information.

Learning Objectives in this Chapter

- Create project templates.
- Use resource projects to store additional system families, details, schedules, and other data.
- Create standard text and dimension types for use in your projects.
- Modify callout, elevation, and section tags and specify which tags are loaded in a template.
- Create title blocks including detail lines, text, labels, symbols, regions, and revision schedules.
- Apply and set view templates to views.
- Create view templates.
- Set up Visibility/Graphic override filters for various categories of elements.

1.1 Preparing Project Templates

A project template is a file that contains information that can be used over and over to create new projects. The goal is to save time by using company standards, enabling you to concentrate on the design. For example, predefined levels (as shown in Figure 1–1 for a residential project) and the associated plan views and elevations provides a starting point for a model.

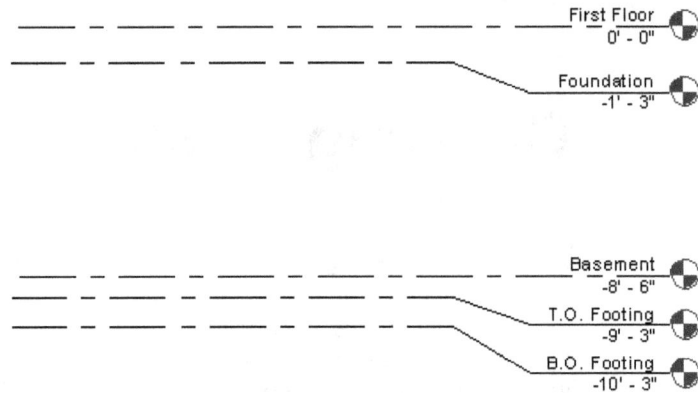

Figure 1–1

- Some items in a project template include:
    - Levels
    - Project-based settings (e.g., Project Units, Object Styles and discipline-specific settings, etc.)
    - Annotation Types
    - Sheets with associated title blocks
    - Views and View Templates
    - Schedules and Legends
    - System Families
    - Component Families

- You can have several project templates for different types of projects or building types, such as residential, commercial, and industrial.

- If you provide constant work to a specific client (e.g., a school system), you can create a template specific to their projects with associated title blocks and other information.

- You can also store items such as sheets, schedules, families, and drafting views (details) in a separate resource file and add the elements to the current project, as required.

How To: Create a Project Template File

1. In the Application Menu, expand ⬜ (New) and click 📁 (Project).
2. In the New Project dialog box, in the *Template File* area, select a template file to build from or select **None** to use a blank project file.
3. In the *Create new* area, select **Project template**, as shown in Figure 1–2.

Project template files have the extension .RTE.

Figure 1–2

4. Click **OK**.
5. Add settings, families, views, etc., as required to the new file.
6. Save the project template file.

- To save time, use an existing project or template that includes some of the basics you need rather than starting from scratch.

- If you select <None> in the Template file list, you are prompted to specify the initial unit system for the project: **Imperial** or **Metric**, as shown in Figure 1–3.

Figure 1–3

- If you need to modify the units type **UN** to open the Project Units dialog box.

Managing Settings

Most of the settings stored in a template file are found in the *Manage* tab>Settings panel, as shown in Figure 1–4. These settings include Units, Snaps, Temporary Dimensions, Object Styles (Lineweights, Line color, and Line patterns), Line Styles, Materials, Fill Patterns, etc.

Specific Structural Settings, MEP Settings, and Panel Schedule Templates are also included in this panel.

Figure 1–4

System Families in Templates

Walls, Wall Foundations, Floors, Slabs, Ceilings, and Roofs as well as Duct, Pipe, Cable Tray and Conduit types are created by duplicating an existing type and modifying the Type Properties, as shown in Figure 1–5. These are known as System Families, because they are created in the system rather than in a separate family file (component families).

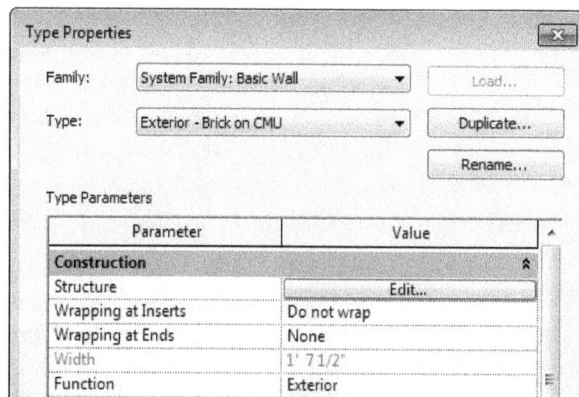

Figure 1–5

- Annotation Styles for text and dimensions are system families and are modified in Type Properties.

- System Families can be added when a project is in process, but it helps to have company standards created in the template.

- Component Families, such as furniture, trees, beams, columns, mechanical equipment, and electrical devices can be loaded directly in a template file if there are types and sizes that are used frequently. Otherwise, they can be loaded from a library or resource project as the project progresses.

- You can duplicate and modify Levels (as shown in Figure 1–6) and Grids (as shown in Figure 1–7).

Figure 1–6

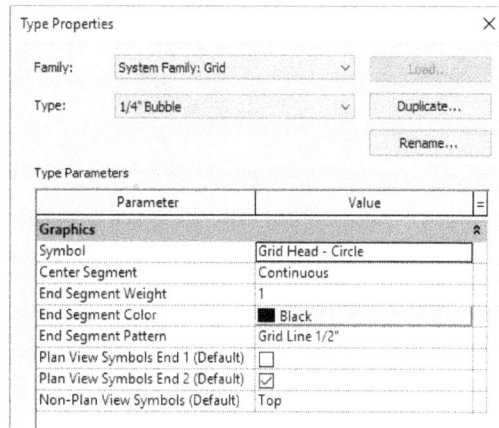

Figure 1–7

Views and Sheets

You can create standard sheets and place empty views on the sheets. They are filled in as you proceed through a project. Views can be a few basic floor and/or ceiling plans for a residential project, as shown in Figure 1–8, or a more complex mix of Mechanical, Electrical, and Plumbing categories as shown in Figure 1–9.

Figure 1–8

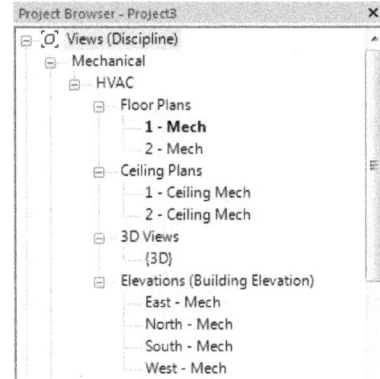
Figure 1–9

- You can create as many sheets as are typically used in a project or you can create a sheet schedule and populate it with sheet names that can be used as placeholder sheets.

- You can also copy sheets from a resource project.

Presetting a Starting View

When you create a project template or project, it can help to specify a starting view. This can be any of the standard views, such as plan, elevation, 3D view, or one that is specifically created. This is often a Drafting View (as shown in Figure 1–10), or a Legend View with information about the project or the cover sheet for the project.

New Project Name

Project Address
Project Address 2

Architect:
Structural Engineer:
MEP Engineer:
Civil Engineer:

Figure 1–10

How To: Set a Starting View

1. Set up the view or sheet that you want to use as the starting view.

2. In the *Manage* tab>Manage Project panel, click 🗐 (Starting View).

3. In the Starting View dialog box, select the view or sheet that you want to use as shown in Figure 1–11.

The Default starting view is <Last Viewed>.

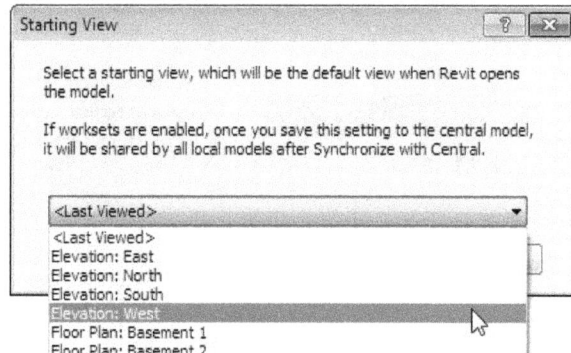

Figure 1–11

4. Click **OK**.

Setting Default Template Files

If your company uses several different templates, you can create a list that displays in the New Project dialog box, as shown in Figure 1–12. The top five templates also display on the Recent Files page.

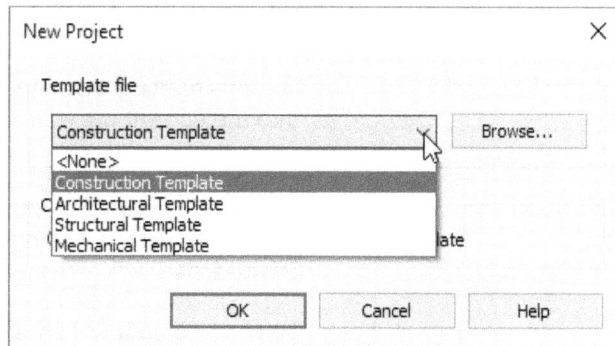

Figure 1–12

- To set the project template file list, in the Application Menu, click **Options**. In the Options dialog box, in the left pane, select **File Locations**, as shown in Figure 1–13. Specify the *Name* and *Path* for each template. Use ✛ (Add Value) to select additional templates.

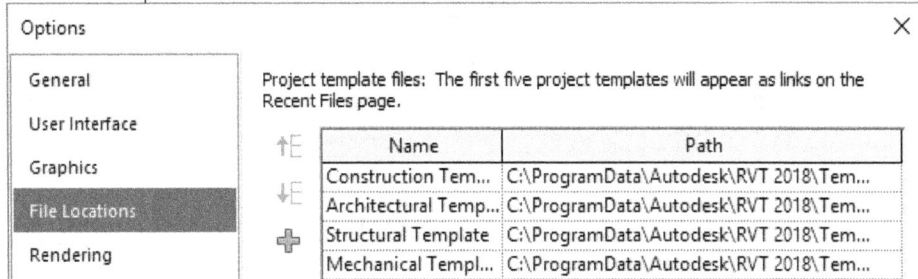

Options		✕
General	Project template files: The first five project templates will appear as links on the Recent Files page.	
User Interface		
Graphics	**Name**	**Path**
File Locations	Construction Tem...	C:\ProgramData\Autodesk\RVT 2018\Tem...
Rendering	Architectural Temp...	C:\ProgramData\Autodesk\RVT 2018\Tem...
	Structural Template	C:\ProgramData\Autodesk\RVT 2018\Tem...
	Mechanical Templ...	C:\ProgramData\Autodesk\RVT 2018\Tem...

Figure 1–13

- Use ⬆E (Move Rows Up) and ⬇E (Move Rows Down) to order the templates. Move the templates that are used most often to the top.

- If you do not require a template anymore, select it and click ▭ (Remove Value).

Using Resource Projects

You can use a template file start a project, but you might also want to have resource projects that include additional custom systems and component families, or even include pre-drawn details in logical groupings. You can then copy these elements into the current project as you need them.

- To copy drafting views (details), sheets, schedules, or reports into the current project, use **Insert Views from File**.

- To copy system families (e.g., wall, floor, duct, pipe, wire types, etc) or annotations (e.g., text and dimension styles, materials, various settings, etc.), use **Transfer Project Standards**.

- To copy component families from a resource project, use **Copy to the Clipboard** and either **Paste Aligned to Selected Levels** or **Paste Aligned to Selected Views**.

How To: Insert Views from an Existing Project

1. In the *Insert* tab>Import panel, expand ⬜ (Insert from File) and click ⬜ (Insert Views from File).
2. In the Open dialog box, select the project file you want to copy from.
3. In the Insert Views dialog box, select the views you want to insert into the current project, as shown in Figure 1–14.

Schedules are completed with the information in the current project. Sheets are added, but do not include any views.

```
Insert Views

Select drafting views, schedules, or reports to be added to the current project.
Views:                                              Preview:

Show all views and sheets                    ⌄

☑ Schedule: Area Schedule (Rentable)
☑ Schedule: Area Schedule Over 10000 SF
☐ Schedule: Brick - Material Takeoff
☐ Schedule: CMU - Material Takeoff
☐ Schedule: EIFS - Material Takeoff
☑ Schedule: Room Schedule
☑ Schedule: Room Style Schedule
☐ Sheet: A303 - Elevations - Other
☐ Sheet: A601 - Schedules
☐ Sheet: A701 - Details

        Check All          Check None

☑ Preview selection
```

Figure 1–14

4. Click **OK**. The views are added to the file.

How To: Transfer Project Standards

1. Open the project from which you want to transfer information.
2. Switch to the current project you are copying to.
3. In the *Manage* tab>Settings panel, click ⬚ (Transfer Project Standards).
4. In the Select Items To Copy dialog box, a list of the currently open projects displays. Select the file to copy from.

5. Select the items you want to copy into the current project, as shown in Figure 1–15.
   - Click **Check None** or **Check All**, as required.

Select Items To Copy

Copy from: Sample Schedules

- [ ] Analytical Link Types
- [ ] Analytical Pipe Connection Types
- [ ] Annotation Family Label Types
- [ ] Area and Volume Computations
- [ ] Arrowhead Styles
- [ ] Assembly Code Settings
- [ ] Browser Organization
- [ ] Building Type Settings
- [x] Cable Tray Settings
- [x] Cable Tray Sizes
- [x] Cable Tray Types
- [ ] Callout Tags
- [ ] Ceiling Types
- [ ] Color Fill Schemes
- [ ] Conduit Settings

Check All
Check None

OK   Cancel

Figure 1–15

6. Click **OK**.
7. If the Duplicate Types dialog box displays (shown in Figure 1–16), choose **Overwrite** or **New Only** to update the existing project.

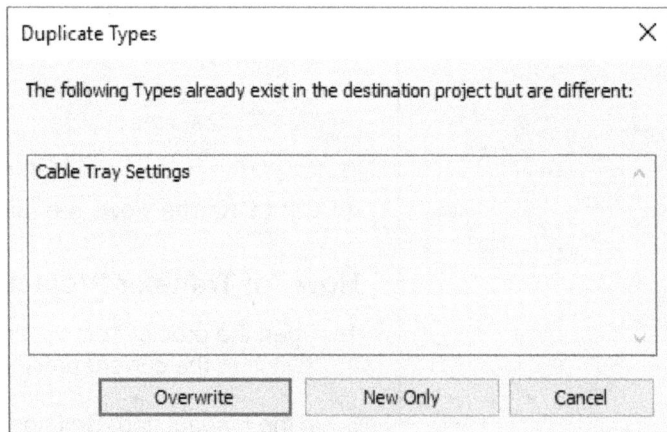

Duplicate Types

The following Types already exist in the destination project but are different:

Cable Tray Settings

Overwrite   New Only   Cancel

Figure 1–16

1.2 Customizing Annotation Types

You can customize Annotation types in your project template file including dimensions, text types, and tags, as shown in Figure 1–17.

Figure 1–17

Text, Dimensions, and Arrowheads are all system families. This means they have a standard set of parameters, which you can modify and save as a type. Callout, Section, and Elevation tags can be modified in the Autodesk Revit software. Most other tags are created using families.

Creating Text Types

Text types are used to standardize text formatting (such as the font, text height, etc.), as shown in Figure 1–18. They can be created for to both annotative text and Model Text.

Figure 1–18

- The **Text** command places text at the height you need for the final plot. The view scale controls the height of the standard text in the views.

- The **Text Size** parameter represents the height of a capital letter. (Verify that the text in projects created in earlier versions of the software displays as expected.)

- The **Model Text** command places text that is typically used on the building, such as the signage shown in Figure 1–19. Text types for Model Text should be the full height of the final element and are not affected by the view scale.

Figure 1–19

How To: Create a Text Type

1. Start the **Text** command. In Properties, click ⊞ (Edit Type) or in the *Annotate* tab>Text panel title, click ⌄ (Text Types).
   - For **Model Text** you first have to place an instance, select it, and modify the type properties.
2. In the Type Properties dialog box, click **Duplicate...**.
3. Type a new name and click **OK**.The new type is activated.
4. Modify the parameters as required for the new type, as shown for annotation text in Figure 1–20.

Type Parameters

Parameter	Value
Graphics	⌃
Color	■ Black
Line Weight	1
Background	Opaque
Show Border	☐
Leader/Border Offset	5/64"
Leader Arrowhead	Arrow 30 Degree
Text	⌃
Text Font	Arial
Text Size	1/4"
Tab Size	1/2"
Bold	☐
Italic	☐
Underline	☐
Width Factor	1.000000

Figure 1–20

5. Click **OK** to finish.

Creating Dimension Types

Dimensions are one of the more complex system families in terms of the number of parameters you can modify. They include options for the Dimension Text, Dimension Line, Tick Marks, and Witness Lines. You can specify information such as the units, color, and all of the gap sizes between elements, as shown in Figure 1–21.

Dimension Text

Dimension Line

Tick Mark

Witness Line

Set gap between witness line and reference

EQ

16' - 0"   13' - 6"

Figure 1–21

How To: Create Dimension Types

1. In the *Annotate* tab>Dimension panel, expand the Dimension panel title (as shown in Figure 1–22), and click 🔧 next to the dimension type you want to create.

You create separate types for each dimension method.

File   Architecture   Structure   Systems   Insert   Annotate   Ana

Modify   Aligned Linear Angular   🏹 Radial   🔶 Spot Elevation
                                   🔵 Diameter   🔶 Spot Coordinate
Select ▾   🏹 Arc Length   🏳 Spot Slope

Modify | 🔧 Linear Dimension Types
Properties   🔧 Angular Dimension Types   🔧 Spot Elevation Types
            🔧 Radial Dimension Types   🔧 Spot Coordinate Types
            🔧 Diameter Dimension Types   🔧 Spot Slope Types
            🖽   Dimension

Figure 1–22

2. In the Type Properties dialog box, click **Duplicate....**
3. Type a new name and click **OK**. The new type is activated.

Values for parameters (such as text size, witness line extension, etc.) are the actual plot size for these elements. The view scale controls how large they are in the specific view.

4. Modify the parameters as required for the new type, as shown in Figure 1–23.

Type Properties

Family:	System Family: Linear Dimension Style ▼	Load...
Type:	Diagonal - 3/32" Arial - Line Leader - Inli ▼	Duplicate...
		Rename...

Type Parameters

Parameter	Value
Graphics	
Dimension String Type	Continuous
Leader Type	Line
Shoulder Length	1/4"
Leader Tick Mark	None
Show Leader When Text Moves	Away From Origin
Tick Mark	Diagonal 3/64"
Line Weight	1
Tick Mark Line Weight	5
Dimension Line Extension	3/32"
Flipped Dimension Line Extensio	3/32"
Witness Line Control	Gap to Element
Witness Line Length	3/32"
Witness Line Gap to Element	1/16"
Witness Line Extension	3/32"
Centerline Symbol	None
Centerline Pattern	Solid
Centerline Tick Mark	Default
Interior Tick Mark	Diagonal 3/64"

| << Preview | OK | Cancel | Apply |

Figure 1–23

5. Click **OK** when you are finished.

• For Linear dimensions, you can specify a *Leader Type, Shoulder Length, Leader Tick Mark, and Show Leader When Text Moves* that is used when the text is pulled away from the dimension string. You can also specify the text inserted for **Equality Text** (the default is still EQ).

• You can specify a *Text Background* option. If you set the value to **opaque**, it automatically masks any elements behind the text. If it is set to **transparent**, anything the text overlaps is still visible.

• If you are dimensioning doors and windows by their widths rather than their centers, you can also have the opening height displayed with the dimension. Select **Show Opening Height**.

Loading Tags in a Template

Tags are families that need to be loaded into a project. Not all types of tags need to be in each project, so you can choose which ones you want to include in your templates. For example, if you are working in an architectural project, you can load tags such as the door, window, and wall shown in Figure 1–24.

Figure 1–24

How To: Specify Loaded Tags

1. In the *Annotate* tab>Tag panel, expand the panel title and click (Loaded Tags).
2. In the Tags dialog box, Use the *Filter* field to limit the types of tags you are looking for by discipline, as shown in Figure 1–25.

Some elements, such as Floors and Structural Fabric Reinforcement, have both tags and symbols. They can both be specified in this dialog box.

Figure 1–25

3. Click **Load Family...**.
4. In the Load Family dialog box, navigate to the appropriate library and folder.
5. Select the required tags and click **Open**. Hold <Ctrl> or <Shift> to select multiple tags.
6. When you have loaded all of the tags that you typically need for a project, click **OK**.

Specifying View Tags

Callout, Elevation, and Section tags can be modified to suit an office standard. The tag is actually part of a view type. For example, you can create a new Elevation view type containing a tag that displays the view name, as shown in Figure 1–26.

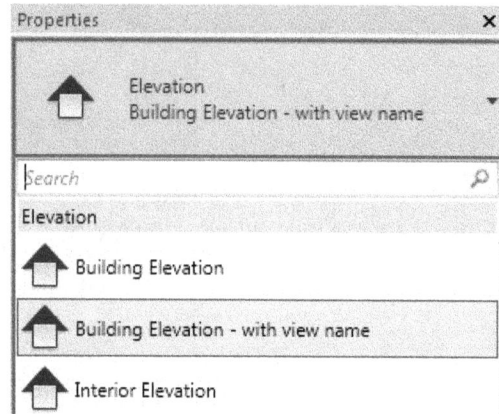

Front Elevation

Figure 1–26

How To: Create Callout, Elevation, and Section Types with Tags

1. Click ⬁ (Callout), ⬆ (Elevation), or ⬖ (Section), as required.

2. In Properties, click ⊞ (Edit Type).
3. In the Type Properties dialog box, duplicate and name the new view type, as shown for an elevation view in Figure 1–27.

Each view type has different parameters.

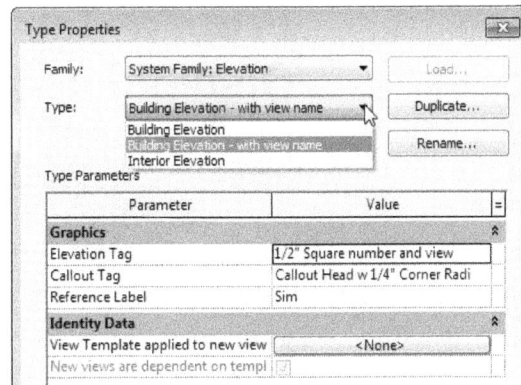

Figure 1–27

4. Beside the **Tag** parameter, click in the *Value* column and then click ⬚ (Browse).

5. In the Type Properties dialog box for the tag, select from an existing type or duplicate a type, and specify a new mark element from a list of families that have been inserted into the project, as shown in Figure 1–28.

Figure 1–28

6. Click **OK** to apply the tag type.

7. Modify the other parameters as required and click **OK** to close the Type Properties dialog box and continue using the command.

• You can also modify the tag type properties and have them ready to use when you create a new view type. In the *Manage* tab>Settings panel, expand 🔧 (Additional Settings) and click ⬠ (Callout Tags), ⬆ (Elevation Tags), or ◇ (Section Tags).

Practice 1a

Prepare Templates for All Disciplines

Estimated time for completion: 15 minutes

Practice Objectives

- Create a new project template file and specify the units and levels.
- Set up text and dimension types and load tags.

In this practice, you will create a new project template file, modify the units, snaps, temporary dimensions, and add several new levels. You will create several text types, add a dimension style that uses arrows (as shown in Figure 1–29), and load typical tags into the project template file.

1/8" Arial   *1/8" Hand*

3/32" Arial   *3/32" Hand*

1/4" Title

R 2' - 6"

78°

14' - 0"

Figure 1–29

Task 1 - Establish a project template file.

1. In the Application Menu, expand ☐ (New) and click ☐ (Project).

2. In the New Project dialog box, select an existing template file similar to your primary discipline. In the *Create New* area, select **Project template** and click **OK**.

3. In the Quick Access Toolbar, click ▦ (Save) and save the template in the practice files folder as **Midrise-Template.rte**.

4. In the *Manage* tab>Settings panel, click ▦ (Project Units) or type **UN**.

5. In the Project Units dialog box, set the *Length* and *Angle* formats as follows:

Length:	Units	Feet and Fractional Inches
	Rounding	To the nearest 1/16"
	Suppress 0 feet	Check
Angle:	Rounding	0 decimal places

6. Click **OK** to close the Units dialog box.

7. Open an elevation view. Change Level 2 to **16'-0"**.

8. In the *Architecture* or *Structure* tab>Datum panel, click
    (Level).

9. In the Options Bar, verify that **Make Plan View** is selected
    and click **Plan View Types...**

10. In the Plan View Types dialog box, select the view types you
    want to create, as shown in Figure 1–30.

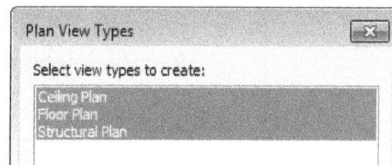

Figure 1–30

11. Add three more levels above the current levels at **12'-0"**
    apart. Add two levels below Level 1 and set them **10'-0"**
    apart. Rename them as **Basement 1** and **Basement 2**, as
    shown in Figure 1–31.

Figure 1–31

*   **MEP only:** Rename above ground levels and
    corresponding views to match the other levels in the
    HVAC sub-discipline (3 - Mech, 4 - Mech, etc) and expand
    the **???** node and select all of the new ceiling plans. In
    Properties, change the *Sub-Discipline* to **HVAC**.

Task 2 - Preset annotation types.

1. Return to the original plan view.

2. Create the following text types:

1/8" Arial	Use the default, but set the *Text Size* to **1/8"**.
1/8" Hand	Use a hand-lettering *Text Font*, such as **Comic Sans MS**, and select *Italic*.
3/32" Hand	Same as above with a *Height* of **3/32"**.
1/4" Title	Use the font of your choice, in bold.
1" Title	Duplicate **1/4" Title** and change the *Height* to **1"**.

3. Create or modify a Linear Dimension type and change the Units Format *Rounding* to the **nearest 1/8"**. Modify the angular dimension type to use arrowheads. Modify other parameters, if required.

4. Load the following tags from the Revit Library>*Annotation* folder subfolders into the discipline-specific project template:

Architecture:

Folder	Tag Name
Architectural	Casework, furniture, and furniture systems
Civil	Parking and planting

MEP:

Folder	Tag Name
Fire Protection	Sprinkler
Electrical	Lighting fixture and panel name

Structure:

Folder	Tag Name
Architectural	Wall and Floor
Structural	Select any different Structural tags you might want to use in place of those already loaded.

5. Save the project template.

1.3 Creating Title Blocks

Title blocks (as shown in Figure 1–32) contain information about the company and consultants designing the project, project information (such as project name and number), and sheet-specific information (such as sheet numbers and drawn by). They are created by sketching detail lines and adding text, symbols, and regions, as well as image files for company logos. The variable information is stored in labels.

Some of these parameters never change, some are project-specific, and some are sheet-specific.

Figure 1–32

How To: Create a Title Block

1. In the Application Menu, expand ▭ (New) and click ▭ (Title Block).

You can select from several preset sizes or create a custom size.

2. In the New Title Block - Select Template File dialog box, select a template file size from the list and click **Open**. A new family file opens and the Family tools display in the ribbon, as shown in part in Figure 1–33.

Figure 1–33

3. Add lines, filled regions, symbols, text, labels, etc., as required.
4. Save and close the file.

- If you select a template with a standard size, a rectangle of that size displays in the view.

- If you select **New Size**, a rectangle with dimensions displays. Edit the dimensions to modify the size.

- You can use dimensions to help place the elements in the title block family, they are not displayed when the title block is inserted.

Adding Labels

Labels are not just text but elements that are assigned to specific parameters and can be added to title blocks or tags. They can change without modifying the rest of the elements. For example, you would use annotation text for the words **Drawn By:** and a label for the initials of the person who did the work (by default displaying DRW in Figure 1–34), because that varies from sheet to sheet.

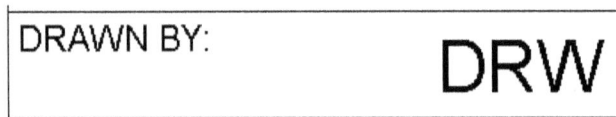

DRAWN BY: DRW

Figure 1–34

- The title block template comes with one text type and one label type already defined. You can create additional types in Properties by duplicating types. The **Text** and **Label** parameters are similar, but you must create separate types for each of them.

- Labels use Rich Text Format so that they match text notes.

Enhanced in 2018

How To: Create a Label

1. In the Family Editor, in the *Create* tab>Text panel, click
   A (Label).

2. In the *Modify | Place Label* tab>Format panel, specify the alignments: **Left**, **Center**, **Right**, **Top**, **Center Middle**, or **Bottom**, as shown in Figure 1–35.

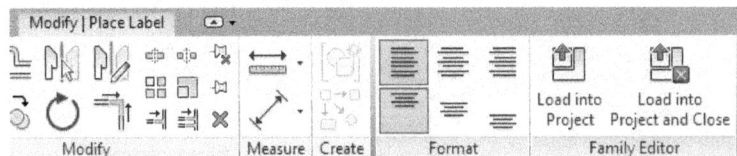

Figure 1–35

3. Click in the view window to place the label, as shown in Figure 1–36.

Figure 1–36

4. In the Edit Label dialog box shown in Figure 1–37, select a label in the *Category Parameters* list and double-click or click

   ⇥ (Add parameter(s) to label). You can select more than one by holding <Ctrl> or <Shift>.

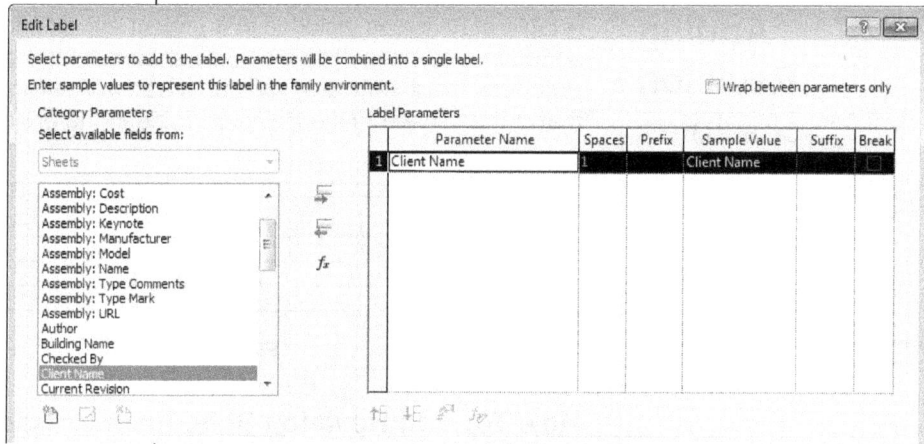

Figure 1–37

5. Enter the *Sample Value* and specify any other options, as required.

   - If you are using several parameters in one label, select **Wrap between parameters only** and **Break** (in column) options to separate them while still permitting a word wrap.

   - Click ⬚ (Add Parameter) to create a new parameter for the project.

   - Click ↑E (Move parameter up) and ↓E (Move parameter down) to reorder multiple parameters.

   - If you select a numerical parameter, click 🔧 (Edit parameter's units format) to change, if required.

   - Click *fx* (Add calculated parameter to label) to use a formula based on other parameters. See the **Advanced Schedule** options for more information on creating calculated parameters.

6. Click **OK** when you have finished editing the label.

- While placing the label, you can rotate or stretch it (as shown in Figure 1–38), or select a point for an additional label.

•DRW

Figure 1–38

- You can also rotate or stretch a label once it has been placed in the title block.

Adding Revision Schedules

A table of revisions included in a project and/or sheet is typically added to a company title block, as shown in Figure 1–39. In the Autodesk Revit software, you can create a Revision Schedule that is then linked to the Revision Table in the project.

No.	Description	Date

Figure 1–39

How To: Add Revision Schedules to Title Blocks

1. In the Family Editor, in the *View* tab>Create panel, click (Revision Schedule).
2. In the Revision Properties dialog box, select the fields you want to use. Several are already selected for you, as shown in Figure 1–40.

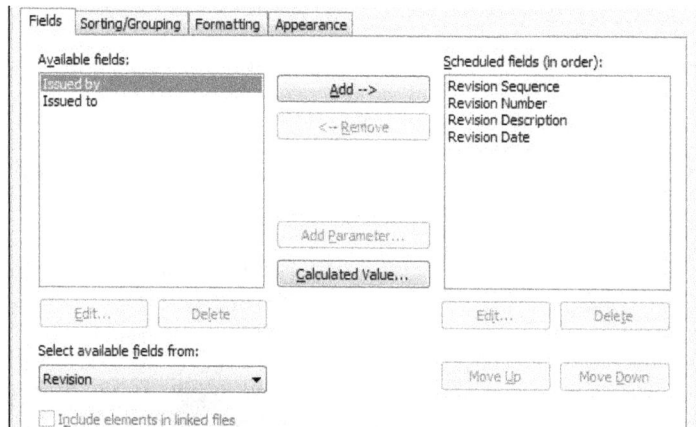

Figure 1–40

3. Modify the options in the *Sorting/Grouping* and *Formatting* tabs, as required.
4. In the *Appearance* tab, select how you want to build the schedule: from the **Top-down** or **Bottom-up**. You can also set the *Height* to **Variable** or **User-Defined**, as shown in Figure 1–41.

Figure 1–41

5. Click **OK**. The schedule view displays.
6. In the Project Browser, open the Sheet view (it has no name).
7. Drag and drop the schedule onto the sheet and modify the controls, as shown in Figure 1–42.

Figure 1–42

* In the Options Bar, you can change the *Rotation on the Sheet* to **None**, **90° Clockwise**, or **90° Counterclockwise**.

*If the height is set to **User-Defined**, an additional control is displayed at the bottom of the schedule. Use it to set the height of the schedule.*

Adding Sheets to Project Templates

You can set up project templates using the custom title block in two ways. Add all or most of the sheets typically required for a project, or create a Sheet List Schedule that can be used to automatically create sheets when they are required.

In most cases, it is best to create sheets that are always used in projects in the template and even put typical views on them, as shown in Figure 1–43. Note that the view is empty in the template, but as you draw elements in the project they automatically display in the view and on the sheet.

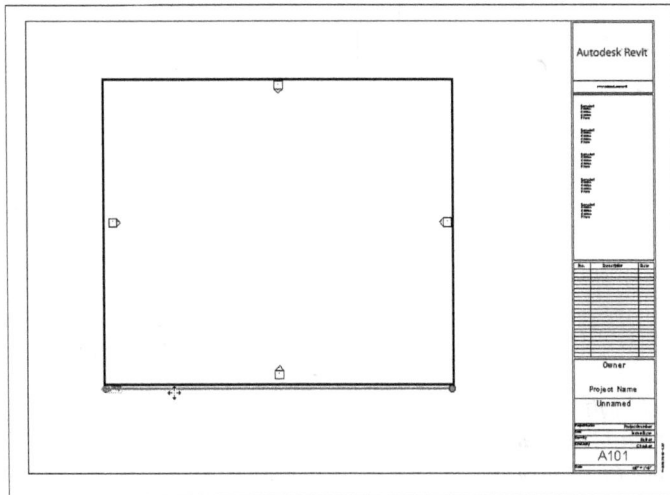

Figure 1–43

How To: Load a Title Block into a Project Template

1. Open the project template and create a sheet, if required.
2. Return to the custom title block family. In the Family Editor panel, click (Load into Project).
3. In the Load into Projects dialog box, select the project you want the title block loaded into and click **OK**. If only one project is open, it is loaded into the project automatically.
4. The title block is now available when you create a sheet.

- If the title block family is not open, select *Insert* tab>Load from Library panel and click (Load Family) to access it, or click **Load...** in the New Sheet dialog box.

Practice 1b

Create Title Blocks for All Disciplines

Practice Objectives

- Draw a custom title block including detail lines, text, labels, and a revision table.
- Set up sheets in the template using the new title block.

Estimated time for completion: 15 minutes

In this practice, you will create a new title block by adding lines, text, labels, logo, and a Revision Schedule similar to Figure 1–44. You will then load it into a project template file and create several standard sheets.

Revision Schedule		
Revision Number	Revision Description	Revision Date

First Floor Plan

Project Name
Enter address here

Site, Inc.

Date	Issue Date
Project Number	Project Number
Drawn By	Author
Sheet Number	A201

Figure 1–44

Task 1 - Create a title block.

1. In the Application Menu, expand ☐ (New) and click ▣ (Title Block).

2. In the New Title Block - Select Template File dialog box, select **D - 36 x24.rft** and click **Open**.

3. In the *Create* tab>Detail panel, click ⌐ (Line) and create lines on the inside of the existing rectangle **1/4"** away from the top, bottom, and right sides. Draw a line **1"** away on the left margin. Trim the lines as required.

4. Draw lines in the lower right corner of the title block, as shown in Figure 1–45.

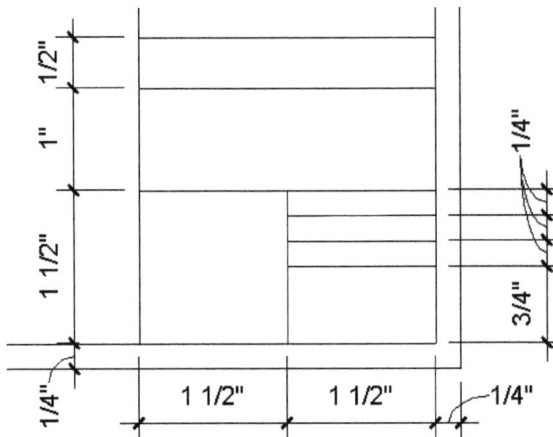

Figure 1–45

5. In the *Create* tab>Text panel, click **A** (Text).

6. In Properties, click ▤ (Edit Type) and create the following Text types:

Type Name	Font	Size	Bold	Background
Arial 1/16"	Arial	1/16"	No	Transparent
Title	Your choice	1"	Yes	Transparent
Logo	Your choice	1/4"	Yes	Transparent

7. In the *Create* tab>Text panel, click 🅰 (Label).

8. In Properties, click 🔳 (Edit Type) and create the following Label types:

Type Name	Font	Size	Bold	Background
Arial 1/8"	Arial	1/8"	No	Transparent
Arial 1/4"	Arial	1/4"	No	Transparent

9. Create a graphic and company name of your own design in the lower left box, for example Jepson+Johnson Architects, as shown in Figure 1–46. Using the following steps, add text, labels, and graphics to the title block.

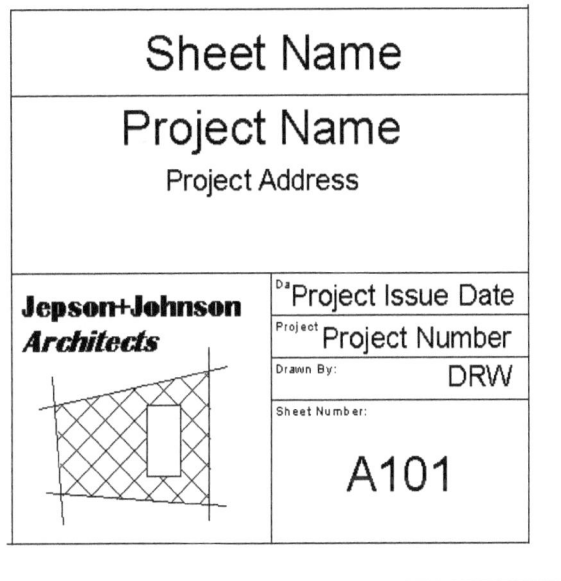

Figure 1–46

- Use 🅰 (Text) with the *text type* **Arial 1/16"** to add text in the lower right spaces for the *Date, Project Number, Drawn By*, and *Sheet Number*.

- Use 🅰 (Label) with the *label type* **Arial 1/4"** and

  ≡ (Align Center) justification to add the *Sheet Name, Project Name*, and *Sheet Number*. Move and stretch the labels to fit in the title block.

- Using the *label type* **Arial 1/8"** and ☰ (Align Center) justification, add the *Project Address* below the *Project Name*.

- Using the *label type* **Arial 1/8"** and ☰ (Align Right) justification, add the *Project Issue Date*, *Project Number*, and *Drawn By*.

- Add the **Logo** text in the box on the lower left side in the title block. Draw lines and add a filled region for a graphic logo, as required.

10. Save the title block in the practice files folder as **TBLK-D.rfa**.

Task 2 - Add a Revision Schedule.

1. In the title block Family Editor, in the *View* tab>Create panel, click 📖 (Revision Schedule).

2. In the Revision Properties dialog box, *Fields* tab, set up the fields as shown in Figure 1–47.

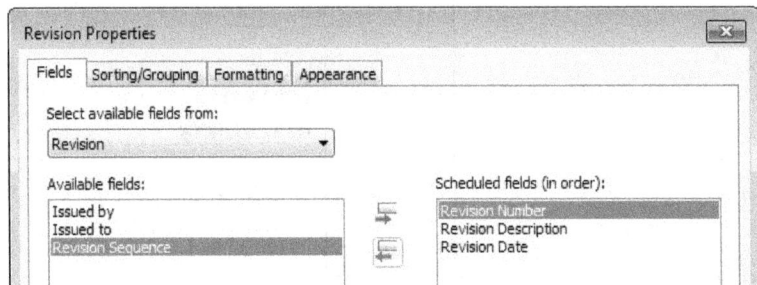

Figure 1–47

3. Accept the defaults for the *Sorting/Grouping* and *Formatting* tabs.

4. Select the *Appearance* tab and change the *Height* to **User defined**.

5. Click **OK**.

6. In the Project Browser, expand *Views (all)* to display the *Schedules* and *Sheets (all)* areas, as shown in Figure 1–48. In the *Sheets (all)* area, open the - view.

Figure 1–48

7. Drag and drop the Revision Schedule onto the sheet.

8. Move it above the sheet name and resize it to display several lines, as shown in Figure 1–49. Align it to the edge of the title block.

Figure 1–49

9. Save and close the title block.

Task 3 - Set up sheets in a project template using the new title block.

---

1. Open the project template **Midrise-Template.rte** that you created in the previous practice. If you did not complete the previous practice, open the template found in the practice files folder:

   • *Architectural*>**Midrise-Template-Architectural.rte**

   • *MEP*>**Midrise-Template-MEP.rte**

   • *Structural*>**Midrise-Template-Structural.rte**

2. In the *View* tab>Sheet Composition panel, click ▢ (Sheet).

3. In the New Sheet dialog box, click **Load...**.

4. In the Load Family dialog box, navigate to the practice files folder, select **TBLK-D.rfa** (that you just created), and click **Open**. If you did not complete the previous task, open the title block found in the corresponding practice files folder:

   - *Architectural*>**TBLK-D-Architectural.rfa**
   - *MEP*>**TBLK-D-MEP.rfa**
   - *Structural*>**TBLK-D-Structural.rfa**

5. Select the title block that you just loaded and click **OK**.

6. In the Project Browser, select the sheet and rename it as **CS000 – Cover Sheet**.

7. Using the **Title** text type, add placeholder text for the project name and address, as shown in Figure 1–50.

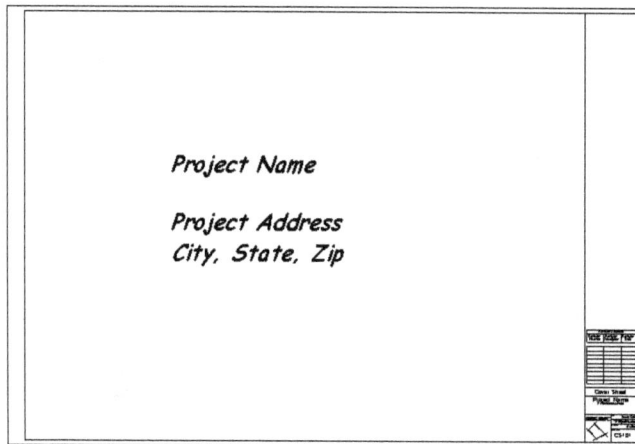

Project Name

Project Address
City, State, Zip

Figure 1–50

8. In the *Manage* tab>Manage Project panel, click ▢ (Starting View).

9. In the Starting View dialog box, select **Sheet: CS000 - Cover Sheet** as shown in Figure 1–51.

Figure 1–51

10. Create another sheet with the new title block and name it according to your discipline:
    *   **A201 – First Floor Plan**
    *   **M201 - First Floor Plan Mechanical**
    *   **E201 - First Floor Plan Electrical**
    *   **P201 - First Floor Plan Plumbing**
    *   **S201 - First Floor Plan Structural**

11. Open this sheet view. Drag the associated **Level 1** floor plan view onto the sheet, as shown in Figure 1–52.

No elements are on the view, but it acts as a placeholder on the sheet. Elements are displayed as they are drawn.

Figure 1–52

12. Save and close the template file.

1.4 Adding View Templates

View templates enable you to set the view properties and visibility options for a view, and then apply these options to other views. For example, you can create a view template that displays spaces, but hides the MEP systems in a view (as shown in Figure 1–53), while another view template displays duct systems but not plumbing fixtures (as shown in Figure 1–54).

Figure 1–53

Figure 1–54

Creating View Templates

You can create view templates to help you ensure that company standards are applied to views. For example, you can create a view template for furniture plans, such as that shown in Figure 1–55. This view template could then be applied to furniture plans for each level in a project. You can also create view types that use a specific view template. When you create a new view, the view template is automatically applied to the view.

Many companies lock in view templates for their sheet views so that users can't deviate from the company standards.

Figure 1–55

How To: Create a View Template from an Existing View

1. Set up a view the way you want it with *Scale*, *Detail Level*, *Visibility Graphic Overrides*, and other *View Settings*.
2. In the Project Browser, right-click on the view and select **Create View Template from View** or, on the *View* tab> Graphics panel, expand ⬜ (View Template), and click 🗐 (Create Template from Current View).
3. In the New View Template dialog box, type a name for the view template.
4. Click **OK**.
5. In the View Template dialog box, make adjustments as required and then click **OK**.

How To: Set up a View Template

1. In the *View* tab>Graphics panel, expand ⬜ (View Template) and then click 🔧 (Manage View Templates).
2. In the Apply View Template dialog box, in the *Names* list, select a view similar to the one you want to create and click 🗐 (Duplicate).
3. In the New View Template dialog box, type a new name for the view template and click **OK**.

4. Select the new view template (as shown in Figure 1–56), and modify the parameter values in the *View Properties* area, as required.

View Templates

View templates

Discipline filter:
<all>

View type filter:
<all>

Names:
Architectural Elevation
Architectural Plan
Architectural Reflected Ceiling Plan
Architectural Section
Electrical Ceiling
Electrical Elevation
Electrical Plan
Electrical Section
Mechanical Ceiling
Mechanical Elevation
Mechanical Plan
Mechanical Section
Plumbing Ceiling

View properties

Number of views with this template assigned: **0**

Parameter	Value	Include
Display Model	Normal	☑
Detail Level	Coarse	☑
Parts Visibility	Show Original	☑
V/G Overrides Model	Edit...	☑
V/G Overrides Annotati	Edit...	☑
V/G Overrides Analytica	Edit...	☑
V/G Overrides Import	Edit...	☑
V/G Overrides Filters	Edit...	☑
Model Display	Edit...	☑
Shadows	Edit...	☑
Sketchy Lines	Edit...	☑
Depth Cueing	Edit...	☑
Lighting	Edit...	☑
Photographic Exposure	Edit...	☑
Background	Edit...	☑
Far Clipping	No clip	☑
Phase Filter	Show All	☑

How do I modify a view template?   OK   Cancel   Apply Properties

Figure 1–56

5. Click **OK** to finish.

• Note that the different view types have different view parameters. For example, 3D views have options for Rendering and Perspectives that plan views do not have. When you apply a view template across various view types, only the options that are mutual are updated.

Hint: Setting the View Scale-to-Detail Level Correspondence

One view parameter is the *Detail Level*. There are three options: **Coarse**, **Medium**, and **Fine**. You can modify the table of scales that are related to the levels. In the *Manage* tab>

Settings panel, expand 🔧 (Additional Settings) and select **Detail Level**. The View scale-to-detail level correspondence dialog box displays, as shown in Figure 1–57.

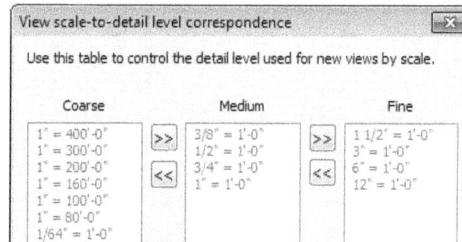

Figure 1–57

How To: Create a New View Type with a View Template

1. Open a view of the type you want to create. For example, if you want to create a new plan view type, select an existing Floor Plan view, or if you want to create a new elevation view type, select an existing Elevation view.
2. In Properties, click **Edit Type**.
3. Duplicate the existing type and give it a new name, as shown in Figure 1–58.

Figure 1–58

4. Specify the *Callout Tag* and *Reference Label*, set the *View Template is applied to new view* option, and select the **New views dependent on template** option, if required.
5. Click **OK**.

- When you create a new view, you can select the view type from the drop-down list, as shown for a new floor plan in Figure 1–59. The view is also placed in its own group in the Project Browser, as shown in Figure 1–60.

Figure 1–59

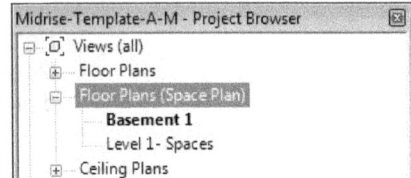

Figure 1–60

Applying View Templates

You can apply view templates by setting a default template in the view properties. When you do this, the view is locked using the parameters set in the view template, and you are prevented from making changes, as shown for the detail level in Figure 1–61. This is useful for views that have been set for printing. You can also apply a view template without locking the view properties.

Figure 1–61

How To: Set the Default View Template for a View

1. In the Project Browser, select one or more views.
2. In Properties, in the *Identity Data* section, click the button next to *View Template*, as shown in Figure 1–62. The name on the button varies according to the template that has already been applied.

Figure 1–62

3. In the Apply View Template dialog box, select the appropriate template and click **OK**.

- To limit the number of view templates that display, filter the list by selecting an option in the *Discipline filter* and *View type filter* drop-down lists, as shown in Figure 1–63.

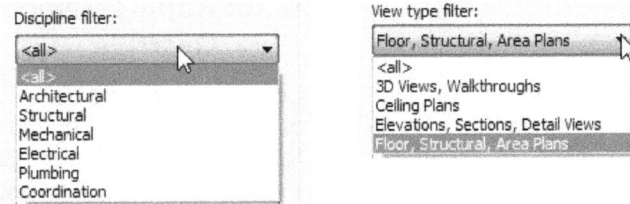

Figure 1–63

• You can apply view templates to any view as many times as required, unless it is set as the default template in the view properties.

• If you want to start a new view template based on an existing view, select **Show Views**. The *Names* list expands to include all of the related views in the project.

Hint: Temporary View Properties

As you are working, it can be helpful to temporarily override the view. You can do this by selecting a view template from the View Control Bar, as shown in Figure 1–64.

Figure 1–64

1. In the View Control Panel, expand (Temporary View Properties) and select **Enable Temporary View Properties**.

2. Expand (Temporary View Properties) again and select **Temporarily Apply Template Properties**. Alternatively, if you have already used the process, you can select from a list of view templates, as shown in Figure 1–64.

3. In the dialog box, select the view template you want to apply and click **OK**.

4. When you are finished, expand (Temporary View Properties) and select **Restore View Properties**.

• Some companies create a "working view" template to be used as a temporary override, rather than having separate working views.

How To: Apply a Temporary View Template Override

Use this method if you are not presetting the view template for views.

1. Select one or more views in the Project Browser. (Hold <Ctrl> or <Shift> to select multiple views.)
2. Right-click in the Project Browser and select **Apply Template Properties**, or on the *View* tab>Graphics panel, expand ⬚ (View Template) and click ⬚ (Apply Template Properties to Current View).
3. In the Apply View Template dialog box, select the view template you want to use from the *Names* list, as shown in Figure 1–65. Several standard view templates are available when you create a project using one of the Autodesk Revit project templates.

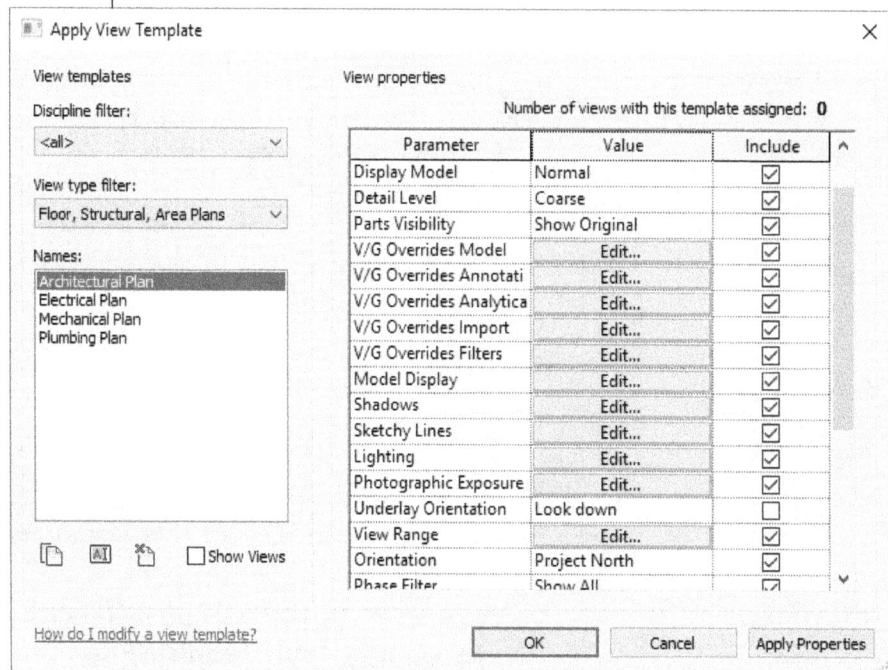

Figure 1–65

4. If you do not want specific view properties to be part of the view template that is applied to views, clear the checkmark in the *Include* column for the parameters you do not want to include. You can also create overrides to the view template by changing parameter values.
5. Click **OK** to finish.

1.5 Setting Up View Filters

View filters can speed up the process of specifying categories that are modified in View Templates. You might want to display certain elements in halftone, or with a different color or lineweight in specific views. For example, a fire evacuation plan might have walls with different fire ratings that display with thicker lineweights, as shown in Figure 1–66. By creating these filters and then applying them in a view template, you can reuse them without having to recreate them each time.

Figure 1–66

- MEP projects frequently use view filters to control which systems display in a view.

How To: Create Filters

1. In the *View* tab>Graphics panel, click (Filters). The Filters dialog box opens as shown in Figure 1–67.

Figure 1–67

- Filters are divided by Rule-based Filters (used in Visibility/Graphic Overrides) and Selection Filters (used by Selection Sets)

2. In the *Filters* area, select the **Rule-based Filters** node or an existing filter and click ⬚ (New) or ⬚ (Duplicate). Name the new filter and click **OK**.

3. In the *Categories* area, filter the list by discipline and then select the categories to include in the filter. Use **Check All** and **Check None** to help select the categories.

4. In the *Filter Rules* area, select what you what to *Filter by*, the filter operator(s), and the value for the filter. If more than one category is selected, the *Filter by* list is limited to parameters shared by the categories you selected. You can create more than one filter rule. They are applied in order. Set *Filter by* to **None** if you do not want to filter by parameters. Filter operators are shown in Figure 1–68.

*You can click **Apply** to save the changes and remain in the dialog box, or **OK** to finish.*

Filter Rules

Filter by: Function

equals
equals
does not equal
is greater than
is greater than or equal to
is less than
is less than or equal to

And:

Figure 1–68

How To: Apply Visibility/Graphic Overrides Filters

1. Type **VG** or **VV** or in the *View* tab>Graphics panel, click

   (Visibility/Graphics) to open the Visibility/Graphic Overrides dialog box. Select the *Filters* tab, as shown in Figure 1–69.

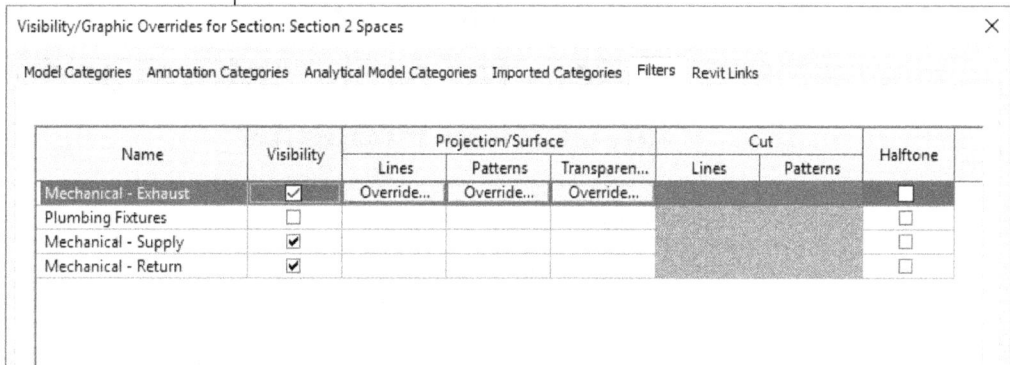

Visibility/Graphic Overrides for Section: Section 2 Spaces   ×

Model Categories   Annotation Categories   Analytical Model Categories   Imported Categories   Filters   Revit Links

Name	Visibility	Projection/Surface			Cut		Halftone
		Lines	Patterns	Transparen...	Lines	Patterns	
Mechanical - Exhaust	☑	Override...	Override...	Override...			☐
Plumbing Fixtures	☐						☐
Mechanical - Supply	☑						☐
Mechanical - Return	☑						☐

Figure 1–69

2. Click **Add** to add a filter to the list.
3. In the Add Filters dialog box, select the filter(s) you want to add, as shown in Figure 1–70, and click **OK**.

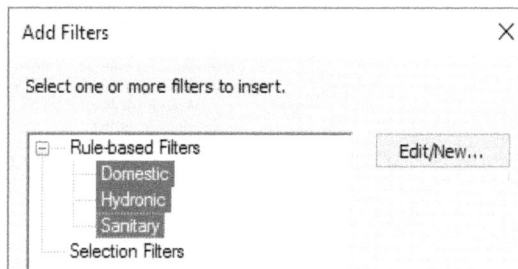

Add Filters   ×

Select one or more filters to insert.

⊟ Rule-based Filters   Edit/New...
      Domestic
      Hydronic
      Sanitary
   Selection Filters

Figure 1–70

- If the filter you want is not defined, click **Edit/New...** to open the Filters dialog box, where you can define a new filter or edit an existing one.

4. In the Visibility/Graphic Overrides dialog box, assign the overrides you want for the filter, as shown in Figure 1–71.

Name	Visibility	Projection/Surface			Cut		Halftone
		Lines	Patterns	Transparen...	Lines	Patterns	
Mechanical - Exhaust	☑	Override...	Override...	Override...			☐
Domestic	☐						☐
Hydronic	☐						☐
Sanitary	☐						☐
Plumbing Fixtures	☐						☐
Mechanical - Supply	☑						☐
Mechanical - Return	☑						☐

Figure 1–71

5. Click **OK**.

Practice 1c

Add View Templates and View Filters for Architectural and Structural Projects

Practice Objectives

- Create visibility filters.
- Create a view template and apply it to several views.

Estimated time for completion: 15 minutes

In this practice, you will create filters that you will use in a structural view template, and apply the view template to several structural plan views, as shown in Figure 1–72. When the filter is working correctly you can add the same information to a project template file.

Figure 1–72

Task 1 - Create filters.

1. Open the project found in the practice files folder, either:

   - *Architectural*>**Office-Architectural.rvt**
   - *Structural*>**Office-Structural.rvt**

2. In the *View* tab>Graphics panel, click (Filters).

3. In the Filters dialog box, click (New), name the new filter **All But Structural**, and click **OK**.

4. In the *Categories* area, set the *Filter list* to **Architecture** and **Structure**.

5. Click **Check All**, and clear **Columns**, all categories starting with **Analytical**, **Structural**, and **Walls**. Click **Apply**.

6. Click (New). Name the new filter **Non-Structural Walls** and click **OK**.

7. In the *Categories* area, click **Check None** and select **Walls**.

8. In the *Filter Rules* area, set *Filter by* to **Structural Usage**, **equals**, and **Non-bearing**, as shown in Figure 1–73.

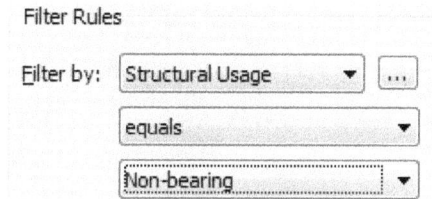

Filter Rules

Filter by: Structural Usage ▼ ...

equals ▼

Non-bearing ▼

Figure 1–73

9. Click **OK** to close the Filters dialog box.

Task 2 - Create a View Template.

---

1. In the Project Browser, in the Floor Plans area, right-click on the **Level 1** view and select **Create View Template From View**.

2. Name the new view template **Structural Plan** and click **OK**.

3. In the View Templates dialog box, set the *View Scale* to **1/16"=1'-0"** and the *Detail Level* to **Coarse**.

4. Next to **V/G Override Filters**, click **Edit...** The Visibility/Graphic Overrides dialog box opens with the *Filter* tab selected.

5. Click **Add**.

6. In the Add Filters dialog box, select the two filters you just created and click **OK**.

7. Place a checkmark in the *Halftone* column for both filters. Continue working in the Visibility/Graphics Overrides dialog box.

8. In the *Annotation Categories* tab, toggle off everything except Grids and all Structural annotations and tags.

9. In the *Model Categories* tab, toggle off items, such as **Casework**, **Furniture**, **Furniture Systems** and **Plumbing Fixtures**, and **Mechanical Equipment**.

10. Click **OK** to close the Visibility/Graphic Overrides dialog box, and click **OK** to complete the view template.

Task 3 - Apply a View Template to several views.

1. In the *Floor Plans* area, use *Duplicate with Detailing* on the **Level 1**, **Level 2**, **Level 3**, and **Level 4** views. Rename them as **Level 1 - Structural**, **Level 2 - Structural**, **Level 3 - Structural**, and **Level 4 - Structural**.

2. Select one of the new Structural views.

3. Right-click and select **Apply Template Properties**.

4. In the Apply View Template dialog box, select the **Structural Plan** view template you just created and click **OK** to apply it.

5. Select the other structural views. In Properties, in the *Identity Data* group, select the button beside *View Template*.

6. In the Assign View Template dialog box, select **Structural Plan**, and then click **OK**.

7. Review the View Control Bar options. Note that you can't make any changes to the view controls of this view, as shown in Figure 1–74.

Figure 1–74

8. Open the **Level 1 - Structural** view. Note that you can still make changes to the View Controls of this view.

9. Look at the different views and compare them to the standard floor plan views. Finish with the **Level 1** view.

10. Save the project.

Practice 1d

Add View Templates and View Filters for MEP Projects

Practice Objectives

- Create visibility filters.
- Create a view template and apply it to several views.

Estimated time for completion: 15 minutes

In this practice, you will create velocity based filters for ductwork that you will use in a mechanical view template, and apply the view template to a duplicated plan view, as shown in Figure 1–75. When the filter is working correctly, you can add the same information to a project template file.

Figure 1–75

Task 1 - Create filters.

1. In the practice files *MEP* folder, open **Office-MEP.rvt**.

2. In the *View* tab>Graphics panel, click 🔲 (Filters).

3. In the Filters dialog box, click 🗋 (New), name the new filter **Mechanical - Low Velocity**, and click **OK**.

4. In the *Categories* area, set the *Filter list* to **Mechanical**. Select **Ducts** and **Flex Ducts**.

5. In the *Filter Rules* area, set *Filter by* to **Velocity**, **is less than or equal to**, and **900 FPM**, as shown in Figure 1–76.

Figure 1–76

6. Click **Apply** and remain in the Filters dialog box.

7. Select the new **Mechanical-Low Velocity** filter and click

   (Duplicate). Right-click on the duplicated filter and click

   (Rename). In the Rename dialog box type **Mechanical-Medium/High Velocity** and click **OK**.

8. In the *Filter Rules* area, set *Filter by* to **Velocity**, **is greater than**, and **1900 FPM**, as shown in Figure 1–77.

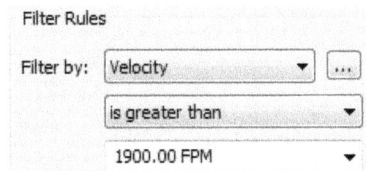

Figure 1–77

9. Click **OK** to close the Filters dialog box.

Task 2 - Create a View Template.

---

1. In the Project Browser, in the *Mechanical>Floor Plans* area, right-click on the **1 - Mech** view and select **Create View Template From View**.

2. Name the new view template **Velocity Duct Plan** and click **OK**.

3. Next to **V/G Override Filters**, click **Edit...** The Visibility/Graphic Overrides dialog box opens with the *Filter* tab selected.

4. Click **Add**.

5. In the Add Filters dialog box, select the two filters you just created and click **OK**.

6. For the **Mechanical-Low Velocity** filter, in the *Projection/Surface>Lines* column, select **Override**.

7. In the Line Graphics dialog box, change *Weight* to **6** and the *Color* to an orange, as shown in Figure 1–78. Click **OK**.

Figure 1–78

8. Repeat for the **Mechanical-Medium/High Velocity** filter and set the *Weight* to **6** and the *Color* to a green. Click **OK**.

9. In the Visibility/Graphics Overrides dialog box, move the new filters to the top of the list. For **Mechanical-Exhaust**, in the *Visibility* column, clear the checkbox as shown in Figure 1–79.

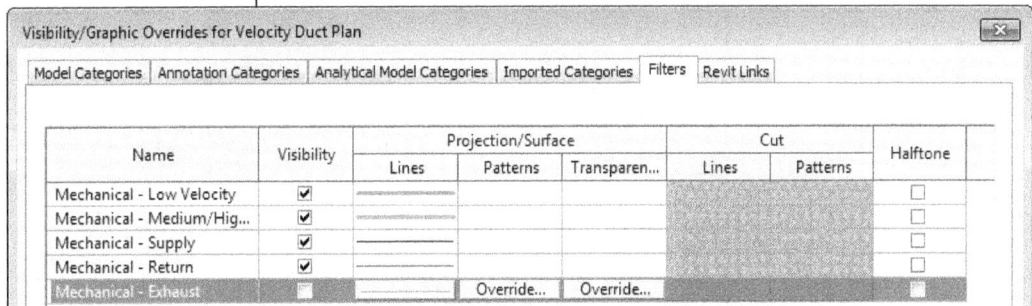

Figure 1–79

10. Click **OK** to close the Visibility/Graphic Overrides dialog box, and click **OK** to complete the view template.

Task 3 - Apply a View Template the views.

1. In the Project Browser, use *Duplicate with Detailing* to duplicate the **1 - Mech** view. Rename it **1 - Mech - Velocity.**

2. Right-click and select **Apply Template Properties**.

3. In the Apply View Template dialog box, select the **Velocity Duct Plan** view template you just created and click **OK** to apply it.

4. Compare the new floor plan view with the existing **1 - Mech** view.

5. Duplicate the **2 - Mech** view, rename it as **2 - Mech - Velocity**.

6. In Properties, in the *Identity Data* group, select the button beside *View Template*.

7. In the Assign View Template dialog box, select **Velocity Duct Plan** and click **OK**.

8. Review the View Control Bar options. Note that you can't make any changes to the view controls of this view, as shown in Figure 1–80.

Figure 1–80

9. Open the **1 - Mech - Velocity** view. Note that you can still make changes to the View Controls of this view.

10. Finish with the **1 - Mech** view.

11. Save the project.

Chapter Review Questions

1. Which of the following items are NOT set in a template file?

    a. Units

    b. Annotation Types

    c. Title blocks

    d. Keyboard Shortcuts

2. What is a label?

    a. A text type used in title blocks.

    b. A dimension with text instead of numbers.

    c. A type of text with variable information.

3. When you want to create new Text Types, such as those shown in Figure 1–81, you need to copy an existing one.

    # A FANCY FONT AT 1/4"

    A HAND LETTERING FONT AT 1/8"

    A HAND LETTERING FONT AT 5/32"

    Figure 1–81

    a. True

    b. False

4. Which of the following enables you to assign a view template consistently to a view so that no changes can be made to the view parameters?

    a. In the View Status Bar, lock the view.

    b. In Properties, select a View Template.

    c. In the Project Browser, right-click on the view and select **Lock**.

    d. In the Apply View Template dialog box, select a template.

5. Which of the following parameters are included in a View Template (as shown in Figure 1–82)? (Select all that apply.)

Figure 1–82

a. View Scale

b. V/G Overrides

c. Project Units

d. Detail Level

Command Summary

Button	Command	Location
Templates		
	Callout Tags	• **Ribbon:** *Manage* tab>Settings panel> expand Additional Settings
	Elevation Tags	• **Ribbon:** *Manage* tab>Settings panel> expand Additional Settings
	Floor Plan	• **Ribbon:** *View* tab>Create panel> expand Plan Views
	Loaded Tags	• **Ribbon:** *Annotate* tab>Tag panel> expand the panel title
	Project Units	• **Ribbon:** *Manage* tab>Settings panel • **Shortcut:** UN
	Section Tags	• **Ribbon:** *Manage* tab>Settings panel> expand Additional Settings
Annotation		
	Dimension Types	• **Ribbon:** *Annotate* tab>Dimensions panel>expand the panel title
	Text	• **Family Editor** • **Ribbon:** *Create* tab>Text panel
Title Blocks		
	Label	• **Family Editor** • **Ribbon:** *Create* tab>Text panel
	New Title Block	• **Application Menu:** expand New> Title block
	Revision Schedule	• **Family Editor** • **Ribbon:** *View* tab>Create panel
View Templates and Filters		
	ApplyTemplate Properties to Current View	• **Ribbon:** *View* tab>Graphics panel> expand View Templates • **Project Browser:** (*right-click on a view*) **Apply Template Properties...**
	Create View Template From View	• **Ribbon:** *View* tab>Graphics panel> expand View Templates • **Project Browser:** (*right-click on a view*)
	Filters	• **Ribbon:** *View* tab>Graphics panel
	Manage View Templates	• **Ribbon:** *View* tab>Graphics panel> expand View Templates
	Temporary View Properties	• View Control Bar

Creating Schedules

Schedules are a critical component of BIM projects. They gather information about the model that is used in construction documents, and can also be used to test your model (for example, to verify the amount of air flow in a space). Several types of schedules can be created, including: building component schedules, key schedules, and material takeoff schedules. These schedules are all created using the same basic methods.

Learning Objectives in this Chapter

- Schedule building components.
- Customize schedule tables using filters, sorting/grouping, formatting, and appearance.
- Modify the appearance and content of individual schedule cells.
- Create a Key Style schedule by defining keys for elements with similar characteristics.
- Create additional parameters including Calculated Value Fields and Percentage Fields.
- Apply conditional formatting to fields in a schedule.
- Embed a schedule into an existing schedule (MEP only).
- Create material takeoff schedules.

2.1 Introduction to Schedules

Schedules can be created at any point in a project or included in template files. Each schedule is a separate view and can be inserted on a sheet, as shown in Figure 2–1.

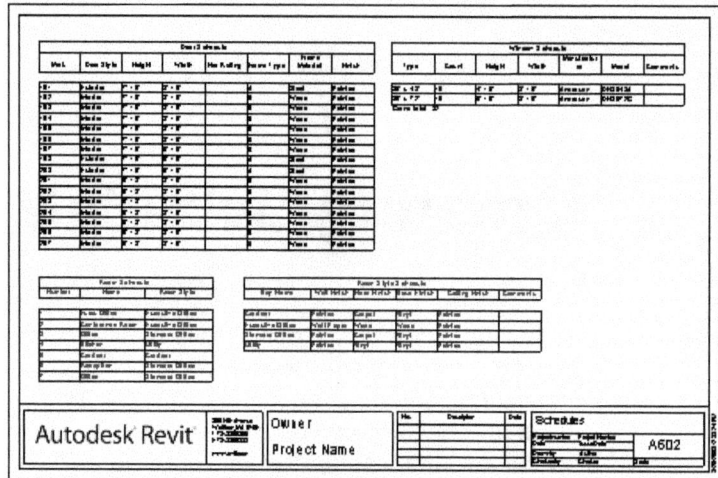

Figure 2–1

You can create the following types of schedules:

(Schedule/ Quantities)	Generates schedules using parameters available at category level. There are two types of Schedule/ Quantities schedules: **Building Component** and **Key**.
(Material Takeoff)	Generates schedules from information about materials in a project and can be used to do quantity takeoffs.
(Sheet List)	Generates schedule from sheet information including who has designed and checked the sheet.
(Note Block)	Generates schedules that keep count of all of the symbols used in the project.
(View List)	Generates schedules that keep count of all of the views in the project, including their scale, phase, and use on sheets.
(Graphical Column Schedule)	(Structural only) Generates graphical schedules displaying heights of all columns in a project compared to levels.

Importing and Exporting Schedules

Schedules are views and can be copied into your project from other projects. Only the formatting information is copied; the information about individually scheduled items is not included. That information is automatically gathered from the elements in the current project. You can also export the schedule information to be used in spreadsheets.

How To: Import Schedules

1. In the *Insert* tab>Import panel, expand (Insert From File) and click (Insert Views From File).
2. In the Open dialog box, locate the project file containing the schedule that you want to use.
3. Select the schedules that you want to import, as shown in Figure 2–2.

If the referenced project contains many types of views, change Views: to **Show schedules and reports only***.*

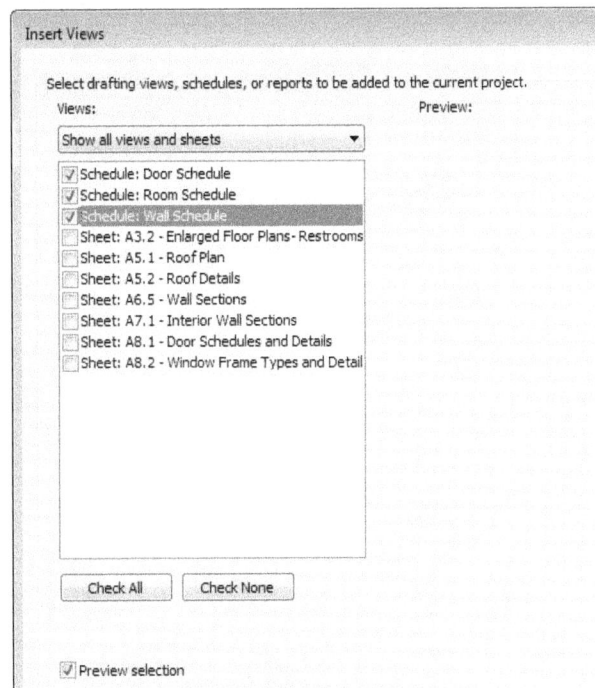

Figure 2–2

4. Click **OK**.

How To: Export Schedule Information

1. Switch to the schedule view that you want to export.

2. In the Application Menu, expand ⬒ (Export), expand
   ⬚ (Reports), and click ⬚ (Schedule).

3. In the Export Schedule dialog box, select a location and
   name for the text file and click **Save**.

4. In the Export Schedule dialog box, set the options in the
   Schedule appearance and *Output options* areas that best suit
   your spreadsheet software, as shown in Figure 2–3.

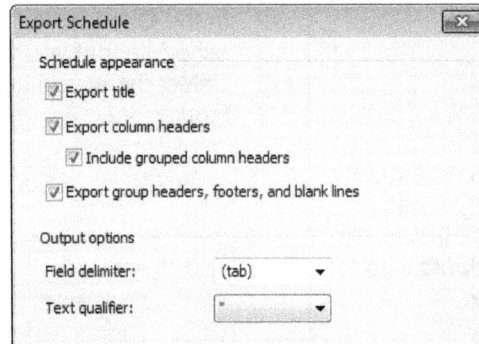

Figure 2–3

5. Click **OK**. A new text file is created that you can open in a
   spreadsheet, as shown in Figure 2–4.

Figure 2–4

2.2 Creating Building Component Schedules

A Building Component schedule is a table view of selected parameters of an element such as air terminals, structural foundations or doors, as shown in Figure 2–5. They can include instance parameters that are automatically filled in (such as the **Height** and **Width**) and type parameters (such as the **Fire Rating** and **Frame**) which need to be added.

<Door Schedule>

A	B	C	D	E	F	G	H
Mark	Height	Width	Fire Rating	Frame Type	Frame Material	Finish	Function
2	7' - 0"	10' - 0"	A	A	Steel	Brushed	Exterior
3	6' - 8"	3' - 0"	B	B	Wood	Paint	Interior ▼
4	6' - 8"	3' - 0"	B	B	Wood	Paint	Interior
5	6' - 8"	3' - 0"	B	B	Wood	Paint	Interior
6	6' - 8"	3' - 0"	B	B	Wood	Paint	Interior

Figure 2–5

How To: Create a Building Component Schedule

1. In the *View* tab>Create panel, expand ▦ (Schedules) and click ▦ (Schedule/Quantities) or in the Project Browser, right-click on the Schedule/Quantities node and select **New Schedule/Quantities**.
2. In the New Schedule dialog box, select the type of schedule you want to create (e.g., Doors) from the *Category* list, as shown in Figure 2–6.

In the Filter list drop-down list, you can specify the discipline(s) to show only the categories that you want to display.

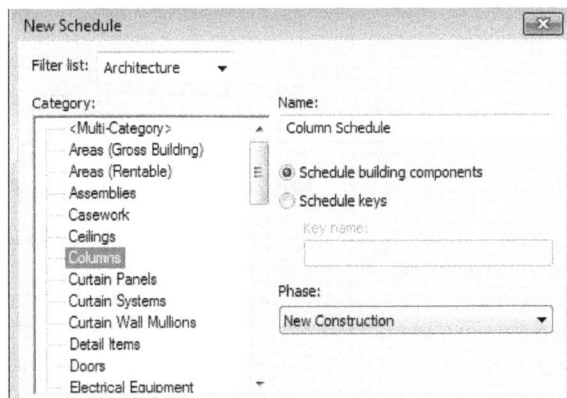

Figure 2–6

3. Type a new *Name*, if the default does not suit.
4. Select **Schedule building components.**
5. Specify the *Phase* as required.
6. Click **OK**.
7. Fill out the information in the Schedule Properties dialog box. This includes the information in the *Fields*, *Filter*, *Sorting/Grouping*, *Formatting*, and *Appearance* tabs.
8. Once you have entering the schedule properties, click **OK**. A schedule report is created in its own view.

- Other elements that can be scheduled include model groups and Revit links.

Enhanced
in 2018

Fields Tab

In the *Fields* tab, you can select from a list of available fields and organize them in the order in which you want them to display in the schedule, as shown in Figure 2–7.

Figure 2–7

How To: Fill out the Fields Tab

You can also double-click on a field to move it from the Available fields to the Scheduled fields list.

1. In the *Available fields* area, select one or more fields you want to add to the schedule and click 🔽 (Add parameter(s)). The field(s) are placed in the *Scheduled fields (in order)* area.
2. Continue adding fields, as required.

- Click ⬅ (Remove parameter(s)) to move a field from the *Scheduled fields* area back to the *Available fields* area.

- Use ⬆E (Move parameter up) and ⬇E (Move parameter down) to change the order of the scheduled fields.

Other Fields Tab Options

Select available fields from	Enables you to select additional category fields for the specified schedule. The available list of fields depends on the original category of the schedule. Typically, they include room information.
Include elements in links	Includes elements that are in files linked to the current project, so that their elements can be included in the schedule.
📄 **(New parameter)**	Adds a new field according to your specification. New fields can be placed by instance or by type.
f_x **(Add Calculated parameter)**	Enables you to create a field that uses a formula based on other fields.
📋 **(Combine parameters)**	Enables you to combine two or more parameters in one column. You can put any fields together even if they are used in another column.
✏ **(Edit parameter)**	Enables you to edit custom fields. This is grayed out if you select a standard field.
📄 **(Delete parameter)**	Deletes selected custom fields. This is grayed out if you select a standard field.

Filter Tab

In the *Filter* tab, you can set up filters so that only elements meeting specific criteria are included in the schedule. For example, you might only want to show information for one level, as shown in Figure 2–8. You can create filters for up to eight values. All values must be satisfied for the elements to display.

Figure 2–8

- The parameter you want to use as a filter must be included in the schedule. You can hide the parameter once you have completed the schedule, if required.

Filter by	Specifies the field to filter. Not all fields are available to be filtered.
Condition	Specifies the condition that must be met. This includes options such as **equal**, **not equal**, **greater than**, and **less than**.
Value	Specifies the value of the element to be filtered. You can select from a drop-down list of appropriate values. For example, if you set *Filter By* to **Level**, it displays the list of levels in the project.

Sorting/ Grouping Tab

In the *Sorting/Grouping* tab, you can set how you want the information to be sorted, as shown in Figure 2–9. For example, you can sort by **Mark** (number) and then **Type**.

Figure 2–9

Sort by	Enables you to select the field(s) you want to sort by. You can select up to four levels of sorting.
Ascending/ Descending	Sorts fields in **Ascending** or **Descending** order.
Header/ Footer	Enables you to group similar information and separate it by a **Header** with a title and/or a **Footer** with quantity information.
Blank line	Adds a blank line between groups.
Grand totals	Selects which totals to display for the entire schedule. You can specify a name to display in the schedule for the Grand total.
Itemize every instance	If selected, displays each instance of the element in the schedule. If not selected, displays only one instance of each type, as shown in Figure 2–10.

Figure 2–10

Formatting Tab

In the *Formatting* tab, you can control how the headers of each field display, as shown in Figure 2–11.

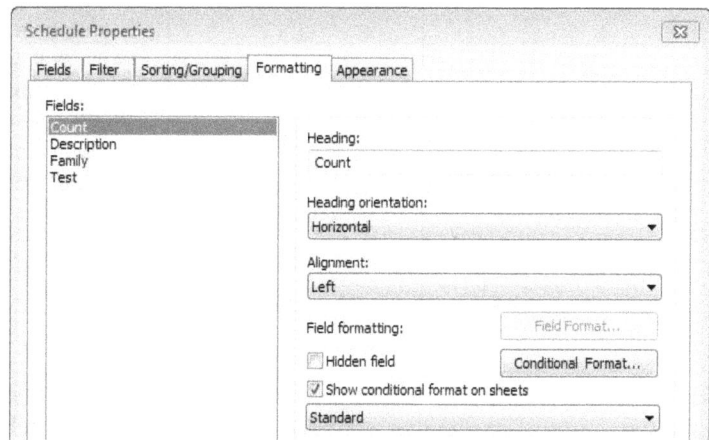

Figure 2–11

Fields	Enables you to select the field for which you want to modify the formatting.
Heading	Enables you to change the heading of the field if you want it to be different from the field name. For example, you might want to replace **Mark** (a generic name) with the more specific **Door Number** in a door schedule.
Heading orientation	Enables you to set the heading on sheets to **Horizontal** or **Vertical**. This does not impact the schedule view.
Alignment	Aligns the text in rows under the heading to be **Left**, **Right**, or **Center**.
Field Format...	Sets the units format for the length, area, volume, angle, or number field. By default, this is set to use the project settings.
Conditional Format...	Sets up the schedule to display visual feedback based on the conditions listed.
Hidden field	Enables you to hide a field. For example, you might want to use a field for sorting purposes, but not have it display in the schedule. You can also modify this option in the schedule view later.
Show conditional format on sheets	Select if you want the color code set up in the Conditional Format dialog box to display on sheets.
Calculation options	Select the type of calculation you want to use. All values in a field are: • **Standard** - Calculated separately. • **Calculate totals** - Added together. • **Calculate minimum** - Reviewed and only the smallest amount is displayed. • **Calculate maximum** - Reviewed and only the largest amount is displayed. • **Calculate minimum and maximum** - Reviewed and both the smallest and largest amounts are displayed. • This is often used with rebar sets.

Hint: Hiding Columns

If you want to use the field to filter or sort, but do not want it to display in the schedule, select **Hidden field**. Alternatively, once the schedule is completed, select the column header, right-click on it, and select **Hide Columns**.

Appearance Tab

In the *Appearance* tab, you can set the text style and grid options for a schedule, as shown in Figure 2–12.

Figure 2–12

Grid lines	Displays lines between each instance listed and around the outside of the schedule. Select the style of lines from the drop-down list; this controls all lines for the schedule, unless modified.
Grid in headers/ footers/spacers	Extends the vertical grid lines between the columns.
Outline	Specify a different line type for the outline of the schedule.
Blank row before data	Select this option if you want a blank row to be displayed before the data begins in the schedule.
Show Title/Show Headers	Select these options to include the text in the schedule.
Title text/Header text/Body Text	Select the text style for the title, header, and body text.

Schedule Properties

Schedule views have properties including the *View Template, View Name, Phases* and methods of returning to the Schedule Properties dialog box as shown in Figure 2–13. In the *Other* area, select the button next to the tab that you want to open in the Schedule Properties dialog box. In the dialog box, you can switch from tab to tab and make any required changes to the overall schedule.

Figure 2–13

Figure 2–14

Just like other views, schedules can have View Templates applied. When you specify a view template directly in the view, as shown in Figure 2–14, none of the schedule properties can be modified.

- Schedule view templates are type-specific. If you apply one to a different type of element, only the *Appearance* information is applied.

- If you apply a schedule view template to a schedule of the same type, it overrides everything in the existing schedule including the fields.

- If you have a complicated schedule, you might want to create a view template for it to avoid losing that organization.

- To create schedule view templates, you need to create at least one from an existing view. Then, you can modify it and duplicate it in the View Templates dialog box.

Filtering Elements from Schedules

When you create schedules based on a category you might need to filter out some of the element types in that category. For example, in the Autodesk Revit software, doors (and windows) in curtain walls are automatically added to a door schedule, as shown at the top in Figure 2–15, but are typically estimated as part of the curtain wall rather than as a separate door. To remove them from the schedule, as shown at the bottom in Figure 2–15, assign a parameter that identifies them and then use that parameter to filter them out of the schedule.

						Door Schedule- 1st
	Door Size			Frame		
Door Type	Width	Height	Thickness	Frame Type	Frame Material	Head Detail
	8' - 3 1/2"	9' - 4 1/4"				
	3' - 0"	7' - 0"	0' - 2"	A	Aluminum	
	3' - 0"	7' - 0"	0' - 2"	B	Aluminum	
	3' - 0"	6' - 8"	0' - 2"	C	Aluminum	

Curtain Wall Doors Displayed

						Door Schedule- 1st
	Door Size			Frame		
Door Type	Width	Height	Thickness	Frame Type	Frame Material	Head Detail
	3' - 0"	7' - 0"	0' - 2"	A	Aluminum	
	3' - 0"	7' - 0"	0' - 2"	B	Aluminum	
	3' - 0"	6' - 8"	0' - 2"	C	Aluminum	
	3' - 0"	6' - 8"	0' - 2"	C	Aluminum	

Curtain Wall Doors Filtered Out

Figure 2–15

- This type of filtering can be used for any schedule in any discipline.

How To: Filter Elements in a Schedule

Create a type specifically for this if you are using one that is also used elsewhere.

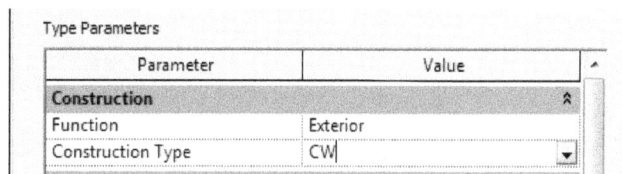

1. Select an element (such as a door used in curtain walls) and modify the Type Parameters. Add a value to one of the parameters that you are not otherwise using in your schedule. For example, set *Construction Type* to **CW**, as shown Figure 2–16

Type Parameters	
Parameter	**Value**
Construction	☆
Function	Exterior
Construction Type	CW

Figure 2–16

2. Create a schedule and include the field, such as *Construction Type.*

3. Modify the *Filter* of the schedule so the parameter does not equal the specified value. In the example shown in Figure 2–17, *Construction Type* **does not equal CW**. Any types that match this filter are excluded from the schedule.

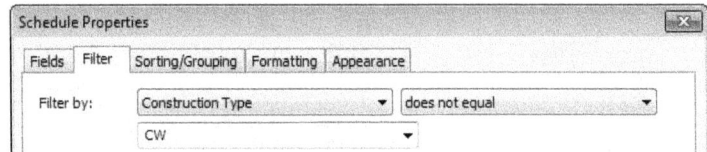

Figure 2–17

4. In the final schedule, the elements display with the specified value. Right-click on the column header and select **Hide Column(s)**, as shown in Figure 2–18. It is just used as a filter and not part of the final schedule.

Figure 2–18

Practice 2a

Create Schedules for Architectural Projects

Practice Objectives

- Create building component schedules.
- Apply filters.
- Enter information.
- Place schedules on a sheet.

Estimated time for completion: 15 minutes

In this practice, you will create Door and Window schedules, filter out curtain wall doors, and add information to cells in the door schedule. You will also place the schedules on a sheet, as shown in Figure 2–19.

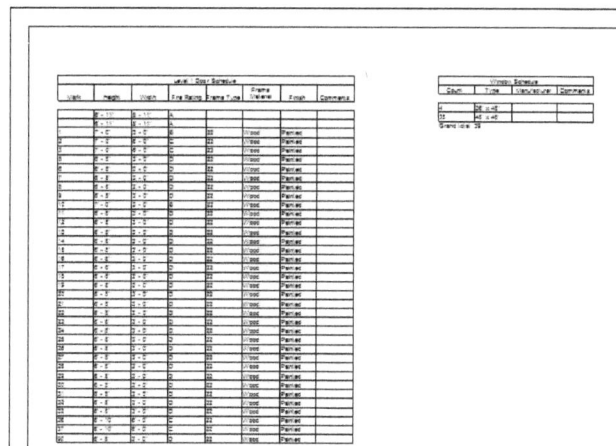

Figure 2–19

Task 1 - Create a Door schedule.

1. In the practice files *Architectural* folder, open **Clark-Hall-Schedules-Create.rvt**.

2. In the *View* tab>Create panel, expand (Schedules) and click (Schedule/Quantities).

3. In the New Schedule dialog box, set the *Filter List* to **Architecture** only to limit the number of categories and then set the *Category* to **Doors.**

4. Name the schedule **Door Schedule-Level 1**. Click **OK**.

5. In the Schedule Properties dialog box, in the *Fields* tab, add the following fields, as shown in Figure 2–20:

- *Level*
- *Mark*
- *Height*
- *Width*
- *Fire Rating*

- *Frame Type*
- *Frame Material*
- *Finish*
- *Comments*
- *Construction Type*

Figure 2–20

6. Click **OK** to create the schedule. Note that Level 1, Level 2, and Level 3 doors are included.

7. In Properties, in the *Other* category, next to **Filter**, click **Edit...**. The Schedule Properties dialog box opens with the *Filter* tab selected. Set *Filter by* to **Level - equals - Level 1**.

8. In the dialog box, in the *Sorting/Grouping* tab, sort the doors by **Mark**, and click **OK** to update the schedule.

9. Save the project.

Task 2 - Remove the Curtain Wall Doors from the schedule.

1. Continue working in the new **Door Schedule-Level 1** view,
   The doors in the curtain walls do not display with a **Mark**, as
   shown in Figure 2–21. Additionally, they are not included in
   door schedules and need to be removed.

A	B	C	D
Level	Mark	Height	Width
Level 1		6' - 11"	5' - 11"
Level 1		6' - 11"	5' - 11"
Level 1	1	7' - 0"	3' - 0"
Level 1	2	7' - 0"	6' - 0"
Level 1	3	7' - 0"	6' - 0"
Level 1	4	6' - 8"	3' - 0"
Level 1	5	6' - 8"	3' - 0"

Figure 2–21

2. In Properties, in the *Other* category, next to **Filter**, click
   Edit....

3. In the Schedule Properties dialog box, in the *Filter* tab, add
   the additional Filter: **Construction Type - does not equal -
   CW**, as shown in Figure 2–22, and click **OK**.

*You need to type **CW**
because the option
does not yet exist in the
project.*

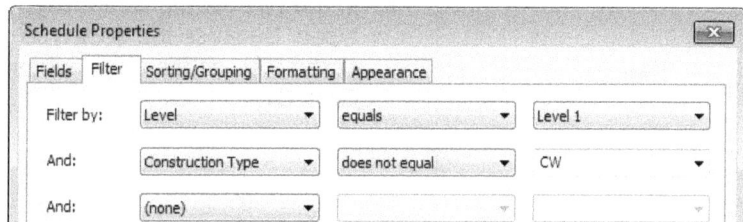

Schedule Properties					
Fields	Filter	Sorting/Grouping	Formatting	Appearance	
Filter by:	Level ▼	equals ▼	Level 1 ▼		
And:	Construction Type ▼	does not equal ▼	CW ▼		
And:	(none) ▼				

Figure 2–22

4. In the Schedule, next to one of the curtain wall doors, in the
   Construction Type column, type **CW**. An alert displays
   prompting you that this is a type property. Click **OK** and the
   curtain wall doors are no longer included in the schedule, as
   shown in Figure 2–23.

A	B	C	D
Level	Mark	Height	Width
Level 1	1	7' - 0"	3' - 0"
Level 1	2	7' - 0"	6' - 0"
Level 1	3	7' - 0"	6' - 0"
Level 1	4	6' - 8"	3' - 0"

Figure 2–23

5. Right-click on the *Level* column header and select **Hide Columns**. Repeat the procedure with the *Construction Type column* header. This removes the columns from the schedule (as shown in Figure 2–24), while still enabling you to use the fields as filters.

			<Door Schedule - Level 1>				
A	B	C	D	E	F	G	H
Mark	Height	Width	Fire Rating	Frame Type	Frame Material	Finish	Comments
1	7' - 0"	3' - 0"					
2	7' - 0"	6' - 0"					
3	7' - 0"	6' - 0"					
4	6' - 8"	3' - 0"					
5	6' - 8"	3' - 0"					
6	6' - 8"	3' - 0"					
7	6' - 8"	3' - 0"					
8	6' - 8"	3' - 0"					

Figure 2–24

6. Save the project

Task 3 - Fill in additional information in the Door Schedule

1. Continue working in the **Door Schedule-Level 1** view,

2. In the *Fire Rating* column, type a letter for one of the door types. Because the door type controls the **Fire Rating** parameter, an alert box opens, as shown in Figure 2–25. Click **OK**.

Figure 2–25

3. Repeat with the other doors until they all have a fire rating.

4. Open the **Floor Plans: Level 1** view and select one of the interior single doors.

5. Right-click and select **Select All Instances>In Entire Project** in Properties. Set the following parameters:

   - *Frame Type:* **22**
   - *Frame Material:* **Wood**
   - *Finish:* **Stained**

6. Switch back to the schedule to verify that it has updated with the new information, as shown in Figure 2–26.

	A	B	C	D	E	F	G	H
	Mark	Height	Width	Fire Rating	Frame Type	Frame Material	Finish	Comments
1	7' - 0"	3' - 0"	A	21	Aluminum	Brushed	
2	7' - 0"	6' - 0"	A	21	Aluminum	Brushed	
3	7' - 0"	6' - 0"	A	21	Aluminum	Brushed	
4	6' - 8"	3' - 0"	B	22	Wood	Stained	
5	6' - 8"	3' - 0"	B	22	Wood	Stained	
6	6' - 8"	3' - 0"	B	22	Wood	Stained	
7	6' - 8"	3' - 0"	B	22	Wood	Stained	
8	6' - 8"	3' - 0"	B	22	Wood	Stained	

<Door Schedule - Level 1>

Figure 2–26

7. In the schedule view, set the rest of the doors to the following parameters:

- *Frame Type:* **21**
- *Frame Material:* **Aluminum**
- *Finish:* **Brushed**

8. Save the project.

Task 4 - Create a Window schedule.

1. Create a new window schedule with the following fields: **Count**, **Type**, **Manufacturer**, and **Comments**.

2. In the *Sorting/Grouping* tab, sort the windows by **Type**. Toggle on **Grand totals** and toggle off **Itemize every instance**.

3. Click **OK** to create the schedule. It lists the total count for a single type (only one type is used in the project), as shown in Figure 2–27.

A	B	C	D
Count	Type	Manufacturer	Comments
39	48" x 48"		
Grand total: 39			

<Window Schedule>

Figure 2–27

4. In the **Floor Plans: Level 1** view, select the three windows in the Conference Room in the office wing. In Properties change the type to **Fixed with Trim: 36" x 72"**.

5. Switch back to the schedule view. A change should display in the schedule that reflects the new window type, as shown in Figure 2–28.

<Window Schedule>			
A	B	C	D
Count	Type	Manufacturer	Comments
3	36" x 72"		
36	48" x 48"		
Grand total: 39			

Figure 2–28

6. Open the **A601- Schedules** sheet. Drag and drop the schedules to this sheet. Modify the width of each field as required.

7. Save the project.

Practice 2b

Create Schedules for MEP Projects

Practice Objectives

- Create building component schedules.
- Place the schedules on a sheet.

Estimated time for completion: 15 minutes

In this practice, you will create schedules for two types of typical MEP schedules: a system schedule and a fixture schedule. In this case, they will be for duct systems and plumbing fixtures. If time permits, you will also create schedules for electrical circuits and lighting fixtures. You will then place the schedules on a sheet, as shown in Figure 2–29.

Duct Systems		
System Name	Comments	Flow
Exhaust Air		
Mechanical Exhaust Air 1		2000 CFM
Mechanical Exhaust Air 7		420 CFM
Mechanical Exhaust Air 9		200 CFM
Return Air		
Mechanical Return Air 1		0 CFM
Mechanical Return Air 2		0 CFM
Mechanical Return Air 3		205 CFM
Mechanical Return Air 4		500 CFM
Mechanical Return Air 5		500 CFM
Mechanical Return Air 6		500 CFM
Mechanical Return Air 10		0 CFM
Mechanical Return Air 14		205 CFM
Supply Air		
Mechanical Supply Air 1		4000 CFM
Mechanical Supply Air 2		2400 CFM
Mechanical Supply Air 3		2900 CFM
Mechanical Supply Air 4		3500 CFM
Mechanical Supply Air 8		0 CFM
Mechanical Supply Air 9		2900 CFM
Mechanical Supply Air 10		3900 CFM
Mechanical Supply Air 15		3090 CFM
Mechanical Supply Air 19		2400 CFM

Figure 2–29

Task 1 - Create a Duct System schedule.

1. In the practice files *MEP* folder, open
    Freel-Office-Create.rvt.

2. In the *View* tab>Create panel, expand ▦ (Schedules) and
    click ▦ (Schedule/Quantities).

3. In the New Schedule dialog box, set the *Filter list* to
    Mechanical and the *Category* to **Duct Systems** and name it
    Duct Systems, as shown in Figure 2–30.

Figure 2–30

4. Click **OK**.

5. In the Schedule Properties dialog box, in the *Fields* tab, add
    the following fields:
    *   *System Classification*
    *   *System Name*
    *   *Comments*
    *   *Flow*

6. In the *Sorting/Grouping* tab, sort by **System Classification**.
    Select **Ascending** and **Header**.

7. Click **OK** to create the schedule. Stretch the columns so that you can read all of the information, as shown in Figure 2–31.

<Duct System Schedule>			
A	B	C	D
System Classification	System Name	Comments	Flow
Exhaust Air			
Exhaust Air	Mechanical Exhaust Air 1		2000 CFM
Exhaust Air	Mechanical Exhaust Air 7		420 CFM
Exhaust Air	Mechanical Exhaust Air 9		200 CFM
Return Air			
Return Air	Mechanical Return Air 1		0 CFM
Return Air	Mechanical Return Air 2		0 CFM
Return Air	Mechanical Return Air 3		205 CFM
Return Air	Mechanical Return Air 4		500 CFM
Return Air	Mechanical Return Air 5		500 CFM
Return Air	Mechanical Return Air 6		500 CFM
Return Air	Mechanical Return Air 10		0 CFM
Return Air	Mechanical Return Air 14		205 CFM
Supply Air			
Supply Air	Mechanical Supply Air 1		4000 CFM
Supply Air	Mechanical Supply Air 2		2400 CFM
Supply Air	Mechanical Supply Air 3		2900 CFM
Supply Air	Mechanical Supply Air 4		3500 CFM
Supply Air	Mechanical Supply Air 8		0 CFM
Supply Air	Mechanical Supply Air 9		2900 CFM
Supply Air	Mechanical Supply Air 10		3900 CFM
Supply Air	Mechanical Supply Air 15		3090 CFM
Supply Air	Mechanical Supply Air 19		2400 CFM

Figure 2–31

8. Right-click on the *System Classification* column and select **Hide Columns**. (The System Classification is specified by the Header).

9. Open the **M601- Mechanical Schedules** sheet. Drag and drop the duct system schedule to this sheet. Modify the width of each field as required.

10. Save the project.

Task 2 - Create a Plumbing Fixture schedule.

---

1. In the *View* tab>Create panel, expand ▦ (Schedules) and click ▦ (Schedule/Quantities).

2. In the New Schedule dialog box, set the *Filter list* to **Piping**, set *Category* to **Plumbing Fixtures**, and name it **Plumbing Fixtures**. Click **OK**.

3. In the Schedule Properties dialog box, in the *Fields* tab, add the following fields:
   - *Family*
   - *Type*
   - *Manufacturer*
   - *Count*

4. In the *Sorting/Grouping* tab, sort by **Family**, and clear **Itemize every instance**.

5. Click **OK** to create the schedule. Stretch the columns such that all the words are visible, as shown in Figure 2–32.

Plumbing Fixture Schedule			
Family	Type	Manufacturer	Count
Drinking Fountain-Hi-Lo-3D	Drinking Fountain-Hi-Lo-3D		2
Shower Base-Round Corner	36" x 36"		1
Sink Kitchen-Double	42" x 21"		3
Sink Vanity-Round	19" x 19"		8
Toilet-Commercial-Wall-3D	15" Seat Height		6
Urinal-Wall-3D	Urinal-Wall-3D		2

Figure 2–32

6. Open the **P601- Plumbing Schedules** sheet. Drag and drop the schedule to this sheet. Modify the width of each field as required.

7. Save the project.

Task 3 - Create electrical-related schedules.

---

1. If time permits, create an electrical circuit schedule similar to the duct system schedule and a lighting fixture schedule similar to the plumbing fixture schedule. Place these schedules on the **E601 - Electrical and Lighting Schedules** sheet.

   - No electrical circuits are established in the project. Add them to fill in the schedule.

2. Save the project.

Practice 2c

Create Schedules for Structural Projects

Practice Objectives

- Create a structural schedule that includes all types of structural elements.
- Reorganize the schedule content by sorting and grouping.
- Place the schedule on a sheet.

Estimated time for completion: 15 minutes

In this practice, you will create a schedule displaying structural elements by category, You will then place it on a sheet and modify it to fit, as shown in Figure 2–33.

Structural Schedule		
Type Mark	Family and Type	Count
Structural Columns		
P-1	Concrete-Rectangular-Column: 24 x 24	22
	W-Wide Flange-Column: W10X33	1
	W-Wide Flange-Column: W10X49	22
Structural Foundations		
F-2	Footing-Rectangular: 14'x14'x2'-0"	1
F-1	Footing-Rectangular: 36" x 36" x 12"	21
	Foundation Slab: 6" Foundation Slab	1
	Step Footing: Step Footing	4
	Wall Foundation: Bearing Footing - 24" x 12"	6
	Wall Foundation: Bearing Footing - 36" x 12"	4
	Wall Foundation: Retaining Footing - 24" x 12" x 12"	1
Structural Framing		
	HSS-Hollow Structural Section: HSS6X6X.500	9
	K-Series Bar Joist-Rod Web: 16K5	65
	W-Wide Flange: W8X10	6
	W-Wide Flange: W12X26	63
	W-Wide Flange: W14X48	62
	W-Wide Flange: W16X45	1

Figure 2–33

Task 1 - Create a structural schedule.

1. In the practice files *Structural* folder, open **Axiom-Building-Create.rvt**.

2. In the *View* tab>Create panel, expand ▦ (Schedules) and click ▦ (Schedule/Quantities).

3. In the New Schedule dialog box, set *Filter list* to **Structure**, set *Category* to **<Multi-Category>**, and name it **Structural Schedule**. Click **OK**.

4. In the Schedule Properties dialog box, in the *Fields* tab, add the following fields:

- *Type Mark*
- *Family and Type*
- *Count*
- *Category*

5. Use ⬆ (Move Up) and ⬇ (Move Down) to change the order of the scheduled fields, if required, so they display as shown in Figure 2–34.

Scheduled fields (in order):

Type Mark
Family and Type
Count
Category

Figure 2–34

6. Click **OK**. The new schedule displays with all of the structural elements in the project in a long list, as shown in part in Figure 2–35.

		\<Structural Schedule\>	
A	B	C	D
Type Mark	Family and Type	Count	Category
	W-Wide Flange-Colum	1	Structural Columns
	W-Wide Flange-Colum	1	Structural Columns
	W-Wide Flange-Colum	1	Structural Columns
	W-Wide Flange-Colum	1	Structural Columns
	W-Wide Flange-Colum	1	Structural Columns
	W-Wide Flange-Colum	1	Structural Columns
	W-Wide Flange-Colum	1	Structural Columns
	W-Wide Flange-Colum	1	Structural Columns
	W-Wide Flange-Colum	1	Structural Columns
	W-Wide Flange-Colum	1	Structural Columns
	W-Wide Flange-Colum	1	Structural Columns
	W-Wide Flange-Colum	1	Structural Columns
	W-Wide Flange-Colum	1	Structural Columns
	W-Wide Flange-Colum	1	Structural Columns
	W-Wide Flange-Colum	1	Structural Columns
	W-Wide Flange-Colum	1	Structural Columns
	W-Wide Flange-Colum	1	Structural Columns
	W-Wide Flange-Colum	1	Structural Columns
	W-Wide Flange-Colum	1	Structural Columns
	Wall Foundation: Beari	1	Structural Foundati
	Wall Foundation: Beari	1	Structural Foundati
	Wall Foundation: Beari	1	Structural Foundati

Figure 2–35

7. Save the project.

Task 2 - Add filtering, sorting, and grouping to the schedule.

1. In Properties, in the *Other* category, next to **Sorting/ Grouping**, click **Edit....** The Schedule Properties dialog box opens with the *Sorting/Grouping* tab selected.

2. In the *Sorting/Grouping* tab, sort by **Category**, and select **Header**. Then sort by **Family and Type** with no header. Clear **Itemize every instance**, as shown in Figure 2–36.

Figure 2–36

3. In the Schedule Properties dialog box, in the *Filter* tab, add the *Filter* **Category does not equal Structural Rebar**, as shown in Figure 2–37.

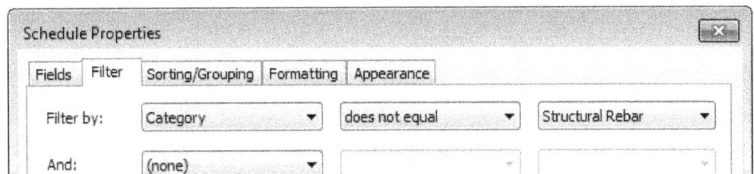

Figure 2–37

4. Click **OK** to update the schedule.

5. Resize the columns to see the information. Right-click on the *Category* column and select **Hide Columns**. The schedule displays as shown in Figure 2–38.

A	B	C
	<Structural Schedule>	
Type Mark	Family and Type	Count
Structural Columns		
P-1	Concrete-Rectangular-Column: 24 x 24	22
	W-Wide Flange-Column: W10X33	1
	W-Wide Flange-Column: W10X49	22
Structural Foundations		
F-2	Footing-Rectangular: 14'x14'x2'-0"	1
F-1	Footing-Rectangular: 36" x 36" x 12"	21
	Foundation Slab: 6" Foundation Slab	1
	Step Footing: Step Footing	4
	Wall Foundation: Bearing Footing - 24" x 12"	6
	Wall Foundation: Bearing Footing - 36" x 12"	4
	Wall Foundation: Retaining Footing - 24" x 12" x 12"	1
Structural Framing		
	HSS-Hollow Structural Section: HSS6X6X.500	9
	K-Series Bar Joist-Rod Web: 16K6	65
	W-Wide Flange: W8X10	6
	W-Wide Flange: W12X26	63
	W-Wide Flange: W14X48	62
	W-Wide Flange: W16X45	1

Figure 2–38

6. Open the **S601- Schedules** sheet. Drag and drop the schedule to this sheet. Modify the width of each field as required.

7. Save the project.

Task 3 - (Optional) Additional Schedules.

1. If time permits, create schedules that incorporate the information shown in Figure 2–39 and Figure 2–40.

<Structural Foundation Schedule>				
A	B	C	D	E
Type Mark	Count	Type	Width	Length
F-1	21	36" x 36" x 12"	3' - 0"	3' - 0"
F-2	1	14"x14"x2'-0"	14' - 0"	14' - 0"

Grand total: 22

Figure 2–39

Hint: Filter by **Type Mark begins with "F"** so that only the individual footing foundations display and sort by Type Mark.

<Structural Foundation Column Schedule>				
A	B	C	D	E
Type Mark	Count	Type	Top Level	Base Level
P-1	22	24 x 24	Level 1	T.O. Footing

Figure 2–40

- **Hint:** Create a Structural Column Schedule, change the name and Filter by **Type Mark begins with "P"** so that only the foundation columns display.

2. Save the project.

2.3 Modifying Schedule Appearance

While you assign global appearance settings in the Schedule Properties dialog box, you can also modify the appearance of each cell in a schedule and add other rows and columns. Title and Heading cells can include both text and parameter values and have different text formatting, as shown in Figure 2–41. You can also add images to title cells and to individual rows in a schedule.

<Window Schedule>						
<Toronto Towers>				Project No.	<1234-5678>	
A	B	C	D	E	F	G
Type	Count	Height	Width	Manufacturer	Model	Comments
36 x 36	72	3' - 0"	3' - 0"	Anderson	FX3636	
36" x 48"	84	4' - 0"	3' - 0"	Anderson	FX3648	
Grand total: 156						

Figure 2–41

- These modifications work with all types of schedules.

- Most of these modifications can be accessed in the *Modify Schedule/Quantities* tab (as shown in Figure 2–42), which is available when you are in a schedule view.

Figure 2–42

- Many of these options are also found in the shortcut menu.

Setting up Parameter Values

Parameter values and options can be set up by cells. The type of cell determines the options you can use.

- **Title Cells:** Select either **Schedule** or **Project Information**, as shown in Figure 2–43. Then, choose from the parameters available, as shown in Figure 2–44.

Figure 2–43

Figure 2–44

- **Header or Data Cells:** Select options based on the type of element the schedule is made for, as shown in Figure 2–45. Then, choose from the parameters available, as shown in Figure 2–46. Changing this information also changes the field specified for the selected column.

Figure 2–45

Figure 2–46

- Parameter values in titles are displayed in the schedule view with **<>** at either end of the value. This does not display on the sheet view.

- Additional options for modifying the parameters include

  (Format Unit), f_x (Calculated), and (Combine Parameters). These are covered in more depth in the *Advanced Schedule Options* topic.

Modifying Columns and Rows

The options for Columns and Rows (as shown in Figure 2–47), vary according to the type of cell selected. You can **Insert**, **Delete**, and **Resize** title columns and rows. If you select a header column you can insert, delete, resize, and hide the column.

Figure 2–47

- Be careful about making changes in the ribbon when you are in a data cell because any changes you make apply to the entire row or column.

How To: Hide a Column

1. Select any cell in the column that you want to hide.
2. In the *Modify Schedule/Quantities* tab>Columns panel, click

   (Hide). Alternatively, if you have selected the header cell, right-click and select **Hide Columns**.
3. The column is hidden.

- If you have hidden any columns and no longer want them

  hidden, you can click (Unhide All) or right-click and select **Unhide All Columns** at any time.

- Hiding columns is typically used when you want to sort or filter and do not want them to display in the final schedule.

How To: Resize a Row or Column

1. Select a cell. If the cell is a title cell you can resize both the row and column
2. In the *Modify Schedule/Quantities* tab>Columns panel, click

   (Resize) or in the Rows panel, click (Resize).
3. In the Resize Column (or Row) dialog box (as shown in Figure 2–48), type a size and click **OK**.

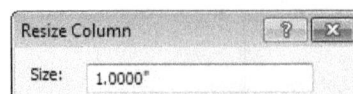

Figure 2–48

4. The column or row is resized in the schedule view and sheet.

Modifying Titles and Headers

The more complex and extensive a schedule, the more it can help to modify the title and header cells, using the commands shown in Figure 2–49. The title cells can be merged or unmerged. You can also insert images and delete the contents of title cells. Header cells can be grouped and ungrouped.

Figure 2–49

How To: Add and Merge Title Cells

1. Click inside a title cell.
2. In the *Modify Schedule/Quantities* tab>Rows panel, expand

    (Insert) and click (Above Selected) or (Below Selected). When inserting below the primary cell it typically comes in matching the number of header cells as shown in Figure 2–50.

<Door Schedule>						
A	B	C	D	E	F	G
Mark	Family and Type	Height	Width	Fire Rating	Frame Material	Frame Type

Before

<Door Schedule>						
A	B	C	D	E	F	G
Mark	Family and Type	Height	Width	Fire Rating	Frame Material	Frame Type

After

Figure 2–50

3. Pick and drag across the cells that you want to merge.

4. Click (Merge Unmerge).
5. The cells are now merged together, as shown in Figure 2–51.

<Door Schedule>						
A	B	C	D	E	F	G
Mark	Family and Type	Height	Width	Fire Rating	Frame Material	Frame Type

Figure 2–51

---

6. Add a parameter, text, or image in the newly merged cell.

•   If you no longer want the cells to be merged, select the cell and click 🔲 (Merge Unmerge).

•   To insert an image file (such as a .BMP, .JPG, or .PNG) in a title cell, select the title cell and click 🖼️ (Insert Image) and select the image from the list.

•   Use 🖼️ (Clear Cell) to delete the text, image, or parameter used in that cell (Titles only).

How To: Group Sub-headers

1. In the Schedule view, drag the cursor over the headers you want to group.
2. In the *Modify Schedule/Quantities* tab>Titles & Headers panel, click 🔲 (Group).
3. A new header area is created above the selected columns. Enter a new name, as shown in Figure 2–52.

A	B	C	D	E
		Window Dimensions		
Window Type	Count	Height	Width	Sill Height
36 x 36	72	3' - 0"	3' - 0"	3' - 0"
36" x 48"	84	4' - 0"	3' - 0"	3' - 0"
Grand total: 156				

Figure 2–52

•   If you no longer need the grouped header cell, select the grouped cell and click 🔲 (Ungroup).

Setting the Appearance

The overall appearance of a schedule, including the text types used in the various cells, is set up in the Schedule Properties. You can also modify individual title and header cells using the options in the Appearance panel, as shown in Figure 2–53.

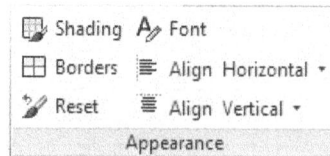

Figure 2–53

(Shading)	Opens the Color dialog box in which you can select a background color for the selected cells.
(Borders)	Opens the Edit Borders dialog box in which you can specify the line style and locations of borders around the selected cells.
(Reset)	Returns the formatting of selected cells to the original specified in the schedule properties.
(Font)	Opens the Edit Font dialog box in which you can specify the **Font**, **Font size**, **Font Style** (**Bold**, **Italic**, or **Underline**) and **Font Color** for the selected cells.
(Align Horizontal)	Aligns the text in the selected cells to the **Left**, **Center**, or **Right** justification.
(Align Vertical)	Aligns the text in the selected cells to the **Top**, **Middle**, or **Bottom** justification.

- The changes you make the tools in the Appearance panel are not included in a schedule view template.

Adding Image Fields and Images

In addition to adding images in the title cells of a schedule you can assign images to elements and have them display in the schedule on a sheet, as shown in Figure 2–54.

Lighting Fixture Types			
Type Mark	Image	Family	Count
A		Troffer Light - 2x2 Parabolic	17
B		Troffer Light - 2x4 Parabolic	48
C		Pendant Light - Hemisphere	10

Figure 2–54

- Images can be set by instance or by type.

How To: Add Images to Schedules

1. In the schedule view, open the Schedule Properties dialog box in the *Fields* tab.
2. Add the *Image* (or *Type Image*) field to the scheduled fields, as shown in Figure 2–55.

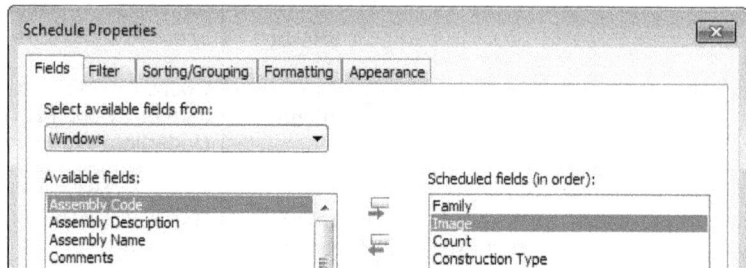

Figure 2–55

3. Complete the rest of your schedule design and click **OK**.
4. In the schedule view, the *Image* (or *Type Image*) column displays as part of the schedules, as shown in Figure 2–56.

<Lighting Fixture Types>			
A	**B**	**C**	**D**
Type Mark	Image	Family	Count
A	<None>	Troffer Light - 2x2 Parabolic	17
B	<None>	Troffer Light - 2x4 Parabolic	48
C	<None>	Pendant Light - Hemisphere	10

Figure 2–56

5. Assign the appropriate image file to the instances or types.

   - Type images for component families (such as light fixtures) are assigned directly in the family file and are read-only in the project. Type images for system families (such as walls) are assigned in the Type Properties.
   - Instance images are assigned in Properties for each instance of the element.

6. To display the images, place the schedule on a sheet.

How To: Assign Image Files

1. Navigate to the appropriate place at which to assign the Image or Type Image. (Type Images for component families are assigned in the family file, not the project.)
2. Next to the **Image** or **Type Image** parameter, click

    (Browse), as shown in Figure 2–57.

Figure 2–57

3. In the Manage Images dialog box, select the image that you want to use, as shown in Figure 2–58.

Figure 2–58

4. Click **OK**

- To add images to the Manage Image dialog box, click **Add...** and navigate to the location in which the images are stored.

- You can also delete and reload images as you would reload linked files.

- Image file formats include BMP, JPG, JPEG, PNG, and TIF.

Practice 2d

Modify Schedules for Architectural Projects

Practice Objectives

- Modify the look of the schedule using parameters, and by merging and grouping cells.
- Add images to a schedule.

Estimated time for completion: 15 minutes

In this practice, you will modify the appearance of a schedule by adding parameters and text to the title and by merging group headers, as shown in Figure 2–59 (on a sheet). You will also add an image field (column) and assign images to a schedule.

Door Schedule - Level 1							
Clark Hall Performing Arts Building				Project Number: 1234.56			
	Door Size			Frame Information			
Mark	Height	Width	Fire Rating	Frame Type	Frame Material	Finish	Comments

Figure 2–59

Task 1 - Modify the appearance of the schedule.

1. In the practice files *Architectural* folder, open **Clark-Hall-Schedules-Modify.rvt**.

2. Open the **Door Schedule-Level 1** view.

3. Select the top title row of the schedule.

4. In the *Modify Schedule/Quantities* tab>Row panel, expand ⌐ᵗᴇ (Insert) and click ⌐ᴳᴱ (Below Selected).

5. Drag the cursor over approximately half of the new heading columns on the left and, in the Titles & Headers panel, click ⊞ (Merge Unmerge). The cells are merged as shown in Figure 2–60.

<Door Schedule - Level 1>							
A	B	C	D	E	F	G	H
Mark	Height	Width	Fire Rating	Frame Type	Frame Material	Finish	Comments

Figure 2–60

The name of the project displays in brackets indicating that it is a parameter rather than text.

6. Select the newly merged cell. In the Parameters panel, expand **Category** and select **Project Information**. Expand **Parameter** and select **Project Name**.

7. Merge the other cells and add text (**Project Number**) and another parameter (**Project Number**), as shown in Figure 2–61.

<Door Schedule - Level 1>							
<Clark Hall>				Project Number:		<1234.56>	
A	B	C	D	E	F	G	H
Mark	Height	Width	Fire Rating	Frame Type	Frame Material	Finish	Comments

Figure 2–61

8. In the *Manage* tab>Settings Panel, click (Project Information).

9. In the Project Properties dialog box, update the *Project Name* to **Clark Hall Performing Arts Building**. Click **OK**. The *Project Name* updates, as shown in Figure 2–62.

<Door Schedule - Level 1>							
<Clark Hall Performing Arts Building>				Project Number:		<1234.56>	
A	B	C	D	E	F	G	H
Mark	Height	Width	Fire Rating	Frame Type	Frame Material	Finish	Comments

Figure 2–62

10. Drag the cursor over the *Height* and *Width* header cells.

11. In the *Modify Schedule/Quantities* tab> Titles & Headers panel, click (Group).

12. Select the new cell and type **Door Size**.

13. Repeat for *Frame Type*, *Frame Material*, and *Finish* and enter **Frame Information**, as shown in Figure 2–63.

A	B	C	D	E	F	G	H
	Door Size			Frame Information			
Mark	Height	Width	Fire Rating	Frame Type	Frame Material	Finish	Comments

Figure 2–63

14. Save the project.

Task 2 - Modify the Appearance of the Title

1. Select the title cell and, in the *Schedules/Quantities* tab> Appearance panel, click ${}^{A_{\mathscr{D}}}$ (Font).

2. In the Edit Font dialog box, change the *Font size* to **1/4"** and set the *Font style* to **Bold**.

3. Modify the other title and header cells as required. In the example shown in Figure 2–64, in addition to changing the font appearance, the Project Number text and parameter have been aligned horizontally to be closer to each other and the border between the two of them has been removed.

<Door Schedule - Level 1>							
<Clark Hall Performing Arts Building>				Project Number: <1234.56>			
A	B	C	D	E	F	G	H
	Door Size				Frame Information		
Mark	Height	Width	Fire Rating	Frame Type	Frame Material	Finish	Comments

Figure 2–64

4. Open the **A601-Schedules** view to display the images and adjust it as required.

5. Save the project.

Task 3 - Add Images to a schedule.

1. Open the **Window Schedule** view.

2. In the Schedule Properties dialog box, in the *Fields* tab add the **Type Mark** and **Image** parameters to the *Scheduled Fields* above the **Type** parameter. Move the **Count** parameter to the bottom of the list, as shown in Figure 2–65, and click **OK**.

In this situation the Type Image is only accessible by opening and adjusting the family file. Therefore, you can use the instance Image parameter.

Figure 2–65

3. In the **Window Schedule** view, select the *Image* cell for the first type and click [...].

4. In the Manage Images dialog box, click **Add...**

5. In the Import Image dialog box, navigate to the practice files *Architectural>Images* folder, select the two window images, and click **Open**.

6. In the Manage Images dialog box, select the image that matches the window row in which you are working and click **OK**.

7. Repeat the process with the other window image. The schedule should look similar to Figure 2–66.

<Window Schedule>					
A	B	C	D	E	F
Type Mark	Image	Type	Manufacturer	Comments	Count
18	Window Rectangle.png	36" x 72"			3
19	Window Square.png [...]	48" x 48"			36
Grand total: 39					

Figure 2–66

8. Open the **Sheets (all): A601 - Schedules** view. The images should display as shown in Figure 2–67

Figure 2–67

9. If time permits, modify the schedule appearance to match the Door schedule.

10. Save the project.

Practice 2e

Modify Schedules for MEP Projects

Practice Objectives

- Modify the look of the schedule using parameters and by merging and grouping cells.
- Add images to a schedule.

Estimated time for completion: 15 minutes

In this practice, you will modify the appearance of a schedule by adding parameters and text to the title and by merging headers. You will also add an image field (column) and assign images to a schedule, as shown on a sheet in Figure 2–68.

Lighting Fixture Types			
Type Mark	Image	Family	Count
A		Troffer Light - 2x2 Parabolic	17
B		Troffer Light - 2x4 Parabolic	48
C		Pendant Light - Hemisphere	10

Figure 2–68

Task 1 - Modify the appearance of the schedule.

1. In the practice files *MEP* folder, open **Freel-Office-Modify.rvt**.

2. Open the **Plumbing Fixtures** schedule view.

3. Select the top title row of the schedule.

4. In the *Modify Schedule/Quantities* tab>Row panel, expand ⌐⌐ (Insert) and click ⌐⌐ (Below Selected).

5. Drag the cursor over half of the new heading columns on the left. In the Titles & Headers panel, click ⊞ (Merge Unmerge). The cells are merged, as shown in Figure 2–69.

<Plumbing Fixtures>			
A	B	C	D
Family	Type	Manufacturer	Count

Figure 2–69

6. Select the newly merged cell. In the Parameters panel, expand **Category** and select **Project Information**. Then expand **Parameter** and select **Project Name**. The name of the project displays in brackets, indicating that it is a parameter

7. In the other cells and add text (**Project Number:**) and another parameter (**Project Number**), as shown in Figure 2–70.

<Plumbing Fixtures>			
<Project Name>		Project Number:	<Project Number>
A	B	C	D
Family	Type	Manufacturer	Count

Figure 2–70

8. In the *Manage* tab>Settings Panel, click ⊡ (Project Information).

9. In the Project Properties dialog box, update *Project Name* to **Freel Office Building** and *Project Number* to **1234.56**. Click **OK**. The parameters update as shown in Figure 2–71.

<Plumbing Fixtures>			
<Freel Office Building>		Project Number:	<1234.56>
A	B	C	D
Family	Type	Manufacturer	Count

Figure 2–71

10. Save the project.

Task 2 - Modify the Appearance of the Title

1. Select the title cell and, in the Schedules/Quantities tab> Appearance panel, click $^{A_{\mathscr{D}}}$ (Font).

2. In the Edit Font dialog box change the *Font size* to **1/4"** and set the *Font style* to **Bold**.

3. Modify the other title and header cells, as required. In the example shown in Figure 2–72, besides changing the font appearance, the **Project Number** text and parameter have been aligned horizontally so they are closer to each other and the border between the two of them has been removed.

<Plumbing Fixtures>			
<Freel Office Building>		Project Number: <1234.56>	
A	B	C	D
Family	Type	Manufacturer	Count

Figure 2–72

4. Save the project.

Task 3 - Add Images to a schedule.

1. Open the **Lighting Fixture Types** view.

2. In the Schedule Properties dialog box, in the *Fields* tab, add the **Image** parameter to the Scheduled Fields after the **Type Mark** parameter, as shown in Figure 2–73, and click **OK**.

In this situation the Type Image is only accessible by opening and adjusting the family file. Therefore, you can use the instance Image parameter.

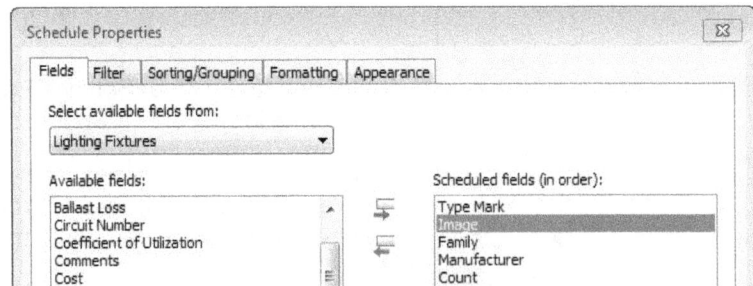

Figure 2–73

3. In the **Lighting Fixture Types** view, select the *Image* cell for the first type and click ⟨...⟩.

4. In the Manage Images dialog box, click **Add...**

5. In the Import Image dialog box, navigate to the practice files *MEP>Images* folder, select the three light images, and click **Open**.

6. In the Manage Images dialog box, select the image that matches the row in which you are working and click **OK**.

7. Repeat the process with the other lighting fixture images. The schedule should look similar to the one shown in Figure 2–74.

A	B	C	D
Type Mark	Image	Family	Count
A	Troffer Light Square.jpg [...]	Troffer Light - 2x2 Parabolic	17
B	Toffer Light rectangle.jpg	Troffer Light - 2x4 Parabolic	48
C	Pendant Light.jpg	Pendant Light - Hemisphere	10

<Lighting Fixture Types>

Figure 2–74

8. Open the **Sheets (all): E601 - Electrical and Lighting Schedules** view. The images should display as shown in Figure 2–75

Figure 2–75

9. If time permits, modify the schedule appearance to match the other schedule.

10. Save the project.

Practice 2f

Modify Schedules for Structural Projects

Practice Objective

- Modify the look of the schedule using parameters, and merging and grouping cells.

Estimated time for completion: 15 minutes

In this practice, you will modify the appearance of a schedule by adding parameters and text to the title and by merging cells, as shown in Figure 2–76.

\<Structural Schedule\>		
\<Axiom Building\>		**Project Number: \<1234.56\>**
A	B	C
Type Mark	Family and Type	Count

Figure 2–76

Task 1 - Modify the appearance of the schedule.

1. In the practice files *Structural* folder, open **Axiom-Building-Modify.rvt**.

2. Open the **Structural Schedule** view.

3. Select the top title row of the schedule.

4. In the *Modify Schedule/Quantities* tab>Row panel, expand ⯯ (Insert) and click ⯯ (Below Selected).

5. If there are more than three new cells, drag the cursor over half of the new heading columns on the left and, in the Titles & Headers panel, click ▥ (Merge Unmerge). The cells are merged as shown in Figure 2–77.

\<Structural Schedule\>		
A	B	C
Type Mark	Family and Type	Count

Figure 2–77

6. Select the newly merged cell. In the Parameters panel, expand **Category** and select **Project Information**. Then expand **Parameter** and select **Project Name**. The name of the project displays in brackets indicating that it is a parameter rather than text, as shown in Figure 2–78.

7. Add text (**Project Number:**) and another parameter (**Project Number**) as shown in Figure 2–78.

<Structural Schedule>		
<Project Name>	Project Number:	<Project Number>
A	B	C
Type Mark	Family and Type	Count

Figure 2–78

8. In the *Manage* tab>Settings Panel, click ⬚ (Project Information).

9. In the Project Properties dialog box, update *Project Name* to **Axiom Building** and *Project Number* to **1234.56**. Click **OK**. The project name and number update as shown in Figure 2–79.

<Structural Schedule>		
<Axiom Building>	Project Number:	<1234.56>
A	B	C
Type Mark	Family and Type	Count

Figure 2–79

10. Save the project.

Task 2 - Modify the appearance of the title.

1. Select the title cell. In the *Schedules/Quantities* tab> Appearance panel, click ᴬ⁄ (Font).

2. In the Edit Font dialog box, change the *Font size* to **1/4"** and set the *Font style* to **Bold**.

3. Modify the other title and header cells as required. In the example shown in Figure 2–80, in addition to changing the font appearance, the **Project Number** text and parameter have been aligned horizontally to be closer to each other and the border between them has been removed.

<Structural Schedule>		
<Axiom Building>	Project Number: <1234.56>	
A	B	C
Type Mark	Family and Type	Count

Figure 2–80

4. Modify the other two schedules to match the appearance.

5. Save the project.

2.4 Creating Key Schedules

A *key schedule* lists type information that is not automatically included in an element, such as the finish or frame type of a door. By grouping this information into keys, you can enter it more quickly.

Schedule key styles are useful when you have a large number of elements that need to have the same finish information, as shown in Figure 2–81. Fields in key styles are typically controlled by instance rather than by type. Grouping styles together makes it easier to apply this information to large numbers of instances.

<Room Style Schedule>					
A	B	C	D	E	F
Key Name	Wall Finish	Floor Finish	Base Finish	Ceiling Finish	Comments
Corridor	Painted	Carpet	Vinyl	Painted	
Executive Office	Wall Paper	Wood	Wood	ACT	
Standard Office	Painted	Carpet	Vinyl	ACT	
Utility	Painted	Vinyl	Vinyl	ACT	

Figure 2–81

How To: Create a Schedule Key Style

1. Start a new schedule.
2. In the New Schedule dialog box, select a category.
3. Select the **Schedule keys** option and type a *Name* for the key, as shown in Figure 2–82. This adds an **Instance** parameter in the Properties dialog box for the selected category and adds a field to the schedule properties.

Use the Filter list to limit the number of categories with which you can work.

Figure 2–82

4. Click **OK**.
5. In the Schedule Properties dialog box, the *Fields* tab displays the new **Key Name** that has already been added to the *Scheduled fields*, as shown in Figure 2–83.
6. Add other fields from the list of *Available fields*, as shown in Figure 2–83.

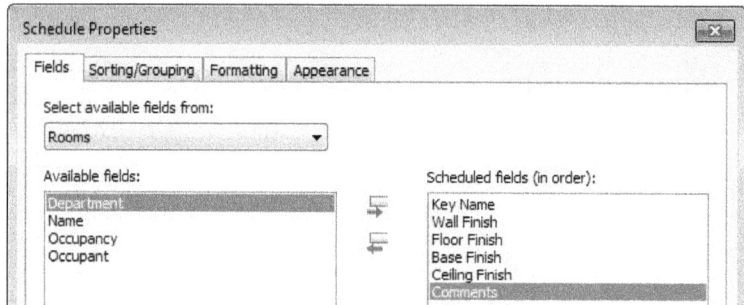

Figure 2–83

7. Fill out the rest of the tabs as required and click **OK**. The new schedule opens with only the fields displayed, as shown in Figure 2–84.

<Room Style Schedule>					
A	B	C	D	E	F
Key Name	Wall Finish	Floor Finish	Base Finish	Ceiling Finish	Comments

Figure 2–84

8. In the *Modify | Schedule/Quantities* tab>Rows panel, click

   (Insert Data Row) or right-click on the schedule and select **Insert Data Row**. A new row with the default label **1** is displayed, as shown in Figure 2–85. Type a new name for the row.

<Room Style Schedule>					
A	B	C	D	E	F
Key Name	Wall Finish	Floor Finish	Base Finish	Ceiling Finish	Comments
1					

Figure 2–85

9. Continue adding rows and names as shown in Figure 2–86.

<Room Style Schedule>					
A	B	C	D	E	F
Key Name	Wall Finish	Floor Finish	Base Finish	Ceiling Finish	Comments
Corridor					
Executive Office					
Standard Office					
Utility					

Figure 2–86

10. Fill in the values for the rows as shown in Figure 2–87.

<Room Style Schedule>					
A	B	C	D	E	F
Key Name	Wall Finish	Floor Finish	Base Finish	Ceiling Finish	Comments
Corridor	Painted	Carpet	Vinyl	Painted	
Executive Office	Wall Paper	Wood	Wood	ACT	
Standard Office	Painted	Carpet	Vinyl	ACT	
Utility	Painted	Vinyl	Vinyl	ACT	

Figure 2–87

11. To assign the key style, add a column to the schedule (such as the *Room Style* column in a Room Schedule shown in Figure 2–88).

<Room Schedule>		
A	B	C
Number	Name	Room Style
101	Office	(none)
102	Conference	(none)
103	Office	Corridor
104	Office	Executive Office
105	Office	Standard Office
106	Office	Utility
107	Work Room	Utility
108	Reception	Standard Office
109	Library	Executive Offic

Figure 2–88

You can also modify the properties of various instances in the project as shown in Figure 2–89.

Figure 2–89

2.5 Advanced Schedule Options

When you are working in a variety of schedules, you might want to include additional parameters, create fields that include formulas, as shown for a rounded area in Figure 2–90, or combine parameters. You can also add conditional formatting that adds a background color to cells that meet the condition. For MEP projects you can also create nested schedules.

<Room Schedule>			
A	B	C	D
Number	Name	Area	Floor Area
101	Office	280.49 SF	280 SF
102	Conference	337.38 SF	340 SF
103	Office	199.63 SF	200 SF
104	Office	199.63 SF	200 SF
105	Office	193.17 SF	190 SF
106	Office	243.22 SF	240 SF
107	Work Room	154.77 SF	150 SF
108	Reception	327.48 SF	330 SF
109	Library	404.78 SF	400 SF

Figure 2–90

Enhanced in 2018

Project Parameters can be added to building elements and items, such as model groups, RVT Links, and Schedules.

Creating Project Parameters

Two types of custom parameters can be used in schedules: project parameters and shared parameters.

• Project parameters can be used in schedules, but not in tags.

• Shared parameters can be used in schedules and in tags. They can also be used in other projects and exported to a database.

How To: Create a Project Parameter in a Schedule

1. In the Schedule Properties dialog box, in the *Fields* tab, click

   (New parameter) (or other Project Parameter access).

2. In the Parameter Properties dialog box, select **Project parameter**, as shown in Figure 2–91.

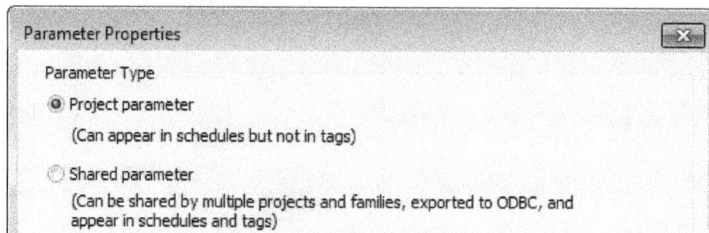

Figure 2–91

3. In the *Parameter Data* area shown in Figure 2–92, Set the value as an **Instance** or a **Type**. and then specify a new *Name* for the parameter and select the *Discipline*, *Group*, and *Type of Parameter* in the drop-down lists. You can also add a custom tooltip.

Figure 2–92

- **Instance parameters:** Set for each instance of the associated element. For example, if you create a **Material** parameter when you are creating a furniture schedule, you can assign a different material to each instance of the component.

- **Type parameters:** Modify all instances of a specific type. For example, if you create a **Material** parameter for a furniture component, changing the material for one component changes all of them.

- **Values are aligned per group type:** (Instance Parameters only.) If an element that includes this parameter is part of multiple groups, the value remains the same for all of the groups. Changing the value in one group changes the value in all of the groups.

- Values can vary by group instance: (Instance Parameters only.) If an element that includes this parameter is part of multiple groups, the value can vary according to the group. Changing the value in one group changes the value for all other instances of that group, but does not change the value for instances of other groups that also include the element.

- The *Discipline* can be set to **Common**, **Structural**, **HVAC, Electrical**, **Piping**, or **Energy**.

- The *Type of Parameter* specifies how the parameter value is stored, The options available for Discipline impact the types of parameters in the list, as shown in Figure 2–93.

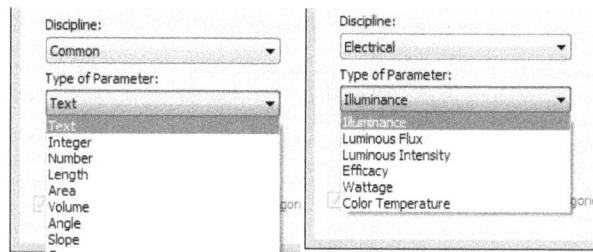

Figure 2–93

Common Parameter Types

Text	A text parameter can host any type of information that consists of both numbers and letters. Examples could be the fabric color or part number of the element.
Integer	Any value that is always represented by a whole number. Examples could be the number of chairs that fit around a conference table or the number of shelves in a bookcase.
Number	Any numeric value: whole, decimal, or fraction. You can use formulas with **Number** parameters.
Length	When you label dimensions, you create **Length** parameters. You can use formulas with **Length** parameters.
Area	Establishes the area of an element. It is numeric and can have formulas applied to it.
Volume	Establishes the volume of an element. It is numeric and can have formulas applied to it.

Angle	Establishes the angle of an element. It is numeric and can have formulas applied to it.
Slope	Displays a slope, as set up in the Field Format.
Currency	Displays the amount in dollars or other currencies, as set up in the Field Format.
Mass Density	Displays the mass per unit volume of material.
URL	Specifies a link to a web site.
Material	Provides a place to assign a material from the list of materials that are set up in the project.
Image	Creates a parameter in which you can add a raster image connected to the family.
Yes/No	Used with instance parameters where you need a **Yes** or **No** answer to a question listed in the name. The default is **Yes**.
<Family Type>	Opens a dialog box where you can select from the list of family types, such as doors, furniture, or tags.

The Group parameter under drop-down list lists groups that categorize parameters in the Properties and Family Types dialog boxes, as shown in Figure 2–94.

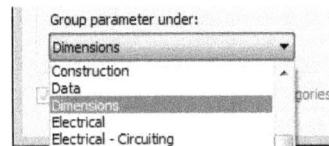

Figure 2–94

To add information to display when you hover the cursor over the new parameter in Properties, click **Edit Tooltip...**, as shown in Figure 2–95.

Figure 2–95

How To: Create Parameters Outside of Schedules

1. In the *Manage* tab>Settings panel, click 📖 (Project Parameters).
2. In the Project Parameters dialog box, click **Add**.
3. In the Parameter Properties dialog box, select **Project parameter** and set up the Parameter Data (i.e., the same information that is in the Parameter Properties dialog box for the schedule).
4. In the *Categories* area, select one or more related categories, as shown in Figure 2–96. Use the Filter list drop-down box to specify the discipline to limit the number of items that are displayed.

Figure 2–96

5. Click **OK**. The parameter is now available in the properties of the selected categories.

Creating Fields from Formulas

In a variety of schedules, you need to gather numerical information and apply formulas to it for a new parameter. For example, you can include cost and quantity information in a Material Takeoff, as shown in the schedule in Figure 2–97.

\<Brick - Material Takeoff\>					
A	B	C	D	E	F
Material: Name	Material: Area	Material: Manufacturer	Material: Cost	Total Cost	Total Units of Brick
Masonry - Brick	22160 SF	XYZ Masonry	3.00	$66480	155123
Masonry - Brick: 14	22160 SF			$66480	155123

Figure 2–97

- You can create calculated value fields to add formulas to a schedule, or create a percentage field using values in the schedule.

- Gather the information you need to use to create formulas, including the exact name of any fields, before you start the process of creating the calculated value.

- Formula outcomes can be rounded off.

How To: Create a Calculated Value Field

1. In the Schedule Properties dialog box, in the *Fields* tab, click
   f_x (Add calculated parameter). The Calculated Value dialog box opens, as shown in Figure 2–98.

*A formula has been added for this figure: (Material: Area / 1 SF) * Material: Cost.*

Figure 2–98

2. Type a *Name* for the new field.
3. Specify **Formula** as the type of field.
4. Select the *Discipline* and *Type*, as required.

5. Type the formula you want to use in the *Formula* field.

   • If a warning displays about inconsistent units, clarify the units by adding ***1** or **/1** to a formula. After doing this, the software should then apply the correct units.

   • To ensure you get the exact field name, click ⌷ (Browse) to select from a list of fields, as shown in Figure 2–99.

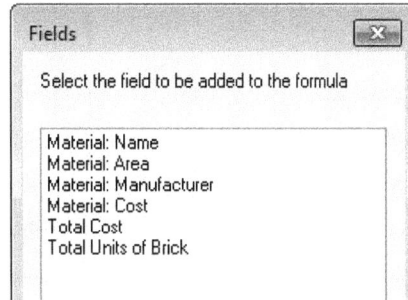

Formulas can only reference fields that are already included in the schedule.

Fields

Select the field to be added to the formula

Material: Name
Material: Area
Material: Manufacturer
Material: Cost
Total Cost
Total Units of Brick

Figure 2–99

6. Click **OK**.

Percentage Fields

Percentage fields can be used with area schedules, as shown in Figure 2–100.

<Area Schedule (Rentable)>		
A	**B**	**C**
Name	Area	Percent of Total Area
Office	2657 SF	9%
Auditorium	9694 SF	33%
Classrooms	13533 SF	46%
Area	3682 SF	12%

Figure 2–100

How To: Create a Percentage Field

1. In the Schedule Properties dialog box, in the *Fields* tab, click

   f_x (Add calculate parameter). The Calculated Value dialog box opens, as shown in Figure 2–101.

Figure 2–101

2. Type a *Name* for the new field.
3. Specify **Percentage** as the type of field.
4. Select the field you want to take a percentage *Of*.
5. Select the field you want to take a percentage *By*.

   • The default option is **<Grand total>**, which calculates the percentage based on the total of the entire schedule.

   • If you have created groups in the *Sorting/Grouping* tab, they are also available. For example, if Fields are sorted by **Level**.

6. Click **OK**.

Combining Parameters

Parameters can be combined into a new parameter. For example, you might want to include the height, width and depth of casework in one **Size** parameter, as shown in Figure 2–102

<Casework Schedule>

A	B	C	D	E
Family	Size	Cost	Count	Comments
Base Cabinet-2 Bin	2' - 10 1/2" x 1' - 6" x 2' - 0"		1	
Base Cabinet-4 Drawers	2' - 10 1/2" x 2' - 0"		2	
Base Cabinet-Double Door Sink Unit	2' - 10 1/2" x 3' - 0" x 2' - 0"		1	
Base Cabinet-Single Door & Drawer	2' - 10 1/2" x 2' - 0" x 2' - 0"		1	

Figure 2–102

   • Combined parameters are schedule-specific and need to be created for each schedule.

How To: Create Combined Parameters

1. In the Schedule Properties dialog box, in the *Fields* tab, click

   ▣ (Combine Parameters).
2. In the Combine Parameters dialog box, in the *Combined Parameter Name* text box, type a new name for the parameter.
3. Select two or more *Schedule Parameters* from the list on the

   left and click ⤵ (Add parameter(s)) to add it to the *Combined Parameter* list on the right.
4. Modify the Separator between each parameter, as shown in Figure 2–103.

Figure 2–103

- Check the preview of the value that displays at the bottom of the dialog box.
- You can also add a Prefix or Suffix and modify the *Sample Value* name.
5. Click **OK**.

Conditional Formatting

Conditional formatting can be applied to any field where you need to display some specific information that can easily be seen at a glance. For example, in Figure 2–104, the *Area* field is highlighted according to a conditional test for any size over 10000 SF.

Conditional formatting is typically used for testing and does not carry over when placed on a sheet.

Area Schedule Over 10000 SF			
A	B	C	D
Number	Name	Area Type	Area
1	Office	Building Common Area	2657 SF
2	Auditorium	Building Common Area	9694 SF
3	Classrooms	Building Common Area	13533 SF
4	Area	Building Common Area	3682 SF

Figure 2–104

How To: Add Conditional Formatting in a schedule

1. Open the schedule you want to work in and select the *Formatting* tab.
2. Select the field to which you want to apply the conditional formatting.
3. Click **Conditional Format...**.
4. In the Conditional Formatting dialog box, select the *Field*, *Test*, and specify a *Value*, as shown in Figure 2–105.

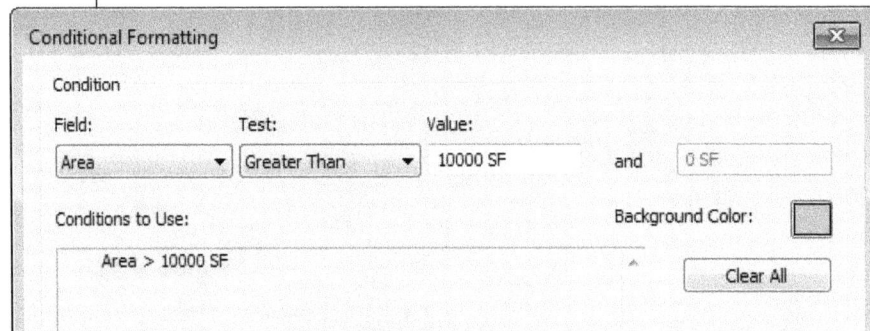

Figure 2–105

5. Click the **Background Color** button and select a color to display in the schedule when the conditions are met.
6. You can select additional fields, test, and values to further refine the conditional statements.
7. When you are finished, click **OK** to close the dialog box and continue working on the Schedule Properties as required.

Embedded Schedules (MEP only)

When working with MEP schedules that refer to spaces or rooms, you can use embedded schedules. For example, in Figure 2–106, a space schedule that is displaying the Space **Number** and **Name**, also has an embedded schedule displaying information about the air terminals in each space.

A	B
SPACE NO.	NAME
DIFFUSER ID	DIFFUSER TYPE
1501	CLASSROOM
29	Supply Diffuser - Perforated - Round Neck - Ceiling Mounted:
30	Supply Diffuser - Perforated - Round Neck - Ceiling Mounted:
31	Supply Diffuser - Perforated - Round Neck - Ceiling Mounted:
32	Supply Diffuser - Perforated - Round Neck - Ceiling Mounted:
1502	CLASSROOM
45	Supply Diffuser - Perforated - Round Neck - Ceiling Mounted:
46	Supply Diffuser - Perforated - Round Neck - Ceiling Mounted:
47	Supply Diffuser - Perforated - Round Neck - Ceiling Mounted:
48	Supply Diffuser - Perforated - Round Neck - Ceiling Mounted:

Figure 2–106

How To: Add an Embedded Schedule

1. Create the base Space or Room schedule.
2. In the Schedule Properties dialog box, select the *Embedded Schedule* tab.
3. Select the **Embedded Schedule** option, and then select a category type from the Category list, as shown in Figure 2–107.

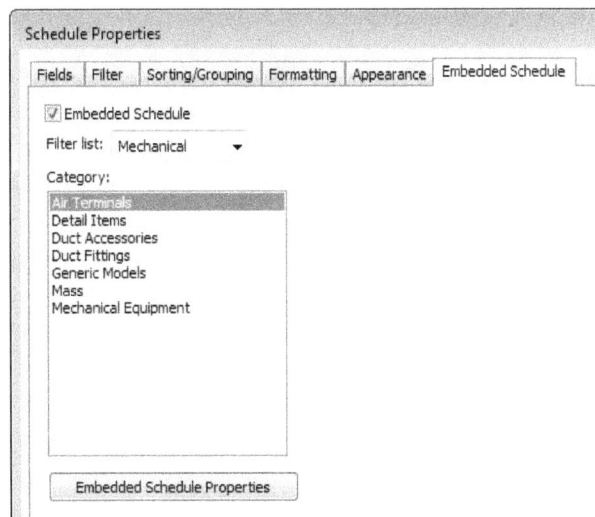

Figure 2–107

4. Click **Embedded Schedule Properties**.

5. In the Schedule Properties dialog box, in the *Field* tab, add the required fields. The fields display in order directly under the base schedule columns, as shown in Figure 2–108.

Base Schedule Fields
Embedded Schedule Fields <SPACE AIRFLOW CHECK>

A	B	C	D
SPACE NO.	NAME	Condition Type	ACTUAL SUPPLY AIRFLOW
DIFFUSER ID	DIFFUSER TYPE	DIFFUSER AIRFLOW	

Figure 2–108

6. Add any filters, sorting, and formatting as required.
7. Click **OK** until the schedule displays.

2.6 Creating Material Takeoff Schedules

Schedules are powerful features that interact with all parts of an Autodesk Revit project. A special schedule, called a Material Takeoff, gathers information about the materials in a project (such as the area and volume) and user-designated properties (such as the cost or manufacturer). You can also create formulas or percentages based on material properties to include in a schedule using the **Calculated value** option, as shown in Figure 2–109. Custom parameters are also permitted in Material Takeoffs.

Figure 2–109

- Creating material takeoff schedules follows the same procedure as when creating building component schedules, except that it uses a different command. In the *View* tab>

  Create panel, expand ▦ (Schedules) and click

  🛒 (Material Takeoff) or in the Project Browser, right-click on the Schedule/Quantities node and select **New Material Takeoff**.

- The options for fields include all of the material parameters, as shown in Figure 2–110.

Figure 2–110

- When creating a Material Takeoff Schedule, it can help to modify the unit settings for the various fields. In the Formatting tab, select a field and click **Field Format...**. In the Format dialog box, clear the **Use project settings** option and modify the options, as shown in Figure 2–111. This is only available for numerical fields.

Figure 2–111

- A numerical value can be assigned a currency. Zeros can be suppressed. Spaces can be suppressed and large numbers can include commas as separators.

Hint: Material Properties

Most material properties used in material takeoff schedules can be set by material. In the *Manage* tab>Settings panel, click

(Materials). In the Material Browser, select the material that you want to modify. In the *Identity* tab, you can add information, such as **Manufacturer** and **Cost** as shown in Figure 2–112.

Figure 2–112

Practice 2g

Create Complex Schedules for Architectural Projects

Practice Objectives

- Create material takeoff schedules.
- (Optional) Create a percentage-based calculated value field for use in a schedule.

Estimated time for completion: 15 minutes

In this practice, you will create a material takeoff schedule that includes several calculated value formulas. You will then add it to a sheet, as shown in Figure 2–113, and test it and other material takeoff schedules by modifying the wall type and material properties. As an optional task, you will create a percentage-based field for an area schedule.

Brick - Material Takeoff					
Material: Name	Material: Area	Material: Manufacturer	Material: Cost	Total Cost per SF	Total Units of Brick
Masonry - Brick	2749 SF	XYZ Masonry	3.00	$8250	19242
Masonry - Brick: 11	2749 SF			$8250	19242

Figure 2–113

Task 1 - Create a material takeoff schedule.

1. In the practice files *Architecture* folder, open **Mall-Addition.rvt**.

2. In the *View* tab>Create panel, expand ▦ (Schedules) and click ▦ (Material Takeoff).

3. In the New Material Takeoff dialog box, in the *Filter* list, select **Architecture**, and in the *Category* list, select **Walls**. Name the schedule **Brick – Material Takeoff** and select **New Construction** from the *Phase* list.

4. Click **OK**.

5. In the *Fields* tab of the Material Takeoff Properties dialog box, add the fields **Material: Name**, **Material: Area**, **Material: Manufacturer**, and **Material: Cost**, as shown in Figure 2–114.

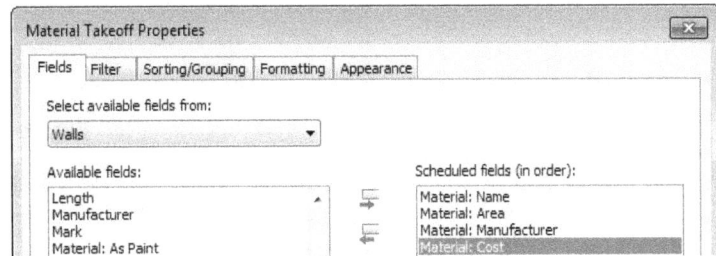

Figure 2–114

Area and Cost are two different types of parameters. Therefore, in this practice, you need to divide the **Material: Area** *parameter by 1 to get the correct result.*

6. Click f_x (Add calculated value) and set the following parameters, as shown in Figure 2–115. (Ensure that you account for the spaces in the field names when typing the formulas. There should be a space after the colon for the software to recognize **Material: Area** as a field.)
    *   *Name:* **Total Cost per SF**
    *   *Discipline:* **Common**
    *   *Type:* **Number**
    *   *Formula:* **(Material: Area / 1SF) * Material: Cost**

You can click

⌞...⌟ *(Browse) to select from a list of fields as you are creating the formula to prevent you from misspelling parameter names.*

Figure 2–115

7. Create another calculated value field using the following parameters. (There are seven standard bricks in a square foot. The type and size of bricks being used might vary and that can affect the number of bricks.)
    *   *Name:* **Total Units of Brick**
    *   *Discipline:* **Common**
    *   *Type:* **Number**
    *   *Formula:* **(Material: Area / 1) *7**

8. In the *Filter* tab, filter the schedule using **Material: Name equals Masonry - Brick**, as shown in Figure 2–116.

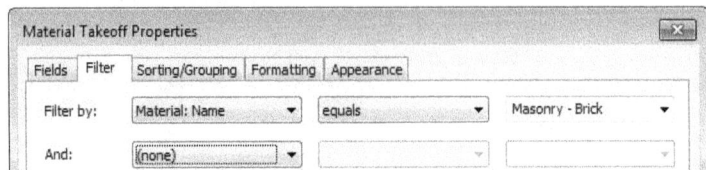

Figure 2–116

9. In the *Sorting/Grouping* tab, sort by **Material: Name** and select **Footer**, as shown in Figure 2–117.

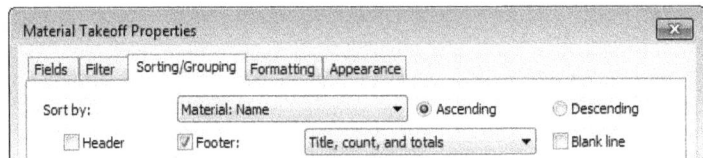

Figure 2–117

10. In the *Formatting* tab, in the *Fields* list, select **Material: Area, Total Cost per SF**, and **Total Units of Brick.** In the *Field formatting* area, select **Calculate totals** from the drop-down list, as shown in Figure 2–118.

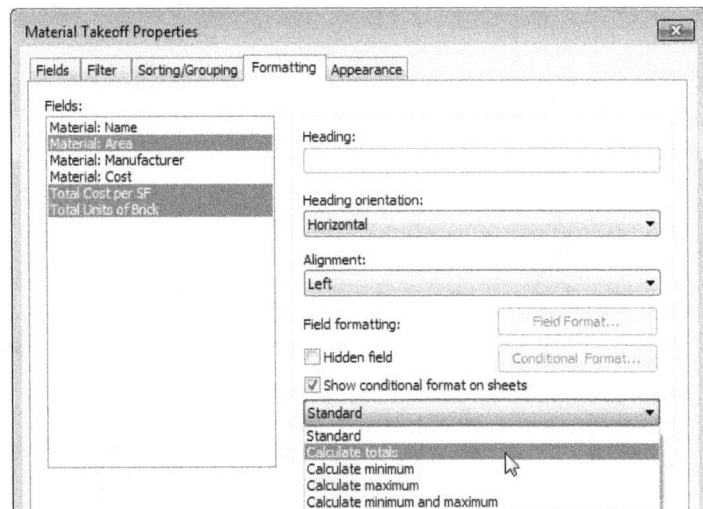

Figure 2–118

11. In the *Appearance* tab, modify the grid lines or text fonts as required and click **OK**.

Task 2 - Modify the material takeoff schedule.

1. The units for the *Total Cost per SF* and *Total Units of Brick* fields have six decimal places, as shown in Figure 2–119. This is more than required.

<Brick - Material Takeoff>					
A	B	C	D	E	F
Material: Name	Material: Area	Material: Manufact	Material: Cost	Total Cost per SF	Total Units of Brick
Masonry - Brick	192 SF		4.00	769.675167	1346.931543
Masonry - Brick	756 SF		4.00	3023.630924	5291.354117

Figure 2–119

2. In Properties, next to *Formatting*, click **Edit...**. The Material Takeoff Properties dialog box opens with the *Formatting* tab selected.

3. Select the *Total Cost per SF* field and click **Field Format...**.

4. In the Format dialog box, clear the **Use default settings** option. Set the *Units* to **Currency**, *Rounding* to **To the nearest 10** and *Unit symbol* to **$**, as shown in Figure 2–120. Click **OK**.

Figure 2–120

5. Select the *Total Units of Brick* field and click **Field Format...**.

6. In the Format dialog box, clear the **Use default settings** option. Set the *Units* to **Fixed** and *Rounding* to **0 decimal places**. Click **OK**.

7. Click **OK** to close the dialog box.

8. In the schedule view, add a manufacturer's name and change the *Material: Cost* of the Brick to **3.00**. The Total Cost updates, but the Total Units of Brick remains the same.

Task 3 - Test the material takeoff schedule.

1. Open the **A102 – Plan and Schedules** sheet.

2. Zoom in on the existing schedules to one side.

3. Add the new **Brick – Material Takeoff** schedule to the sheet. Use grips to modify the size of the schedule as required.

4. This schedule is different from other schedules because it includes all the instances of Brick. In the Project Browser, select the **Brick - Material Takeoff** schedule (you do not have to open it to change the properties).

5. In Properties, in the *Other* area, next to Sorting/Grouping, click **Edit...**.

6. In the Material Takeoff Properties dialog box, in the *Sorting/Grouping* tab, clear the **Itemize every instance** option. The schedule updates on the sheet.

7. Open the **3D Views: Front View**. Arrange the views so that you can see the 3D view and the top two schedules on the sheet, as shown in Figure 2–121.

Figure 2–121

8. In the 3D view, select one of the walls on the tower to the left and change its wall type to **Basic Wall: FCE – Exterior – EIFS on Mtl.Stud**, as shown in Figure 2–122.

EIFS on Mtl.Stud

Figure 2–122

9. The schedules change to display a smaller amount of the stone used and add to the EIFS schedule that was blank before, as shown in Figure 2–123.

Stone - Material Takeoff			
Material: Description	Material: Area	Material: Cost	Total Cost
Facestone	865 SF	0.00	0
Facestone: 6	865 SF		0

EIFS - Material Takeoff			
Material: Description	Material: Area	Material: Cost	Total Cost
EIFS	298 SF	12.00	3574
EIFS: 1	298 SF		3574

Figure 2–123

10. Double-click on the Stone - Material Takeoff schedule in the sheet to open the related schedule view.

11. Change the *Material: Cost* to **10**.

12. The *Material: Cost* and *Total Cost* fields update on the sheet as well.

13. Modify these fields so that they display as currency.

Task 4 - (Optional) Create a percentage-based Calculated Value field.

1. Using ⊞ (Schedule/Quantities), create a new area schedule called **Area Schedule (Rentable)**.

2. Add the fields *Name* and *Area*.

3. Click f_x (Add calculated parameter) and add the new *Calculated Value* field, as shown in Figure 2–124.

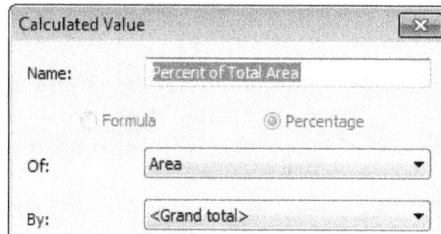

Figure 2–124

4. Click **OK** twice to create the schedule.

5. Open the **A103 – Area Plans** sheet and add the new area schedule to the sheet next to the colored legend, as shown in Figure 2–125.

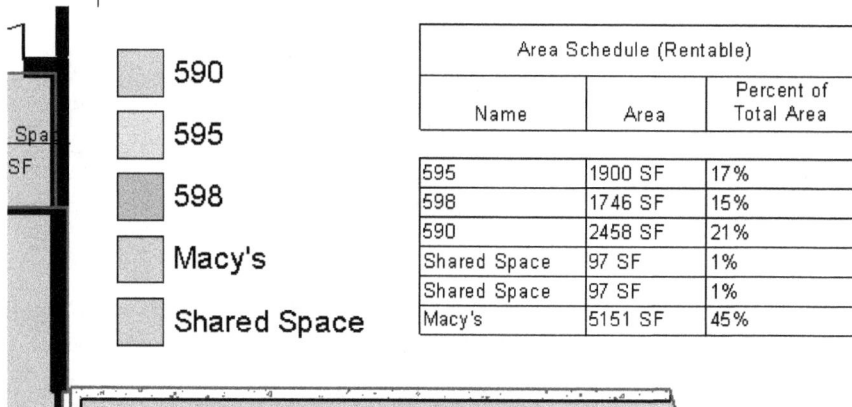

Area Schedule (Rentable)		
Name	Area	Percent of Total Area
595	1900 SF	17%
598	1746 SF	15%
590	2458 SF	21%
Shared Space	97 SF	1%
Shared Space	97 SF	1%
Macy's	5151 SF	45%

Figure 2–125

6. Save and close the project.

Practice 2h

Create Complex Schedules for MEP Projects

Practice Objectives

- Create a base schedule and add an embedded schedule into it.
- Test the scheduled information using conditional formatting.

Estimated time for completion: 20 minutes

In this practice, you will create a base schedule including a Calculated Value and Conditional Formatting. You will then add an embedded schedule to create an Space Air Flow Check schedule, as shown in Figure 2–126.

\<Space Air Flow Check\>					
A	B	C	D	E	F
Space Number	Name	Condition Type	Actual Supply Airfl	Calculated Supply	Airflow Check
Diffuser ID	Diffuser Type	Diffuser Airflow			
101	Office Area 1	Heated and cooled	0 CFM	2833 CFM	-2833 CFM
102	Office Area 2	Heated and cooled	0 CFM	2546 CFM	-2546 CFM
103	Vestuble 1	Heated and cooled	0 CFM	351 CFM	-351 CFM
104	Foyer 1	Heated and cooled	0 CFM	718 CFM	-718 CFM
105	Conf. Room	Heated and cooled	800 CFM	519 CFM	281 CFM
1	Supply Diffuser	400 CFM			
2	Supply Diffuser	400 CFM			
106	Women's 1	Heated and cooled	500 CFM	203 CFM	297 CFM
13	Supply Diffuser	500 CFM			
107	Mens 1	Heated and cooled	500 CFM	201 CFM	299 CFM
14	Supply Diffuser	500 CFM			
108	Hall 1	Heated and cooled	500 CFM	864 CFM	-364 CFM
8	Supply Diffuser	500 CFM			
109	Mech. Room	Heated and cooled	100 CFM	90 CFM	10 CFM
50	Supply Diffuser	100 CFM			
110	Elec. Room	Heated and cooled	100 CFM	168 CFM	-68 CFM
49	Supply Diffuser	100 CFM			
111	Utility	Heated and cooled	0 CFM	54 CFM	-54 CFM
112	Break Room 1	Heated and cooled	500 CFM	527 CFM	-27 CFM
9	Supply Diffuser	500 CFM			
113	Vestuble 2	Heated and cooled	0 CFM	150 CFM	-150 CFM
114	Stair	Heated and cooled	0 CFM	53 CFM	-53 CFM
115	Elev.	Heated and cooled	0 CFM	25 CFM	-25 CFM
201	Office Space 3	Heated and cooled	0 CFM	7327 CFM	-7327 CFM
202	Office Space 4	Heated and cooled	0 CFM	6196 CFM	-6196 CFM
203	Foyer 2	Heated and cooled	0 CFM	867 CFM	-867 CFM
204	Womens 2	Heated and cooled	0 CFM	203 CFM	-203 CFM
205	Mens 2	Heated and cooled	140 CFM	201 CFM	-61 CFM
37	Supply Diffuser	140 CFM			
206	Hall 2	Heated and cooled	0 CFM	1003 CFM	-1003 CFM
25	Supply Diffuser	500 CFM			
207	Stair	Heated and cooled	0 CFM	238 CFM	-238 CFM
208	Break Room 2	Heated and cooled	410 CFM	497 CFM	-87 CFM
24	Supply Diffuser	205 CFM			
34	Supply Diffuser	205 CFM			
209	Mechanical Ro	Heated and cooled	0 CFM	268 CFM	-268 CFM

Figure 2–126

Task 1 - Create a Base schedule.

1. In the practice files *MEP* folder, open **Office-Airflow.rvt**.

2. Create a new Schedules/Quantities schedule.

3. In the New Schedule dialog box, filter the list by *Mechanical*, if required, and select **Spaces**. Name the schedule **Space Air Flow Check** and click **OK**.

4. Add the following fields: **Number**, **Name**, **Condition Type**, **Actual Supply Airflow**, and **Calculated Supply Airflow**, as shown in Figure 2–127.

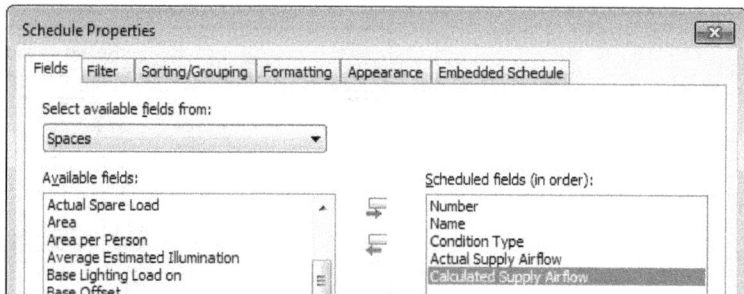

Figure 2–127

5. While still in the *Fields* tab, click f_x (Add calculated parameter).

6. In the Calculated Value dialog box, specify the *Name* as **Airflow Check**, *Discipline* as **HVAC**, and *Type* as **Air Flow**.

By browsing for the fields, you save time by not misspelling or mis-capitalizing the field names.

7. For the Formula, click ⟦...⟧ and select **Actual Supply Airflow** and click **OK**. Type a minus sign (-) and then click ⟦...⟧ again and select **Calculated Supply Airflow**. Click **OK**.

8. In the *Sorting/Grouping* tab, sort by **Number**.

9. In the *Formatting* tab, select **Airflow Check** and click **Conditional Format...**.

10. In the Conditional Formatting dialog box, specify the different fields, as shown in Figure 2–128. You can select any color you want.

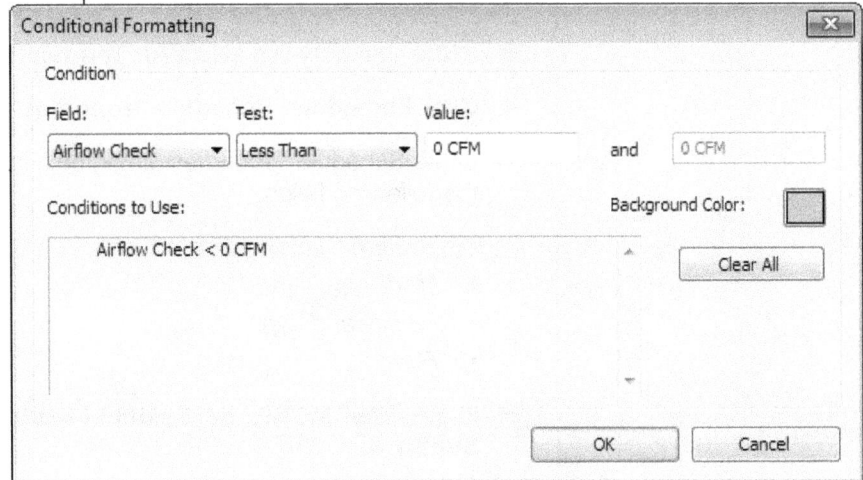

Figure 2–128

11. Click **OK** to display the schedule (shown in part) up to this point. Expand the columns, as shown in Figure 2–129.

\<Space Air Flow Check\>					
A	B	C	D	E	F
Number	Name	Condition Type	Actual Supply Airfl	Calculated Supply	Airflow Check
101	Office Area 1	Heated and cooled	0 CFM	2833 CFM	-2833 CFM
102	Office Area 2	Heated and cooled	0 CFM	2546 CFM	-2546 CFM
103	Vestuble 1	Heated and cooled	0 CFM	351 CFM	-351 CFM
104	Foyer 1	Heated and cooled	0 CFM	718 CFM	-718 CFM
105	Conf. Room	Heated and cooled	800 CFM	519 CFM	281 CFM
106	Women's 1	Heated and cooled	500 CFM	203 CFM	297 CFM
107	Mens 1	Heated and cooled	500 CFM	201 CFM	299 CFM
108	Hall 1	Heated and cooled	500 CFM	864 CFM	-364 CFM

Figure 2–129

12. Click inside the **Number** heading and change it to **Space Number**.

13. Save the project.

Task 2 - Add an embedded schedule.

1. While still in the Space Air Flow Check schedule view, in Properties, beside *Embedded Schedule*, click **Edit...**.

2. In the Schedule Properties dialog box, in the *Embedded Schedule* tab, select **Embedded Schedule**.

3. In the Category list, select **Air Terminals**.

4. Click **Embedded Schedule Properties**.

5. In the Schedule Properties dialog box, in the *Fields* tab, add the following fields:

   - *System Classification*
   - *Mark*
   - *Family and Type*
   - *Flow*

6. In the *Filter* tab, filter by: **System Classification equals Supply Air**.

7. In the *Sorting/Grouping* tab, set *Sort by as* **Mark** and *Then by* as **Family and Type**, as shown in Figure 2–130.

Figure 2–130

8. In the *Formatting* tab, select the *Field* **System Classification** and select **Hidden field**.

9. Select **Mark** and set *Heading* as **Diffuser ID**. Set *Heading orientation* as **Horizontal** and *Alignment* as **Right**.

10. Select **Family and Type** and set *Heading* as **Diffuser Type**. Set *Heading orientation* as **Horizontal** and *Alignment* as **Left**.

11. Select **Flow** and set *Heading* as **Diffuser Airflow**. Set *Heading orientation* as **Horizontal** and *Alignment* as **Left**.

12. Click **OK** until the schedule displays, as shown in part in Figure 2–131.

A	B	C	D	E	F
\<Space Air Flow Check\>					
Space Number	Name	Condition Type	Actual Supply Airfl	Calculated Supply	Airflow Check
Diffuser ID	Diffuser Type	Diffuser Airflow			
101	Office Area 1	Heated and cooled	0 CFM	2833 CFM	-2833 CFM
102	Office Area 2	Heated and cooled	0 CFM	2546 CFM	-2546 CFM
103	Vestuble 1	Heated and cooled	0 CFM	351 CFM	-351 CFM
104	Foyer 1	Heated and cooled	0 CFM	718 CFM	-718 CFM
105	Conf. Room	Heated and cooled	800 CFM	519 CFM	281 CFM
1	Supply Diffuser	400 CFM			
2	Supply Diffuser	400 CFM			
106	Women's 1	Heated and cooled	500 CFM	203 CFM	297 CFM
13	Supply Diffuser	500 CFM			

Figure 2–131

13. Save the project.

14. If time permits, work with the project to establish the correct air flow for the various spaces.

Practice 2i

Create Complex Schedules for Structural Projects

Practice Objectives

- Create project parameters and modify an existing schedule using them.
- Modify and group headers in a schedule to graphically link the parameter types.

Estimated time for completion: 20 minutes

In this practice, you will create project parameters for structural footing types. Your will then add the new parameters to a schedule, add an additional parameter, add headers to the schedule, and fill in the schedule, as shown in Figure 2–132.

	<Structural Foundation Schedule>
A	B	C	D	E	F	G	H	I	J
		Dimensions			Reinforcement				
					Cover		Bars			
Type	Length	Width	Thickness	Top Cover	Bottom Cover	Major Bars	Minor Bars	Count	Volume
FC3.0		3' - 0"	1' - 0"	0' - 3"	0' - 1 1/2"	#4 @ 1'-0"	#4 @ 1'-0"	4	715.22 CF
FC5.0	139' - 10"	5' - 0"	1' - 0"	0' - 3"	0' - 2"	#4 @ 0'-9"	#4 @ 0'-9"	1	553.47 CF
FS6.0	6' - 0"	6' - 0"	1' - 0"	0' - 3"	0' - 1 1/2"	#4 @ 1'-0"	#4 @ 1'-0"	27	972.00 CF
FS8.0	8' - 0"	8' - 0"	1' - 0"	0' - 3"	0' - 2"	#4 @ 0'-9"	#4 @ 1'-0"	3	192.00 CF
Grand total: 35								35	2432.69 CF

Figure 2–132

Task 1 - Add Project parameters.

1. In the practice files *Structural* folder, open **Century-Building.rvt**.

2. In the Project Browser, in the *Schedules/Quantities* area, open the **Structural Foundation Schedule**, as shown in Figure 2–133. This schedule is limited to existing parameters and does not include any rebar information. Also, the **Foundation Thickness** parameter is recorded for continuous footing (FC) types but not for spot footings (FS) types.

	<Structural Foundation Schedule>
A	B	C	D	E	F
		Dimensions			
Type	Length	Width	Foundation Thickness	Count	Volume
FC3.0		3' - 0"	1' - 0"	4	715.22 CF
FC5.0	139' - 10"	5' - 0"	1' - 0"	1	553.47 CF
FS6.0	6' - 0"	6' - 0"		27	972.00 CF
FS8.0	8' - 0"	8' - 0"		3	192.00 CF
Grand total: 35				35	2432.69 CF

Figure 2–133

3. Open the **Structural Plans: T.O.F.** view.

4. Select one of the spot footings.

5. In Properties, click ⊞ (Edit Type).

*You can see a **Thickness** parameter, but this does not link into schedules.*

6. In the Type Properties dialog box, there are parameter groups for *Dimensions* and *Identity Data*, as shown in Figure 2–134, but no information about the rebar that typically needs to be included in a foundation schedule.

Figure 2–134

7. Click **Cancel** to close the dialog box and click in the view to clear the foundation selection.

8. In the *Manage* tab>Settings panel, click 🗓 (Project Parameters).

9. In the Project Parameters dialog box, click **Add**.

10. In the Parameter Properties dialog box, create a *Project parameter* named **Bottom Cover**. Make it a **Type** parameter and set *Discipline* to **Common**, *Type of Parameter* to **Length**, and *Group parameter under* to **Rebar Set**. In *Categories*, set the *Filter list* to **Structure**, and select **Structural Foundations**, as shown in Figure 2–135.

Figure 2–135

11. Click **OK**.

12. Add additional Type parameters. Set *Discipline* as **Common** and *Group parameter under* as **Rebar Set** with the following additional information:

Name	Type of Parameter	Categories
Top Cover	Length	Structural Foundations
Major Bars	Text	Structural Foundations and Walls
Minor Bars	Text	Structural Foundations and Walls

13. When you are finished, the four parameters display as shown in Figure 2–136. Click **OK**.

Figure 2–136

14. Select a footing again and open the Type Properties dialog box. This time the **Rebar Set** group of parameters is also displayed, as shown in Figure 2–137. Click **OK**.

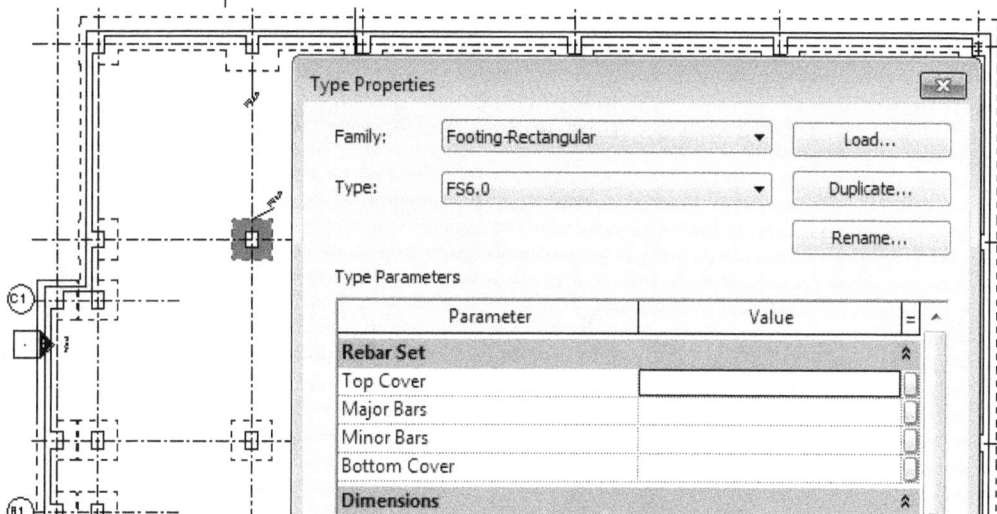

Figure 2–137

15. Save the project.

Task 2 - Modify a Foundation schedule.

1. Switch back to the Structural Foundation Schedule.

2. In Properties, in the *Other* area, next to *Fields*, click **Edit...**.

3. In the Schedule Properties dialog box, in the *Fields* tab, add the following fields: **Top Cover**, **Bottom Cover**, **Major Bars** and **Minor Bars**. Place them in the order shown in Figure 2–138.

Figure 2–138

4. In the *Scheduled fields (in order)* area, remove the existing **Foundation Thickness** parameter.

5. In the *Fields* tab, click ⬚ (New parameter).

6. In the Parameter Properties dialog box, select **Project parameter**, and enter the *Name* **FS and FC Foundation Thickness**. Set it as a **Type** parameter with *Discipline* set to **Common**, *Type of Parameter* set to **Length**, and *Group* with **Dimensions**.

7. Click **OK**.

8. Click ⬆E (Move parameter up) to place it below the existing **Width** parameter.

9. Select the new parameter and click ✏ (Edit parameter).

10. The full Parameter Properties dialog box opens. The **Structural Foundations** category is already selected because you are working in that type of schedule. Additionally, select the **Walls** category.

11. Click **OK** twice to close the dialog boxes.

12. The schedule displays as shown in Figure 2–139.

A	B		C	D	E	F	G	H	I	J
	Dimensions			FS and FC Foundation						
Type	Length		Width		Top Cover	Bottom Cover	Major Bars	Minor Bars	Count	Volume
FC3.0			3' - 0"						4	715.22 CF
FC5.0	139' - 10"		5' - 0"						1	553.47 CF
FS6.0	6' - 0"		6' - 0"						27	972.00 CF
FS8.0	8' - 0"		8' - 0"						3	192.00 CF
Grand total: 35									35	2432.69 CF

Figure 2–139

13. Save the project.

Task 3 - Modify and apply headers.

A column cannot be added under an existing header. Therefore, delete the header and then remake it with the correct associations.

1. Click inside the header for FS and FC Foundation Thickness. Delete **FS and FC Foundation** so it displays as only *Thickness*.

2. In the schedule view, select the *Dimensions* header and in the *Modify Schedule/Quantities* tab>Titles & Headers panel, click ⬚ (Ungroup).

3. Press and drag the cursor over the columns from *Length* to *Thickness*.

4. In the Titles & Headers panel, click ⬚ (Group).

5. Type a header name of **Dimensions**.

6. Repeat the process to create a header from *Top Cover* to *Minor Bars* with the name **Reinforcement**.

7. Group *Top Cover* and *Bottom Cover* and name the header **Cover**.

8. Group *Major Bars* and *Minor Bars* and name the header **Bars**. The schedule displays as shown Figure 2–140.

A	B	C	D	E	F	G	H	I	J
		Dimensions			Reinforcement				
					Cover		Bars		
Type	Length	Width	Thickness	Top Cover	Bottom Cover	Major Bars	Minor Bars	Count	Volume
FC3.0		3' - 0"						4	715.22 CF
FC5.0	139' - 10"	5' - 0"						1	553.47 CF
FS6.0	6' - 0"	6' - 0"						27	972.00 CF
FS8.0	8' - 0"	8' - 0"						3	192.00 CF
Grand total: 35								35	2432.69 CF

Figure 2–140

9. Set the *Thickness* to **1'-0"** for each of the types.

10. Open the **Structural Plans: T.O.F.** view and select one of the larger **FS8.0** spot footings.

11. In Properties, click ⊞ (Edit Type). The **FS and FC Foundation Thickness** parameter has been added and set to **1'-0"**. Fill out the rest of the information for the *Cover* and *Bars*, as shown in Figure 2–141, and close the Type Properties dialog box.

Figure 2–141

12. In the Type Properties of each foundation type or in the schedule view, fill out the rest of the information as shown in the schedule in Figure 2–142.

A	B	C	D	E	F	G	H	I	J
		Dimensions			Reinforcement				
				Cover		Bars			
Type	Length	Width	Thickness	Top Cover	Bottom Cover	Major Bars	Minor Bars	Count	Volume
FC3.0		3' - 0"	1' - 0"	0' - 3"	0' - 1 1/2"	#4 @ 1'-0"	#4 @ 1'-0"	4	715.22 CF
FC5.0	139' - 10"	5' - 0"	1' - 0"	0' - 3"	0' - 2"	#4 @ 0'-9"	#4 @ 0'-9"	1	553.47 CF
FS6.0	6' - 0"	6' - 0"	1' - 0"	0' - 3"	0' - 1 1/2"	#4 @ 1'-0"	#4 @ 1'-0"	27	972.00 CF
FS8.0	8' - 0"	8' - 0"	1' - 0"	0' - 3"	0' - 2"	#4 @ 0'-9"	#4 @ 1'-0"	3	192.00 CF
Grand total: 35								35	2432.69 CF

Figure 2–142

13. Save the project.

Chapter Review Questions

1. In the Schedule Properties dialog box (shown in Figure 2–143), in which tab do you define the order of the list of elements?

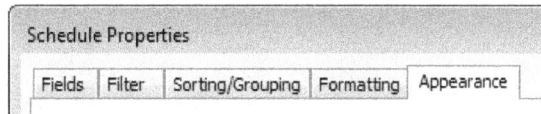

   Schedule Properties

   | Fields | Filter | Sorting/Grouping | Formatting | Appearance |

   Figure 2–143

   a. *Fields*

   b. *Filter*

   c. *Sorting/Grouping*

   d. *Formatting*

   e. *Appearance*

2. Which type of schedule lists style information that is not automatically included in an element, such as the finish or frame type of a door?

   a. Material Takeoff

   b. Quantities

   c. Key

   d. Building Component

3. When creating *Calculated Value* fields (such as shown in Figure 2–144), the parameters you use must first be added to the list of fields in the schedule.

   Calculated Value

   Name: Airflow Check

   ⊙ Formula   ○ Percentage

   Discipline: HVAC

   Type: Air Flow

   Formula: Actual Supply Airflow - Calculated

   OK   Cancel   Help

   Figure 2–144

   a. True

   b. False

4. When creating a Material takeoff schedule, where do you modify information about the material, such as the cost or manufacturer, as shown in Figure 2–145? (Select all that apply.)

Stone - Material Takeoff			
Material: Description	Material: Area	Material: Cost	Total Cost
Stone	865 SF	0.00	0
Stone: 6	865 SF		0

EIFS - Material Takeoff			
Material: Description	Material: Area	Material: Cost	Total Cost
EIFS	298 SF	12.00	3574
EIFS: 1	298 SF		3574

Figure 2–145

a. In the Type Properties dialog box.

b. In the schedule, fill out the columns related to the type information.

c. In the Material Editor.

d. In the Material Browser.

5. (MEP only) Which of the following should be created before you can create an embedded schedule, as shown in Figure 2–146?

A	B
SPACE NO.	NAME
DIFFUSER ID	DIFFUSER TYPE
1501	CLASSROOM
29	Supply Diffuser - Perforated - Round Neck - Ceiling Mounted:
30	Supply Diffuser - Perforated - Round Neck - Ceiling Mounted:
31	Supply Diffuser - Perforated - Round Neck - Ceiling Mounted:
32	Supply Diffuser - Perforated - Round Neck - Ceiling Mounted:
1502	CLASSROOM
45	Supply Diffuser - Perforated - Round Neck - Ceiling Mounted:
46	Supply Diffuser - Perforated - Round Neck - Ceiling Mounted:
47	Supply Diffuser - Perforated - Round Neck - Ceiling Mounted:
48	Supply Diffuser - Perforated - Round Neck - Ceiling Mounted:

Figure 2–146

a. Rooms or Spaces.

b. Elements covered in the schedule.

c. The schedule that you want to embed.

d. A key schedule.

Command Summary

Button	Command	Location
Schedule Types		
NA	Graphical Column Schedule	• **Ribbon:** *View* tab>Create panel> expand Schedules (*Structural Columns only*)
	Material Takeoff Schedule	• **Ribbon:** *View* tab>Create panel> expand Schedules
	Note Block	• **Ribbon:** *View* tab>Create panel> expand Schedules
	Schedule/ Quantities	• **Ribbon:** *View* tab>Create panel> expand Schedules
	Sheet List	• **Ribbon:** *View* tab>Create panel> expand Schedules
	View List	• **Ribbon:** *View* tab>Create panel> expand Schedules
Schedule Appearance		
	Align Horizontal	• **Ribbon:** *Modify Schedule/Quantities* tab>Appearance panel
	Align Vertical	• **Ribbon:** *Modify Schedule/Quantities* tab>Appearance panel
	Borders	• **Ribbon:** *Modify Schedule/Quantities* tab>Appearance panel
	Font	• **Ribbon:** *Modify Schedule/Quantities* tab>Appearance panel
	Reset	• **Ribbon:** *Modify Schedule/Quantities* tab>Appearance panel
	Shading	• **Ribbon:** *Modify Schedule/Quantities* tab>Appearance panel
	Delete (Columns)	• **Ribbon:** *Modify Schedule/Quantities* tab>Columns panel
	Hide (Columns)	• **Ribbon:** *Modify Schedule/Quantities* tab>Columns panel
	Insert (Columns)	• **Ribbon:** *Modify Schedule/Quantities* tab>Columns panel
	Resize (Columns)	• **Ribbon:** *Modify Schedule/Quantities* tab>Columns panel
	Unhide All (Columns)	• **Ribbon:** *Modify Schedule/Quantities* tab>Columns panel
	Calculated	• **Ribbon:** *Modify Schedule/Quantities* tab>Parameters panel
	Combine Parameters	• **Ribbon:** *Modify Schedule/Quantities* tab>Parameters panel

	Format Unit	• **Ribbon:** *Modify Schedule/Quantities* tab>Parameters panel
	Delete (Rows)	• **Ribbon:** *Modify Schedule/Quantities* tab>Rows panel
	Insert (Rows)	• **Ribbon:** *Modify Schedule/Quantities* tab>Rows panel
	Insert Data Row	• **Ribbon:** *Modify Schedule/Quantities* tab>Rows panel
	Resize (Rows)	• **Ribbon:** *Modify Schedule/Quantities* tab>Rows panel
	Clear Cell	• **Ribbon:** *Modify Schedule/Quantities* tab>Titles & Headers panel
	Group	• **Ribbon:** *Modify Schedule/Quantities* tab>Titles & Headers panel
	Insert Image	• **Ribbon:** *Modify Schedule/Quantities* tab>Titles & Headers panel
	Merge Unmerge	• **Ribbon:** *Modify Schedule/Quantities* tab>Titles & Headers panel
	Ungroup	• **Ribbon:** *Modify Schedule/Quantities* tab>Titles & Headers panel

Custom System Families

System families are embedded in an Autodesk® Revit® project or template file. They are modified by editing the type properties of the family. Walls, roofs, floors, and compound ceiling types each have an assembly of layers that can be modified along with other parameters. MEP system families include duct, pipe, conduit, and cable tray families.

Learning Objectives in this Chapter

- Create system family types for walls, roofs, floors, and ceilings.
- Modify wall types vertically to include split materials, profiles, and reveals.
- Create a vertically stacked wall type from two or more wall types.
- Create duct and pipe types using routing preferences.
- Create cable tray and conduit types using type properties.

3.1 Creating Wall, Roof, Floor, and Ceiling Types

System families are created and modified in a project or template file by duplicating an existing element type. Some of these system families (such as walls, roofs, floors, and some ceilings) are compound or layer-based. For example, to modify a compound wall, you edit the type and select the **Structure** parameter. This opens the Edit Assembly dialog box (as shown in Figure 3–1) which enables you to specify each layer of the assembly.

Figure 3–1

- Walls are used as the primary example, but floors, roofs, and compound ceilings follow the same pattern.

- Structural Floors often use profiles for metal decking. Creating this type of floor is covered in the profile families topic.

How To: Create a Compound Wall, Floor, Roof, or Ceiling

1. Start the wall, floor, roof or ceiling command.
2. In Properties, select a type similar to the one you want to create and click ⊞ (Edit Type).
3. In the Type Properties dialog box, click **Duplicate...**.
4. In the Name dialog box, enter a name for the new type and click **OK**.
5. Next to the **Structure** parameter, click **Edit...**.
6. In the Edit Assembly dialog box, modify the layers of the assembly as required, and then click **OK**.
7. Modify any Type Parameters in the Type Properties dialog box.
8. Click **OK** to close the dialog box.

Hint: Basic Ceilings

The basic ceiling system family does not include a structure parameter. Instead, modify the Type by specifying a *Material* for the entire thickness of the ceiling.

Editing Wall, Roof, and Floor Assemblies

In the Edit Assembly dialog box, you can define the layers that make up the compound structure, as shown in Figure 3–2.

To better visualize the wall, click << Preview to open a view of the layers in the structure. You can preview the structure in a plan or section view, and zoom or pan in the preview screen.

Figure 3–2

Assembly Information

The top of the dialog box lists the *Family* (such as **Basic Wall** or **Floor**), the *Type* that you gave to the new type, and the *Total thickness* (which is the sum of the layers defined in the wall), as shown in Figure 3–3. It also includes *Resistance (R)* and *Thermal Mass* which are automatically calculated from the materials assigned to the layers. You can also set a *Sample Height* for your wall design.

Family:	Basic Wall		
Type:	Exterior - Brick on CMU		
Total thickness:	1' 7 1/2"	Sample Height:	20' 0"
Resistance (R):	0.6455 (h·ft²·°F)/BTU		
Thermal Mass:	6.2429 BTU/°F		

Figure 3–3

Layers

When you specify the layers for the compound element, you assign them a *Function*, *Material*, and *Thickness*, as shown in Figure 3–4.

Layers

EXTERIOR SIDE

	Function	Material	Thickness	Wraps	Structural Material
3	Thermal/	Insulation	0' 3"	✓	
4	Membran	Vapor / M	0' 0"	✓	
5	**Core Bound**	**Layers Abov**	**0' 0"**		
6	Structure [	Masonry -	0' 7 5/8"		✓
7	**Core Bound**	**Layers Belo**	**0' 0"**		
8	Substrate	Metal - Fu	0' 1 5/8"	✓	
9	Finish 2 [5	Gypsum	0' 0 5/8"	✓	

INTERIOR SIDE

Insert	Delete	Up	Down

Figure 3–4

- Use the buttons to insert additional layers and to rearrange them in the layer list. You can also delete layers from the list.

- The *Core Boundary* function defines the layers above and below the wrapping; a heavier line is displayed when a plan or section view is cut.

- Editing a wall assembly works from the exterior side at the top of the list to the interior side at the bottom. For floors and roofs, you work around the layers above and below the wrap of the *Core Boundary*.

Options

Function	Select from a set list of functions in the drop-down list with a priority of highest (1) to lowest (5). High priority layers connect before low priority layers.
Structure [1]	The structural support for the wall, floor, or roof.
Substrate [2]	A material that acts as a foundation for another material, such as plywood or gypsum board.
Thermal/ Air Layer [3]	An open layer for air space.
Finish 1 [4]	The exterior finish layer, such as brick for a wall.
Finish 2 [5]	The interior finish layer, such as drywall for a wall.
Membrane Layer	A vapor barrier. Typically, this is set to a zero thickness. Therefore, it does not have a priority code.
Structural Deck (1)	(Floors only) A structural support based on a Deck Profile. You can also specify the Deck Usage with a Bound Layer Above or a Standalone Deck.
Material	Select from a list of available materials. Layers clean up if they share the same material. If they do not, a line displays at the join.
Thickness	Set the thickness of the particular layer.

Wall Only Options

Sample Height	Displays the height of a wall in section when you are creating it. It does not impact the height of the wall in the project.
Default Wrapping	Set up how the heavy line style wraps around openings in walls: *at Inserts* (**Do not wrap**, **Interior**, **Exterior**, or **Both**), and *at Ends* (**None**, **Exterior**, or **Interior**). Wrapping is only visible in plan view.
Wraps	Set up individual layers to wrap—select the Wraps option at the end of each layer.

- Wall wrapping can be set in the assembly or in the Type Properties, as shown in Figure 3–5.

Wrapping at Inserts	Do not wrap
Wrapping at Ends	None

Figure 3–5

- Roofs, floors, and structural slabs have an additional parameter that relates to sloping for drains. When *Variable* is not selected, the slab is set to a constant thickness and the entire element slopes, as shown on the top in Figure 3–6. When *Variable* is selected, only the top layer slopes, as shown on the bottom in Figure 3–6.

Level 1

Variable not checked

Level 1

Variable checked

Figure 3–6

Practice 3a

Create Compound Wall Types

Practice Objectives

- Create an exterior wall with two different types of layers on the interior and the exterior.
- Create an interior wall that has the same material on either side of the structural core.

Estimated time for completion: 15 minutes

In this practice, you will create interior and exterior wall types, and then draw walls using them, as shown in Figure 3–7.

Figure 3–7

Task 1 - Create a Wall type.

1. Start a new project based on the default architectural template and save it as **SW House.rvt**.

2. In the *Architecture* tab>Build panel or *Structure* tab> Structure panel, click ⬜ (Wall).

For creating a wall type, it does not matter which command you started with.

3. In Properties, click ⊞ (Edit Type).

4. In the Type Properties dialog box, click **Duplicate...**.

5. In the Name dialog box, type **Exterior – Adobe** and click **OK**.

6. Next to the **Structure** parameter, click **Edit...**.

7. Next to the **Structure [1]** layer, select the *Material* column and click ⬚ (Browse).

8. Expand the Library panel to display it more clearly and select **AEC Materials>Masonry>Brick, Adobe** as shown in Figure 3–8.

Figure 3–8

9. Double-click on **Brick, Adobe** to add it to the list of materials that are available in the project. **Brick, Adobe** is now selected in the Material Browser. Click **OK** to apply the material.

10. In the Edit Assembly dialog box, in the *Thickness* column, type **1'-0"** and verify that **Structural Material** is selected, as shown in Figure 3–9.

Layers

EXTERIOR SIDE

	Function	Material	Thickness	Wraps	Structural Material
1	Core Boundar	Layers Above	0' 0"		
2	Structure [1]	Brick, Adobe	1' 0"		☑
3	Core Boundar	Layers Below	0' 0"		

INTERIOR SIDE

Insert   Delete   Up   Down

Figure 3–9

11. In the *Layers* area, click **Insert**.

In the Material Browser,
type **wood** *in the search*
field to narrow the list of
materials.

12. Set this layer with *Function* set to **Substrate (2)**, *Material* to **Plywood, Sheathing**, *Thickness* to **1 5/8"**. Click **Down** until the new layer is below the Layers Below Wrap, as shown in Figure 3–10.

13. Add one more layer on the interior side and set *Function* to **Finish 2**, *Material* to **Cherry**, *Thickness* to **5/8"**. Select **Wraps** but not **Structural Material**, as shown in Figure 3–10.

Layers

EXTERIOR SIDE

	Function	Material	Thickness	Wraps	Structural Material
1	Core Boundar	Layers Above	0' 0"		
2	Structure [1]	Brick, Adobe	1' 0"	☐	☑
3	Core Boundar	Layers Below	0' 0"		
4	Substrate [2	Plywood, Sh	0' 1 5/8"	☑	☐
5	Finish 2 [5]	Cherry	0' 0 5/8"	☑	☐

INTERIOR SIDE

Figure 3–10

14. Click **OK** to close the Edit Assembly dialog box.

15. Repeat the process to create another new wall type named **Interior – Wood Panel**. In the Type Properties dialog box, change the *Function* to **Interior**.

16. Set up the layer structure as shown in Figure 3–11.

The **Softwood, Lumber**
material is found in the
AEC Materials list if it is
not in the document list.

Layers

EXTERIOR SIDE

	Function	Material	Thickness	Wraps	Structural Material
1	Finish 2 [5]	Cherry	0' 0 5/8"	☑	☐
2	Core Boundar	Layers Above	0' 0"		
3	Structure [1]	Softwood, L	0' 3 5/8"	☐	☑
4	Core Boundar	Layers Below	0' 0"		
5	Finish 2 [5]	Cherry	0' 0 5/8"	☑	☐

INTERIOR SIDE

Figure 3–11

17. Click **OK** twice to close the dialog boxes.

Task 2 - Draw walls using the new Wall types.

1. Set the *Detail Level* to ▢ (Medium).

2. Draw the house shown in Figure 3–12.

   - **Exterior: Exterior – Adobe** and *Height* of **10'-0"**
   - **Interior: Interior – Wood Panel** and *Height* of **10'-0"**

Figure 3–12

- For the Interior walls, set the Location Line to **Finish Face – Interior** or **Finish Face – Exterior** to place the horizontal walls and **Wall Centerline** for the vertical walls.

3. Save the project.

3.2 Vertically Compound Walls

Vertically Compound walls are made of regions of different materials, as well as optional permanent sweeps or reveals, as shown in Figure 3–13. Several options help you create these walls: **Modify**, **Split Region**, **Merge Regions**, **Assign Layers**, **Wall Sweeps**, and **Reveals**.

Figure 3–13

You must be have the *View:* set to **Section: Modify Type Attributes** to work with the **Modify Vertical Structure** tools, as shown in Figure 3–14.

Figure 3–14

How To: Modify the Vertical Structure of a Wall Type

1. Open the wall type you want to modify and edit the structure.
2. Create any additional layers that might be required.
3. In the Edit Assembly dialog box, open the preview and set the *View:* to **Section: Modify Type Attributes**. This activates the *Modify Vertical Structure* tools, as shown in Figure 3–15.

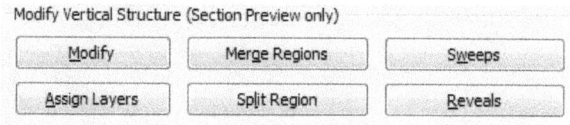

Modify Vertical Structure (Section Preview only)

| Modify | Merge Regions | Sweeps |
| Assign Layers | Split Region | Reveals |

Figure 3–15

4. Zoom in as required to see the various layers.
5. In the Layers list, select the layer you want to work with.
6. Use the various tools that are outlined below.
7. Click **OK** until all of the dialog boxes are closed to save the wall type.

- When making changes to the vertical structure of a wall type it helps to have the *Sample Height* set to the shortest expected height for the wall type so the changes are displayed more clearly.

How To: Split Regions and Assign Layers

1. In the Edit Assembly dialog box, click **Split Region**.
2. In the section preview, move the cursor up the wall to the place where you want the region to be cut. Select the wall at that point and a dimension is displayed as shown in Figure 3–16

Figure 3–16

3. In the *Layers* area, highlight the layer that you want to use and click **Assign Layers**.
4. In the section view, select the wall part that you want to change and click **Modify**.

- You can create as many split regions as required in one layer.

- To change the dimension, click **Modify** and select the border between the two regions that have been split. Then type a new distance using the temporary dimension.

- You can modify the width of the layer in the section view or in the *Thickness* column in the *Layers* area.

- You can add additional functions as required. In the example shown in Figure 3–17, two layers have the function **Finish 1**, and each layer has a different material. The *Thickness* is set by the selected layer and cannot be modified.

Layers

	Function	Material	Thickness	Wraps
1	Finish 1 [4]	Masonry - Bric	0' 3 5/8"	✓
2	Finish 1 [4]	Masonry - Co	0' 3 5/8"	✓
3	Thermal/Air L	Misc. Air Layer	0' 3"	✓
4	Membrane La	Air Barrier - Ai	0' 0"	✓
5	Substrate [2]	Wood - Sheat	0' 0 3/4"	✓

EXTERIOR SIDE

Figure 3–17

Merging Regions

To link regions together, click **Merge Regions** and select the line between the layers you want to merge, as shown in Figure 3–18. Watch the arrow cursor. It tells you which way the merge takes place. The tooltip also tells you names of the layers that are being merged. You can only merge layers that are next to each other.

Figure 3–18

- You can merge layers vertically or horizontally. For example, to create the situation shown in Figure 3–18, you need to split the regions horizontally before merging some of the vertical lines.

Wall Sweeps and Reveals

When you split regions, the parts you create cannot have different widths. To create a protrusion or a reveal, add a wall sweep, as shown in Figure 3–19.

Figure 3–19

How To: Add a Sweep

1. In the Edit Assembly dialog box, click **Sweeps** to open the Wall Sweeps dialog box.
2. In the Wall Sweeps dialog box, click **Add**. A default row is added, as shown in Figure 3–20.

Wall Sweeps

Wall Sweeps

	Profile	Material	Distance	From	Side	Offset	Flip	Setback	Cuts Wall	Cutt:
1	Default	<By Cate	0' 0"	Ba	Exte	0' 0"	☐	0' 0"	☑	☐

Figure 3–20

3. Select the *Profile* column and select from the list of the existing profiles in the project.

4. Continue setting up the profile by selecting a *Material* and setting the *Distance* from the top or bottom, interior or exterior *Side*, and the *Offset* from that side. If required, place a checkmark in the *Flip* column to flip the profile, as shown in Figure 3–21.

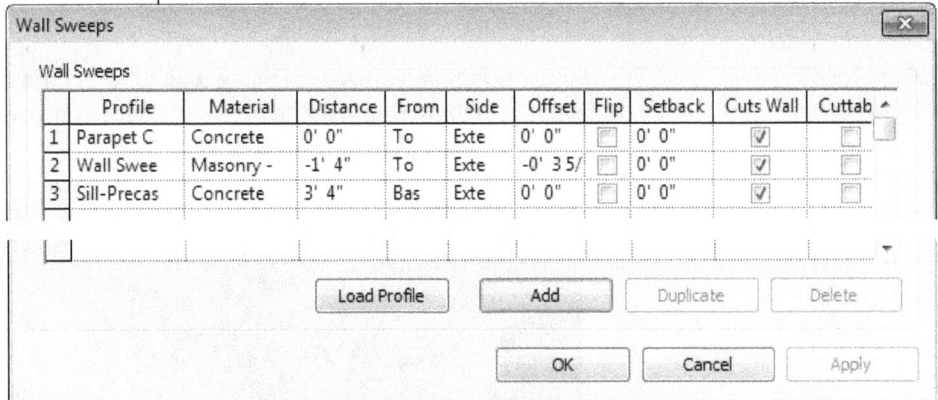

	Profile	Material	Distance	From	Side	Offset	Flip	Setback	Cuts Wall	Cuttab
1	Parapet C	Concrete	0' 0"	To	Exte	0' 0"	☐	0' 0"	☑	☐
2	Wall Swee	Masonry -	-1' 4"	To	Exte	-0' 3 5/	☐	0' 0"	☑	☐
3	Sill-Precas	Concrete	3' 4"	Bas	Exte	0' 0"	☐	0' 0"	☑	☐

Figure 3–21

5. Click **Apply** to see the addition before you click **OK** to finish.

- Reveals work the same way, except that you do not assign a material to a reveal. The whole shape of the reveal profile is visible in the section view, but you only see the cut in the project.

- You can also click **Load Profile** to add a profile in the Wall Sweeps or Reveals dialog box.

Practice 3b

Create Vertically Compound Walls

Estimated time for completion: 15 minutes

Practice Objective

- Create a vertically compound wall.

In this practice, you will modify a wall type to create a wooden wainscot (**Split Region** and **Assign Layers**) below a chair rail (**Sweep**), as shown in Figure 3–22.

Figure 3–22

Task 1 - Split regions and assign layers in a wall type.

1. In the practice files *Architectural* folder, open **SW-House-Vertical.rvt.**

2. Select one of the **Interior – Wood Panel** walls and in Properties, click ⊞ (Edit Type).

3. Edit the *Structure* parameter.

4. In the Edit Assembly dialog box, change the *Sample Height* to **9'-0"**. This sets the correct wall height for the preview.

5. Click **<< Preview** and set the *View:* to **Section: Modify type attributes**.

6. In the *Layers* area, insert an additional finish on both sides of the structure. Set the material to **Plaster and Lathe**. Do not specify a thickness. Once you apply it to part of the split region, it takes on the appropriate thickness.

7. In the *Modify Vertical Structure* area, click **Split Region**.

8. In the Section view, move the cursor to a point **3'-6"** above the base, as shown in Figure 3–23. Zoom in to ensure that you split the finish layer and not the central structural layer.

Figure 3–23

9. Repeat with the opposite finish layer.

10. Stay zoomed in, close to the place where you made the split.

11. In the *Layers* area, select the **Plaster and Lathe** layer on the Exterior Side.

12. In the *Modify Vertical Structure* area, click **Assign Layers**.

13. In the preview, select the top part of the exterior wall where you want the finish applied. Click **Modify**. The color should change as shown in Figure 3–24.

Figure 3–24

14. Repeat with the other finish and the side of the wall.

15. Click **Modify** to finish the process. The list of layers displays as shown in Figure 3–25.

Layers

EXTERIOR SIDE

	Function	Material	Thickness	Wraps	Structu Mater
1	Finish 2 [5]	Plaster and Lathe	0' 0 5/8"	☑	
2	Finish 1 [4]	Cherry	0' 0 5/8"	☑	
3	Core Boundar	Layers Above Wrap	0' 0"		
4	Structure [1 ▾	Softwood, Lumber	0' 3 5/8"		☑
5	Core Boundar	Layers Below Wrap	0' 0"		
6	Finish 2 [5]	Plaster and Lathe	0' 0 5/8"	☑	
7	Finish 1 [4]	Cherry	0' 0 5/8"	☑	

INTERIOR SIDE

Insert	Delete	Up	Down

Figure 3–25

16. Click **OK** twice to close the dialog boxes.

17. Look at the interior walls in a 3D or section view. Shade the view. You should see the difference above and below the paneling, as shown in Figure 3–26.

Figure 3–26

Task 2 - Add sweeps to the wall type.

1. Edit the structure of the same wall type.

2. In the Edit Assembly dialog box, *Modify Vertical Structure* area, click **Sweeps**.

3. In the Wall Sweeps dialog box, click **Load Profile**.

4. In Load Family dialog box, navigate to the *Profiles>Finish Carpentry* folder, select **Base 2.rfa** and click **Open**.

5. In the Wall Sweeps dialog box, click **Add** and set up two wall sweeps using the following information, as shown in Figure 3–27.
   - *Profile:* **Base 2: 3 1/2" x 3/4"** (or similar)
   - *Material:* **Cherry**
   - *Distance:* **3'-6"**
   - *From:* **Base**
   - *Side:* **Interior** for one sweep and **Exterior** for the other

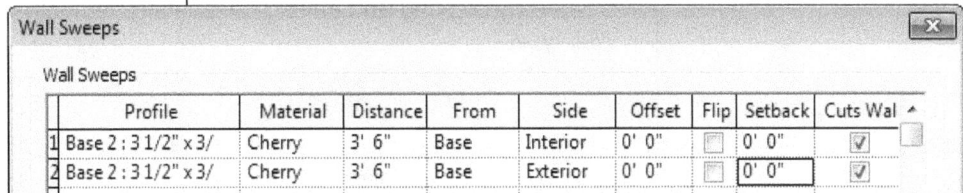

	Profile	Material	Distance	From	Side	Offset	Flip	Setback	Cuts Wal
1	Base 2 : 3 1/2" x 3/	Cherry	3' 6"	Base	Interior	0' 0"	☐	0' 0"	☑
2	Base 2 : 3 1/2" x 3/	Cherry	3' 6"	Base	Exterior	0' 0"	☐	0' 0"	☑

Figure 3–27

6. Click **OK** to exit the Wall Sweeps dialog box.

7. In the preview of the Edit Assembly dialog box, you should see the two sweeps when you zoom in, as shown in Figure 3–28.

Figure 3–28

8. Click **OK** twice to close the dialog boxes. The entire set of interior walls updates with the new information.

9. Add an additional interior wall using this type so that you can see how it automatically uses the information.

10. If time permits, modify the **Exterior-Adobe** wall so that the inside of that wall matches the interior walls.

11. Save the project.

3.3 Stacked and Embedded Walls

A vertically stacked wall is a specific system family that takes two or more existing basic walls and stacks them on top of each other at specific heights, as shown in Figure 3–29. One wall must be variable in height. The basic wall types have to be in place before you create the stacked wall. These walls are created by copying and editing an existing Vertically Stacked Wall type.

Figure 3–29

How To: Create a Vertically Stacked Wall

1. Start the **Wall** command.
2. In Properties, select an existing stacked wall type and click

   ⊞ (Edit Type).
3. Duplicate the wall type and give it a new name.
4. In the Type Properties dialog box, next to the **Structure** parameter, click **Edit...**.
5. In the Edit Assembly dialog box, set the *Offset* for how the walls are stacked, and a *Sample Height* for the preview, as shown in Figure 3–30.

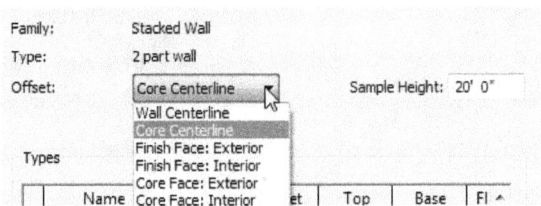

Figure 3–30

6. In the *Name* column, select the basic wall types you want to add to the stacked wall, as shown in Figure 3–31.

Types

TOP

	Name	Height	Offset	Top	Base	▲
1	Exterior - Brick on ▾	Variable	0' 0"	0' 0"	0' 0"	
2	Exterior - CMU on	3' 0"	0' 0"	0' 0"	0' 0"	

Figure 3–31

7. For each wall type, set the appropriate height and location (Up or Down) in the list. One height must be variable. Set the *Offset* of the wall as required.
8. Click **<< Preview** to see the wall, as shown in Figure 3–32.

Figure 3–32

9. Click **OK** until all of the dialog boxes are closed.

Hint: Embedding a Wall Inside Another Wall

Another way of creating a compound wall is to embed one wall inside another wall, as shown in Figure 3–33. When you have drawn a host wall, draw another wall on top of, or parallel to it near the host. A warning box opens and recommends that you use **Cut Geometry** to embed the wall in the host wall.

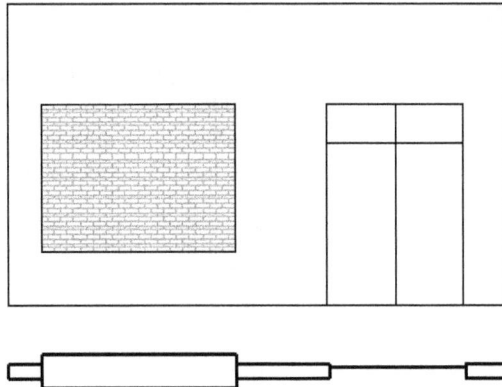

Figure 3–33

1. Add the embedded wall to the host wall.
2. Close the warning box.
3. In the *Modify* tab>Geometry panel, click ⬚ (Cut).
4. Select the host wall.
5. Select the wall that cuts the host wall.

- Embedded walls work similar to windows. You can modify the embedded wall with controls.

- Some curtain wall types are created to be automatically embedded in another wall. The type **Curtain Wall: Storefront** is an example. The Type Parameter *Automatically Embed* is available for all curtain wall types.

- You can separate embedded walls. In the *Modify* tab> Geometry panel, expand ⬚ (Cut) and click ⬚ (Uncut Geometry).

Practice 3c

Create Stacked and Embedded Walls

Estimated time for completion: 10 minutes

Practice Objectives

- Create a vertically stacked wall type.
- Embed a wall into a stacked wall.

In this practice, you will create a vertically stacked wall and use it in a project. You will also embed a curtain wall and another wall type into a host wall, as shown in Figure 3–34.

Figure 3–34

Task 1 - Create a stacked wall.

1. Start a new project based on the default architectural or structural template and save it as **Warehouse.rvt**.

2. Start the **Wall** command and select the **Stacked Wall: Exterior – Brick Over CMU w Metal Stud** type.

3. Edit the type and duplicate it to create a new wall type named **Exterior – EIFS over Brick/CMU**.

4. Edit the structure of the new wall.

5. For the top wall, select **Exterior – EIFS on Mtl. Stud**. Leave the *Height* as **Variable** and set the *Offset* to **4"**.

6. For the bottom wall, select **Exterior – Brick on CMU** and set the *Height* to **6'-0"**.

7. Click **OK** to close all of the open dialog boxes.

8. Draw a rectangular building **50'-0" x 30'-0"** using the new wall style.

9. Display the walls in 3D to verify that the Brick/EIFS are displayed on the exterior.

10. Save the project.

Task 2 - Create an embedded wall.

1. Open the **Floor Plans: Level 1** view.

2. On the south face of the building, add a wall using **Curtain Wall: Storefront** at an *Unconnected Height* of **8'-0"**. Place it directly on the center line of the existing wall along only a portion of the wall. It automatically cuts the existing wall.

3. Open the **Floor Plans: Level 2** view.

4. Add another wall on the same face using **Basic Wall: Exterior – Brick on Mtl. Stud**. This time a warning box opens.

5. Close the warning box.

6. In the *Modify|Place Wall* tab>Geometry panel, click ⌀ (Cut).

7. Select the host wall.

8. Select the wall that cuts the host wall.

9. In the *Elevations* area, open the **South** view.

10. Flip the orientation of the brick insert as required.

11. Change the size of the embedded wall using the controls, but do not move it down into the lower brick wall.

12. Save the project.

3.4 Creating MEP System Families

Autodesk Revit MEP system templates are preloaded with families for Ducts, Pipes, Cable Trays and Conduits. You can also duplicate and modify these families to create new family types. Ducts (as shown in Figure 3–35) and Pipes are set using Routing Preferences. Flex Ducts and Flex Pipes as well as Cable Tray and Conduit are set up by defining fittings in the Type Properties.

Figure 3–35

How To: Create Duct Types

1. Start the **Place Duct** command, select one of the existing types, and click ▦ (Edit Type).
2. In the Type Properties dialog box, click **Duplicate...**, type a new name in the Name dialog box, and click **OK**.
3. Next to the **Routing Preferences** parameter, click **Edit...**.

4. The Routing Preferences dialog box, displays as shown in Figure 3–36.

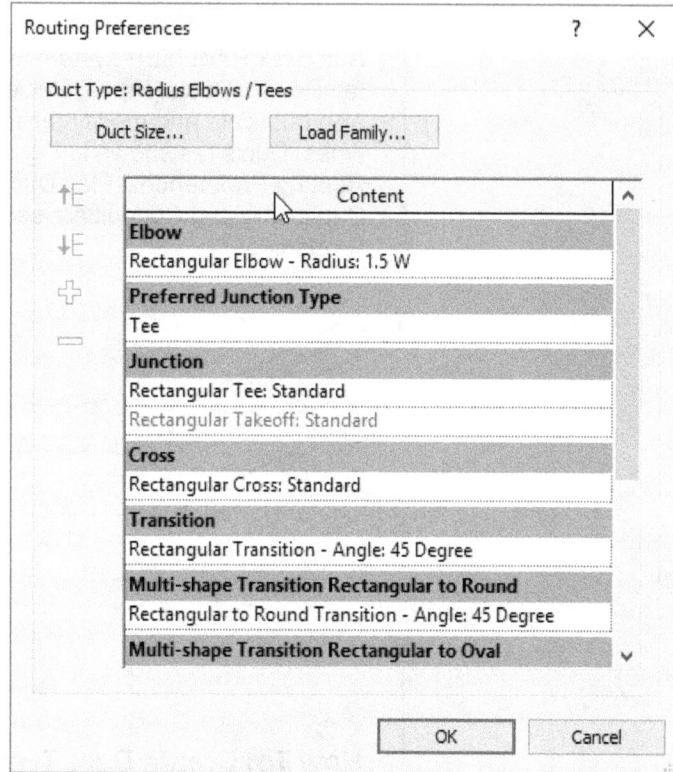

Figure 3–36

5. Click **Duct Size...** to open the Mechanical Settings dialog box to the Duct Settings so that you can add or remove the typical sizes used in the project.

6. Click **Load Family...** to add any duct fittings that you want to use in the type that are not already loaded in the project.

7. For each of the fittings, expand the drop-down list and select the size that you want use, as shown in Figure 3–37.

Figure 3–37

8. If you want to include more than one option for a fitting, click

   ✥ (Add row) and select the secondary option for the fitting.

   You can also use ⬆E (Move row up) or ⬇E (Move row down) to specify the order in which the fittings are applied by

   default or click ▬ (Remove Row) to delete the ones you do not need to use.
9. When you have finished assigning fittings, click **OK** to close the Routing Preference dialog box.
10. Fill in the other Parameters for the Type Properties as required and click **OK** to finish the new duct type.

- Flex ducts do not have routing preferences, the Fitting selection takes place directly in the Type Properties, as shown in Figure 3–38.

Type Properties ✕

Family: System Family: Flex Duct Round   Load...

Type: Flex - Round   Duplicate...

Rename...

Type Parameters

Parameter	Value	=
Construction		≫
Roughness	0.0003'	
Fittings		≫
Preferred Junction Type	Tap	
Tee	Round Tee: Standard	
Tap	Round Takeoff: Standard	
Transition	Round Transition - Angle: 45 Degre	
Multi Shape Transition Rect to R	Rectangular to Round Transition -	
Multi Shape Transition Rect to O	None	
Multi Shape Transition Oval to R	None	
Union	Round Union: Standard	
Identity Data		≫

Figure 3–38

How To: Create Pipe Types

1. Start the **Place Pipe** command, select one of the existing types, and click ⊞ (Edit Type).
2. In the Type Properties dialog box, click **Duplicate...**, type a new name in the Name dialog box, and click **OK**.
3. Next to the **Routing Preferences** parameter, click **Edit...**.
4. The Routing Preferences dialog box opens, as shown in Figure 3–39.

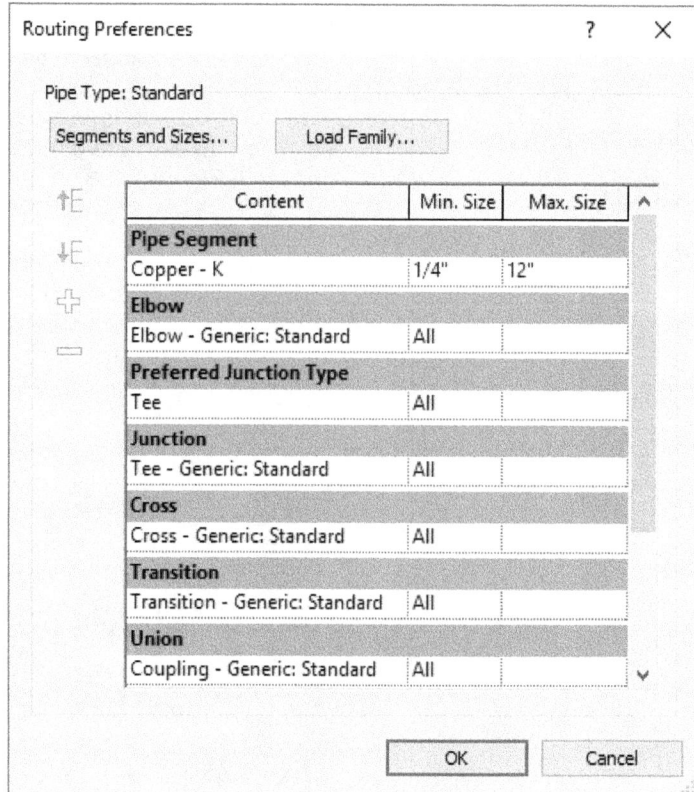

Routing Preferences			? ✕
Pipe Type: Standard			
Segments and Sizes...	Load Family...		

	Content	Min. Size	Max. Size
	Pipe Segment		
	Copper - K	1/4"	12"
	Elbow		
	Elbow - Generic: Standard	All	
	Preferred Junction Type		
	Tee	All	
	Junction		
	Tee - Generic: Standard	All	
	Cross		
	Cross - Generic: Standard	All	
	Transition		
	Transition - Generic: Standard	All	
	Union		
	Coupling - Generic: Standard	All	

OK   Cancel

Figure 3–39

5. Click **Segments and Sizes...** to open the Mechanical Settings dialog box to the Pipe Settings. In this dialog box, specify the Segment types and sizes for the various types of pipe as shown in Figure 3–40.

Segment types can be added or removed here.

Figure 3–40

6. Click **Load Family...** to add any pipe fittings that you want to use in the type that have not already been loaded in the project.

7. For the Pipe Segment type and each of the fittings, expand the drop-down list and select the size that you want to use as shown in Figure 3–41.

Figure 3–41

8. If you want to include more than one option for a fitting, click ✚ (Add row) and select the secondary option for the fitting.

You can also use ↑E (Move row up) or ↓E (Move row down) to specify the order in which the fittings are applied by default or ▭ (Remove Row) to delete the ones you do not need to use.

9. When you have finished assigning fittings, click **OK** to close the Routing Preference dialog box.

10. Fill in the other Parameters for the Type Properties as required and click **OK** to finish the new pipe type.

- Flex pipes do not have routing preferences, the Fitting selection takes place directly in the Type Properties as shown in Figure 3–42.

Type Properties			×
Family:	System Family: Flex Pipe Round	∨	Load...
Type:	Flex - Round	∨	Duplicate...
			Rename...

Type Parameters

Parameter	Value	=	∧
Fittings			⤬
Preferred Junction Type	Tee		
Tee	Tee - Generic: Standard		
Tap	None		
Transition	Transition - Generic: Standard		
Union	Coupling - Generic: Standard		
Mechanical			⤬
Roughness	0.00180"		
Identity Data			⤬

Figure 3–42

How To: Set up Cable Tray and Conduit Types

1. Start the **Cable Tray** or **Conduit** command, select one of the existing types, and click 🔲 (Edit Type).

2. In the Type Properties dialog box, click **Duplicate**, type a new name in the Name dialog box, and click **OK**.

3. Select the fittings that you want to use as shown in Figure 3–43.

The fitting families need to be in the project before you get to this point.

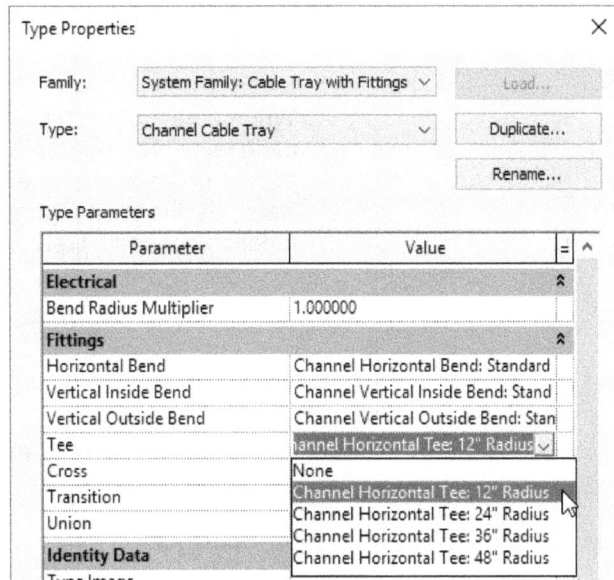

Figure 3–43

- For Conduit you first need to specify the Electrical Standard that you are using, as shown in Figure 3–44. Ensure that you also load the correct fittings that match the specific standard as well.

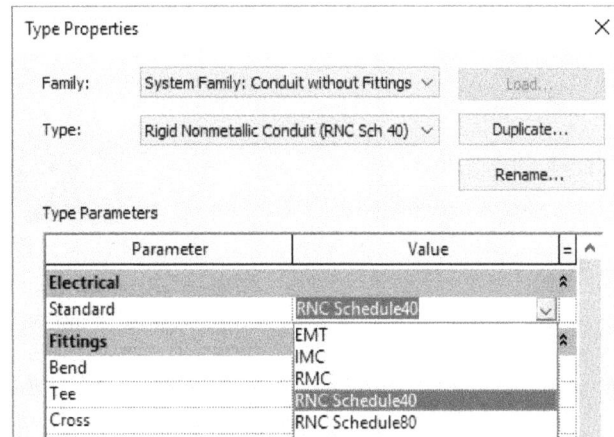

Figure 3–44

4. Fill in the values for any of the Identity Data information you might have and click **OK** to finish.

Chapter Review Questions

1. When creating a compound wall, you assign a Function for each layer. The numbers after the function names is the priority of the layers when they are joined together with other walls, as shown in Figure 3–45. Which of the following function connects first?

Figure 3–45

    a. Membrane Layer

    b. Substrate

    c. Structure

    d. Thermal/Air Layer

    e. Finish

2. How do you create a wall type that has more than one finish material on the vertical plane in the one type, as shown for stone and stucco in Figure 3–46?

Figure 3–46

    a. Create separate wall types for the stone and stucco. Duplicate an existing Stacked Wall type and set the wall types to stone and stucco.

    b. Draw two walls on top of each other and use (Join Geometry) to link them.

    c. Duplicate an existing Basic Wall type and use **Split Region** and **Assign Layers** to apply the stone and stucco materials to separate parts of the wall.

    d. Draw the first wall, draw the other wall on top of the first, and use (Cut Geometry) to cut the second wall out of the first wall.

3. Which command do you need to use to embed a wall inside another wall?

    a. **Wall Joins**

    b. **Cut Geometry**

    c. **Cope**

    d. **Split Face**

4. (MEP only.) When setting up a new duct or pipe type, which of the following items can be set by type?

    a. System Type

    b. Width and Height

    c. Preferred Junction Type

    d. Justification

5. (MEP only.) When creating a new conduit or cable tray type you need to assign Routing Preferences.

    a. True

    b. False

Command Summary

Button	Command	Location
	Cable Tray	• **Ribbon:** *Systems* tab>Electrical panel • **Shortcut:** CT
	Conduit	• **Ribbon:** *Systems* tab>Electrical panel • **Shortcut:** CN
	Cut Geometry	• **Ribbon:** *Modify* tab>Geometry panel
	Duct	• **Ribbon:** *Systems* tab>HVAC panel • **Shortcut:** DT
	Edit Type	• **Ribbon:** *Modify* tab>Properties panel • **Properties Palette**
	Pipe	• **Ribbon:** *Systems* tab>Plumbing & Piping panel • **Shortcut:** PI
	Uncut Geometry	• **Ribbon:** *Modify* tab>Geometry panel> expand Cut
	Wall: Architectural	• **Ribbon:** *Architecture* tab>Build panel or *Structure* tab>Structure panel>expand Wall • **Shortcut:** WA
	Wall: Structural	• **Ribbon:** *Architecture* tab>Build panel or *Structure* tab>Structure panel>expand Wall • **Shortcut:** WA

Component Family Concepts

Component (or loadable) families are the heart of the Autodesk® Revit® software. They include furniture; doors and windows; mechanical, electrical, and plumbing equipment; and structural framing. While some families are included with the software, it is important to know how to create custom families yourself. The basics include creating a parametric framework, adding solid geometry, and creating family types.

Learning Objectives in this Chapter

- Understand the different types of families that can be created in the software.
- Set up a parametric framework using reference planes, dimensions, and labels.
- Flex the framework to test all of the parameters.
- Create solid/void forms including extrusions, blends, revolves, sweeps, and swept blends.
- Create family types.
- Load and test families in a project.

4.1 Creating Component Families

Loadable component families are model or annotation elements that have been grouped together and set up with dimensions and other parameters. Families are parametric, meaning that they can be changed without having to recreate the elements. For example, when you change the *Height* and *Depth* of the storage pedestal shown in Figure 4–1, other parts move as well.

Figure 4–1

- *Component Families* (e.g., doors, air handling units, columns, etc.) are defined in the Family Editor and loaded into a project. One family can have many types.

- Many families are complex and time-consuming to create, but creating them all follows the same basic process.

How To: Create a Component Family (Overview)

1. In the Application Menu, click ☐ (New) and select **Family**.
2. In the New Family - Select Template File dialog box, select the template you want to use and click **Open**.
3. Set the parametric framework by adding reference planes/lines in plan and elevation views. This is a very important step when working with parametric families.
4. Label and dimension the reference planes/lines to control the movement of the elements and create parameters.
5. Flex the model to ensure the parameters change as expected.
6. Use the Forms tools (shown in Figure 4–2) to draw the elements.

Flexing a model: Changing the dimensions of a model to test its parametric features.

Figure 4–2

7. Lock the elements to the reference planes/lines.
8. Flex the elements again by changing the parameters to ensure that they are working.
9. Create family types with different parameters, as required.
10. Save the family.

11. Click ☐ (Load into Project) to test the family in a project.

Hint: Other Family Types

- *System Families* are preset in the templates used to create projects (e.g., walls, roofs, slabs, ducts, pipes, and conduit). You create new types by modifying existing parameters.

- *In-Place Families* are component families created directly in a project and are dependent on the model geometry (e.g., custom gutters, special trim, or built-in columns).

Preparing to Create Families

As you create families, you should plan ahead by asking a variety of questions, including:

- Is this family going to be used by one project (in-place) or by many projects (component)?

- Do you need different 2D representations in different views? What about 3D elements?

- Is this going to be a host-based or stand-alone family?

- Do you need various sizes of this family component?

Hint: Host-based vs. Stand-alone Families

Host-based families are dependent on a host. Examples include downlights (which require a ceiling) and sconces (which require a wall), as shown in Figure 4–3.

Stand-alone families do not need a host. Examples include the desk and table lamp shown in Figure 4–3.

Ceiling-based family — / Stand-alone family — / Wall-based family —

Figure 4–3

Saving Custom Family Files

When you create custom family files, you should save them to a location shared by the entire company, similar to the Autodesk Revit library. For easy access, set the custom library as the primary or secondary library available when you load a family.

How To: Specify the File Location for Custom Libraries

1. In the Application Menu, click **Options**.
2. In the Options dialog box, select the *File Locations* tab.
3. Click **Places...**.
4. In the Places dialog box, click ➕ (Add Value). A new *Library Name* is added to the list. Specify the name and path for the library, as shown in Figure 4–4.

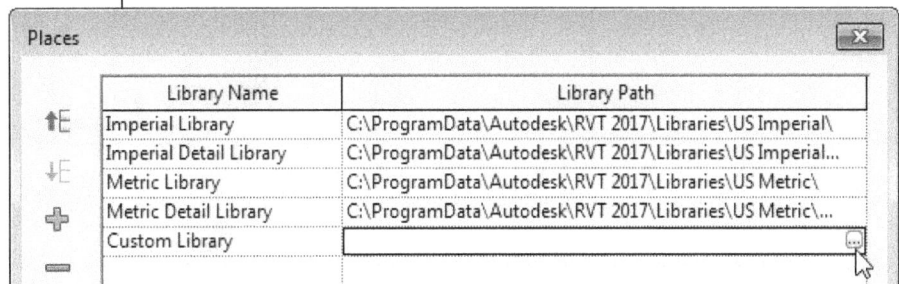

Figure 4–4

5. Click 🔼E (Move Rows Up) and 🔽E (Move Rows Down) to reorder the list of library names.
6. Click **OK** to close the dialog boxes.

- The library at the top of the list will be the default location when loading families.

4.2 Creating the Parametric Framework

Autodesk Revit families can be parametric (i.e., controlled by parameters). These parameters are the framework for creating family elements. They are based on reference planes that are dimensioned and labeled, as shown in Figure 4–5.

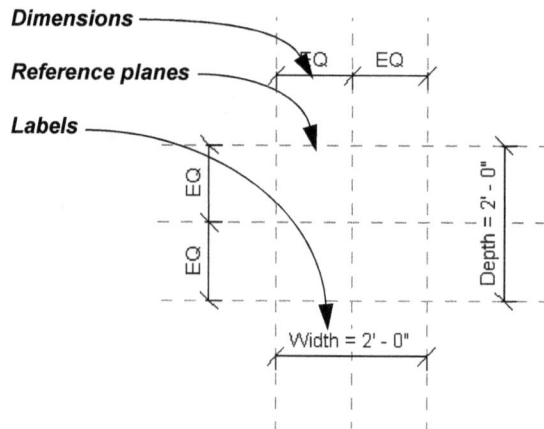

Figure 4–5

Before you draw any elements in a family, set up the parametric framework:

1. Place reference planes at critical locations.
2. Dimension the reference planes and label some of them so they can be manipulated.
3. Flex the dimensioned and labeled reference planes to ensure that they function as expected.

How To: Draw Reference Planes

1. In the Family Editor, in the *Create* tab>Datum panel, click

   (Reference Plane).
2. In the *Modify | Place Reference Plane* tab>Draw panel, click

   (Line) or (Pick Lines).
3. Draw or select the lines that define the location of the plane.
4. Draw or select other lines as required.

- The number of reference planes you need depends on what you are drawing.

- Reference planes display in plan and elevation views, but not in 3D views.

Reference Plane Options

- By default, the origin of a family is the center of the space where you create the family. In most templates, this is located at the intersection of the existing reference planes. You can also specify your own origin by modifying the properties of two intersecting reference planes to specify that they define the origin, as shown in Figure 4–6.

Figure 4–6

- Reference planes do not display in the project when you insert the family type, but might impact snap and alignment behavior.

  - In Properties, under *Other*, set the **Is Reference** parameter to the plane you want to use, as shown in Figure 4–7.

  - If you do not want a reference plane to be a snap or an alignment, set the **Is Reference** parameter to **Not a Reference**.

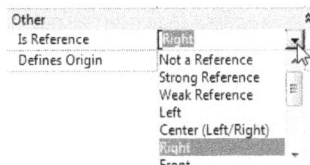

Figure 4–7

- After placing a reference plane, you can name it by clicking on **<Click to name>** and typing in the text box, as shown in Figure 4–8, or in Properties.

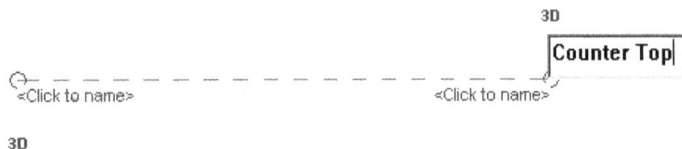

Figure 4–8

- Naming a reference plane enables you to use it to set the work plane when you are ready to add geometry to the family.

Reference Lines

Reference Lines, as shown in Figure 4–9, are similar to reference planes, but have distinct start and end points. They can be drawn using a wide variety of geometry, such as rectangles, circles, or arcs. Typically, they are used for angled elements.

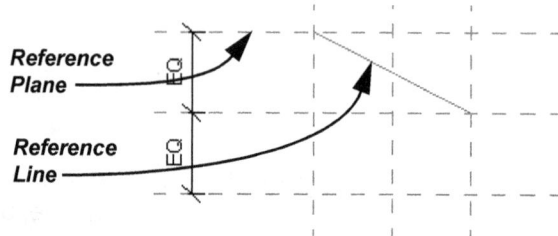

Figure 4–9

- In the Family Editor, in the *Create* tab>Datum panel, click ⌐ (Reference Line).

- Reference lines cannot be named.

Adding Dimensions and Labels

Add dimensions and labels to reference planes to start the constraining process, as shown in Figure 4–10. For example, you might want to run a string of dimensions and then set the distances to be equal by clicking on the associated **EQ** symbol. This moves the reference planes into place. Labeling a dimension creates a parameter that can be modified in the Family Types dialog box.

Figure 4–10

How To: Label a Dimension

1. Select the dimension you want to label.
2. In the *Modify | Dimensions* tab>Label Dimension panel, select an existing label from the drop-down list, as show in Figure 4–11. You can also right-click on the dimension text, select **Label**, and choose from the list as shown in Figure 4–12.

Figure 4–11

Figure 4–12

How To: Add a Label

1. Select the dimension you want to label.
2. In the *Modify | Dimensions* tab>Label Dimension panel, click

   (Create Parameter).

3. In the Parameter Properties dialog box, in the *Parameter Type* area, select **Family**, as shown in Figure 4–13.

To use this option, shared parameters must be created in your system.

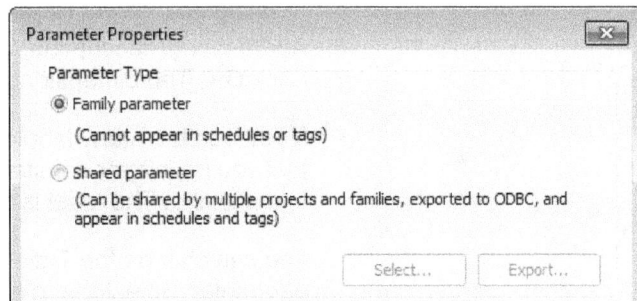

Figure 4–13

4. In the *Parameter Data* area, specify the *Name*, as shown in Figure 4–14. The *Type of Parameter* is automatically set to **Length** and the *Group parameter under* is set to **Dimensions**, because the parameter is a dimension.

When naming a parameter, it is good practice to use title casing and a short name without abbreviations. Parameters are case sensitive.

Figure 4–14

5. Select **Type** or **Instance**.
   - **Type** applies it to all instances of a family when it is inserted into a project. To modify it, you need to change the Type Properties.
   - **Instance** applies it to individual instance when inserted into a project. It can be modified directly in Properties.
   - For an instance property, if you want the dimension information to be used in a formula or placed in a schedule, select **Reporting Parameter**.
6. Add a tooltip description, if required.
7. Click **OK**. The dimension is labeled and ready to be flexed.

- If you add too many labeled dimensions, the software warns that you have over-constrained the sketch. You cannot ignore this warning. The label is not created in this case.

- You can change the *Type* or *Instance* setting of a label parameter. Select the related dimension and in the *Modify Dimension* tab>Label Dimension panel, select (or clear) **Instance Parameter**, as shown in Figure 4–15.

Figure 4–15

Flexing Geometry

Once you have established dimensions and labeled them, you need to verify that the parameters work correctly with each other. To do this, flex the geometry by changing the value of a label (as shown in Figure 4–16), or using the Family Types dialog box.

Figure 4–16

*   Select the labeled dimension and then the dimension text to change the value.

*   To see all of the values you can flex at one time and to add formulas and non-dimension parameters, you need to work in the Family Types dialog box.

How To: Flex the Geometry in the Family Types Dialog box

1. In the *Create* or *Modify* tab>Properties panel, click

    (Family Types). The Family Types dialog box displays as shown in Figure 4–17.

You might have to move the dialog box to display the elements you are adjusting.

Figure 4–17

2. Change the labeled parameters and click **Apply**.
3. Do the elements move correctly? Try several modifications.
4. Set the parameters as required and click **OK** to finish the command.

- When you open a family file, the Autodesk Revit software automatically checks the constraints in the family. If there are any issues, a dialog box offers information.

New in **2018**

Creating and Modifying Parameters

In addition to creating labels (parameters specifically for dimensions), you can add parameters that store other information (such as the material of the element, as shown in Figure 4–18, the wattage of a light fixture, or the reinforcement cover setting in concrete). You can also add formulas to parameters so that they change when a related parameter changes.

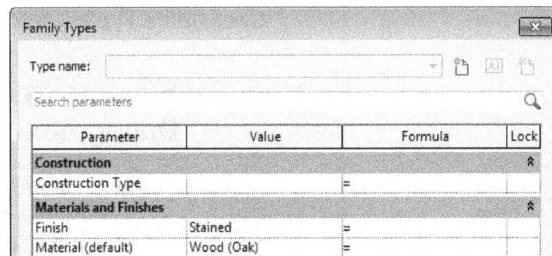

Figure 4–18

- Instance parameters include (default) after the name, as shown in Figure 4–18. The assigned value is then used when the component is inserted into a project. It can be changed in Properties when the component is selected.

Other options are covered in later topics.

- The Family Types dialog box contains options for editing, creating, and organizing parameters, as shown in Figure 4–19Figure 4–19.

Figure 4–19

	Edit Parameter	Displays the Parameter Properties dialog box, where you can change the name, group, or tooltip, or switch between **Type** and **Instance**. You can also change the parameter to reference a shared parameter.

🗋	**New Parameter**	Opens the Parameter Properties dialog box, where you can setup a new parameter.
↑E , ↓E	**Move parameter up/down**	Enables you to organize the parameters in each group.
🗋	**Delete parameter**	Removes the selected parameter.
A↓Z , A↑Z	**Sort parameters in ascending/ descending order**	Sets the order of the parameters to alphabetical order and removes any changes you might have made.

How To: Create Parameters

1. In the Family Editor, in the *Create or Modify* tab>Properties panel, click 🔲 (Family Types).

2. In the Family Types dialog box click 🗋 (New Parameter).
3. In the Parameter Properties dialog box, set up the Parameter Data, as shown in Figure 4–20.

The Discipline can be set to **Common**, **Structural**, **HVAC**, **Electrical**, **Piping**, *or* **Energy**. *The Type of Parameter list changes according to the discipline.*

Figure 4–20

4. Click **OK**.

Common Parameter Types

Text	A text parameter can host any type of information that consists of both numbers and letters. Examples could be the fabric color or part number of the element.
Integer	Any value that is always represented by a whole number. Examples could be the number of chairs that fit around a conference table or the number of shelves in a bookcase.
Number	Any numeric value: whole, decimal, or fraction. You can use formulas with **Number** parameters.
Length	When you label dimensions, you create **Length** parameters. You can use formulas with **Length** parameters.
Area	Establishes the area of an element. It is numeric and can have formulas applied to it.
Volume	Establishes the volume of an element. It is numeric and can have formulas applied to it.
Angle	Establishes the angle of an element. It is numeric and can have formulas applied to it.
Slope	Displays a slope, as set in the Field Format.
Currency	Displays the amount in dollars or other currencies, as set up in the Field Format.
Mass Density	Displays the mass per unit volume of material.
URL	Specifies a link to a web site.
Material	Provides a place to assign a material from the list of materials that are set up in the project.
Image	Creates a parameter at which you can add a raster image connected to the family.
Yes/No	Used with instance parameters where you need a **Yes** or **No** answer to a question listed in the name. The default is **Yes**.
\<Family Type\>	Opens a dialog box where you can select from the list of family types, such as doors, furniture, or tags.

How To: Add Formulas to Parameters

1. In the *Create* or *Modify* tab>Properties panel, click

   ⬚ (Family Types).

2. In the Family Types dialog box, in the *Formula* column, add formulas to the parameters. In the example shown in Figure 4–21, the *Shelf Height* is defined as the **Height** divided by **4**. When you change the *Shelf Height* or *Height*, the other value updates according to the formula.

Dimensions				≈
Depth	2' 0"	=		☑
Height	6' 0"	=		☑
ShelfHeight	1' 6"	= Height / 4		☑
TrimWidth	0' 2"	=		☐
Width	4' 0"	=		☑

Figure 4–21

You can use several types of formulas with families:

Arithmetic	Basic arithmetic operations in formulas include addition (+), subtraction (-), multiplication (*), division (/), exponentiation, logarithms, and square roots.
Trigonometric	Trigonometric functions include sine, cosine, tangent, arcsine, arccosine, and arctangent.
Conditional	Conditional functions include comparisons in a condition (e.g., <, >, =, etc.) and Boolean operators with a conditional statement (e.g., AND, OR, NOT, etc.). See the Autodesk Revit Help files for more information about creating conditional statements.

- You can enter numbers as integers, decimals, or fractions. Conditional statements can include numeric values, numeric parameter names, or **Yes/No** parameters.

- Formulas are case-sensitive. Therefore, if you have created a dimension label named **Height**, ensure that the formula that uses this label also has the H capitalized (e.g., **Height * 2**).

Hint: Formulas in Projects

You can use a formula to specify the length of a wall by typing it in the temporary dimension. Start with an equal sign (e.g., =12 / 3 + 4). The example shown in Figure 4–22 returns the number 8 (interpreted as 8'-0") in the dimension. Formulas also work with numerical values in Properties.

=12/3+4

Figure 4–22

Practice 4a

Set up a Bookcase Family

Practice Objectives

- Add reference planes.
- Dimension and label reference planes.
- Add a formula to a parameter.
- Flex the framework.

Estimated time for completion: 20 minutes

In this practice, you will create a family file based on a template and view the existing reference planes. You will also create reference planes, dimension them, and label the dimensions, as shown in Figure 4–23. You will add a formula to control a parameter and then test the framework by changing parameter values.

Figure 4–23

Task 1 - Open a family template.

1. Close all open projects.

2. On the Start page, under the *Families* area, select **New**.

3. In the New Family - Select Template File dialog box, select the template **Furniture.rft** from the Revit Library and click **Open**.

4. In the *View* tab>Windows panel, click ⊟ (Tile) (or type **WT**).

5. The four open views display so you can see each of them. Type **ZA** (the shortcut for **Zoom All to Fit**) to fit the view in all of the windows.

6. Two existing reference planes are included in the file, as well as **Ref.Level**.

7. Save the family in the practice files *Architectural* folder as **Barrister Bookcase.rfa**.

Task 2 - Create plan view reference planes.

---

1. Maximize the **Ref. Level** view.

2. Create four new reference planes, one on each side of the existing planes, as shown in Figure 4–24. Do not worry about the exact location yet.

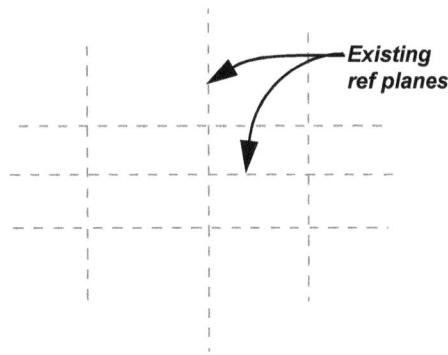

Figure 4–24

3. Add dimensions between each reference plane and across the top and side, as shown in Figure 4–25. Set the interior dimensions to **Equal**.

Your dimensions might vary depending on where you originally placed the reference planes.

Figure 4–25

4. Select the overall horizontal dimension. In the *Modify | Dimensions* tab>Label Dimension panel, click (Create Parameter).

5. In the Parameter Properties dialog box, in the *Parameter Data* area, ensure that **Type** is selected and then type the name **Width**. Click **OK**.

6. Repeat the process for the overall vertical dimension and name the parameter **Depth**.

7. Select the *Width* dimension and click on the text. Change it to **3'-0"**. Repeat the process and set the *Depth* to **1-'4"**, as shown in Figure 4–26.

Figure 4–26

8. Create one more horizontal reference plane **1"** inside the front reference plane and name it **Door Face**. Dimension and lock it in place, as shown in Figure 4–27.

Figure 4–27

9. Flex the framework by changing the *Width* dimension to **3'-6"** and the *Depth* dimension to **1'-1"**.

10. Verify that the other reference planes have remained in place.

11. Save the family file.

Task 3 - Create front view reference planes.

1. Open the **Elevations: Front** view.

2. Create the reference planes and dimensions and label them, as shown in Figure 4–28.

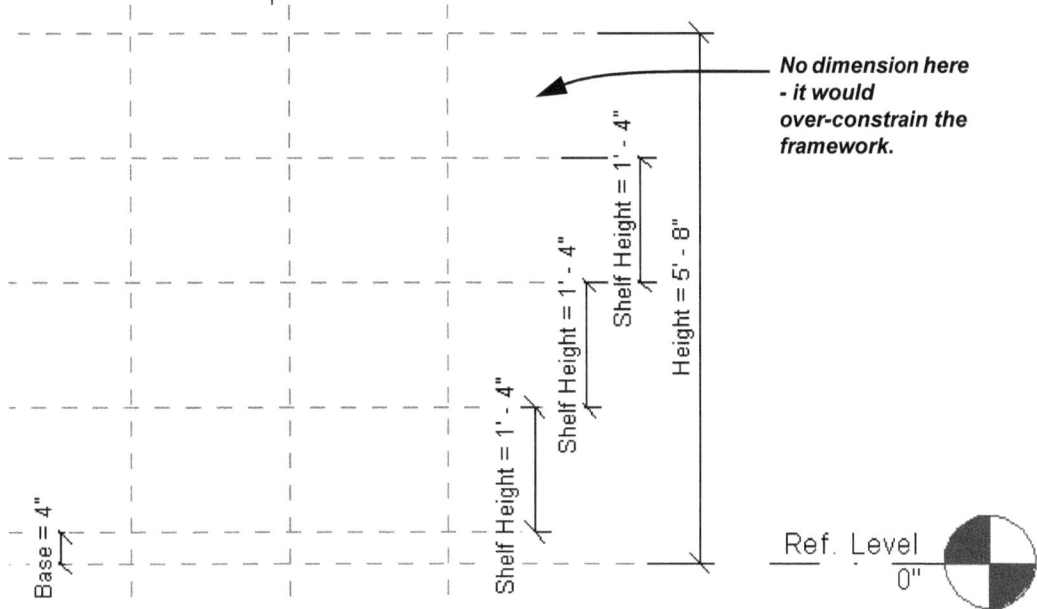

No dimension here - it would over-constrain the framework.

Base = 4"

Shelf Height = 1' - 4"

Shelf Height = 1' - 4"

Shelf Height = 1' - 4"

Shelf Height = 1' - 4"

Height = 5' - 8"

Ref. Level

0"

Figure 4–28

- Each of the shelf height dimensions must be separate. Once you have created one shelf height parameter, you can apply the same label to the other dimensions.

3. In the *Modify* (or *Create*) tab>Properties panel, click

   (Family Types).

The parameters automatically display in alphabetical order. You can reorganize them as required.

4. In the Family Types dialog box, set up a formula for the *Shelf Height*, as shown in Figure 4–29. Lock the **Height** parameter and the **Shelf Height** parameter also locks.

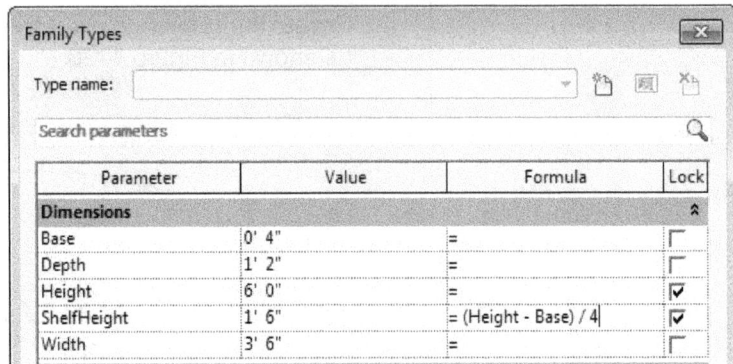

Parameter	Value	Formula	Lock
Dimensions			⌃
Base	0' 4"	=	☐
Depth	1' 2"	=	☐
Height	6' 0"	=	☑
ShelfHeight	1' 6"	= (Height - Base) / 4	☑
Width	3' 6"	=	☐

Family Types

Type name:

Search parameters

Figure 4–29

5. Move the dialog box to one side and try several different values. Click **Apply** to apply the changes to the family. Verify that all of the reference planes move together. Click **OK**.

6. Save the family.

Practice 4b

Set up a Heat Pump Family

Practice Objectives

- Add reference planes.
- Dimension and label reference planes.
- Add a formula to a parameter.
- Flex the framework.

Estimated time for completion: 20 minutes

In this practice, you will create a family file based on a template and view the existing reference planes. You will also create reference planes, dimension them, label the dimensions, as shown in Figure 4–30, and use a formula in parameters, as shown in Figure 4–31.

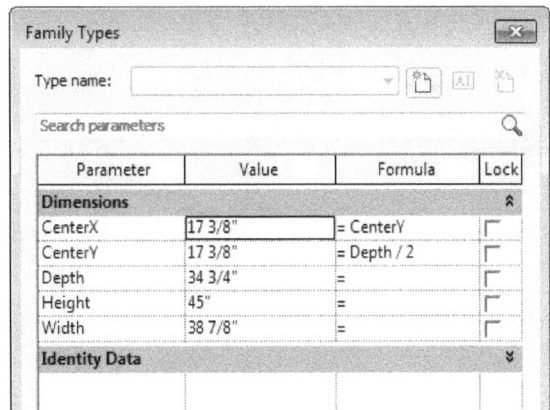

Width = 38 7/8"

CenterY = 17 3/8"

Depth = 34 3/4"

CenterX = 17 3/8"

Figure 4–30

Parameter	Value	Formula	Lock
Dimensions			⌃
CenterX	17 3/8"	= CenterY	☐
CenterY	17 3/8"	= Depth / 2	☐
Depth	34 3/4"	=	☐
Height	45"	=	☐
Width	38 7/8"	=	☐
Identity Data			⌄

Family Types — Type name: — Search parameters

Figure 4–31

Task 1 - Open a family template.

1. Close all open projects.

2. On the Start page, under the *Families* area, click **New**.

3. In the New Family - Select Template File dialog box, select the template **Mechanical Equipment.rft** from the Revit Library and click **Open**.

4. In the *View* tab>Windows panel, click ⊟ (Tile) or type **WT**.

5. The four open views display. Type **ZA** (the shortcut for **Zoom All to Fit**) to fit the view in all of the windows.

6. Two existing reference planes are included in the file, as well as **Ref.Level**.

Changing the units so that they display as inches makes it easier to work with the dimensions.

7. Type **UN** to open the Project Units dialog box. Click the button under *Format* for *Length* and change the *Units* to **Fractional inches**. Then, set the *Rounding* **To the nearest 1/8"**.

8. Click **OK** until all of the dialog boxes are closed. Save the family in the practice files *MEP* folder as **Heat Pump.rfa**.

Task 2 - Create plan view reference planes.

1. Maximize the **Ref. Level** view.

2. Create two new reference planes, above and to the right of the existing planes, as shown in Figure 4–32. Do not worry about the exact location yet.

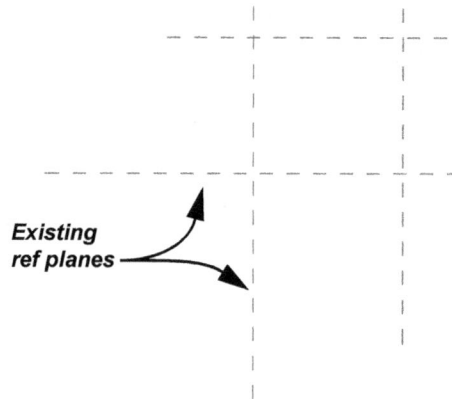

Figure 4–32

3. Add the dimensions shown in Figure 4–33.

Your dimensions might vary depending on where you originally placed the reference planes.

Figure 4–33

The scale in the graphics have been changed to display the dimensions more clearly.

4. Select the horizontal dimension. In the *Modify | Dimensions* tab>Label Dimension panel, click ⬜ (New Parameter).

5. In the Parameter Properties dialog box, in the *Parameter Data* area, ensure that **Type** is selected and then type the name **Width**. Click **OK**.

6. Repeat the process for the overall vertical dimension and name the parameter **Depth**.

7. Add two more reference planes inside the other reference planes. Dimension and label them, as shown in Figure 4–34.

These new dimensions are not at the center of the unit but a specific distance from the right side and the top reference planes. The exact distance is not required at this time.

Figure 4–34

8. Open the Elevations: **Front** view.

9. Create the reference planes and dimensions shown in Figure 4–35. Name the **Top of Unit** and **Top of Base** reference planes. Label the *Height* dimension and lock the **1"** and **EQ** dimensions into place.

   • Note that you might need to zoom in to do this.

Name: Top of Unit (lowest of the three reference planes)

Name: Top of Base

Ref. Level

0"

Figure 4–35

10. Save the family.

Task 3 - Flex the parameters.

1. Remain in elevation view.

2. Select the **Height** parameter and change it to a different height. Verify that the top dimensions moves with the height and the bottom one stays in place.

3. Try a different height to fully check it.

4. Return to the **Floor Plans: Ref. Level** view.

5. In the *Modify* (or *Create*) tab>Properties panel, click (Family Types).

6. In the Family Types dialog box, set up a formula for *CenterY* and *CenterX*, as shown in Figure 4–36. Lock one of the center parameters and the related parameters also lock.

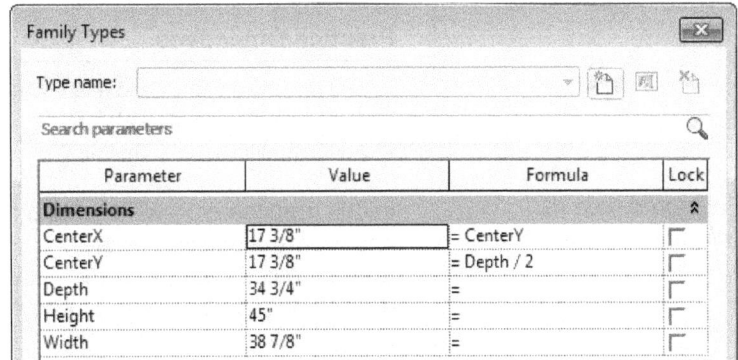

Parameter	Value	Formula	Lock
Dimensions			⌃
CenterX	17 3/8"	= CenterY	☐
CenterY	17 3/8"	= Depth / 2	☐
Depth	34 3/4"	=	☐
Height	45"	=	☐
Width	38 7/8"	=	☐

Family Types

Type name:

Search parameters

Figure 4–36

7. Move the dialog box to one side and try several different values. Click **Apply** to apply the changes to the family. Verify that all of the reference planes move together. Click **OK**.

8. Save the family.

Practice 4c

Set up a Structural Column Family

Practice Objectives

- Add reference planes and reference lines.
- Add dimensions and labels.
- Add a formula to a parameter.

Estimated time for completion: 10 minutes

In this practice, you will create a family file based on a template and view the existing reference planes. You will also create reference lines and reference planes, dimension them, label the dimensions, as shown in Figure 4–37, and use a formula in parameters.

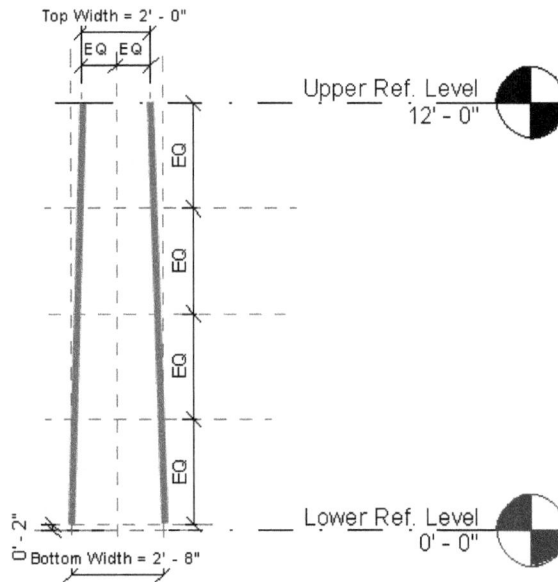

Figure 4–37

Task 1 - Open a family template.

1. Close all open projects.

2. On the Start page, in the *Families* area, select **New**.

3. In the New Family - Select Template File dialog box, select the template **Structural Column.rft** from the Revit Library and click **Open**.

4. Open a 3D view and the **Elevations: Front** views.

5. In the *View* tab>Windows panel, click ⊟ (Tile) or type **WT**. The three open views display so you can see each of them. Type **ZA** (the shortcut for **Zoom All to Fit**) to fit the view in all of the windows.

6. Several existing reference planes and some dimensions are included in the file, as well as **Lower Ref.Level** and **Upper Ref. Level** which set the height of the column once it is used in a project.

7. Save the family in the practice files *Structural* folder as **Trellis Column.rfa**.

Task 2 - Create reference planes.

---

1. Maximize the **Elevations: Front** view.

2. Change the *Upper Ref. Level* to **12'-0"**.

3. Extend the reference planes past the upper level marker.

4. Draw four new horizontal reference planes between the **Lower** and **Upper Ref. Levels**, as shown in Figure 4–38. Do not worry about the exact location yet but the lowest one is close to the **Lower Ref. Level** and the others are more or less equally spaced in the remaining area.

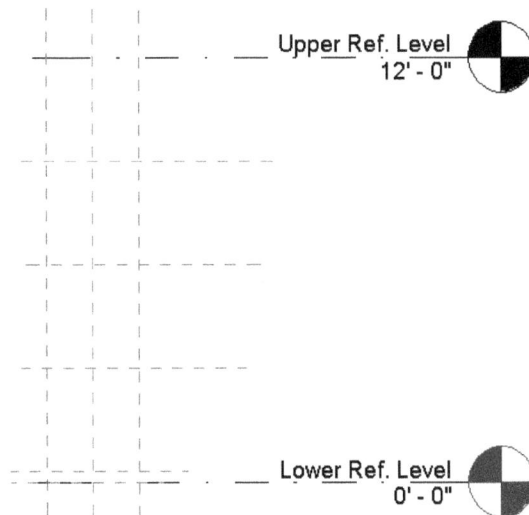

Figure 4–38

5. Dimension the lowest reference plane to the **Lower Ref. Level**. Set the dimension to **2"** and lock the dimension as shown in Figure 4–39. Name the reference plane **Top of Base**.

Figure 4–39

6. Add a string of dimensions between the evenly spaced reference planes and the lowest reference plane, as shown in Figure 4–40. Set the dimension string to **Equal**.

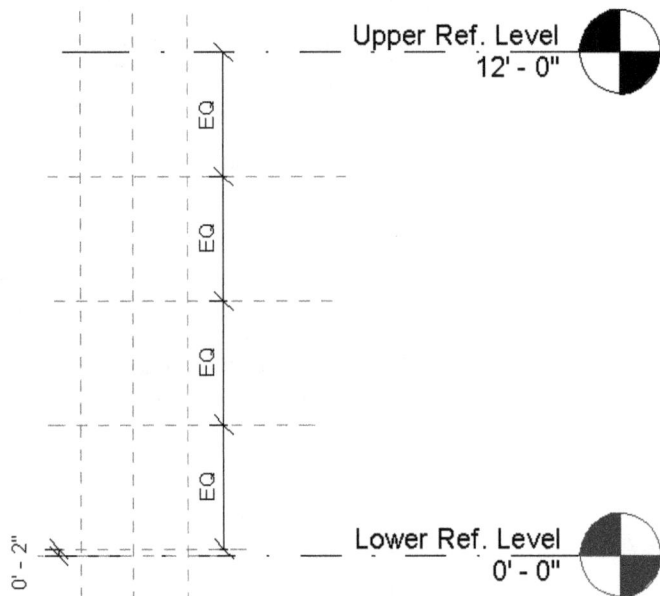

Figure 4–40

7. Add two short vertical reference planes crossing the **Upper Ref. Level**.

8. Dimension and set them as equal, as shown in Figure 4–41.

Figure 4–41

9. Add an overall dimension to the new short reference planes.

10. Select the overall dimension.

11. In the *Modify | Dimensions* tab>Label Dimension panel, click

    ⬜ (New Parameter).

12. In the Parameter Properties dialog box, name it **Top Width**
    and click **OK**. The new parameter displays with the
    dimension, as shown in Figure 4–42.

Your dimensions might vary depending on where you originally placed the reference planes.

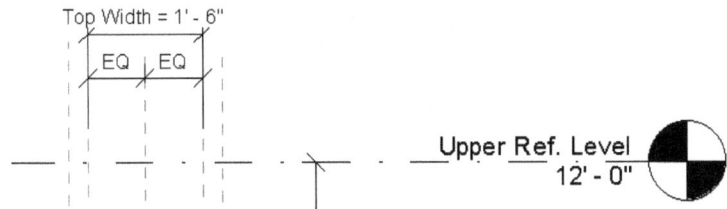

Figure 4–42

13. Add another dimension to the overall vertical reference
    planes below the **Lower Ref. Level** and label it **Bottom
    Width**, as shown in Figure 4–43.

14. In the *Create* tab>Datum panel, click ⬏ (Reference Line).

15. Draw reference lines from the **Top of Base** reference plane
    to the **Upper Ref. Level**, as shown in Figure 4–43. Ensure
    that you snap to the intersections of the reference planes.

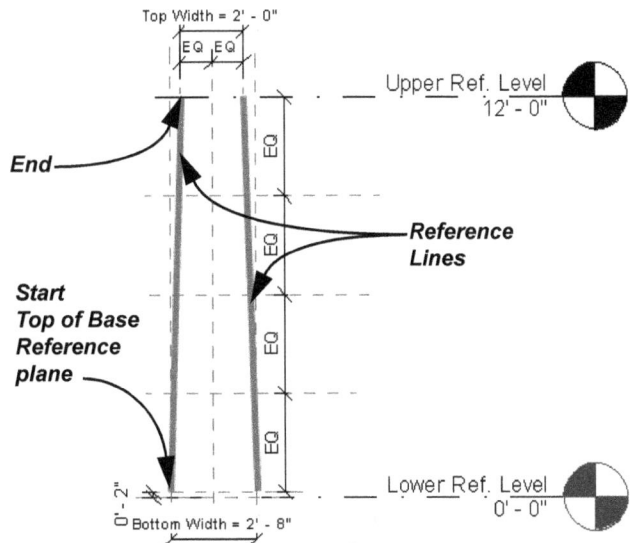

Figure 4–43

16. In the *Modify* (or *Create*) tab>Properties panel, click
    (Family Types).

17. Set up the formula for the *Top Width,* **Bottom Width / 1.3**, as
    shown in Figure 4–44.

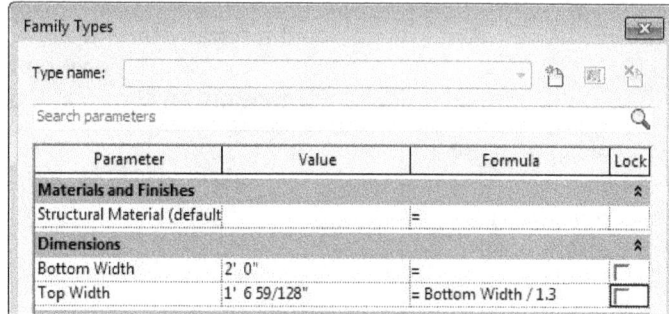

Family Types			
Type name:			
Search parameters			
Parameter	**Value**	**Formula**	**Lock**
Materials and Finishes			⌃
Structural Material (default		=	
Dimensions			⌃
Bottom Width	2' 0"	=	
Top Width	1' 6 59/128"	= Bottom Width / 1.3	

Figure 4–44

18. Move the dialog box to one side and try several different
    values for the bottom width. Click **Apply** to apply the changes
    to the family. Verify that all of the reference planes and lines
    move together. Click **OK**.

19. Change the height of the **Upper Ref. Level** to flex the frame
    work.

20. Save the family.

4.3 Creating Family Elements

Once parametric framework has been created, it is recommended to add actual geometry to the family file, as shown in Figure 4–45. The components in a family can include 3D solids and voids as well as 2D symbolic lines. You can also include model lines, model text, and annotation text.

Figure 4–45

Creating 3D Elements

There are five methods of creating solid forms, as shown in Figure 4–46. Each method uses a sketched 2D profile as the basis of the 3D shape.

Figure 4–46

Void forms use the same creation methods.

- **Extrusion** pushes the profile out in one direction.
- **Blend** links two profiles together.
- **Revolve** rotates the profile around an axis.
- **Sweep** extends a profile along a path.
- **Swept Blend** connects two different profiles along a path.

> **Hint: Selecting Void Forms**
>
> Solids and voids are considered separate categories. You can use the **Filter** command to select them separately, as shown in Figure 4–47.
>
>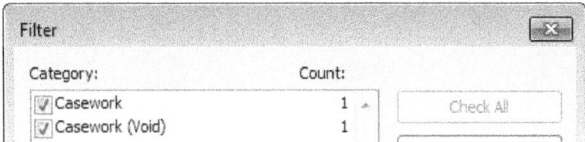
>
> **Figure 4–47**

Extrusions

Extrusions are the simplest elements to create. All you need to do is draw a closed profile using Autodesk Revit sketch tools and assign a depth for the extrusion, as shown in Figure 4–48.

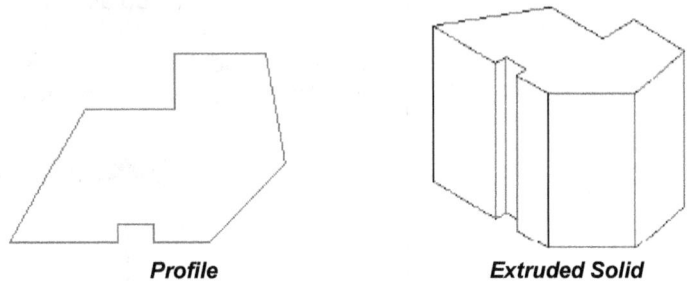

Profile   *Extruded Solid*

Figure 4–48

How To: Create Solid Extrusions

1. In the *Create* tab>Forms panel, click ⬚ (Extrusion).
2. In the Options Bar, set the *Depth* for the extrusion, as shown in Figure 4–49.

Depth	12"		☑ Chain	Offset: 0"		☐ Radius:	12"

Figure 4–49

   - A positive value for the depth extrudes up or toward you depending on the work plane. A negative value extrudes down or away from you.
3. In the *Modify | Create Extrusion* tab>Draw panel, use the sketch tools to create the profile for the extrusion. You can add dimensions and reference planes as required, to create the profile. They will not display when the extrusion is finished.

4. In the Mode panel, click ✔ (Finish Edit Mode) to create the extrusion.
5. In the *Modify | Extrusion* tab, make changes to the extrusion as required.

*By default, **Start** is at the work plane and **End** is at the depth.*

6. In Properties, you can adjust the *Extrusion Start* and *Extrusion End*, the *Visible* and *Visibility/Graphics Overrides*, and *Material*. You can also change it from a **Solid** to a **Void** or vice versa, and place it in the *Subcategory* of **Hidden Lines** or **Overhead Lines**.

   - In the *Create* tab>Work Plane panel, click ⊞ (Set) to select the plane on which you want to draw a profile (e.g., on top of another extrusion).

Blends

If the entire blended element is not displayed in plan view, select the View name in the Project Browser, and then in Properties, modify the View Range Cut Plane.

Blends are defined by two profiles: one for the base (bottom) and one for the top. The two profiles are connected by the solid element. If the base and top do not have the same number of corners, adjust the vertex connection, as shown in Figure 4–50.

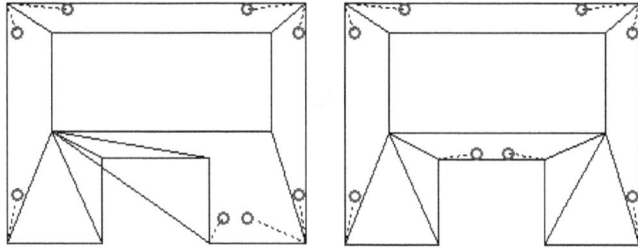

Figure 4–50

How To: Create Solid Blends

1. In the *Create* tab>Forms panel, click ⬙ (Blend).
2. In the *Modify | Create Blend Base Boundary* tab>Draw panel, use the sketch tools to draw the base profile.

3. In the Mode panel, click ⬙ (Edit Top).
4. In the Options Bar, set the *Depth* for the top.
5. Draw the top profile using the sketch tools.

6. If the intersections are complex, click ⬙ (Edit Vertices) and ensure that all of the connections work correctly.

7. Click ✓ (Finish Edit Mode) to create the blend.
8. The *Modify | Blend* tab displays, where you can edit the base or the top. You also have access to the Properties of the blend.

- When you click ⬙ (Edit Vertices), open blue dots are displayed on the dotted lines. These lines are suggested connections. Select the dot to toggle the connection on or off, and repeat with other corners to obtain the required connections. Use the tools in the *Edit Vertices* tab>Vertex Connect panel, as shown in Figure 4–51, to modify the vertices.

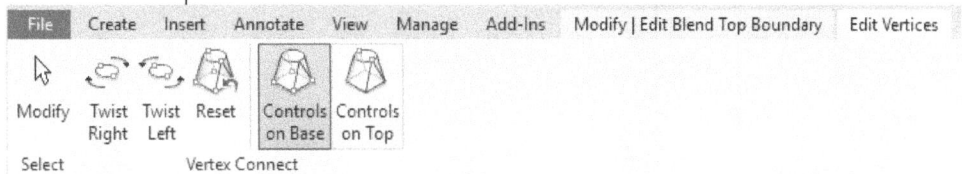

Figure 4–51

Revolves

A revolved solid form requires a profile and an axis around which it is revolved, as shown in Figure 4–52. The profile often needs to be sketched in a work plane perpendicular to the *ground*. Before sketching the profile, create a reference plane that you can use for the work plane. For example, if you are creating a dome, create two intersecting reference planes at the center of the dome and name them. Then, when you start the revolution, you can select one reference plane for your work plane and the other for your axis.

You can name a reference plane in Properties.

Profile with axis   **Revolved solid**

Figure 4–52

How To: Create Solid Revolves

1. In the *Create* tab>Forms panel, click 🔲 (Revolve).
2. In the *Modify | Create Revolve* tab>Work Plane panel, click

   ▦ (Set). In the Work Plane dialog box, select the plane on which you want to draw the profile. A prompt warns you if you need to change views to draw in that work plane.

3. In the Draw panel, click ⬐ (Boundary Line) and draw the profile.

The axis can be an edge of the profile or some distance away if there is an opening.

4. In the Draw panel, click 🔄 (Axis Line) and draw or select the axis about which the profile will rotate.

5. Click ✓ (Finish Edit Mode) to create the solid.
6. The *Modify | Revolve* tab displays, where you can edit the revolve. You can also change the Properties (such as the *End Angle* and *Start Angle*).

Sweeps

A sweep is similar to an extrusion. However, instead of only extruding in one direction, it follows a path that can have multiple segments, as shown in Figure 4–53. You define the path first and then create the profile on the path.

Figure 4–53

How To: Create Solid Sweeps

1. In the *Create* tab>Forms panel, click 🖱 (Sweep).

2. In the *Modify | Sweep* tab>Sweep panel, click ✏️ (Sketch Path) or 🖱 (Pick Path). Draw or select the path you want the sweep to follow.

3. Click ✔ (Finish Edit Mode).
4. In the Sweep panel, select a profile from the list or click
   🖱 (Select Profile), and then click 🖱 (Edit Profile) to sketch a profile.
   - The Go To View dialog box opens if you need to change views to draw the profile. Select the view in which you want to draw the profile and click **Open View**.
5. Draw the profile for the sweep on the profile plane, as shown in Figure 4–54.

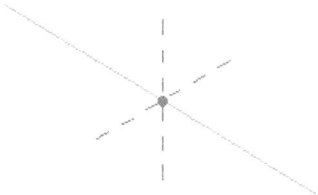

Figure 4–54

6. Click ✔ (Finish Edit Mode) twice to complete the process.
7. The *Modify | Sweep* tab displays, where you can edit the sweep. In Properties, you can change several options of the profile along with the other standard options.

Click 🖱 (Load Profile) to load additional profiles into the family file for use with the sweep.

The profile plane is automatically drawn on the first line of the path. It is the red dot with the green line through it, as shown in a 3D view in Figure 4–54. The red dot is the place where the profile and path intersect.

Swept Blends

Swept blends consist of a path and two profiles, as shown in Figure 4–55. The profiles can have different shapes. The path must be one segment, which can be a line, an arc, or a spline.

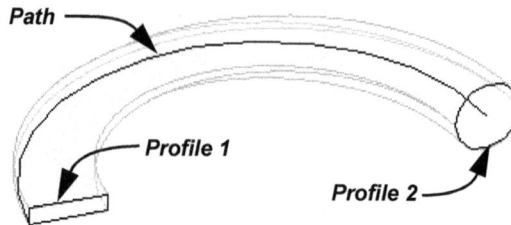

Figure 4–55

How To: Create Solid Swept Blends

1. In the *Create* tab>Forms panel, click ➿ (Swept Blend).
2. In the *Modify | Swept Blend* tab>Swept Blend panel, click

    ➿ (Sketch Path) or ➿ (Pick Path). Draw or select the path you want the swept blend to follow. You can only have one segment in the path.

3. Click ✓ (Finish Edit Mode).

4. In the Swept Blend panel, click ➿ (Select Profile 1).
5. Select a profile from the list or create a new profile using

    ➿ (Edit Profile).

6. Click ➿ (Select Profile 2) and repeat the process. It does not need to be the same size or shape as the first profile.

7. In the Swept Blend panel, click ➿ (Edit Vertices) and align the vertices. This controls the twist of the swept blend.

8. Click ✓ (Finish Edit Mode).
9. In the *Modify | Swept Blend* tab, make any changes as required.
10. In Properties, set any options as required.

Aligning and Locking

It is important to lock and align sketches to reference planes (rather than other family elements) so that they can be flexed parametrically. The padlock symbol displays when you snap to reference planes while drawing. Select the padlock to lock the element to the reference plane, as shown in Figure 4–56.

Figure 4–56

- When using the (Pick Line) option, in the Options Bar, you can select **Lock** to automatically lock the sketch line to the selected reference plane.

- You can also use the **Align** command to align and lock elements to reference planes.

- You can temporarily hide other elements before sketching to ensure that you only work with the reference planes.

- Tangency Locks display when you add arcs that are tangent to other lines, as shown in Figure 4–57. Close the padlock to keep the tangency as the element is flexed.

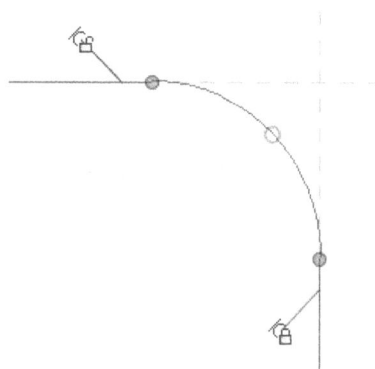

Figure 4–57

Practice 4d

Create Family Geometry for the Bookcase

Practice Objectives

- Create solid extrusion elements.
- Align and lock the elements to reference planes.
- Join the geometry of elements.

Estimated time for completion: 20 minutes

In this practice, you will create extruded solids for the base, frame, shelves, and back of a bookcase, and lock them in place with dimensions. You will also join the solid elements together to form one unit, as shown in Figure 4–58.

Figure 4–58

Task 1 - Create a base for the bookcase.

1. In the practice files *Architectural* folder, open **Barrister-Bookcase-Geometry.rfa**.

2. Open the **Floor Plans: Ref. Level** view.

3. In the *Create* tab>Forms panel, click (Extrusion). In the Options Bar, set the *Depth* to **4"**.

4. In the *Modify | Create Extrusion* tab>Draw panel, use the sketch tools to draw a rectangle across the outside intersections of the reference planes. Lock all four lines to the reference planes, as shown in Figure 4–59.

Figure 4–59

5. Click ✓ (Finish Edit Mode).

6. Open the **Elevations: Front** view.

7. In the *Modify* tab>Modify panel, click (Align). Align the top of the extrusion to the *Base* reference plane and lock it.

8. Save the family.

Task 2 - Create the frame and shelves for the bookcase.
---

1. In the *Create* tab>Work Plane panel, click (Set).

2. In the Work Plane dialog box, set the *Name* to **Reference Plane : Door Face** and click **OK**.

3. Start the **Extrusion** command.

4. Draw four reference planes inside the existing reference planes. Dimension and label them as shown in Figure 4–60.

Drawing the reference planes inside the extrusion helps to keep the primary views from getting cluttered.

Figure 4–60

5. In the Family Types dialog box, flex the *Height* and *Width* of the overall bookcase to verify that the new **Frame Width** parameters move as expected.

6. Return to the *Modify | Create Extrusion* tab and select **Rectangle**.

7. In the Options Bar, set the *Depth* to **1'-0"**.

8. Draw and lock two rectangular sketches to the reference planes, as shown in Figure 4–61.

Hint: type **SI** to force the snap to the intersection of the reference planes.

Figure 4–61

9. Click ✔ (Finish Edit Mode).

10. Start the **Extrusion** command again.

11. Draw two reference planes on either side of the shelf height reference plane. Dimension and label them as shown in Figure 4–62. Repeat with the other two shelf height locations.

Shelf Thickness = 1"

Figure 4–62

- To make the labels more readable, change the scale to **1"=1'-0"**. You can also create an additional dimension type with the *Read Convention* set to **Horizontal** and use it for the **Shelf** parameters, as shown in Figure 4–62.

12. In the *Modify | Create Extrusion* tab>Draw panel, select **Rectangle**.

13. In the Options Bar, ensure that the *Depth* is set to **1'-0"**.

14. Draw the sketch around each shelf, as shown in Figure 4–63. Lock the sketches to the reference planes.

Figure 4–63

15. Click ✓ (Finish Edit Mode).

16. Open the Family Types dialog box and move the *Height*, *Width*, and *Depth* to the top of the parameters list.

17. Flex the *Height* and *Width* of the overall bookcase to verify the new **Shelf Thickness** parameters move as expected. Finish the flexing with the *Height* set to **5'-0"** and the *Width* to **3'-0"**.

18. Save the family.

Task 3 - Create the back of the bookcase.

1. Open the **Elevations: Left** view.

2. Align and lock the back of the frame and shelf extrusions to the back reference plane (on the left).

3. Open the **Floor Plans: Ref. Level** view.

4. Start the **Extrusion** command again.

5. Add a reference plane **1/4"** from the back of the bookcase. Dimension and lock it in place, as shown in Figure 4–64.

Create a label if you want to change the size of the back.

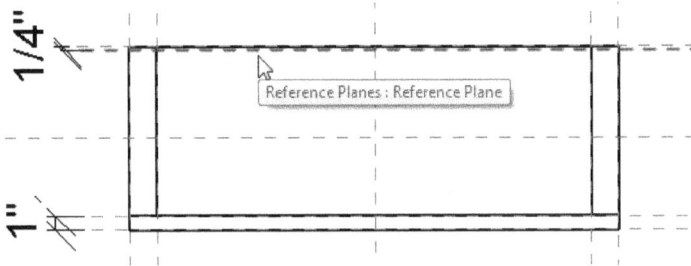

Figure 4–64

6. Return to the *Modify | Create Extrusion* tab and select **Rectangle**.

7. In the Options Bar, set the *Depth* to **2'-6"**. (This is less than the bookcase height. You will adjust it later.)

8. Draw a rectangular sketch across the back and lock it to the reference planes.

9. Click ✓ (Finish Edit Mode).

10. Open the **Elevations: Left** view. Switch the **Visual Style** to
     (Hidden Line). The back extrusion is shown in
    Figure 4–65.

11. Align and lock the top of the back panel with the top reference
    plane, as shown in Figure 4–66.

Figure 4–65

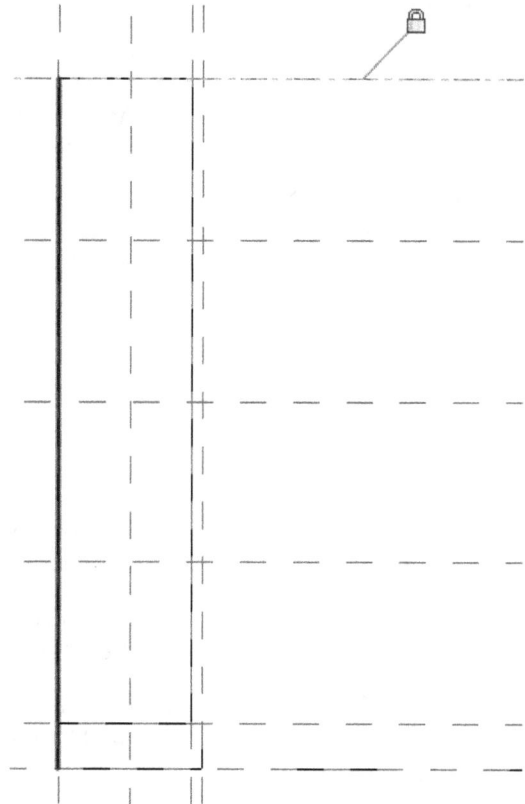

Figure 4–66

12. Switch to a 3D view. The base, frame, shelves, and back are all separate elements, as shown in Figure 4–67.

13. In the *Modify* tab>Geometry panel, click (Join) and join the four elements. The bookcase should display as shown in Figure 4–68.

Figure 4–67

Figure 4–68

14. Save the family.

Practice 4e

Create Family Geometry for the Heat Pump

Practice Objective

- Create extrusions and blends.

Estimated time for completion: 20 minutes.

In this practice, you will create extruded and blended solids for the base, cabinet, top, and fan unit of a heat pump, as shown in Figure 4–69.

Figure 4–69

Task 1 - Create the main cabinet of a heat pump.

1. In the practice files *MEP* folder, open **Heat-Pump-Geometry.rfa.**

2. Ensure that the **Floor Plans: Ref. Level** view is open.

3. Add four reference planes 3" to the inside of each exterior reference plane. Dimension and lock them into place, as shown in Figure 4–70.

4. In the *Create* tab>Datum panel, click ⌐ (Reference Line).

5. In the Options Bar, toggle off **Chain**, if required.

6. Draw a reference line at each of the four corners, as shown in Figure 4–70. Ensure that you lock any open padlocks that display as you draw each line.

Figure 4–70

7. Flex the framework by changing the *Width* and *Depth*.

8. In the *Create* tab>Work Plane panel, click ⊞ (Set).

9. In the Work Plane dialog box, set *Name* as **Reference Plane : Top of Base** and click **OK**.

10. In the *Create* tab>Forms panel, click ⬚ (Extrusion). In the Options Bar, set the *Depth* to **30"**.

11. Sketch and lock the shape to the reference lines shown in Figure 4–71. (**Hint:** Use **Pick Lines** with the **Lock** option set and then trim the excess, as required.)

Width = 38 7/8"

3"

3"

3"

CenterY = 17 3/8"

Depth = 34 3/4"

3"

CenterX = 17 3/8"

Figure 4–71

12. Click (Finish Edit Mode).

13. Open the **Elevations: Front** view. Align and lock the top of the unit extrusion to the **Top of Unit** reference plane, as shown in Figure 4–72.

Top of Unit
reference plane

Ref. Le

Figure 4–72

14. Save the family.

Task 2 - Create the top and base of the heat pump.

1. Return to the **Floor Plans: Ref. Level** view.

2. Temporarily hide the existing extrusion.

3. Set the Work Plane to the **Top of Unit** reference plane.

4. In the *Create* tab>Forms panel, click ⬙ (Blend).

5. In the *Modify | Create Blend Base Boundary* tab>Draw panel, click ⬨ (Pick Lines).

6. In the Options Bar, set the *Depth* to **1/2"**, and the *Offset* to **1"**.

7. Position the offset inside the reference planes and click on the outer-most reference planes and reference lines. Use **Trim/Extend to Corner** to clean up the sketch for the base, as shown in Figure 4–73.

8. Click ⬙ (Edit Top). Select **Pick Lines**, and then set the *Depth* to **1/2"** and the *Offset* to **1-1/2"**.

9. Use and trim the same reference planes and reference lines to create a sketch for the top, as shown in Figure 4–73.

Using reference planes to establish the sketch of the blend, rather than other elements, ensures the accuracy of the elements.

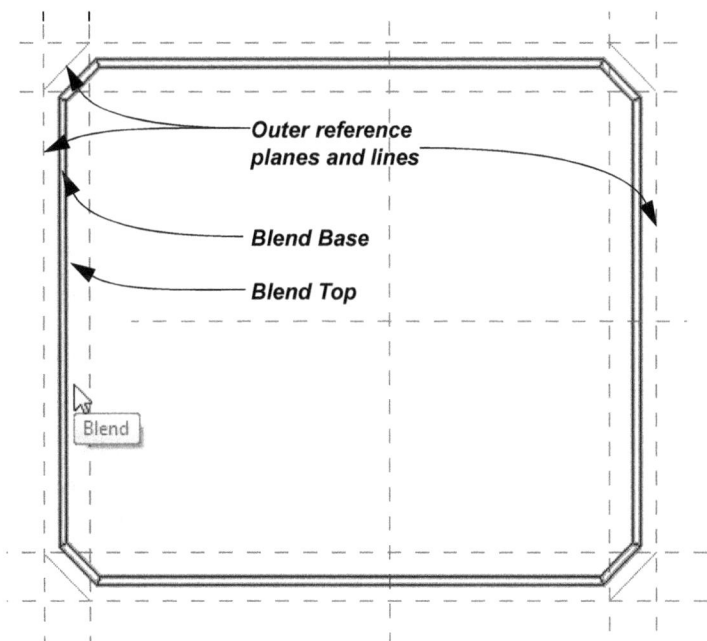

Outer reference planes and lines

Blend Base

Blend Top

Blend

Figure 4–73

10. Click ✓ (Finish Edit Mode).

11. Flex the framework to ensure that the blend is working.

12. Return to the **Floor Plans: Ref. Level** view, if you switched to a 3D view.

13. Select the blend and temporarily hide it.

14. Set the *Work Plane* to **Level: Ref. Level**.

15. In the *Create* tab>Forms panel, click 🗍 (Extrusion). In the Options Bar, set the *Depth* to **1"**.

16. In the *Modify | Create Extrusion* tab>Draw panel, use the **Pick Lines** tool to draw a boundary at **1/2"** inside the unit reference planes, as shown in Figure 4–74.

Figure 4–74

17. Click ✓ (Finish Edit Mode).

18. Reset Temporary Hide/Isolate.

19. Open the **Elevations: Front** view.

20. Temporarily hide the main cabinet extrusion.

21. In the *Modify* tab>Modify panel, click ⬜ (Align) and align the top of the base extrusion to the *Top of Base* reference plane and lock it, as shown in Figure 4–75.

Figure 4–75

22. Reset Temporary Hide/Isolate.

23. Open a 3D view.

24. Open the Family Types dialog box and reorder the parameters so that *Width*, *Height,* and *Depth* are at the top.

25. Flex the dimensions to check that everything is working as expected. Save the family.

Task 3 - Add the fan.

---

1. Return to the **Floor Plans: Ref. Level** view.

2. Set the Work Plane to the **Top of Unit** reference plane.

3. Start the **Extrusion** command and in the Options Bar, set the *Depth* to **1"**.

4. Draw a circle from the intersection of the CenterX and CenterY reference planes with a radius close to the outside, as shown in Figure 4–76. The exact dimension does not matter for this step.

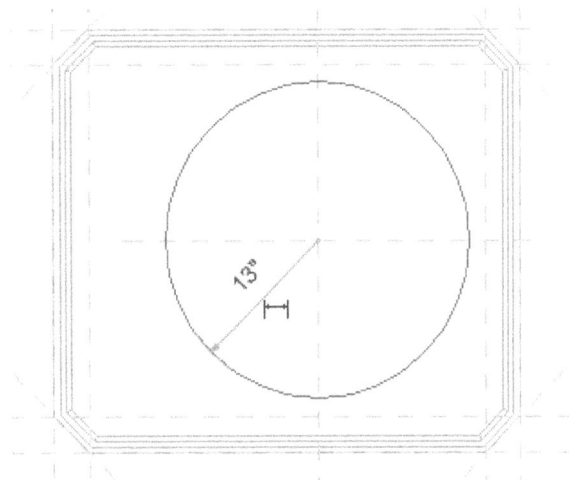

Figure 4–76

5. Dimension the radius of the circle and create a new Label based on the dimension named **Radius of Fan**.

6. Open the Family Types dialog box and move the **Radius of Fan** parameter below all of the others.

7. Next to **Radius of Fan**, in the *Formula* area, type **Depth / 2 - 1"**.

8. Click **Apply**.

9. Flex the element by changing the *Depth*. When it works as expected, click **OK**.

10. Click ✓ (Finish Edit Mode).

11. Open the **Elevations: Front** view. Align and lock the top of the fan to the top reference level, as shown in Figure 4–77.

Figure 4–77

12. In the *Modify* tab>Geometry panel, click 🔲 (Join).

13. Join the unit and the beveled blend together. Then join the fan to the unit and the base to the unit.

14. View the unit in 3D, as shown in Figure 4–78.

Figure 4–78

15. Save the family.

Practice 4f

Create Family Geometry for the Structural Column

Practice Objectives

- Create extrusions.
- Add dimensions and labels.

Estimated time for completion: 10 minutes.

In this practice, you will create extruded solids for the base and open framework of the column. You will lock them in place with the **Align** tool. You will also test the geometry by modifying the height and widths of the columns. The final version is shown in Figure 4–79.

Figure 4–79

Task 1 - Create a base for the column.

1. In the practice files *Structural* folder, open **Trellis-Column-Geometry.rfa**.

2. Open the **Floor Plans: Lower Ref. Level** view.

3. In the *Create* tab>Forms panel, click ▯ (Extrusion). In the Options Bar, set the *Depth* as **2"**.

4. Draw four reference planes to the outside of the existing reference planes. Dimension and lock them at 2", as shown in Figure 4–80.

Figure 4–80

5. In the *Modify | Create Extrusion* tab>Draw panel, use the sketch tools to draw a rectangle across the outside intersections of the reference planes. Lock all four lines to the reference planes, as shown in Figure 4–81.

Figure 4–81

6. Click ✓ (Finish Edit Mode).

7. Open the **Elevations: Front** view.

8. In the *Modify* tab>Modify panel, click 🔲 (Align). Align the top of the extrusion to the lower reference plane and lock it, as shown in Figure 4–82.

0' - 2"

0' Bottom Width = 2' - 8"

Figure 4–82

9. Save the family.

Task 2 - Create the open work frame for the column.

---

1. Continue working in the **Elevations: Front** view.

2. In the *Create* tab>Work Plane panel, click ▦ (Set).

3. In the Work Plane dialog box, set *Name* as **Reference Plane : Front**, as shown in Figure 4–83, and click **OK**.

All of these reference planes were added and named in the family template file.

Figure 4–83

---

4. Temporarily hide the base extrusion.

5. In the *Create* tab>Datum panel, click ⮢ (Reference Line).

6. Draw four angled reference lines, as shown in Figure 4–84.

   - Ensure that you are snapping to the intersections of the horizontal reference planes and the angled reference lines that establish the taper.
   - Use the shortcut **SI** to snap to the intersections and not the end points.

Figure 4–84

7. Change the height of the **Upper Ref. Level** and the Bottom Width and verify that all of the reference planes and lines are working as expected. End with the **Upper Ref. Level** set to **12'-0"** and the **Bottom Width** set to **2'-8"**.

8. Start the **Extrusion** command.

9. Draw the sketch shown in Figure 4–85. On the Options Bar, use ⬚ (Pick Lines) with Lock selected.

   - Use offsets, ⬚ (Split Element), and ⬚ (Trim Element) to create the lines, as required.
   - Ensure that the sketch is completely closed.
   - Zoom in to make adjustments.
   - All dimensions are **2"** total thickness (1" halfwidth).

Be very careful when trimming the lines. If you get a warning, cancel and try again.

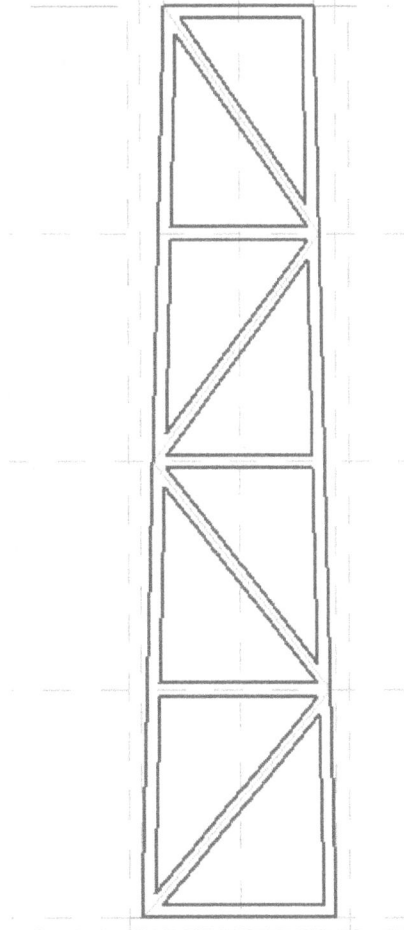

Figure 4–85

10. Click ✓ (Finish Edit Mode).

11. Open the **Floor Plans: Lower Ref. Level** view.

12. Align and lock the extrusion to the Front and Back Reference planes as shown in Figure 4–86.

Figure 4–86

13. Open the **3D Views: View 1** view.

14. In the View Control Bar, set the Visual Style to 🗗 (Shaded).

15. Rotate the view so you can see the open framework.

16. Save the family.

Task 3 - Dimension the framework for flexing.

---

1. Open the **Elevations: Front** view.

2. Open the Family Types dialog box and move it so you can see the column.

3. In the Family Types dialog box, change the **Top Width** *Formula* to **Bottom Width /1.5** and click **Apply**.

4. You can see how the connections of the open framework deform, as shown in the detail in Figure 4–87.

Figure 4–87

5. Close the dialog box and undo the change.

6. Verify that the **Upper Ref. Level** is set as **12'-0"**.

It is important to work with the exact sizes when you create the extrusion, otherwise the angled lines are not exactly parallel and you cannot dimension them.

7. Select the extrusion. In the *Modify | Extrusion* tab>Mode panel, click ⬚ (Edit Extrusion).

8. Dimension each part of the framework, as shown in part in Figure 4–88.

Figure 4–88

• The dimensions around the outside of the framework are constrained to a reference line, but the ones that are offset on both sides of the reference line are not. Therefore, you have to add a 1" dimension to the reference line for the constraints to be satisfied.

9. Open the Family Types dialog box and change the formula again. Does everything work as expected? If not, click **Cancel** to close the dialog box and fix the dimensions.

10. Click ✔ (Finish Edit Mode).

11. View the family in 3D.

12. Save the family.

4.4 Creating Family Types

An important aspect of Family Types is that it helps you *flex* or test the parametric dimensions you set up, as well as helps you create formulas for parameters. A further use for Family Types is the ability to create preset sizes for insertion into a project. When you select the related command, the types display in the Type Selector, as shown in Figure 4–89 for a desk component.

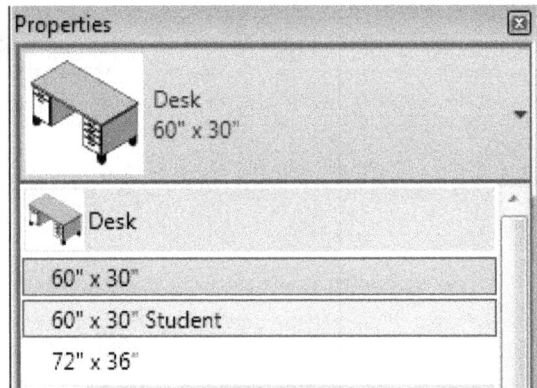

Figure 4–89

How To: Create Family Types

1. In the Family Editor, in the *Create* or *Modify* tab>Properties panel, click ⊞ (Family Types).

2. At the top of the Family Types dialog box, click 📄 (New Type), as shown Figure 4–90.

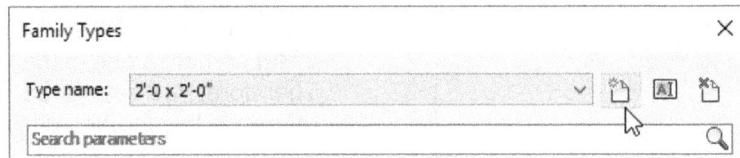

Figure 4–90

- You can type a part or all of a parameter's name to limit the number of parameters that display. This enables you to modify the values more quickly.

3. In the Name dialog box, type a name for the Family Type (as shown in Figure 4–91) and click **OK**.

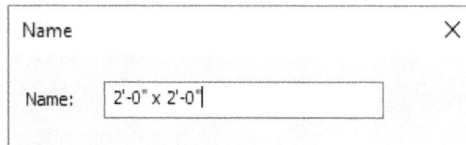

Name	✕
Name:	2'-0" x 2'-0"

Figure 4–91

*   Select a name that is useful for the entire set of types, typically a size.
*   The name of the family always precedes the name of the type. Therefore, you do not need to re-enter that information.

4. In the Family Types dialog box, set the *Value(s)* for that size (as shown in Figure 4–92) and click **Apply**.

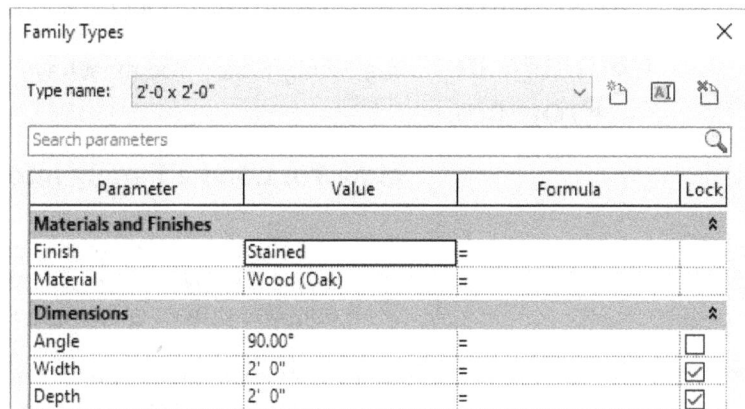

Parameter	Value	Formula	Lock
Materials and Finishes			
Finish	Stained	=	
Material	Wood (Oak)	=	
Dimensions			
Angle	90.00°	=	
Width	2' 0"	=	✓
Depth	2' 0"	=	✓

Family Types — Type name: 2'-0 x 2'-0" — Search parameters

Figure 4–92

5. Repeat the process. You can create as many different types as you need.
6. Verify that all of the types are functioning correctly.
7. Click **OK** to finish the command.
8. Save the family.
9. Load the family into a project and test the new types you have created.

*   In the *Family Types* area, click [AI] (Rename Type) and (Delete Type) as required, to modify the list.

*   To edit a type, select the type name, change the value(s), and click **Apply**.

Hint: Exporting and Importing Family Types

Family Types can be exported to a text file and then imported into a related family. This can save you time when creating different versions of the same basic category.

- In the Application Menu, expand ⬜ (Export), scroll down and click ⬜ (Family Types). In the Export As dialog box, select a location and name. Click **Save**.

- In the *Insert* tab>Import panel, click ⬜ (Import Family Types). In the Import Family Types dialog box, select the required text file, and click **Open**.

Working with Families in Projects

To continue testing your family it helps to see how it works in a project. You can load a family into one or more projects while in the Family Editor. You must have a project open before doing this.

How To: Load a Family into a Project

1. In the Family Editor panel, click ⬜ (Load into Project). The panel is displayed in all of the Family Editor tabs.
2. If only one project is open, the family is automatically loaded into it. If you have more than one project open, the Load into Projects dialog box opens. Select the project(s) to load into, as shown in Figure 4–93.

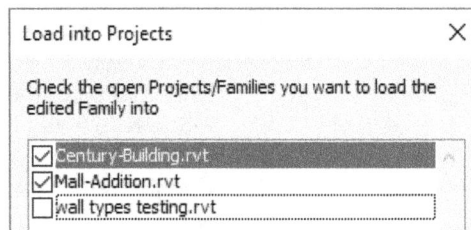

Load into Projects ✕

Check the open Projects/Families you want to load the edited Family into

☑ Century-Building.rvt
☑ Mall-Addition.rvt
☐ wall types testing.rvt

Figure 4–93

3. The project opens with the family loaded. Often, the related command is started with the new family selected in the Type Selector.

- If you have finished working on the family you can click ⬜ (Load into Project and Close).

Practice 4g

Create Family Types for the Bookcase

Practice Objectives

- Create family types of different sizes.
- Test the family in a project.

Estimated time for completion: 10 minutes

In this practice, you will create Family Types for different sizes of the bookcase. Your will then test the bookcase family in a project by placing each of the different types, as shown in Figure 4–94.

Figure 4–94

Task 1 - Create Family Types.

1. In the practice files *Architectural* folder, open **Barristers-Bookcase-Types.rvt**.

2. In the *Create* or *Modify* tab>Properties panel, click (Family Types).

3. In the Family Types dialog box, click (New Type).

4. In the Name dialog box, type **3'-0" x 5'-0"** and click **OK**.

5. In the *Dimensions* area, verify or set the following values for the parameters as shown in Figure 4–95:

- *Width:* **3'-0"**
- *Height:* **5'-0"**
- *Depth:* **1'-1"**
- *Base:* **4"**

Parameter	Value	Formula	Lock
Dimensions			
Width	3' 0"	=	☐
Height	5' 0"	=	☑
Depth	1' 1"	=	☐
Base	0' 4"	=	☑
Frame Width	0' 2"	=	☐
Shelf Thickness	0' 1"	=	☐
Shelf Height	1' 2"	= (Height - Base) / 4	☑

Family Types — Type name: 3'-0" x 5'-0"

Figure 4–95

6. Click **Apply**.

7. Repeat these steps for the following sizes:

- **3'-0" x 6'-0"**
- **3'-6" x 5'-0"**
- **3'-6" x 6'-0"**

8. In the Family Types dialog box, test each of the new named types.

9. Click **OK**.

10. Save the family.

Task 2 - Use the family in a project.

1. In the practice files *Architectural* folder, open **Barristers-Bookcase-Project.rvt**.

2. In the *View* tab>Windows panel, expand ⬚ (Switch Windows). Select a Barrister-Bookcase family view.

3. In the Family Editor panel, click ⬚ (Load into Project).

   • If there is only one project open, the family file is automatically loaded into that project.

   • If more than one project is open, the Load into Projects dialog box opens. Select the project you want to load and click **OK**.

4. The **Component** command is automatically started with the Barristers Bookcase family selected.

5. Place one of each type in the project.

6. Create a 3D view to see the differences.

7. Save the project.

Practice 4h

Create Family Types for the Heat Pump

Practice Objectives

- Create family types of different sizes.
- Test the family in a project.

Estimated time for completion: 10 minutes.

In this practice, you will create and apply Family Types of different sizes to a heat pump and test the family in a project, as shown in Figure 4–96.

Figure 4–96

Task 1 - Create Family Types.

1. In the practice files *MEP* folder, open **Heat-Pump-Types.rfa**

2. In the *Create* tab>Properties panel, click (Family Types).

3. In the Family Types dialog box, click (New Type).

4. In the Name dialog box, type **HP060C** as the name.

5. In the *Dimensions* area, verify or set the following values for the parameters, as shown in Figure 4–97:

- *Width:* **38 7/8"**
- *Height:* **44 3/4"**
- *Depth:* **34 3/4"**

Family Types			
Type name:	HP060C		
Search parameters			🔍

Parameter	Value	Formula	Lock
Dimensions			⌃
Width	38 7/8"	=	☐
Height	44 3/4"	=	☐
Depth	34 3/4"	=	☐
CenterX	17 3/8"	= CenterY	☐
CenterY	17 3/8"	= Depth / 2	☐
Radius of Fan	16 3/8"	= Depth / 2 - 1"	☐

Figure 4–97

6. Click **Apply**. The family resizes to match the new information.

7. Create the other models as follows:

Model	Width	Height	Depth
HP048C	38 7/8"	37"	34 3/4"
HP030C	32 7/8"	32 3/4"	28 3/4"
HP024C	32 7/8"	28 5/8"	28 3/4"

8. In the Family Types dialog box, test the family types by selecting the *Name* and clicking **Apply** after each selection.

9. Click **OK**.

10. Save the family.

Task 2 - Use the family in a project.

1. In the practice files *MEP* folder, open **Heat-Pump-Project.rvt**.

2. Switch back to one of the Heat Pump family views.

3. In the Family Editor panel, click (Load into Project).
   - If there is only one project open, the family file is automatically loaded into that project.
   - If more than one project is open, the Load into Projects dialog box opens. Select the project you want to load and click **OK**.

4. The **Component** command is automatically started with the new family selected.

5. Place one of each type in the project.

6. Create a 3D view to see the differences

7. Save the project and the family.

Practice 4i

Create Family Types for the Structural Column

Practice Objectives

Estimated time for completion: 10 minutes

- Create family types.
- Use the family in a project.

In this practice, you will create and apply Family Types for the column. You will add the column family to a project and test the columns by modifying levels, as shown in Figure 4–98.

Figure 4–98

Task 1 - Create Family Types.

1. In the practice files *Structural* folder, open **Trellis-Column-Types.rfa**.

2. In the *Create* or *Modify* tab>Properties panel, click ⊞ (Family Types).

---

3. In the Family Types dialog box, click ▢ (New Type).

4. In the Name dialog box, set the name as **Over 12'-0"** and click **OK**.

5. In the *Dimensions* area, set the *Bottom Width* to **3'-0"**.

6. Click **Apply**.

7. Create another new Family Type with the name **Under 12'-0"**.

8. In the *Dimensions* area, set the *Bottom Width* to **2'-8"**.

9. Click **OK**.

10. Save the family.

Task 2 - Use the family in a project.

---

1. In the practice files *Structural* folder, open **Trellis-Column-Project.rvt**

2. Open the **Structural Plans: Level 2** view.

3. In the *View* tab>Windows panel, expand ▤ (Switch Windows). Select a Trellis column family view.

4. In the Family Editor panel, click ▤ (Load into Project).
   - If there is only one project open, the family file is automatically loaded into that project.
   - If more than one project is open, the Load into Projects dialog box opens. Select the project you want to load and click **OK**.

5. The **Structural Column** command is automatically started with the Trellis Column family selected. Verify that

   ▯ (Vertical Column) is selected.

6. Place one of each type in the project using the default information.

7. Open the **Elevations: South** view.

Change the Top Level first, so that the column does not go in the wrong direction.

8. Select the **Under 12'-0"** column. In Properties, set the *Top Level* to **Level 2,** the *Top Offset* to (negative) **-6",** and the *Base Level* to **Level 1** with no *Base Offset.*

9. Select the **Over 12'-0"** column. In Properties, set the *Top Level* to **Level 3**, the *Top Offset* to (negative) **-6"**, and the *Base Level* to **Level 1** with no *Base Offset*, as shown in Figure 4–99.

Figure 4–99

10. Change the height of the levels to see how the look of the column changes.

11. Save the project.

Chapter Review Questions

1. In which of the following views do the Reference planes, as shown in Figure 4–100, display? (Select all that apply.)

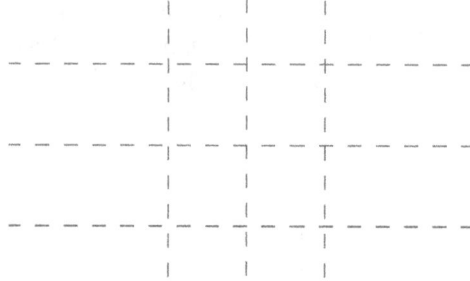

Figure 4–100

   a. Plan

   b. Elevation

   c. 3D

   d. Section

2. Which of the following is created when you label a dimension?

   a. Family

   b. Type

   c. Parameter

   d. Value

3. Which of the following commands, shown in Figure 4–101, require profiles instead of sketches? (Select all that apply.)

Figure 4–101

   a. **Extrusion**

   b. **Blend**

   c. **Revolve**

   d. **Sweep**

   e. **Swept Blend**

4. Which of the following commands creates the element shown in Figure 4–102?

Figure 4–102

a. **Extrusion**

b. **Blend**

c. **Revolve**

d. **Sweep**

e. **Swept Blend**

5. In which dialog box do you specify sizes for component types?

a. Family Editor

b. Family Types

c. Family Categories

d. Family Properties

Command Summary

Button	Command	Location
Forms		
	Blend	• **Ribbon**: *Create* tab>Forms panel
	Extrusion	• **Ribbon**: *Create* tab>Forms panel
	Revolve	• **Ribbon**: *Create* tab>Forms panel
	Sweep	• **Ribbon**: *Create* tab>Forms panel
	Swept Blend	• **Ribbon**: *Create* tab>Forms panel
	Void Forms	• **Ribbon**: *Create* tab>Forms panel
Other Tools		
	Align	• **Ribbon**: *Modify* tab>Modify panel
	Family Types	• **Ribbon**: *Create* or *Modify* tab> Properties panel
	Load Family	• **Ribbon**: *Insert* tab>Load from Library panel
	Load into Project	• **Ribbon**: *all tabs*>Family Editor panel
Reference and Work Plane		
	Reference Line	• **Ribbon**: *Create tab*>Datum panel
	Reference Plane	• **Ribbon**: *Create* tab>Datum panel
	Set	• **Ribbon**: *Create* tab>Work Plane panel

Advanced Family Techniques

Once you have created basic families with parametric framework, geometry, and family types, you can enhance the families with additional parameters, elements and settings. Possible enhancements include controls for flipping the family, or connectors for MEP system elements. You can also nest families into other families, and then coordinate the parameters between the two. Visibility Display settings enable you to specify the elements you want to display at various Detail Levels.

Learning Objectives in this Chapter

- Add controls, room calculation points, connectors, and openings.
- Insert components and associate the parameters.
- Control the display of elements in views at various detail levels using visibility settings.
- Create masking regions to block elements that would otherwise display through a family.
- Add Model and Symbolic lines.

5.1 Additional Tools for Families

Once you have created the basic framework of your family, added solid elements, established family types and tested it in a project, you can start to add items that will make the family even more powerful. Some family-specific functions include the following:

- Controls that flip and mirror the family.

- A room calculation point that makes a family room-aware.

- Connectors (MEP elements only) that contain information such as pipe or duct size and electrical currents.

- Openings in a host, such as a wall or ceiling.

- Nested families made of multiple families as shown in Figure 5–1.

Figure 5–1

Adding Controls

You can place control arrows to flip or mirror geometry in the family, as shown in Figure 5–2. The controls also display on doors and other elements. Some family templates already include controls and you can add others.

Flip the instance left/right across its center

Figure 5–2

How To: Add Controls

1. In the *Create* tab>Control panel, click ⊹ (Control).
2. In the *Modify | Place Control* tab>Control Type panel, click one of the following controls:

   - ⇐ (Single Vertical)

   - ↑ (Single Horizontal)

   - ⇵ (Double Vertical)

   - ⇔ (Double Horizontal)

3. Click on the screen to place the control in the view. Move the controls once you have placed them, as required.

Setting Room Calculation Points

Some families (e.g., lighting fixtures, specialty equipment, casework, furniture, etc.) can be placed so that the default center of the element is not in the room where it needs to be counted, as shown in Figure 5–3. You can adjust this by modifying the Room Calculation Point, making the family a room-aware family.

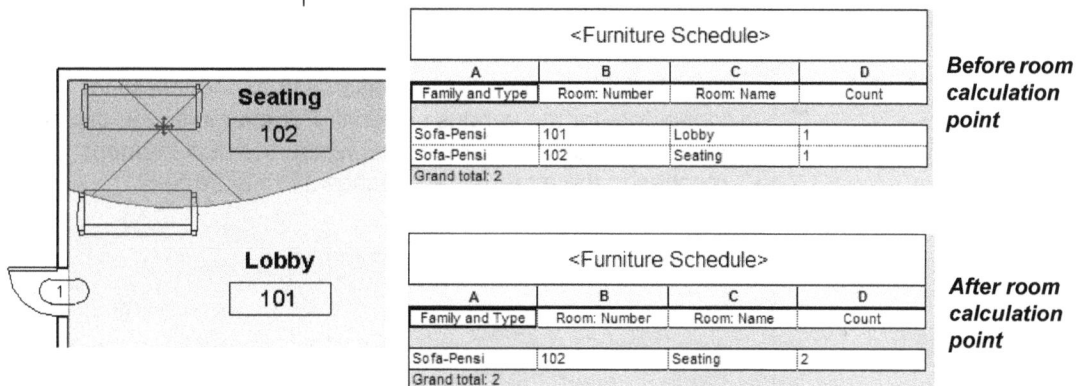

<Furniture Schedule>			
A	B	C	D
Family and Type	Room: Number	Room: Name	Count
Sofa-Pensi	101	Lobby	1
Sofa-Pensi	102	Seating	1
Grand total: 2			

Before room calculation point

<Furniture Schedule>			
A	B	C	D
Family and Type	Room: Number	Room: Name	Count
Sofa-Pensi	102	Seating	2
Grand total: 2			

After room calculation point

Figure 5–3

- Room Calculation Points must be set in the family.

How To: Set a Room Calculation Point

1. Open the Family file.
2. In Properties, select Room Calculation Point, as shown on the left in Figure 5–4.
3. Move the room calculation point to the required location, as shown on the right in Figure 5–5.

Figure 5–4

Figure 5–5

4. Save and load (or reload) the family file into the project.

Adding Connectors

In MEP families there is an additional option for creating connectors for the various systems. For example, you can add a duct connector to an air terminal where the duct element attaches to the air terminal, as shown in Figure 5–6.

Figure 5–6

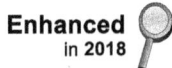
Enhanced in 2018

- If you are using imported 3D shapes in a family, you can place connectors on the geometry.

These tools are found on the *Create* tab>Connectors panel, as shown in Figure 5–7.

Figure 5–7

How To: Add a Connector

1. In the *Create* tab>Connectors panel, select the type of connector you want to use.
2. In the Options Bar, specify the type of connector (if applicable), as shown for an electrical connector in Figure 5–8.

Figure 5–8

3. In the *Modify | Place Connector* tab>Placement panel, click
   (Face) or   (Work Plane).
4. Select a face or workplane that matches the location and direction of the connector.
5. Select the connector and make any required adjustments in Properties.

Adding Openings

The **Opening** command enables you to sketch an opening in a host element. You need to have started the family using one of the host-based templates.

How To: Add an Opening to a Host Element

1. In the *Create* tab>Model panel, click ☐ (Opening).
2. In the *Modify | Create Opening Boundary* tab>Draw panel, use the sketch tools to create the opening. Use reference planes and dimensions as required.

3. Click ✓ (Finish Edit Mode).
4. In the *Modify | Opening cut* tab, make changes as required.
5. In the Options Bar, select when you want the cut to display transparently (in **3D**, **Elevation**, or both), as shown in Figure 5–9.

Modify Opening Cut	Transparent in: ☑ 3D ☐ Elevation

Figure 5–9

Adding Components

Adding a component to a family produces a nested family. In most cases, you want to do this with elements that are used multiple times in other families, such as the hardware shown in Figure 5–10.

Figure 5–10

- Nesting families increase the file size and can impact your computer's performance.

- There are two types of components:

  - ☐ **(Component):** In the *Create* tab>Model panel. places model components that display in all views.

  - ☐ **(Detail Component):** In the *Annotate* tab>Detail panel, places detail components that display only in the current view.

Associating Family Parameters

When you are working with nested families, you might need to associate parameters in the host family with the inserted family. Other types of parameters can also be associated.

How To: Associate Family Parameters

1. Select the element(s) whose parameters need to be associated.
2. In Properties, in the row where you want to connect the parameters, click ▢ (Associate Family Parameter), as shown in Figure 5–11.

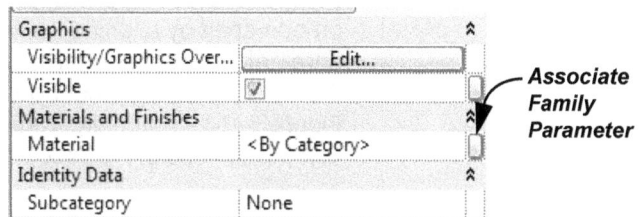

Figure 5–11

3. In the Associate Family Parameter dialog box, select the related parameter (as shown in Figure 5–12) and click **OK**.

Type part of the parameter name in the search box to speed up selection.

Figure 5–12

- The parameter is now grayed out and marked with the **=** sign, as shown in Figure 5–13.

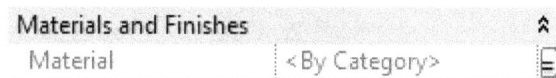

Figure 5–13

Practice 5a

Add a Component to the Bookcase

Estimated time for completion:15 minutes

Practice Objectives

- Add a component to a family.
- Associate parameters between the component and the family.
- Copy and align the component.

In this practice, you will insert a glass door component into the bookcase family. You will fit the component to the correct location on one shelf by aligning it and associating door width and height parameters with the related parameters in the family. You will then copy and align that door to other shelves, as shown in Figure 5–14. Optionally, you will add a Material parameter and test the options in a project.

Figure 5–14

Task 1 - Add door components.

1. In the practice files *Architectural* folder, open **Barrister-Bookcase-Component.rfa**.

2. Open the **Floor Plans: Ref. Level** view.

3. In the *Insert* tab>Load from Library panel, click ⬇ (Load Family).

4. In the Load Family dialog box, in the practice files *Architectural* folder, select **Shelf-Door-Glass.rfa** and click **Open**.

5. In the *Create* tab>Model panel, click ⬜ (Component).

6. Place a copy of the door in the view aligned to the **Center L/R** reference plane, as shown in Figure 5–15. The width might not match the bookcase width.

Nearest

Figure 5–15

7. Use ⬜ (Align) to lock the center of the bookcase with the center reference plane, as shown in Figure 5–16.

Figure 5–16

8. Use ⬜ (Align) to line up the back of the door with the **Door Face** reference plane and lock it, as shown in Figure 5–17.

Select the Door Face reference plane first when you are aligning.

Figure 5–17

9. Save the family.

Task 2 - Associate parameters.

1. Click ⌖ (Modify) and select the door.

2. In Properties, scroll down to the *Other* heading.

3. Beside **Door Width**, at the end of the row. click ▢ (Associate Family Parameter).

4. In the Associate Family Parameter dialog box, select **Width** and then click **OK**.

5. Repeat the process to associate **Door Height** with **Shelf Height**. The parameters in Properties gray out and an equal sign displays in the button, as shown in Figure 5–18. The door should now fit in the shelf, as shown in Figure 5–19.

Other		⌃
Door Width	3' 0"	▤
Door Height	1' 3"	▤
Label	<None>	

Figure 5–18

Figure 5–19

6. Change the *Width* dimension to flex the model to ensure that it works correctly.

7. Save the family.

Task 3 - Align and copy the doors

1. Open the **Elevations: Front** view and set the *Visual Style* to ⬜ (Hidden Line). The door needs to be aligned vertically.

2. Align and lock the top of the door with the shelf height reference planes for the bottom shelf, as shown in Figure 5–20.

Figure 5–20

3. Copy the door to the other shelves.

4. Align and lock the top of each copied door with the associated reference plane, as shown in Figure 5–21.

*Ensure that the **Multiple Alignment** option is not selected in the Options Bar.*

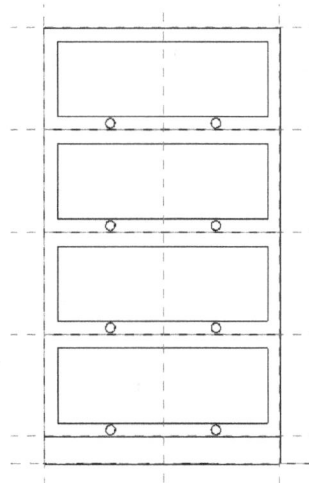

Figure 5–21

5. Change the *Height* dimension to flex the model and check the door alignments.

6. Open the **Elevations: Left** view and align the back of the top three door faces with the **Door Face** reference plane.

7. Switch to a 3D view, as shown in Figure 5–22.

Figure 5–22

8. Use Family Types to flex the model again to ensure that everything is working together.

9. Save the family.

Task 4 - (Optional) Add and test a Material parameter.

---

1. In the *Create* tab>Properties panel, click ⊞ (Family Types).

2. In the Family Types dialog box, click 🗋 (New Parameter).

3. Create a family parameter with the *Parameter Data* set as shown in Figure 5–23. Click **OK**.

Setting the type as an
Instance *makes*
modifying this
parameter in the project
file easier.

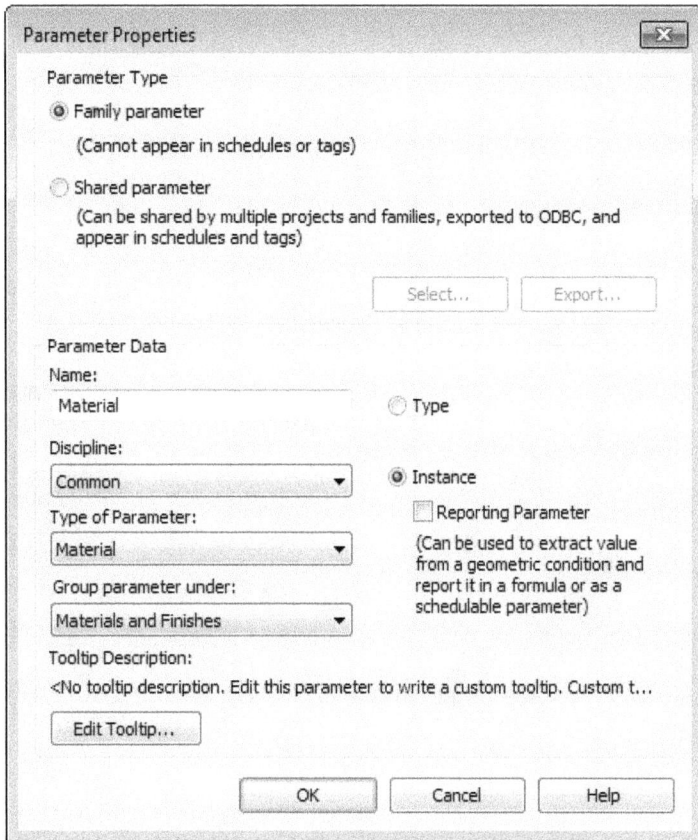

Figure 5–23

4. In the Family Types dialog box, leave the **Material** parameter set to **<By category>**, as shown in Figure 5–24, and click **OK** to close the dialog box.

Figure 5–24

5. In the 3D view, select all of the bookcase components, but not the doors.

6. In Properties, a new instance parameter labeled **Material** displays under *Materials and Finishes*.

7. In the *Material* row, click ⬚ (Associate Family Parameter), as shown in Figure 5–25.

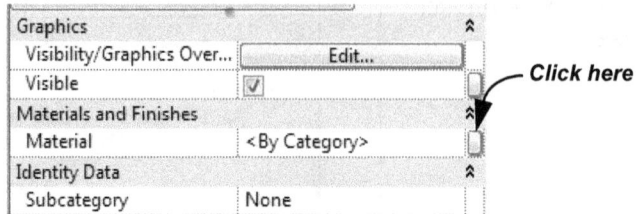

Graphics		⌃
Visibility/Graphics Over...	Edit...	
Visible	☑	
Materials and Finishes		⌃
Material	<By Category>	
Identity Data		⌃
Subcategory	None	

— *Click here*

Figure 5–25

8. In the Associate Family Parameter dialog box, select the **Material** parameter, as shown in Figure 5–26, and click **OK**.

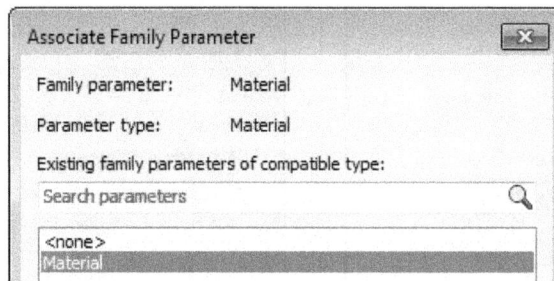

Associate Family Parameter   ✕

Family parameter: Material

Parameter type: Material

Existing family parameters of compatible type:

Search parameters   🔍

<none>
Material

Figure 5–26

- The Material is now marked with the = sign, as shown in Figure 5–27.

Materials and Finishes   ⌃
    Material   <By Category>

Figure 5–27

9. Select one of the bookcase doors.

10. In Properties, click 🔳 (Edit Type).

11. In the Type Properties dialog box, associate the **Door Material** parameter with the **Material** parameter.

12. Click **OK**.

13. Save the family.

14. Open the **Barristers-Bookcase-Project.rvt** file.

15. Delete any existing bookcase elements.

16. Switch to the bookcase family and load it into the project.

17. Place one of each type in the project.

18. Create a 3D view to see the differences.

19. In the View Status Bar, set the *Visual Style* to ▱ (Consistent Colors).

20. Select a bookcase. In Properties, in the *Materials and Finishes* area, next to the **Material** parameter, click **...** (Browse).

21. In the Material Browser, select a material and click **OK** to apply it to the bookcase. (Several materials starting with the word **Bookcase** are available for you to use.)

22. Repeat with the other bookcases using different materials, such as those shown in Figure 5–28.

Figure 5–28

23. Save the project and family.

Practice 5b

Add a Component and Connectors to the Heat Pump

Practice Objectives

- Add a void element.
- Add a component to a family.
- Add electrical and piping connectors
- Associate parameters.

In this practice, you will add a void element to cut out part of the main unit of the heat pump. Your will then insert a panel component into that void. You will create additional extrusions and add connectors to these and other extrusions in the panel component. Finally, you will create and associate parameters to set pipe sizes. The completed family is shown in Figure 5–29.

Estimated time for completion: 20 minutes.

Figure 5–29

Task 1 - Add a void.

1. In the practice files *MEP* folder, open **Heat-Pump-Connectors.rfa**.

2. Open the **3D**, **Ref. Level**, and **Front** views. Tile the views so that all three are visible on the screen.

3. In the **Front** elevation view, add two references planes to the lower left corner of the unit and dimension them as shown in Figure 5–30.

4. Select the lower reference plane and name it **Bottom of Void**, as shown in Figure 5–30.

Figure 5–30

5. Activate the **Ref. Level** view and zoom in on the lower left corner of the equipment.

6. Change the *Scale* to **1 1/2" =1'-0"**.

7. Draw and dimension the reference planes shown in Figure 5–31.

Existing 3" dimensions shown for clarity.

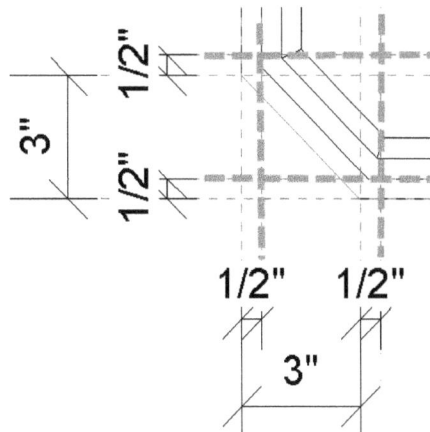

Figure 5–31

8. In the *Create* tab>Forms panel, expand ⬡ (Void Forms) and click ⬚ (Void Extrusion).

9. In the *Modify | Create Void Extrusion* tab>Work Plan panel, click ▦ (Set).

10. In the Work Plane dialog box, select the *Name* **Reference Plane: Bottom of Void** and click **OK**.

11. Draw and lock the sketch, as shown in Figure 5–32.

Figure 5–32

12. In Properties, set the *Extrusion End* to **9"**.

13. Click ✓ (Finish Edit Mode) and click in empty space to release the selection.

14. In the **Elevation: Front** view, align and lock the extrusion end to the top reference plane.

15. Rotate the 3D view so you can see the new void, as shown in Figure 5–33.

Figure 5–33

16. Save the project.

Task 2 - Insert a component.

1. Activate the **Floor Plan: Ref. Level** view.

2. In the *Create* tab>Model panel, click ⬚ (Component).

3. When prompted to load a family, click **Yes**.

4. Navigate to the practice files *MEP* folder and open **Connector Panel.rfa**.

5. Insert the component, as shown in Figure 5–34.

Figure 5–34

6. Align and lock the back and side of the component to the reference planes.

7. In the **Elevations: Front** view, align and lock the top of the component to the top of the void reference plane, as shown in Figure 5–35.

Figure 5–35

8. Save the family.

Task 3 - Add extrusions for piping connections.

---

1. Activate the **Floor Plan: Ref. Level** view.

2. Draw a section in front of the angled reference line at 45 degrees and open it. (This section is not cutting anything, but acts similar to an elevation.)

3. Start the **Extrusion** command.

4. In the Work Plane dialog box, select **Pick a plane**, and then click **OK**. Select the edge of the plane shown in Figure 5–36.

5. Add the reference planes, dimensions, and the extrusion shown in Figure 5–36. Set the extrusion *Depth* to **1/4"**.

You might need to zoom in closer to place the smaller circle.

9 1/4"

6"

Radius 1/2"

Radius 1/4"

Select this face for the Work Plane

Figure 5–36

6. Join the extrusion to the rest of the unit.

7. Save the family.

Task 4 - Add connectors.

---

1. Open the 3D view and modify the view to display the corner of the unit where the connectors need to be applied.

2. In the *Create* tab>Connectors panel, click (Electrical Connector).

3. In the Options Bar, select **Power-Balanced**.

4. Select the face of the top circular extrusion, as shown in Figure 5–37.

5. Click **Modify** and select the new connector.

6. In Properties, in the *Identity Data* area, in the *Connector Description*, type **Electric Power Supply**.

7. Continue adding the other connectors as shown in Figure 5–37. For the Pipe Connectors, before selecting the location, in Properties, set the *Round Connector Dimension* to **Use Radius**.

Pipe Connector:
Other
Connector Description:
Gas Line

Pipe Connector:
Other
Connector Description:
Liquid Line

Electrical Connector:
Power-Balanced
Connector Description:
Electric Power Supply

Electrical Connector:
Power-Balanced
Connector Description:
Low Voltage

Figure 5–37

8. Save the project.

Task 5 - Create and assign new parameters for piping connectors.

1. In the Properties panel, click ⊞ (Family Types).

2. Add the following Type parameters:

Name	Discipline	Type	Group
Gas Line Service Valve	Piping	Pipe Size	Mechanical
Liquid Line Service Valve	Piping	Pipe Size	Mechanical
Gas Line Radius	Piping	Pipe Size	Dimensions
Liquid Line Radius	Piping	Pipe Size	Dimensions

- The **Radius** parameters are going to be linked to **Radius** parameters in the connectors. The Autodesk Revit software reads this and sets the correct diameter for the connector in the family when it is inserted into a project.

3. Assign the following values:
   - *Gas Line Service Valve:* **7/8"**
   - *Liquid Line Service Valve*: **3/8"**

4. Type in the following formulas:
   - *Gas Line Radius*: **Gas Line Service Valve / 2**
   - *Liquid Line Radius:* **Liquid Line Service Valve / 2**

5. Move the two radius parameters to the end of the Dimensions section. The final set of parameters is shown in Figure 5–38.

Parameter	Value	Formula	Lock
Dimensions			☆
Width	38 7/8"	=	☐
Height	44 3/4"	=	☐
Depth	34 3/4"	=	☐
CenterX	17 3/8"	= CenterY	☐
CenterY	17 3/8"	= Depth / 2	☐
Radius of Fan	16 3/8"	= Depth / 2 - 1"	☐
Gas Line Radius	7/16"	= Gas Line Service Valve /	☐
Liquid Line Radius	3/16"	= Liquid Line Service Valve	☐
Mechanical			☆
Gas Line Service Valve	7/8"	=	☐
Liquid Line Service Valve	3/8"	=	☐

Figure 5–38

6. Click **OK**.

7. In Properties, under the *Dimensions* heading, verify that the *Round Connector Dimension* is set to **Use Radius**.

8. Select the Gas Line connector.

9. In Properties, in the *Dimensions* area, in the **Radius** parameter, click ⬚ (Associate Family Parameter).

10. In the Associate Family Parameter dialog box, select **Gas Line Radius**, as shown in Figure 5–39, and click **OK**.

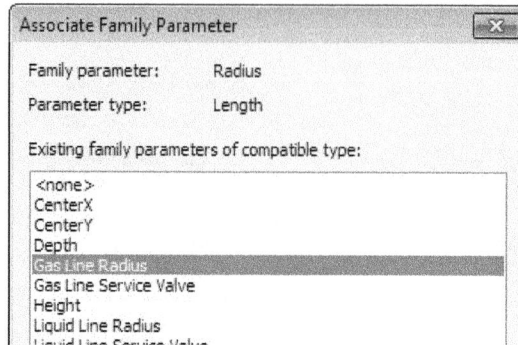

Figure 5–39

11. Repeat the process for the Liquid Line connector and associate the **Liquid Line Radius** to it.

12. When it is finished the connectors should be sized accordingly in the family, as shown in Figure 5–40.

Select the connector and click the Flip control if the Z-axis is pointing into the heat pump.

Figure 5–40

13. Save the family.

Practice 5c

Modify the Structural Column

Practice Objectives

- Add and test material parameters.
- Associate parameters.
- Add parameters to an existing extrusion.

In this practice, you will add a material parameter and test it in a project, as shown in Figure 5–41. You will also modify the trellis extrusion and create parameters so that the side and horizontal members can be a different size than the diagonal members.

Estimated time for completion: 15 minutes

Figure 5–41

Task 1 - Add a material parameter.

1. In the practice files *Structural* folder, open **Trellis-Column-Advanced.rfa.**

2. In the *Create* tab>Properties panel, click ⊞ (Family Types).

3. In the Family Types dialog box, click ⬚ (New Parameter).

Setting the type as an **Instance** makes modifying this parameter in the project file easier.

4. Create a **Family parameter** and set the *Parameter Data,* as shown in Figure 5–42. Click **OK**.

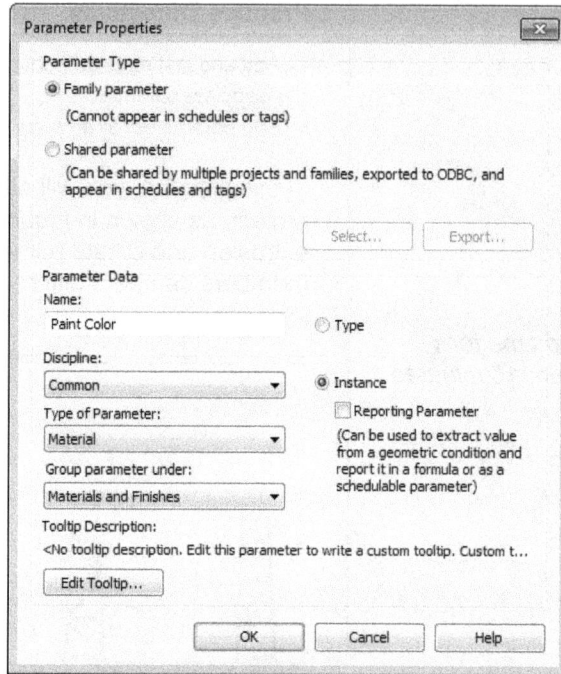

Figure 5–42

5. In the Family Types dialog box, ensure that the **Paint Color** parameter is set to **<By category>**, as shown in Figure 5–43. Click **OK** to close the dialog box.

Parameter	Value	
Materials and Finishes		
Paint Color (default)	<By Category>	=
Structural Material (default)		=

Figure 5–43

6. Click **OK**.

7. In the 3D view, select the column extrusion and the base.

8. In Properties, in the *Materials and Finishes* area, a parameter labeled **Material** displays.

9. In the *Material* row, click ⬚ (Associate Family Parameter), as shown in Figure 5–44.

Figure 5–44

10. In the Associate Family Parameter dialog box, select **Paint Color** (as shown in Figure 5–45), and then click **OK**.

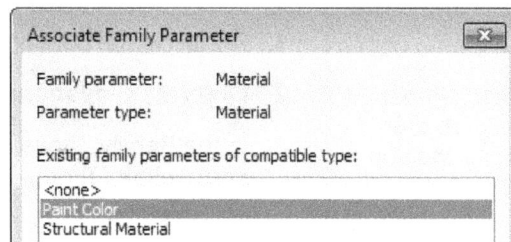

Figure 5–45

- The Material is now marked with the = sign, as shown in Figure 5–46.

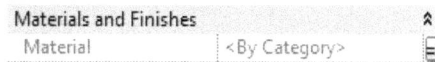

Figure 5–46

11. Save the family.

Task 2 - Modify the material of the columns.

1. Open the **Trellis-Column-Project.rvt** file. Delete any existing columns from previous practices.

2. Switch to the column family and load it into the project.

3. Add several columns at different heights. Set the base and top of each column in properties.

4. Open the **Elevations: South** view.

5. In the View Status Bar, set the *Visual Style* to ⬜ (Consistent Colors).

6. Select one of the columns.

7. In Properties, under the *Materials and Finishes* heading, beside *Paint Color* in the <By Category> box, click
   ⬚ (Browse) to open the Material Browser.

8. In the Material Browser, select a material and click **OK** to apply it to the column.
   - Several materials of different colors (starting with the words **Metal - Paint Finish**) are available for you to use.

9. Repeat with the other columns using different materials.

10. Save the project.

Task 3 - Create parameters for changing the size of the structural members.

---

1. Return to the column family.

2. Open the **Elevations: Front** view and edit the extrusion.

3. In the Family Types dialog box, add the following Length parameters (Type):
   - **Side Bar**
   - **Angled Bar**
   - **Horizontal Bar**
   - **Angled Bar Halfwidth**
   - **Horizontal Bar Halfwidth**

If the extrusion cannot be edited, ensure that the Formula for the Top Width is set to 1.3.

4. Reorder the list and add the formulas shown in Figure 5–47.

Parameter	Value	Formula	Lock
Materials and Finishes			☆
Paint Color (default)	<By Category>	=	
Structural Material (defa		=	
Dimensions			☆
Bottom Width	2' 8"	=	☐
Side Bar	0' 0"	=	☐
Angled Bar	0' 0"	=	☐
Horizontal Bar	0' 0"	= Side Bar	☐
Angled Bar Halfwidth	0' 0"	= Angled Bar / 2	☐
Horizontal Bar Halfwidth	0' 0"	= Horizontal Bar / 2	☐
Top Width	1' 9 85/256"	= Bottom Width / 1.5	☐

Figure 5–47

5. Apply the parameters to the appropriate dimensions, as shown in part in Figure 5–48.

Select more than one dimension with the same information by holding <Ctrl> as you select.

Figure 5–48

- Change the scale of the view to better display the parameters.

6. Change some of the dimensions either directly in the sketch or through the Family Types dialog box to flex the design.

7. Finish the sketch.

8. Open the 3D view and the Family Types dialog box and flex the model.

9. Save the family and test it in the project.

5.2 Visibility Display Settings

You can make families more versatile by controlling what is displayed in various views and at different detail levels. For example, you can set the Coarse view to display only 2D symbolic lines while the Fine detail view displays the full 3D model, as shown in Figure 5–49. To do this, change the visibility of the elements. You can also add Masking Regions to elements in a family to obscure other elements.

Fine detail level   Coarse detail level

Figure 5–49

How To: Control the Display of Elements

1. Select the elements that you want to modify.

2. In the *Modify* contextual tab>Mode panel, click (Visibility Settings).

3. In the Family Element Visibility Settings dialog box, specify the views and detail level in which you want the elements to display, as shown in Figure 5–50.

Figure 5–50

4. Click **OK**.

- All model elements (not detail elements) typically display in 3D views. You can select how they display in plan and elevation views.

- The *Detail Levels* control whether or not the element displays at various scales. If you clear the checkmark from a level, the lines defining the element turn gray in the family file. They do not display at that detail level when inserted into the project.

- The plan is cut at the cut plane specified by the *View Range*. Some elements, such as furniture and mechanical equipment, cannot be cut in plan view, while structural columns can.

- To aid in assigning elements to various detail levels, you can preview the visibility. In the View Control Bar, expand

  ▭ (Preview Visibility Off) and select ▭ (Preview Visibility On). When the preview is on, you can change the *Detail Level* and only the elements assigned to that level display, as shown in Figure 5–51 and Figure 5–52.

Detail Level: Medium

Figure 5–51

Detail Level: Fine

Figure 5–52

- Some elements, such as columns, can be cut in plan views. The option displays in the Family Element Visibility Settings dialog box, as shown in Figure 5–53.

Figure 5–53

- When the category permits, you can also set **Preview Visibility On (Not Cut)**, as shown in Figure 5–54.

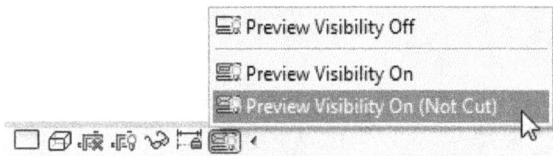

Figure 5–54

Adding Lines

Lines are often used to display the model elements in plan and elevation views at the **Coarse** (and sometimes **Medium**) detail level. There are two types of lines:

- (Model Line) in the *Create* tab>Model panel, shown in all views.

- (Symbolic Line) in the *Annotate* tab>Detail panel, are visible in views parallel to the view in which they were drawn.

Lines can also be used in other situations. For example, you could use model lines to draw door hardware that is not three-dimensional, or use symbolic lines to draw the door swing (as shown in Figure 5–55) so that it does not display in 3D views.

Figure 5–55

- Use the standard sketch tools in the Draw panel to draw model and symbolic lines. You can also specify a subcategory with an associated line type (as shown in Figure 5–56) for a door family.

Figure 5–56

- You can create entire families of model and symbolic lines if they are only going to be used in a 2D view. For example, create a 2D family for a hospital bed, as shown in Figure 5–57, and use it in a large hospital layout where most of the instances do not need to be full 3D.

2D families can still be robust in the number and types of parameters they hold for use in schedules and quantity takeoffs.

Figure 5–57

Creating Masking Regions

A masking region obscures other elements in a project. They can be placed in a family or project. For example, in the Desk family shown in Figure 5–58, a chair placed under the desk is masked but the lamp on top of the desk is not.

Figure 5–58

How To: Create Masking Regions

1. Open a plan or elevation view.

2. In the *Annotate tab*>Detail panel, click ▢ (Masking Region).
3. In the *Modify | Create Masking Region Boundary* tab> Subcategory panel, select the subcategory you want to use for the boundary of the region.
4. In the Draw panel, select the tools to sketch the region. You can also use most of the Modify options as you draw.

5. Click ✓ (Finish Edit Mode) and click in empty space to finish the command.

Practice 5d

Modify the Visibility of Elements in the Bookcase

Practice Objectives

- Modify visibility settings.
- Create symbolic lines.

Estimated time for completion: 10 minutes

In this practice, you will modify the visibility settings of the main 3D elements so that they display at the **Medium** and **Fine** detail levels. You will also create a simple extrusion for 3D views and sketch symbolic lines for 2D views to display at the **Coarse** detail level. The elevation views of the three detail levels are shown in Figure 5–59.

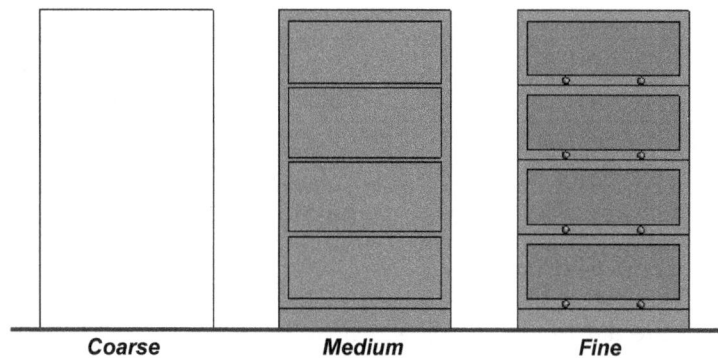

| Coarse | Medium | Fine |

Figure 5–59

Task 1 - Modify the visibility settings of the 3D elements.

1. In the practice files *Architectural* folder, open **Barrister-Bookcase-Visibility.rfa**.

2. Open the **Floor Plans: Ref. Level** and **Elevation: Front** views. Tile the views so you see the 3D view along with the two opened views.

3. Activate the 3D view and set the *Visual Style* to ⬜ (Hidden Line).

4. In the View Control Bar, expand 🖥 (Preview Visibility Off) and select 🖥 (Preview Visibility On).

5. By default, the *Display Level* is set to **Medium** so all elements should be visible.

6. Hover the cursor over part of the bookcase element (but not the doors) and press <Tab> until the **Joined Solid Geometry** highlights, as shown in Figure 5–60. Click to select it.

Figure 5–60

7. In the *Modify | Joined Solid Geometry* tab>Visibility panel, click (Visibility Settings).

8. In the Family Element Visibility Settings dialog box, in the *Detail Levels* area, clear the **Coarse** option and select **Medium** and **Fine**, as shown in Figure 5–61. Then, click **OK**.

This has to be done in two steps because the doors are a different element (a nested family) from the rest of the elements.

Figure 5–61

9. Select the door elements.

10. In the Family Element Visibility Settings dialog box, in the *Detail Levels* area, clear the **Coarse** and **Medium** options and select **Fine**. Click **OK**. The doors no longer display, as shown in Figure 5–62.

11. Change the *Detail Level* to **Fine**. The doors should display as shown in Figure 5–63.

Figure 5–62

Figure 5–63

12. Change the *Detail Level* to **Coarse**. Nothing should display in the 3D view.

13. Save the family.

Task 2 - Create an extrusion for coarse detail in 3D views.

1. In the **Elevation: Front** and **Floor Plans: Ref. Level** views, select ⬛ (Preview Visibility On).

2. The *Detail Level* is set to **Coarse** so none of the 3D elements display.

3. In the **Ref. Level** view, create a new extrusion with the footprint shown in Figure 5–64. Set the *Depth* to **2'-6"** and click ✔ (Finish Edit Mode).

Lock all sketch lines.

Figure 5–64

4. In the **Elevations: Front** view, align and lock the top of the new extrusion to the top reference plane, as shown in Figure 5–65. The simple extrusion also displays in the 3D view as shown in Figure 5–66.

Figure 5–65

Figure 5–66

5. Select the new extrusion.

6. In the *Modify | Extrusion* tab>Mode panel, click (Visibility Settings).

7. In the Family Element Visibility Settings dialog box, clear all of the options for the *View Specific Display* and all the *Detail Levels* except **Coarse**, as shown in Figure 5–67.

You do not want this element displaying in the 2D views at any detail level.

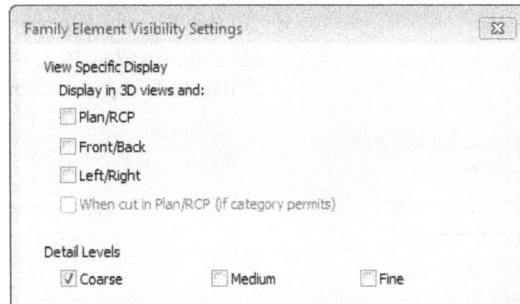

Figure 5–67

8. The simple extrusion should only display in the 3D view.

9. Save the family.

Task 3 - Add symbolic lines to elevation and plan views.

1. In the **Elevations: Front** view, verify that the *Detail Level* is set to **Coarse**.

2. In the *Annotate* tab>Detail panel, click (Symbolic Line).

3. Draw a rectangle around the outside of the bookcase and lock it to the reference planes, as shown in Figure 5–68.

Figure 5–68

4. Select all of the lines.

5. In the *Modify | Lines* tab>Visibility panel, click ⬚ (Visibility Settings).

6. In the Family Element Visibility Settings dialog box, in the *Detail Levels* area, select **Coarse** and clear the **Medium** and **Fine** options, as shown in Figure 5–69. Click **OK**.

*Symbolic lines display in views parallel to the view where they were drawn. Therefore, the lines in the **Front** view will automatically display in the **Back** view.*

Figure 5–69

7. Repeat the process in the **Floor Plans: Ref. Level** view, as shown in Figure 5–70.

Figure 5–70

8. Select all of the lines and set the *Visibility Settings* to **Coarse**.

9. Open the **Elevations: Left** view and repeat the process. (Toggle on **Preview Visibility** to hide the 3D elements at the **Coarse** detail level).

10. Check the detail levels in each of the views.

11. Save the family.

Task 4 - Load and test the family in a project.

1. Open the **Barristers-Bookcase-Project.rvt** file.

2. Open the **Floor Plans: Level 1** view.

3. Delete any existing bookcases.

4. Switch to the bookcase family file and load it into the project.

5. Add at least one copy of the new bookcase.

6. In the View Status Bar, set the *Visual Style* to **Shaded**.

7. Change the detail levels to see the differences, as shown in Figure 5–71.

Detail Level: Coarse

Detail Level: Medium

Detail Level: Fine

Figure 5–71

8. Test in other views to ensure that the detail levels display the way you want them to.

9. Save and close the project and the family.

Practice 5e

Modify the Visibility of Elements in the Heat Pump

Practice Objectives

- Modify visibility settings.
- Create symbolic lines.

Estimated time for completion: 10 minutes

In this practice, you will modify the visibility settings of the 3D elements so that they display differently at various levels of detail, as shown in Figure 5–72. You will also create elements that display at a **Coarse** detail level, including a simple extrusion for 3D views and symbolic lines for plan and elevation views.

Coarse   *Medium*   *Fine*

Figure 5–72

- The electrical and piping connectors are hidden in these views for clarity.

Task 1 - Modify the visibility settings of the 3D elements.

1. In the practice files *MEP* folder, open
   Heat-Pump-Visibility.rfa

2. Open the **Floor Plans: Ref. Level** and **Elevation: Front** views. Tile the views so you see the 3D view along with the two opened views.

3. In each of the views, in the View Control Bar, expand

   ⊟ (Preview Visibility Off) and select ⊟ (Preview Visibility On).

4. Activate the 3D view and set the *Visual Style* to ⬦ (Hidden Line), if required.

5. By default, the *Detail Level* is set to **Medium** so all elements should be visible, as shown in Figure 5–73.

6. Rotate the view as required and select the panel component.

7. In the *Modify | Joined Solid Geometry* tab>Visibility panel, click ⬚ (Visibility Settings).

8. In the Family Element Visibility Settings dialog box in the *Detail Levels* area, clear the **Coarse** and **Medium** options and select **Fine**. Click **OK**.

9. Repeat the process with the connector extrusions. Neither of these elements should display in the **Medium** detail level as shown in Figure 5–74.

Figure 5–73

Figure 5–74

10. Hover the cursor over part of the heat pump element and press <Tab> until the **Joined Solid Geometry** highlights, as shown in Figure 5–75. Click to select it.

Figure 5–75

11. In the Family Element Visibility Settings dialog box, in the *Detail Levels* area, clear the **Coarse** option and select **Medium** and **Fine**, as shown in Figure 5–76. Click **OK**.

Figure 5–76

12. Change the *Detail Level* to **Fine**. The panel and connectors should display.

13. Change the *Detail Level* to **Coarse**. No 3D elements should display in any of the views that are set to **Coarse**.

14. Save the family.

Task 2 - Add elements for the Coarse detail view.

1. Activate the **Floor Plans: Ref. Level** view.

2. Set the Workplane to **Ref. Level.**

3. Create a new extrusion with the footprint shown in Figure 5–77. Set the *Depth* to **40"** and click ✔ (Finish Edit Mode).

Figure 5–77

4. Switch to the **Elevations: Front** view.

5. Set the *Visual Style* to **Shaded** to display the extrusion.

6. Align and lock the top and bottom of the new extrusion to the reference planes, as shown in Figure 5–78.

Figure 5–78

7. Select the extrusion.

8. In the *Modify | Extrusion* tab>Mode panel, click 🔲 (Visibility Settings).

9. In the Family Element Visibility Settings dialog box, clear all of the options except **Coarse**, as shown in Figure 5–79.

You do not want this element displaying in the 2D views at any detail level.

Figure 5–79

*Symbolic lines display in views parallel to the view where they were drawn. Therefore, the lines in the **Front** view will automatically display in the **Back** view.*

10. Activate the **Elevation: Front** view.

11. In the *Annotate* tab>Detail panel, click ▣ (Symbolic Line).

12. Draw a rectangle using the outermost reference planes of the heat pump and lock it to the reference planes.

13. Select all of the lines.

14. In the *Modify | Lines* tab>Visibility panel, click ▣ (Visibility Settings).

15. In the Family Element Visibility Settings dialog box, in the *Detail Levels* area, select **Coarse** and clear the **Medium** and **Fine** options, as shown in Figure 5–80. Click **OK**.

Figure 5–80

16. Return to the **Ref. Level** view and draw and lock symbolic lines to the outer reference planes using the same footprint as the extrusion. Set the visibility settings, as shown in Figure 5–80.

17. Open the **Elevations: Left** view and repeat the process. (Toggle on **Preview Visibility** to hide the 3D elements at the **Coarse** detail level).

18. Check the detail levels in each of the views.

19. Save the family.

Task 3 - Load and test the family in a project.

1. Open the **Heat-Pump-Project.rvt** file.

2. Delete any existing Heat Pump components.

3. Open the Mechanical>HVAC>**Floor Plans: 1 - Mech** view.

4. Switch to the heat pump family file and load it into the project.

5. Add at least one copy of the new heat pump.

6. In the View Status Bar, set the *Visual Style* to **Shaded**.

7. Change the detail levels to display the differences, as shown in Figure 5–81.

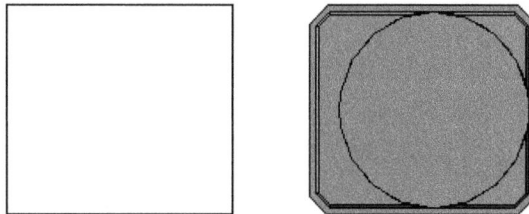

Detail Level: Coarse   *Detail Level: Medium and Fine*

Figure 5–81

8. Open a 3D view, rotate it so that the connector locations display and test the detail levels.

9. Save and close the project and the family.

Practice 5f

Modify the Visibility of Elements in the Structural Column

Practice Objectives

- Modify visibility settings.
- Create a simple extrusion.
- Add symbolic lines.

Estimated time for completion: 10 minutes

In this practice, you will modify the visibility settings of the 3D elements so that they display differently at various levels of detail, as shown in Figure 5–82. You will also create elements that display at a **Coarse** detail level, including a simple extrusion for 3D views and symbolic lines for plan and elevation views.

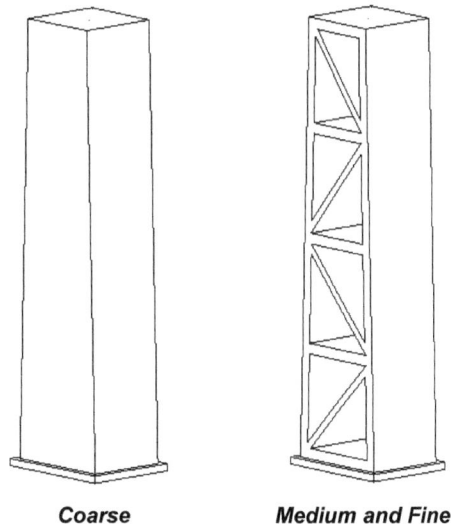

Coarse   *Medium and Fine*

Figure 5–82

Task 1 - Modify the visibility settings of the 3D elements.

1. In the practice files *Structure* folder, open **Trellis-Column-Visibility.rfa**

2. Open the **Floor Plans: Lower Ref. Level** and **Elevation: Front** views. Tile the views so you see the 3D view along with the two opened views.

3. In each of the views, in the View Control Bar, expand

   (Preview Visibility Off) and select (Preview Visibility On).

4. Activate the 3D view and set the *Visual Style* to ⬚ (Hidden Line), if required.

5. By default, the *Detail Level* is set to **Medium** so all elements should be visible, as shown in Figure 5–83.

Figure 5–83

6. Select the main column elements, excluding the base, and click ⬚ (Visibility Settings).

7. In the Family Element Visibility Settings dialog box, in the *Detail Levels* area, clear the **Coarse** option and select **Medium** and **Fine**, as shown in Figure 5–84. Click **OK**.

Figure 5–84

8. Save the family.

Task 2 - Sketch elements for the Coarse detail view.

1. Activate the **Elevations: Front** view.

2. The 3D column elements should not display because the *Detail Level* is set to **Coarse**.

3. Create a new extrusion with the footprint shown in Figure 5–85. Set the *Depth* to (negative) **-2'-0"**.

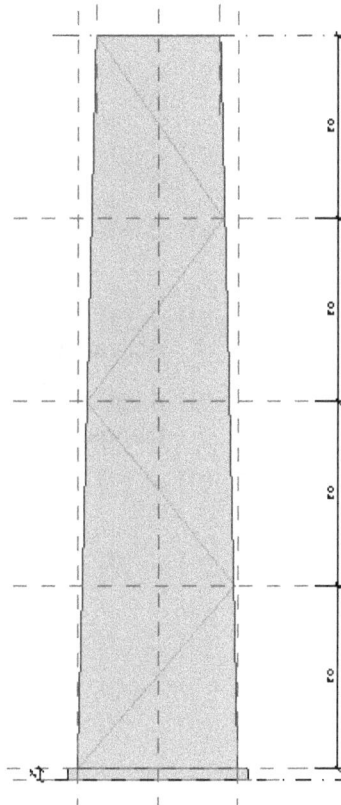

Figure 5–85

4. Select the extrusion.

5. In the *Modify | Extrusion* tab>Mode panel, click (Visibility Settings).

6. In the Family Element Visibility Settings dialog box, clear all of the options except **Coarse** and **When cut in Plan/RCP**, as shown in Figure 5–86.

You do not want this element displaying in the 2D views at any detail level, except when it is cut in plane view, because the size of the tapered column varies according to the cut plane.

Family Element Visibility Settings

View Specific Display
Display in 3D views and:
☐ Plan/RCP
☐ Front/Back
☐ Left/Right
☑ When cut in Plan/RCP (if category permits)

Detail Levels
☑ Coarse   ☐ Medium   ☐ Fine

OK   Cancel   Default   Help

Figure 5–86

7. Activate the **Lower Ref. Level** view.

8. Align and lock the extrusion to the front and back reference planes, as shown in Figure 5–87.

*Set the **Preview Visibility On**, not **Preview Visibility On (Not Cut)**, so that you can see the new extrusion.*

Figure 5–87

9. Save the family.

Task 3 - Add symbolic lines.

1. Activate the **Elevations: Front** view.

2. In the *Annotate* tab>Detail panel, click ▣ (Symbolic Line).

3. Create the same outline as the new extrusion. Ensure that you lock the extrusion to the reference planes and lines.

4. Select all of the lines.

5. In the *Modify | Lines* tab>Visibility panel, click 🔲 (Visibility Settings).

6. In the Family Element Visibility Settings dialog box, in the *Detail Levels* area, select **Coarse** and clear the **Medium** and **Fine** options, as shown in Figure 5–88. Click **OK**.

*Symbolic lines display in views parallel to the view where they were drawn. Therefore the lines in the **Front** view will automatically display in the **Back** view.*

Family element visibility settings   ⊠

Symbolic Element Visibility

Symbolic Elements are view direction specific: they show only in views parallel to their creation view.

☐ Show only if Instance is cut

Detail Levels

☑ Coarse   ☐ Medium   ☐ Fine

| OK | Cancel | Default | Help |

Figure 5–88

- Do not select **Show only if Instance is cut** because the front view is not impacted by the taper of the column.

7. Activate the **Floor Plans: Lower Ref. Level** view.

8. In the View Control Bar, change the *Visibility Preview* to

   🖼 Preview Visibility On (Not Cut). The simple extrusion no longer displays.

9. Add symbolic lines, as shown in Figure 5–89, and set them to display only at the **Coarse** detail level.

Figure 5–89

10. Open the **Elevations: Left** view and add symbolic lines around the edge of the column (but not the base) and set the *Visibility Settings* to match the other lines.

11. Check the detail levels in each of the views.

12. Save the family.

Task 4 - Load and test the family in a project.

1. Open **Trellis-Column-Project.rvt**.

2. Open the **Structural Plans: Level 2** view.

3. Delete any existing columns.

4. Switch to the trellis column family file and load it into the project.

5. Add at least one copy of the new column.

6. Switch to the **Elevations: South** view.

7. Change the detail levels to display the differences, as shown in Figure 5–90.

Detail Level:
Coarse

Detail Level:
Medium and Fine

Figure 5–90

8. Open a 3D view and test the detail levels.

9. Save and close the project and the family.

Chapter Review Questions

1. If your family can be switched from one side to another (such as a door swing) which type of icon would you add?

   a. Mirror

   b. Connector

   c. Control

   d. Calculation

2. (MEP only.) When adding an Electrical Connector, where do you specify the System Type (such as Power-Balanced or Security)?

   a. In the Options Bar

   b. In the shortcut menu

   c. In the expanded Connectors panel

   d. In the Type Properties

3. In which of the following situations would you use a nested family? (Select all that apply.)

   When the family is used multiple times...

   a. in one family

   b. in other families

   c. in one project

   d. in several projects

4. The main reason to associate a family parameter is when:

   a. The parameter will be shared in several projects.

   b. The parameter will be used in a schedule.

   c. You want a user-created parameter to control another parameter.

   d. You want the parameter to reference a parameter in the project.

5. For the elements in a family to display differently at Coarse and Fine detail levels (as shown in Figure 5–91), you must draw everything in 2D.

Detail Level: Coarse

Detail Level: Fine

Figure 5–91

a. True

b. False

Command Summary

Button	Command	Location
Connectors		
	Cable Tray Connector	• **Ribbon**: *Create* tab>Connectors panel> expand Connector
	Conduit Connector	• **Ribbon**: *Create* tab>Connectors panel> expand Connector
	Duct Connector	• **Ribbon**: *Create* tab>Connectors panel> expand Connector
	Electrical Connector	• **Ribbon**: *Create* tab>Connectors panel> expand Connector
	Pipe Connector	• **Ribbon**: *Create* tab>Connectors panel> expand Connector
Other Tools		
	Component	• **Ribbon**: *Create* tab>Model panel
	Control	• **Ribbon**: *Create* tab>Control panel
	Detail Component	• **Ribbon**: *Annotate tab*>Detail panel
	Masking Region	• **Ribbon**: *Annotate tab*>Detail panel
	Model Line	• **Ribbon**: *Create* tab>Model panel
	Opening	• **Ribbon**: *Create* tab>Model panel
	Symbolic Line	• **Ribbon**: *Annotate* tab>Detail panel
	Visibility Settings	• **Ribbon**: Various contextual tabs> Mode panel

Additional Family Types

Beyond the basics of family creation, there are several special cases. These include in-place families that are only available in the current project, 2D profile families used with various elements (such as gutters and sweeps), and annotation families for tags and symbols. Shared parameters are frequently required when you create tags with information you want to include in schedules.

Learning Objectives in this Chapter

- Create in-place families directly in a project.
- Create 2D profiles that are used to create 3D wall sweeps, reveals, railings, nosings, and other elements.
- Create 2D symbol families using drawing tools, filled regions, text, and labels.
- Create shared parameters that can be used in both tags and schedules in multiple projects.

6.1 Creating In-Place Families

In-place families use standard family tools to create elements that are specific to the project in which you create them. These might include built-in furniture, sloped walls, as shown in Figure 6–1, custom door or window openings, and roofs.

Figure 6–1

In-place family elements become the actual element you specify, such as a wall, door, roof, column, ceiling fixture, or floor.

- If the element is a host element, such as a wall, you can add elements to it, such as doors or windows.

- Elements, such as in-place doors and windows, can be copied and moved within their host.

- Complex stairs can be created as an in-place family.

- In-place family elements can be aligned and locked to project elements so they move together.

- Ensure that reference planes are drawn in the family. If you tie an in-place family to an external reference plane and if the reference plane is deleted, you lose the family.

- In-place families are rarely used in the Autodesk® Revit® MEP software.

How To: Create an In-Place Family

1. In a project, in the *Architecture* tab>Build panel, or *Structure* tab>Model panel, or *Systems* tab>Model panel, expand

   ▢ (Component) and click ▢ (Model In-Place).
2. The Family Category and Parameters dialog box opens, as shown in Figure 6–2. You can filter the list to display only the disciplines required.

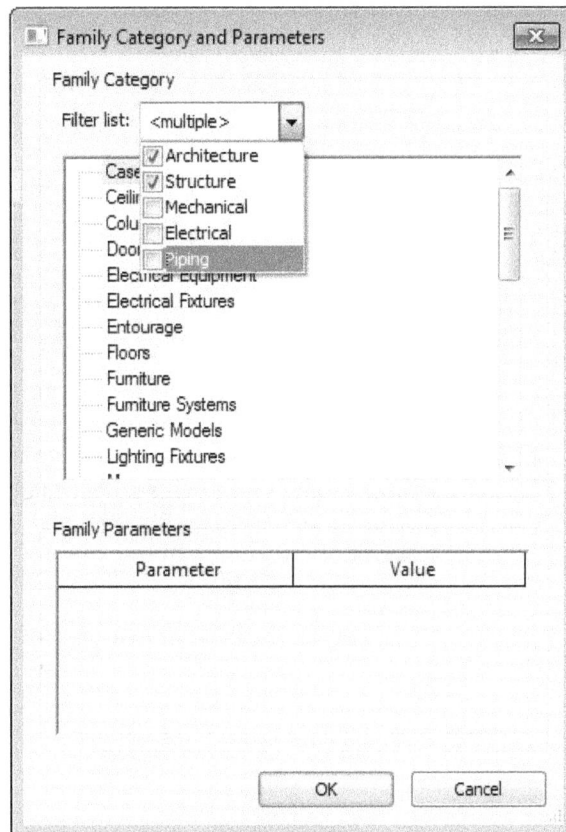

Figure 6–2

3. Select a *Family Category* and click **OK**. In the Name dialog box, enter a name for the new family and click **OK**.
4. The Family Editor tabs display in the ribbon. Use the tools as required to create the elements you want to have in the family.
5. In the In-Place Editor panel, click ✓ (Finish Model) to create the in-place element.

6.2 Creating Profiles

Profiles are 2D elements that are used in a variety of commands to create 3D elements. For example, you need a profile to create wall sweeps (as shown in the Base profile in Figure 6–3) and reveals, gutters, fascias, and floor slab edges. They are also used in families for railings, stair nosings, and solid sweeps.

Profile   *Profile used in a Wall Sweep*

Figure 6–3

Several profile templates are supplied with the Autodesk® Revit® software: **Profile**, **Profile-Hosted**, **Profile-Mullion**, **Profile-Rail**, **Profile-Reveal**, and **Profile-Stair Nosing**. These are created with existing reference planes to help you place the elements correctly on the host element.

- All profiles must be closed shapes.

- Profile families can include detail components.

Practice 6a

In-Place Families and Profiles: Door Opening

Learning Objectives

- Create an in-place door family and opening.
- Add trim for the in-place door family using a sweep based on a 2D profile.

Estimated time for completion: 15 minutes

In this practice, you will create a door in-place family and add an odd-shaped opening. Using a Sweep, you will add a profile for door trim, as shown in Figure 6–4.

Figure 6–4

Task 1 - Create an in-place door family.

1. Start a new project based on the default architectural template.

2. Open the **Floor Plan: Level 1** view and draw a **10'-0"** high wall in the project.

3. In the *Architecture* tab>Build panel, expand (Component) and click (Model In-Place).

4. In the Family Category and Parameters dialog box, Set the *Filter list* to **Architecture** and then set the *Family Category* to **Doors** and click **OK**.

5. Name the in-place family **Odd Shaped Opening**.

6. The Family Editor tools display in the ribbon. In the *Create* tab>Datum panel, click ✐ (Reference Plane) and draw a reference plane along the center of the wall. Name it **Center of Wall**, as shown in Figure 6–5.

The reference plane is used to specify the work plane. It does not impact the shape of the wall.

Figure 6–5

7. Switch to the **Elevations :South** view and zoom in on the wall.

8. In the *Create* tab>Model panel, click ☐ (Opening).

9. If you have more than one wall in the project you are prompted to select a host for the opening. Click **OK** and select the wall.

10. Draw an opening similar to that shown in Figure 6–6.

The exact design does not matter; ensure that it is at least the width and height of a standard door opening. The sketch must be closed.

Figure 6–6

11. Click ✔ (Finish Edit Mode) but do not finish the model.

Task 2 - Add a sweep for the trim and sketch a profile.

1. In the *Create* tab>Work Plane panel, click ▦ (Set).

2. In the Work Plane dialog box, set the *Name* to **Reference Plane: Center of Wall** and click **OK**.

3. In the *Create* tab>Forms panel, click ⬭ (Sweep).

4. In the *Modify | Sweep* tab>Sweep panel, click ✐ (Sketch Path).

5. Draw a path around the edge of the opening. Do not close this sketch.

   - Click ✎ (Pick Lines) and, in the Options Bar, select **Lock**. This locks the sketch to the existing geometry so the sketch updates if the opening is modified.

6. Click ✓ (Finish Edit Mode).

7. In the *Modify | Sweep* tab>Sweep panel, click ▱ (Edit Profile).

8. In the Go To View dialog box, select **Floor Plan: Level 1** and click **Open View**.

9. Zoom in on the red dot. Draw the profile shown in Figure 6–7. The profile must be closed. You do not need to add the dimensions.

Figure 6–7

10. Click ✓ (Finish Edit Mode) to finish the profile.

11. Click ✓ (Finish Edit Mode) again to finish the sweep.

12. Click ✓ (Finish Model).

13. View the new cased opening in several views.

14. Move the opening. You can see that the opening works just like a door.

15. Save the project as **Sample Opening.rvt**.

Drawing the profile in the in-place model keeps the size of the trim directly connected to the selected wall and opening.

Practice 6b

In-Place Families and Profiles: Concrete Corbeling

Practice Objectives

- Create a 2D profile and use it in an in-place family to create a concrete corbel.
- Join the corbeling to the wall.

Estimated time for completion: 15 minutes

In this practice, you will draw a profile of a corbel and then use it in an in-place family to create a sweep, as shown in Figure 6–8.

Walls : Wall Corbelling : Wall Corbelling

Figure 6–8

Corbel: A stepped bracket, designed to support a weight. It projects from a wall and is created from a building material, such as concrete, stone, or wood.

Task 1 - Create the profile.

1. Create a new family based on the **Profile-Hosted.rft** template found in the Autodesk Revit Library.

2. Save the family to your practice folder as **Corbel.rfa**.

3. Draw the four reference planes as shown in Figure 6–9.

The dimensions are for information only.

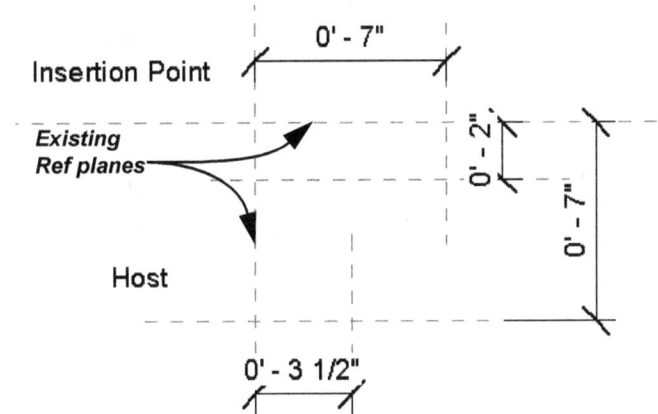

Figure 6–9

4. In the *Create* tab>Detail panel, click ⌐ (Line). Draw the profile shown in Figure 6–10.

The Family Editor does not display as many tabs or panels because fewer commands are required to create a 2D profile.

Figure 6–10

5. Save the family.

Task 2 - Add a new wall sweep using the profile.

---

1. In the practice files *Structural* folder, open **Concrete-Structure.rvt**.

2. Open the **Structural Plans: Level 1** view.

3. In the *Structure* tab>Model panel, expand ⬜ (Component) and click ⬜ (Model In-Place).

4. In the Family Category and Parameters dialog box, set the *Filter list* to **Structure** only, select **Walls**, and click **OK**.

5. In the Name dialog box, type **Wall Corbelling** and click **OK**.

6. In the In-Place Editor, in the *Create* tab>Forms panel, click ⬜ (Sweep).

7. In the *Modify | Sweep* tab>Sweep panel, click ⬜ (Sketch Path).

8. Use the Draw tools to sketch the lines shown in Figure 6–11.

Figure 6–11

9. Click ⬜ (Finish Edit Mode).

10. In the *Modify | Sweep* tab>Sweep panel, click ⬜ (Load Profile).

11. In the Load Family dialog box, navigate to the folder where you saved the **Crobel.rfa** profile created in the previous task. Select it and click **Open**.

12. In the Sweep panel, click ⬜ (Select Profile).

13. In the *Profile* list, select **Corbel**.

14. In the Quick Access Toolbar, click ⬜ (Default 3D View).

15. Zoom in on the profile location, it is facing into the wall as shown in Figure 6–12.

Figure 6–12

16. In the Options Bar, click **Flip**.

17. In the Options Bar or using the temporary dimension, lower the corbel (negative) **-6"** in the Y-direction, as shown in Figure 6–13.

Figure 6–13

18. Click ✓ (Finish Edit Mode).

19. With the new Corbel sweep still selected, in Properties, in the *Materials and Finishes* area, next to Material, click ⌷ (Browse).

20. In the Materials Browser, select **Concrete - Cast-in-Place Concrete** and click **OK**.

21. In the *Modify* tab>In-Place Editor panel, click ✓ (Finish Model).

Task 3 - Join the corbel to the wall.

1. Open the **Structural Plans: Level 1** view.

2. Draw a Wall Section across the wall and corbel, as shown in Figure 6–14.

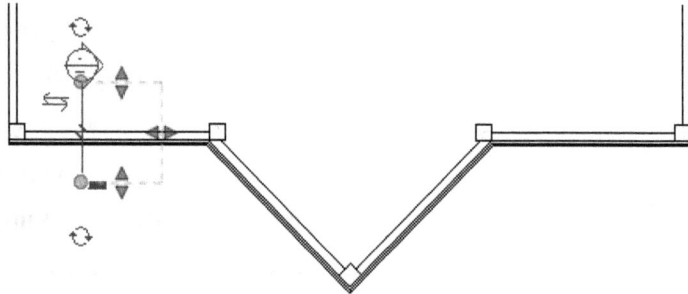

Figure 6–14

3. Open the section. You can see that the wall and corbel are still considered separate entities, as shown in Figure 6–15.

4. In the *Modify* tab>Geometry panel, click (Join). Select the wall and then the corbel. It becomes part of the existing wall, as shown in Figure 6–16.

Figure 6–15

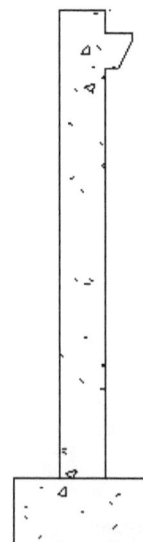

Figure 6–16

5. Save the project.

Practice 6c

In-Place Families and Profiles: Structural Floor Type

Practice Objectives

- Create a profile to use in defining a composite metal deck.
- Load the profile into a project and create a new structural floor type using the profile.
- Test the new floor and change the span direction.

Estimated time for completion: 20 minutes

In this practice, you will create a profile for a composite metal deck and save it to a library. You will then load the profile into a project, use it to create a new Metal Deck Floor type, as shown in Figure 6–17, and test the new floor type.

Figure 6–17

Task 1 - Create a composite Metal Deck profile.

1. Create a new family based on the **Profile.rft** template found in the Autodesk Revit Library.

2. Save the family to your practice folder as **Composite-Metal-Deck.rfa**.

3. Type **UN** to open the Project Units dialog box.

4. Next to *Length Units*, select **Format**.

5. In the Format dialog box, change the units to **Fractional inches**. (This makes the dimensions in the family read in inches only so that it is easier to create the profile.)

6. Click **OK** twice to close the dialog boxes.

7. Set the *Scale* to **3" = 1'-0"**.

8. In the *Create* tab>Datum panel, click (Reference Plane).

9. Add reference planes as shown in Figure 6–18. They help you draw the elements (the dimensions are shown for reference only).

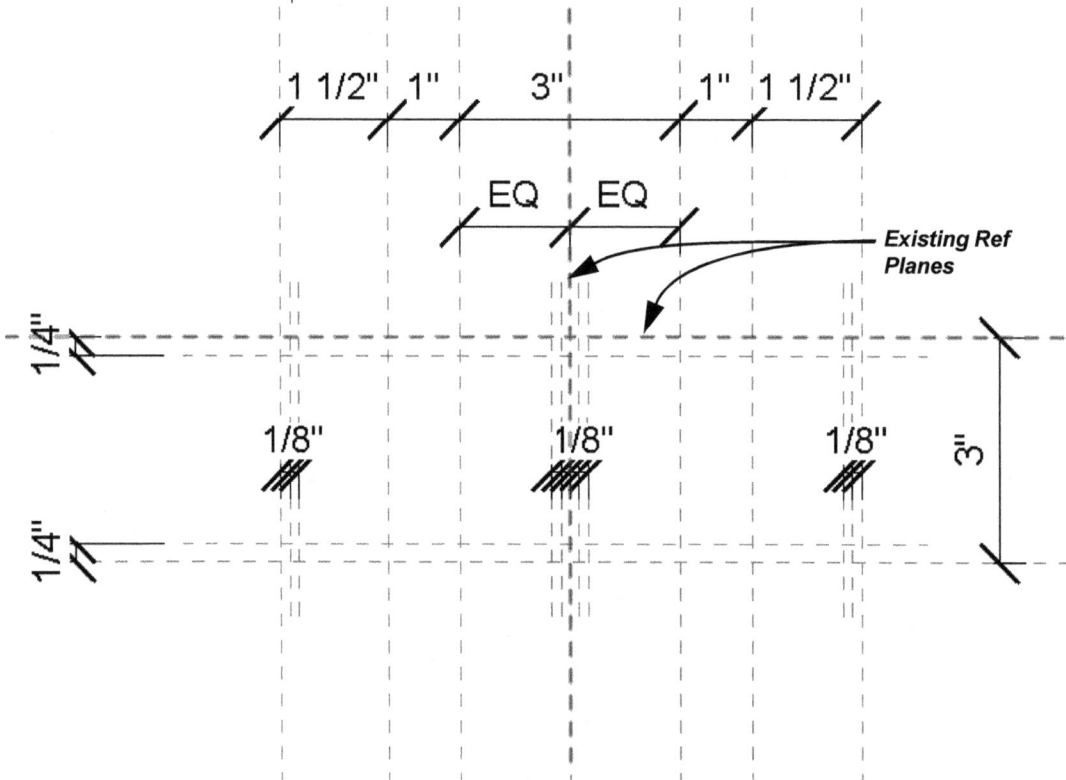

Figure 6–18

10. In the *Create* tab>Detail panel, click (Line). In the Options Bar, verify that the **Chain** option is selected.

11. Sketch the profile as shown in Figure 6–19.

Figure 6–19

12. Click ⬚ (Modify) or press <Esc> when the profile is complete.

13. In the *Create* tab>Properties panel, click ⬚ (Family Types).

14. At the top of Family Types dialog box, click ⬚ (New Type).

15. In the Name dialog box, set the name to **3"**, and click **OK**.

16. Click **OK** again to close the dialog box.

17. Save the family without closing the file.

Task 2 - Load the composite Metal Deck profile.

1. Start a new project based on the default Structural template.

2. In the Quick Access Toolbar or *View* tab>Windows panel, expand ⬚ (Switch Windows), and select **Composite-Metal-Deck.rfa** or press <Ctrl>+<Tab> to toggle back to the family file.

If more than one project is open, select the new one from the list that displays.

3. In the Family Editor panel, click ⬚ (Load into Project) to insert the family into the new project. You should be in the **Structural Plans: Level 2** view of the new project.

4. In the *Structure* tab>Structure panel, click ⌒ (Floor: Structural).

5. in the Type Selector, verify that **Floor: 3"LW Concrete on 2" Metal Deck** is selected.

6. In the *Modify | Create Floor Boundary* tab>Draw panel, use the **Line** or **Rectangle** tool to draw a slab of any type or size. Set the *Span Direction* to **Horizontal**.

7. Click ✓ (Finish Edit Mode).

8. In the Quick Access Toolbar or *View* tab>Create panel, click

   ♦ (Section) and place a section vertically through the slab from north to south.

9. Open the new section view and change the *Scale* to **3/4"=1'-0"** and the *Detail Level* to **Fine**. You might need to adjust the crop region and/or zoom in on the slab section. It should look similar to the one shown in Figure 6–20.

Figure 6–20

10. Select the slab.

11. In Properties, click 🔲 (Edit Type).

12. Duplicate the existing type. Name the duplicated type **6" Concrete on 3" Comp Metal Deck**.

13. In the Type Properties dialog box, next to the **Structure** parameter, click **Edit...**.

14. Modify the **Structure [1], Concrete, Lightweight - 4 ksi** layer to a *Thickness* of **6"**, as shown in Figure 6–21.

Layers

	Function	Material	Thickness	Wraps	Structural Material	Variable
1	Core Boundary	Layers Above Wrap	0' 0"			
2	Structure [1]	Concrete, Lightweig	0' 6"	☐	☑	☐
3	Structural Dec	Metal Deck	0' 0"	☐	☐	☐
4	Core Boundary	Layers Below Wrap	0' 0"			

Figure 6–21

15. For the **Structural Deck** layer, select **Composite-Metal-Deck: 3"** in the Deck Profile drop-down list, as shown in Figure 6–22.

Figure 6–22

16. Click **OK** to close all of the dialog boxes. The section should display the metal deck profile that was previously created, as shown in Figure 6–23.

Figure 6–23

Task 3 - Change the Flute Direction of a comp metal deck.

---

1. Return to the **Structural Plans: Level 2** view.

2. Select the **Span Direction Symbol**. Note that the **Direction Symbol** extends to the edges of the slab. The closed arrowheads represent the flute direction and the open arrowheads represent the extents of the slab in the perpendicular direction.

3. Start the **Rotate** command and rotate the span direction 90 degrees.

4. Return to the section view. The orientation of the composite metal deck has changed, as shown in Figure 6–24.

Figure 6–24

5. Save the project as **New Floor.rvt** and close the project.

6. Save and close the file **Composite-Metal-Deck.rfa**.

6.3 Creating Symbol Families

Annotation symbols are 2D elements that can be inserted into views or sheets to give additional information about a project. You can modify symbols that are supplied with the Autodesk Revit software to fit your company standards. You can also create new symbols using a variety of templates, as shown in Figure 6–25.

Annotation templates in Autodesk Revit

Figure 6–25

The drawing tools for annotation families include the standard line sketching tools, filled region, text, and label. You can also add existing symbols to the family.

• Most annotation symbols do not have family types. They are designed to change size according to the view scale.

• Some annotation family templates include notes to help you create the symbol. Delete them before using the family.

Hint: Modifying Labels

When you add labels, the length of the boundary box impacts the way the text word-wraps. For example, the Viewport: Title w Line tag that comes with the default metric template does not have enough room for a long title, as shown in Figure 6–26.

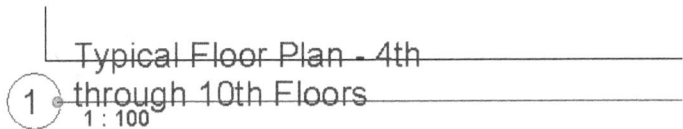

Typical Floor Plan - 4th
1 through 10th Floors
    1 : 100

Figure 6–26

To modify it, open the related family file (in this case **M_View Title.rfa**) and stretch the length of the label boundary as shown in Figure 6–27.

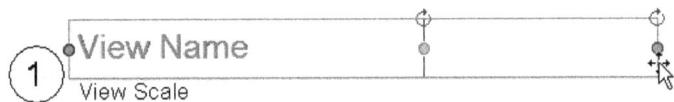

View Name
1
    View Scale

Figure 6–27

Save the annotation family and reload it into the project. The length of the title expands to fit the longer title as shown in Figure 6–28.

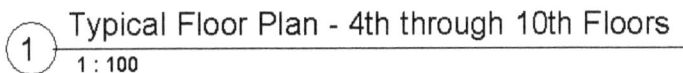

Typical Floor Plan - 4th through 10th Floors
1
    1 : 100

Figure 6–28

Practice 6d

Create Symbol Families: Arrow Symbol

Practice Objectives

- Create an annotation symbol.
- Add a Filled Region.
- Test the symbol in a project.

Estimated time for completion: 10 minutes.

In this practice, you will create an annotation symbol and apply it to a project, as shown in Figure 6–29.

View Scale 1/2"=1'-0"   View Scale 1/4"=1'=0"

Figure 6–29

Task 1 - Create an annotation symbol.

1. Create a new annotation symbol family based on the **Generic Annotation.rft** template found in the Autodesk Revit Library in the *Annotations* folder.

2. Save the family to your practice folder as **Arrow.rfa**.

3. Draw the arrow as shown in Figure 6–30. The dimensions are for reference only; do not add them to the sketch.

Figure 6–30

---

4. In the *Create* tab>Detail panel, click ⬚ (Filled Region). Add a filled region to the arrow, as shown in Figure 6–31. You can use the default solid pattern or create a new pattern if time permits.

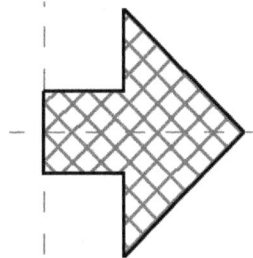

Figure 6–31

5. Delete the notes and save the family.

Task 2 - Add the symbol to a project.

1. Open a project file.

2. In the *Insert* tab>Load from Library panel, click ⬇ (Load Family) and select the new file **Arrow.rfa**, found in the practice files folder.

3. In the *Annotate* tab>Symbol panel, click ✛ (Symbol).

4. Select the **Arrow** type.

5. Add some other full-scale elements near the arrow.

6. Change the *View Scale*, as shown in Figure 6–29. The arrow should resize according to the new view scale.

7. Close the project. You do not need to save it.

6.4 Working with Project and Shared Parameters

The Autodesk Revit software includes many parameters used in families and schedules.

- **Family parameters:** Are specific to a family that constrain or flex geometry and assign attributes, such as material.

- **Project parameters:** Can be assigned to schedules.

- **Shared parameters:** Can be referenced in multiple locations, projects, families, tags, and schedules, and shared between projects.

Project Parameters

Project parameters are created per project in the Parameter Properties dialog box, as shown in Figure 6–32. In the *Manage* tab>Settings panel, click 🗒 (Project Parameters). In the Project Parameters dialog box, click **Add...**. Each parameter is assigned to one or more categories. Use the *Filter list* to specify the discipline to limit the number of items displayed.

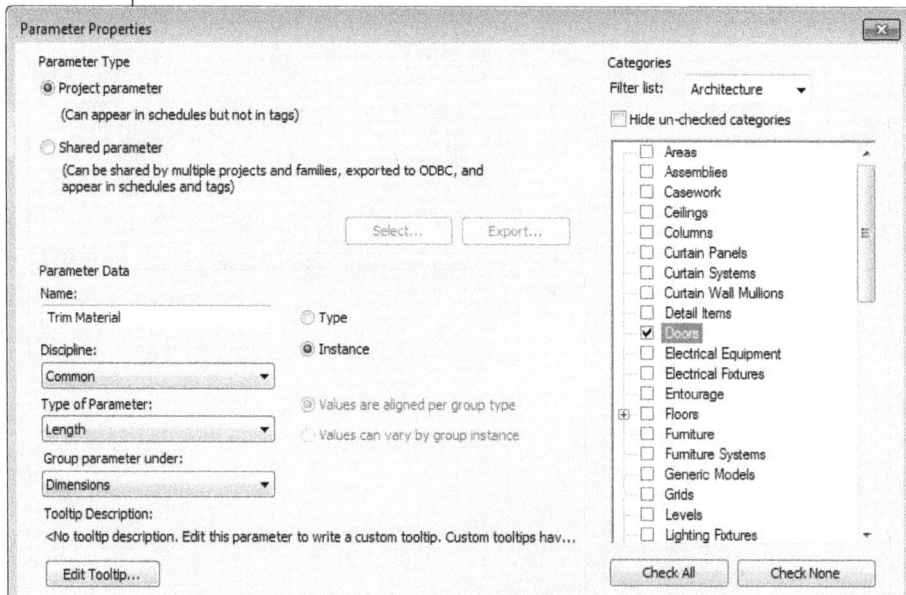

Figure 6–32

- If you want a parameter to be used in a schedule (such as the manufacturer of a desk family) it can be a project parameter.

- If you want to use a parameter in a tag and a schedule, create a shared parameter.

Shared Parameters

Create shared parameters for custom information that needs to be displayed in both tags and schedules, used in multiple projects or families, or exported to ODBC to be put in a database.

- Shared parameters can be created wherever there is an option to create a parameter (as shown in Figure 6–33), including Schedule Properties (creating a Field) and the Family Types dialog box.

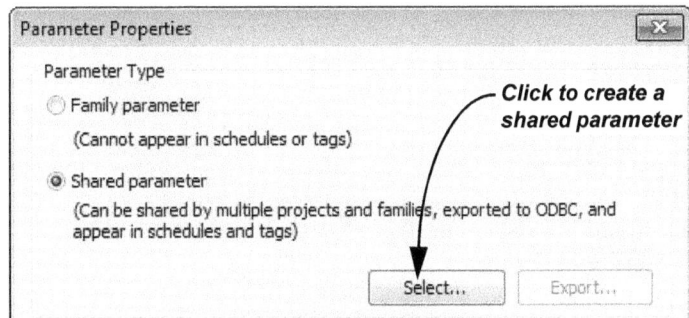

Figure 6–33

- You can also directly open the Edit Shared Parameters dialog box. In the *Manage* tab>Settings panel, click (Shared Parameters).

- If you are creating shared parameters in a family file, do it only for elements that constrain or flex the geometry and are used in a schedule.

How To: Create a Shared Parameter

1. Start the process of adding a parameter in Project Parameters, schedules, or family types.
2. Set the *Parameter Type* to **Shared parameter** in the Parameter Properties dialog box, as shown in Figure 6–34.

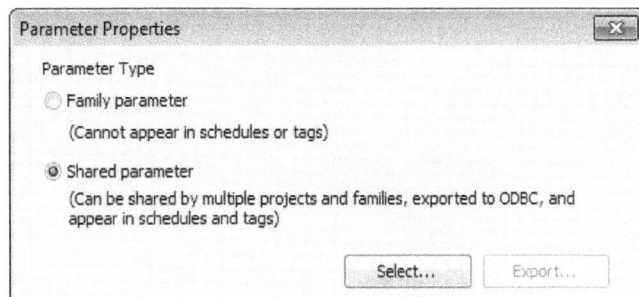

Figure 6–34

3. Click **Select...**.
4. In the Shared Parameters dialog box, you can select from groups and parameters that are already included in your project, or click **Edit...** to create a new shared parameter.
   - If no shared parameter file has been specified, an alert box opens. Click **Yes** to select a shared parameter file.
5. In the Edit Shared Parameters dialog box, as shown in Figure 6–35, click **Create...** to create a shared parameter file or **Browse...** to select an existing one.

Shared parameters are stored in a text file that should be placed in a network location available to everyone. This ensures consistency between projects and team members by maintaining naming standards and limiting typical typing errors with spaces and case sensitivity.

Figure 6–35

6. Creating groups for related parameters makes working with numerous names much easier. In the *Groups* area, click **New** to create a new parameter group.
7. In the New Parameter Group dialog box, as shown in Figure 6–36, type a new name and click **OK**.

Only one shared parameter file can be active in a project at a time. Therefore, create one main file with multiple groups instead of creating many files.

Figure 6–36

8. In the Edit Shared Parameters dialog box, in the *Parameters* area, click **New** to create a new shared parameter.
9. In the Parameter Properties dialog box, type a *Name* for the parameter, and set the *Discipline* (**Common**, **Structural**, or **Electrical**) and *Type of Parameter* in the drop-down lists. You can also add a Tooltip. The dialog box is shown in Figure 6–37.

Figure 6–37

10. Click **OK**.
11. In the Edit Shared Parameters dialog box, once you have the parameters in place, you can:

   • Click **Properties...** to display the contents of the Parameter Properties. You cannot modify them.
   • Click **Move...** to switch a parameter from one parameter group to another.
   • Click **Delete** to remove a parameter. Be careful about using this because it might impact the current project and any other projects that use the parameter.

12. When you have finished creating the shared parameters, click **OK** to close the Edit Shared Parameters dialog box.
13. Continue with the other steps required to add the parameter to the project, family, or schedule.

How To: Add a Shared Project Parameter to a Project

1. In the *Manage* tab>Settings panel, click ⬚ (Project Parameters).
2. In the Project Parameters dialog box, as shown in Figure 6–38, click **Add**.

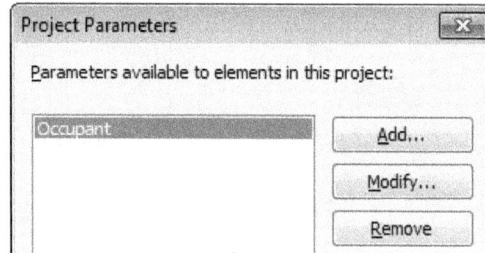

Figure 6–38

3. In the Parameter Properties dialog box, select **Shared parameter** and click **Select...**.
4. In the Shared Parameters dialog box, set the *Parameter group* and *Parameters* that you want to add to the project, as shown in Figure 6–39. Click **OK**.

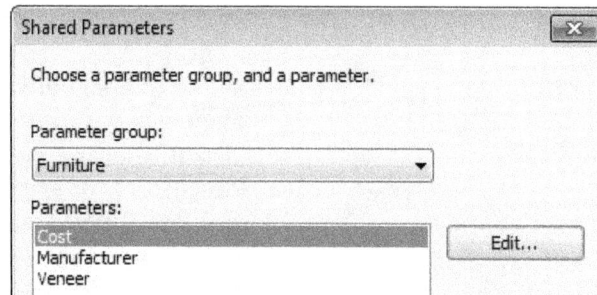

Figure 6–39

- If the parameter you want to use does not exist, click **Edit....** to create a new shared parameter.

Use the Filter List to
limit the number of
categories available.

5. In the Parameter Properties dialog box:

   - In the *Categories* area, select the categories to which you want the parameter to apply, as shown in Figure 6–40.

   Categories

   Filter list: Architecture   ▼

   ☐ Hide un-checked categories

   ☐ Doors
   ☐ Electrical Equipment
   ☐ Electrical Fixtures
   ⊞ ☐ Floors
   ☑ Furniture
   ☑ Furniture Systems
   ☐ Generic Models
   ☐ Grids
   ☐ Levels
   ☐ Lighting Fixtures
   ⊟ ☐ Mass
        ☐ Mass Exterior Wall
        ☐ Mass Floor
        ☐ Mass Glazing

   [Check All]   [Check None]

   Figure 6–40

   - In the *Parameter Data* area, the Name, Discipline, and Type of Parameter drop-down lists are grayed out, while the shared parameter you just selected is displayed.

6. Select an option from the Group parameter under drop-down list (this is where it displays in the Element Properties dialog box) and select **Instance** or **Type**, as shown in Figure 6–41. Add a tooltip description, if required.

   Parameter Data

   Name:
   [Cost]   ○ Type

   Discipline:
   [Common ▼]   ⦿ Instance

   Type of Parameter:
   [Currency ▼]

   Group parameter under:
   [Other ▼]

   Figure 6–41

7. Click **OK** twice to add the parameter to the project.

Practice 6e

Work with Shared Parameters in Architectural Projects

Practice Objectives

- Create shared parameters in a project.
- Create an annotation tag family and link the shared parameters into the tag.
- Add the shared parameters to a family and insert them into the project along with the associated tags.
- Create a schedule using the shared parameters including the project, tag, and family.

Estimated time for completion: 20 minutes

In this practice, you will create shared parameters through project parameters and use them in a family, tag, and schedule, as shown in Figure 6–42.

Furniture System Schedule		
Employee	Extension	Department
	1234	
	1234	
	1234	
Martha Hollowell	2437	Courseware
Jennifer MacMillian	2785	Courseware
Ronda Wiley	1258	Sales
	1234	

Figure 6–42

Task 1 - Create shared parameters.

1. In the practice files *Architectural* folder, open **Office-Layout.rvt**.

2. In the *Manage* tab>Settings panel, click ▦ (Project Parameters).

3. In the Project Parameters dialog box, click **Add...**.

4. In the Parameter Properties dialog box, select **Shared parameter** and click **Select...**.

5. If there is no existing shared parameter file, an alert box displays prompting you to select a shared parameter file. Click **Yes**. If the Shared Parameters dialog box opens, click **Edit...**.

6. In the Edit Shared Parameters dialog box, click **Create...**.

7. Open the practice folder and save the new file as **Office-Parameters.txt**.

8. In the *Groups* area, click **New**. Type the name **Office Information** and click **OK**. This becomes the current group, as shown in Figure 6–43.

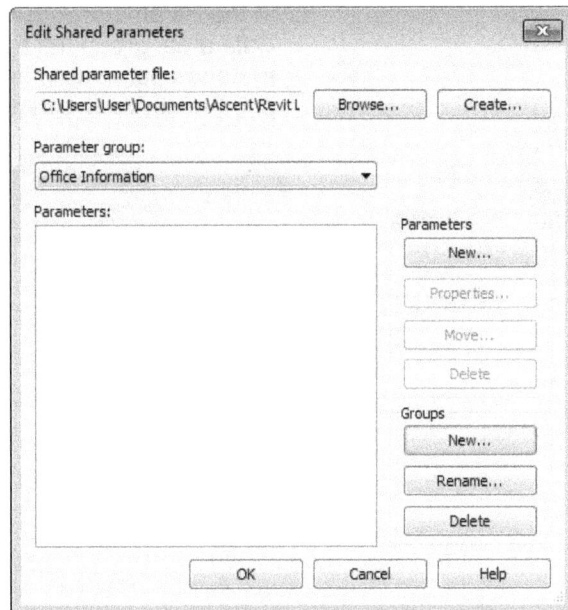

Figure 6–43

9. In the *Parameters* area, click **New...** and create three new shared parameters using the following information:

Name	Discipline	Type of Parameter
Extension	Common	Integer
Employee	Common	Text
Department	Common	Text

10. Click **OK**.

11. In the Shared Parameters dialog box, shown in Figure 6–44, select **Department** and click **OK**.

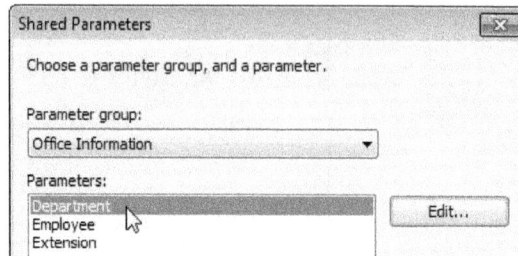

Figure 6–44

12. In the Parameter Properties dialog box, in the *Parameter Data* area, group the parameter under **Other** and make it an **Instance** parameter. In the *Categories* list, select **Furniture** and **Furniture Systems**, as shown in Figure 6–45.

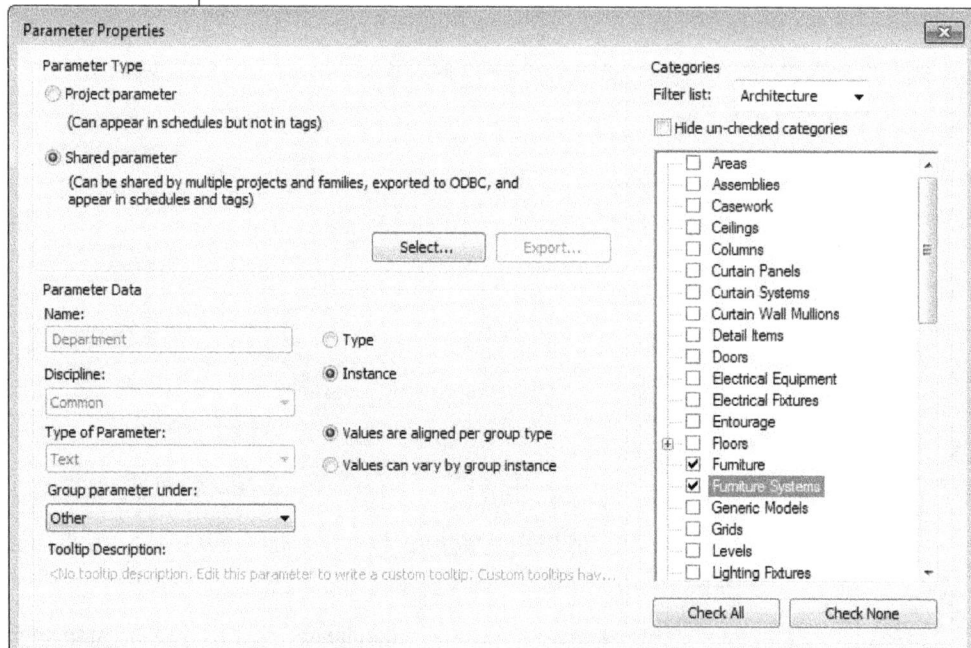

Figure 6–45

13. Click **OK**. **Department** is added to the shared parameters in the project.

14. Repeat the process for **Employee** and **Extension**.

15. Click **OK** to finish creating the project parameters.

16. Save the project.

Task 2 - Create a tag with shared parameters.

1. Create a new family based on the **Generic Tag.rft** template found in the *Annotation* folder of Autodesk Revit Library.

2. Save the family to the practice files folder as **Office-Information.rfa**.

3. Zoom in, read the information in red, and delete the note.

4. In the *Modify* tab>Properties panel, click ⬚ (Family Category and Parameters).

5. In the Family Category and Parameters dialog box, set the *Family Category* to **Furniture Systems Tags**, as shown in Figure 6–46. Click **OK**.

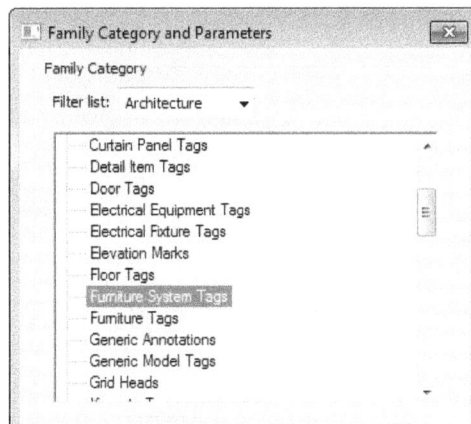

Figure 6–46

6. In the *Create* tab>Detail panel, click ⌐ (Line). Draw a box, starting at the crossing of the two reference lines, as shown in Figure 6–47. Do not add the dimensions; they are for reference only.

Figure 6–47

7. In the *Create* tab>Text panel, click ▨**A** (Label).

8. Use the default type, **Label: 3/32"**.

9. Click inside the box you just created.

10. In the Edit Label dialog box, which includes a list of the multi-category parameters supplied with the Autodesk Revit software, click ▨ (Add Parameter).

In the Parameter Properties dialog box, you can only create shared parameters.

11. In the Parameter Properties dialog box, click **Select...**.

12. The shared parameters you created earlier should be available by default in the Shared Parameters dialog box. Select **Extension**, as shown in Figure 6–48, and click **OK**.

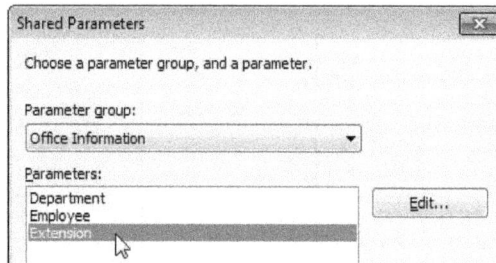

Figure 6–48

13. Click **OK** until you reach the Edit Label dialog box.

14. Select **Extension** and click ⇥ (Add parameter(s) to label). Click **OK** to insert the label into the family.

15. Click ▹ (Modify) and select the new label. Resize the outline of the text box to fit inside the box. Move the label so that it is centered in the box, as shown in Figure 6–49.

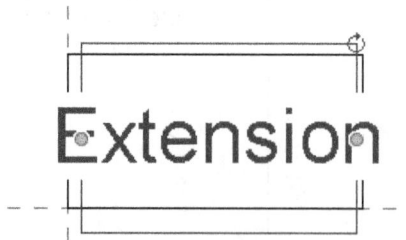

Figure 6–49

16. Save the family and load it into the project **Office-Layout.rvt**.

Task 3 - Add shared parameters to a furniture family.

1. Continue working in the project **Office-Layout.rvt**.

2. In the *Architecture* tab>Build panel, click ▱ (Component).

3. In the *Modify | Place Component* tab>Mode panel, click ▤ (Load Family).

4. In the practice files *Architectural* folder, open **Work-Station-Cubicle.rfa**.

5. Place a workstation in one of the rooms in the wing to the left of the main building.

6. Click ▯ (Modify) and select the new workstation.

7. In the *Modify | Furniture Systems* tab>Mode panel, click ▱ (Edit Family).

8. In the Properties panel, click ▥ (Family Types).

9. In the Family Types dialog box, click ▯ (New Parameter).

10. Select **Shared Parameter** and click **Select...**.

11. The shared parameters you created earlier are also available in this family file. Add each of the parameters from the *Office-Information* category into the family as an Instance parameter in the *Other* category.

12. In the Family Types dialog box, set the *Extension (default)* to **1234**, as shown in Figure 6–50. The other values can be left blank.

Other			☆
Department (default)		=	
Employee (default)		=	
Extension (default)	1234	=	▯

Figure 6–50

13. Click **OK**.

14. Save the family file and load it into the **Office-Layout.rvt** project. Overwrite the existing version and its parameter values.

15. Add several other cubicles in various offices.

Task 4 - Add tags and create a schedule.

1. In the *Annotate* tab>Tag panel, click 🔲 (Tag by Category).

2. Select the workstations and tag each of them. The default **1234** extension number should display on each tag, as shown in Figure 6–51.

Figure 6–51

3. Select a workstation. In Properties, the **Extension**, **Employee**, and **Department** parameters should be available in the *Other* category, as shown in Figure 6–52.

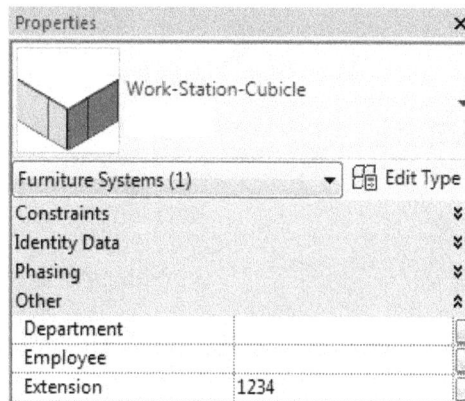

Figure 6–52

4. Change the *Extension*, and add an *Employee* name and *Department*.

5. Repeat with several other workstations.

6. In the *View* tab>Create panel, expand 🗔 (Schedules) and click 🗔 (Schedule/Quantities).

7. In the New Schedule dialog box, create a new Furniture Systems schedule and set the *Phase* is set to **Phase 1**, as shown in Figure 6–53.

Figure 6–53

8. In the *Fields* tab, add the **Family and Type** parameter and then add **Extension**, **Employee**, and **Department**, as shown in Figure 6–54.

Figure 6–54

9. At this point, you can modify the other schedule properties as required. Click **OK** when you are finished. The schedule should display the information you entered in the workstation's properties. Change the name of the schedule to **Office Information** and **Hide** the *Family and Type* column, as shown in Figure 6–55.

<Office Information>		
A	B	C
Employee	Extension	Department
Ronda	1234	Sales
Pual	1235	Engineering
Anne-Marie	1236	Sales
Kareen	1237	Marketing
Martha	1238	Engineering
Jen	1239	Enginering

Figure 6–55

10. Save the project.

11. If time permits, you can copy the Office Information tag and change the *Family Category* to **Furniture Tags**. Then you can use the new tag to tag the desks in the project. Furniture and Furniture Systems are different categories and cannot use the same tag.

Practice 6f

Estimated time for completion: 20 minutes

Work with Shared Parameters in MEP Projects

Practice Objectives

- Create a schedule that uses shared parameters.
- Add the shared parameters to a family file and note the impact on the schedule.

In this practice, you will create a mechanical equipment schedule and add shared parameters to the project through the schedule. You will then modify and add the shared parameters in a family file and update the family in the project. The shared parameters then populate the schedule, as shown in Figure 6–56.

Mechanical Equipment Schedule						
Mark	Type	Dimensions			Gas Line Diameter	Liquid Line Diameter
		Height	Width	Depth		
1	HPD60C	44 3/4"	38 7/8"	34 3/4"	1"	1/2"
2	HPD60C	44 3/4"	38 7/8"	34 3/4"	1"	1/2"
3	HPD60C	44 3/4"	38 7/8"	34 3/4"	1"	1/2"
4	HPD60C	44 3/4"	38 7/8"	34 3/4"	1"	1/2"

Figure 6–56

Task 1 - Create a schedule and add shared parameters.

1. In the practice files *MEP* folder, open **Townhouse-Complex.rvt**. Note that four heat pumps have been added to serve the townhouses.

2. In the *View* tab>Create panel, expand ▦ (Schedules) and click ▦ (Schedule/Quantities).

3. In the New Schedule dialog box, set the *Filter list* to **Mechanical**, select the *Category* of **Mechanical Equipment**, and click **OK**.

4. In the Schedule Properties dialog box, in the *Fields* tab, select the following fields: **Mark** and **Type**. The rest of the parameters need to be shared parameters.

5. Click ▢ (New Parameter).

6. In the Parameter Properties dialog box, select **Shared parameter** and click **Select...**.

7. If there is no existing shared parameter file, an alert box displays prompting you to select a shared parameter file. Click **Yes**. If the Shared Parameters dialog box opens, click **Edit...**.

8. In the Edit Shared Parameters dialog box, click **Create...**.

9. In the Create Shared Parameter File dialog box, navigate to the practice files *MEP* folder and save the new file as **Townhouse-Parameters.txt**.

10. In the *Groups* area, click **New**. Set the name as **Heat Pump Information** and click **OK**. This becomes the current group, as shown in Figure 6–57.

Figure 6–57

11. In the *Parameters* area, click **New**. Create new shared type parameters using the following information:

Name	Discipline	Type of Parameter
Height	Common	Length
Width	Common	Length
Depth	Common	Length
Gas Line Diameter	Common	Length
Liquid Line Diameter	Common	Length

12. Click **OK**.

13. In the Shared Parameters dialog box, select **Height**, as shown in Figure 6–58, and click **OK**.

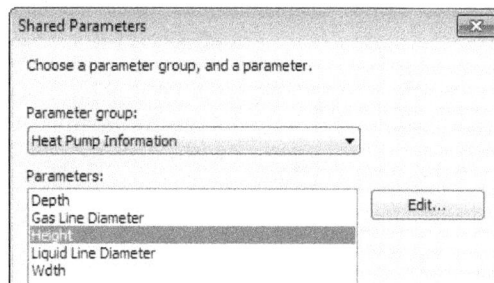

Figure 6–58

14. In the Parameter Properties dialog box, in the *Parameter Data* area, group the parameter under **Dimensions**, as shown in Figure 6–59.

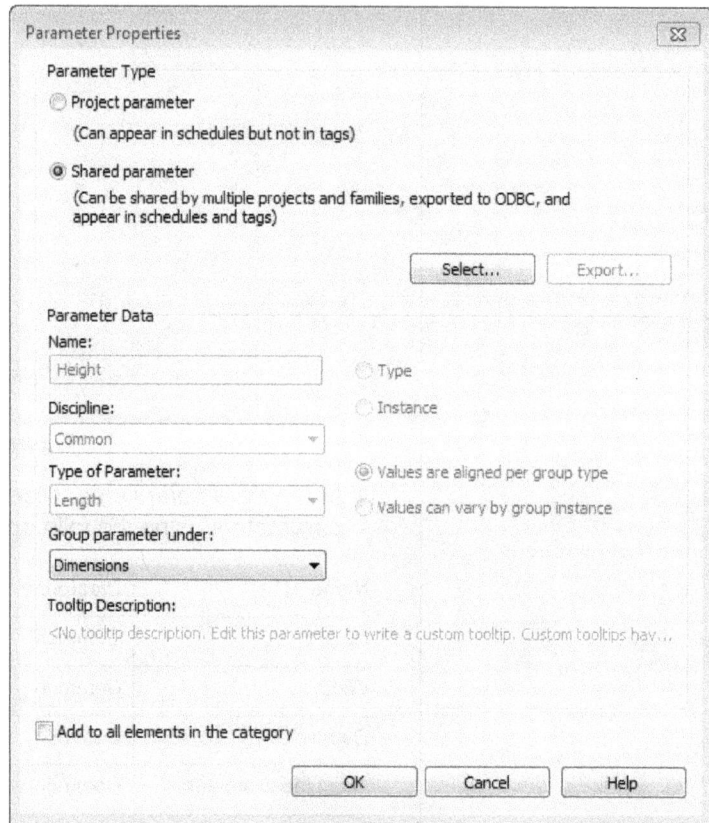

Figure 6–59

15. Click **OK**. Height is added to the scheduled fields.

16. Click ⬚ (New Parameter) again.

17. In the Parameter Properties dialog box, select **Shared parameter** and click **Select...**.

18. This time you do not have to create a shared parameter file, as the files created in the previous steps are available. Select **Width** and click **OK** to apply the parameter to the scheduled fields.

19. Repeat the process and add the rest of the new shared parameters in the order shown in Figure 6–60.

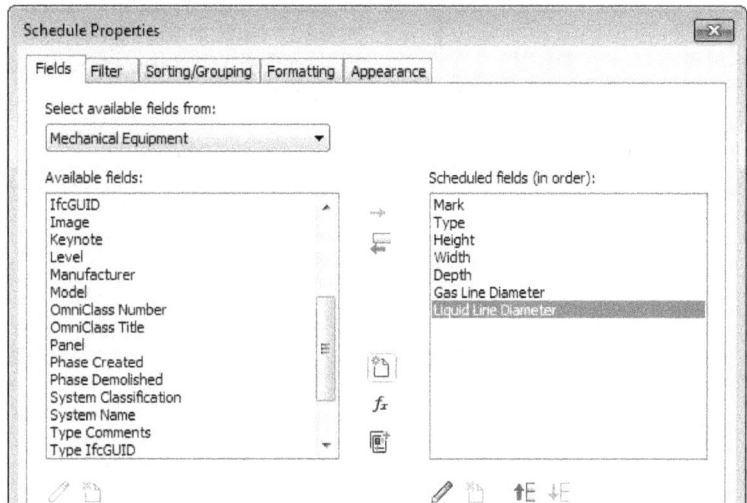

Figure 6–60

20. Click **OK**. The Mechanical Equipment Schedule displays but only includes values for the **Mark** and **Type**, as shown in Figure 6–61. The shared parameters are not yet identified in the Heat Pump family.

<Mechanical Equipment Schedule>						
A	B	C	D	E	F	G
Mark	Type	Height	Width	Depth	Gas Line Diameter	Liquid Line Diamete
1	HP060C					
2	HP060C					
3	HP060C					
4	HP060C					

Figure 6–61

21. Save the project.

Task 2 - Add shared parameters to a family.

1. Open the Mechanical>HVAC>**Floor Plans: Ground-Mech** view and select one of the heat pumps.

2. In the *Modify | Mechanical Equipment* tab>Mode panel, click (Edit Family). The family file opens in the Family Editor.

3. In the Properties panel, click ⊞ (Family Types).

4. In the Family Types dialog box several of the parameters that already exist in the family are displayed, as shown in Figure 6–62, but they are not connected as shared parameters.

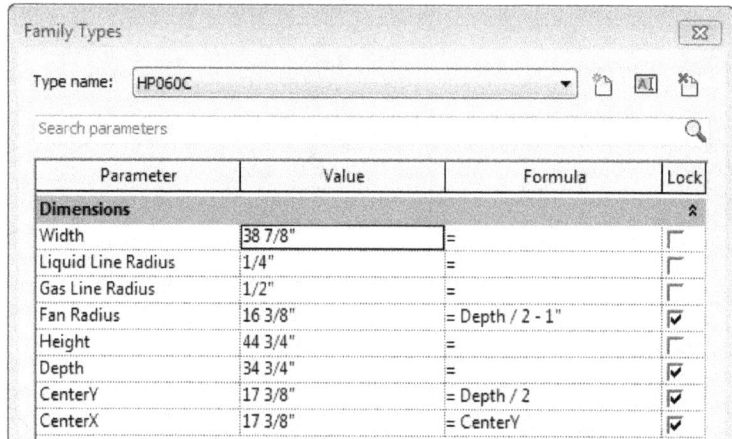

Parameter	Value	Formula	Lock
Dimensions			↕
Width	38 7/8"	=	☐
Liquid Line Radius	1/4"	=	☐
Gas Line Radius	1/2"	=	☐
Fan Radius	16 3/8"	= Depth / 2 - 1"	☑
Height	44 3/4"	=	☐
Depth	34 3/4"	=	☑
CenterY	17 3/8"	= Depth / 2	☑
CenterX	17 3/8"	= CenterY	☑

Figure 6–62

5. Select the **Width** parameter and in the *Parameters* area, click

   ✎ (Edit Parameter).

6. In the Parameter properties dialog box, select **Shared Parameter** and click **Select...**.

7. The shared parameters you created earlier are also available in this family file, as shown in Figure 6–63.

Figure 6–63

8. Select **Width** and click **OK** twice. The existing parameter is now connected with the shared parameter.

The information stored in the Heat Pump family for the Liquid Line and Gas Line are set to a radius, because it is required by the connectors. Therefore, you have to add Parameters and formulas for the diameters.

9. Repeat the process with the **Height** and **Depth** parameters.

10. In the Family Types dialog box, click ⬚ (New Parameter).

11. In the Parameter Properties dialog box, select **Shared parameter** and click **Select...**.

12. In the Shared Parameters dialog box, select **Gas Line Diameter** and click **OK**.

13. Set it as a **Type** parameter and group it with the **Dimensions** group. Click **OK**.

14. Repeat the process for **Liquid Line Diameter**.

15. Set the following formulas for the two diameter parameters, as shown in Figure 6–64.
    - Gas Line Diameter = **Gas Line Radius * 2**
    - Liquid Line Diameter = **Liquid Line Radius * 2**

Family Types			
Type name: HP060C			
Search parameters			
Parameter	**Value**	**Formula**	**Lock**
Dimensions			
Depth	34 3/4"	=	☑
Gas Line Diameter	1"	= Gas Line Radius * 2	☐
Height	44 3/4"	=	☐
Liquid Line Diameter	1/2"	= Liquid Line Radius * 2	☐
Liquid Line Radius	1/4"	=	☐
Gas Line Radius	1/2"	=	☐

Figure 6–64

16. Click **OK** to close the Family Types dialog box.

17. Save the family to the practice folder.

Task 3 - Load the family and modify the schedule.

---

1. In the *Create* tab>Family Editor panel, click ⬆ (Load into Project).

2. Overwrite the existing version and its parameter values.

3. Open the Mechanical Equipment Schedule. The values for the parameters are now included. Add headers for the dimensions, as shown in Figure 6–65.

		Overall Dimensions			Pipe Dimensions	
A	B	C	D	E	F	G
Mark	Type	Height	Width	Depth	Gas Line Diameter	Liquid Line Diameter
1	HP060C	3' - 8 3/4"	3' - 2 7/8"	2' - 10 3/4"	0' - 1"	0' - 0 1/2"
2	HP060C	3' - 8 3/4"	3' - 2 7/8"	2' - 10 3/4"	0' - 1"	0' - 0 1/2"
3	HP060C	3' - 8 3/4"	3' - 2 7/8"	2' - 10 3/4"	0' - 1"	0' - 0 1/2"
4	HP060C	3' - 8 3/4"	3' - 2 7/8"	2' - 10 3/4"	0' - 1"	0' - 0 1/2"

<Mechanical Equipment Schedule>

Figure 6–65

4. Typically the values for these parameters should only be in inches. To fix this, in Properties next to **Formatting** parameter, click **Edit...**.

5. The Schedule Properties dialog box opens with the *Formatting* tab selected.

6. In the *Fields* area, select **Height** and click **Field Format...**.

7. Clear **Use project settings** and change the *Units* to **Fractional inches**. Click **OK**.

8. Repeat this for the rest of the length based parameters so that they display in inches and not in feet and inches.

9. Click **OK** to close the dialog box. The schedule updates as shown in Figure 6–66.

		Overall Dimensions			Pipe Dimensions	
A	B	C	D	E	F	G
Mark	Type	Height	Width	Depth	Gas Line Diameter	Liquid Line Diameter
1	HP060C	44 3/4"	38 7/8"	34 3/4"	1"	1/2"
2	HP060C	44 3/4"	38 7/8"	34 3/4"	1"	1/2"
3	HP060C	44 3/4"	38 7/8"	34 3/4"	1"	1/2"
4	HP060C	44 3/4"	38 7/8"	34 3/4"	1"	1/2"

<Mechanical Equipment Schedule>

Figure 6–66

10. Save the project.

Practice 6g

Work with Shared Parameters in Structural Projects

Practice Objectives

Estimated time for completion: 20 minutes

- Create shared parameters in a project.
- Use the shared parameters in a family, associated tag, and a schedule.

In this practice, you will create shared parameters through project parameters and use them in family, tag, and schedule, as shown in Figure 6–67. The context here is a public plaza with columns, some free-standing and some supporting canopies and roofs. Each column will have custom brackets for banners, flags, etc.

Figure 6–67

Task 1 - Create shared parameters.

1. In the practice files *Structural* folder, open **Events-Plaza.rvt**.

2. In the *Manage* tab>Project Settings panel, click 🗒 (Project Parameters).

3. In the Project Parameters dialog box, click **Add...**.

4. In the Parameter Properties dialog box, select **Shared parameter** and click **Select...**.

5. If there is no existing shared parameter file, an alert box displays prompting you to select a shared parameter file. Click **Yes**. If the Shared Parameters dialog box opens, click **Edit...**.

6. In the Edit Shared Parameters dialog box, click **Create...**.

7. Save the new file as **Plaza-Parameters.txt** in the practice files folder.

8. Create a new parameter group. In the *Groups* area, click **New...**. Set the name as **Columns** and click **OK**. This becomes the current group, as shown in Figure 6–68.

Figure 6–68

9. In the *Parameters* area, click **New...** and create three new shared parameters using the following information:

Name	Discipline	Type of Parameter
Bracket Type	Common	Text
Bracket Offset from Base	Common	Length
Bracket Finish	Common	Material

10. Click **OK**.

11. In the Shared Parameters dialog box, select **Bracket Type**, as shown in Figure 6–69, and click **OK**.

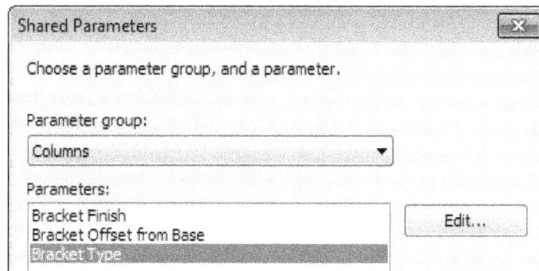

Figure 6–69

12. In the Parameter Properties dialog box, in the *Parameter Data* area, group the parameter under **Other** and make it an **Instance** parameter. In the *Categories* area, filter the list based on **Structure** and select **Structural Columns,** as shown in Figure 6–70.

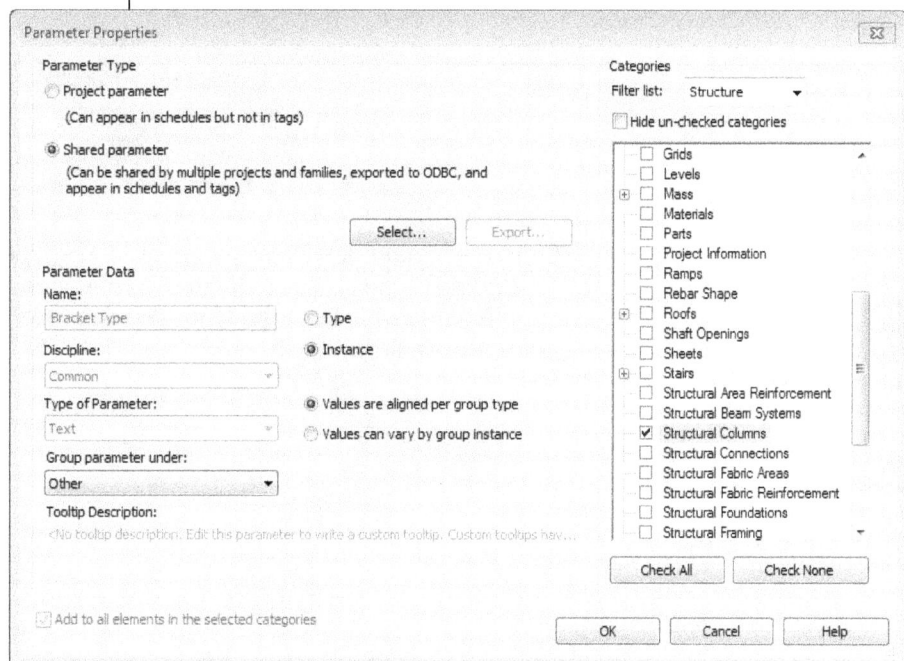

Figure 6–70

13. Click **OK**. **Bracket Type** is added to the shared parameters in the project.

14. Repeat the process to add **Bracket Offset from Base** and **Bracket Finish** to the Project Parameters list.

15. Click **OK** to finish creating the project parameters.

16. Save the project.

Task 2 - Create a Tag with Shared parameters.

1. Start a new family based on the **Generic Tag.rft** template found in the default library's *Annotations* folder.

2. Zoom in, read the information in red, and delete the note.

3. In the Properties panel, click ⬚ (Family Category and Parameters).

4. In the Family Category and Parameters dialog box, set the *Family Category* to **Structural Column Tags**, as shown in Figure 6–71. Click **OK**.

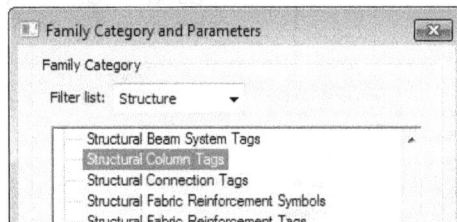

Figure 6–71

5. In the *Create* tab>Detail panel, click ✏ (Line). Draw a box, starting at the crossing of the two reference lines, as shown in Figure 6–72. Do not add the dimensions. They are for reference only.

Figure 6–72

6. In the *Create* tab>Text panel, click 🄰 (Label).

7. Use the default type, **Label: 3/32"**.

8. In the *Modify | Place Label* tab>Format panel, set Justification to ≡ (Align Center) and ≡ (Align Top).

9. Click inside the box you just created.

10. In the Edit Label dialog box, which includes a list of the multi-category parameters supplied with the Autodesk Revit software, click ⬛ (Add Parameter).

In this dialog box, you can only create shared parameters.

11. In the Parameter Properties dialog box, click **Select...**.

12. In the Shared Parameters dialog box, the shared parameters you created earlier should be available by default. Select **Bracket Type**, as shown in Figure 6–73, and click **OK**.

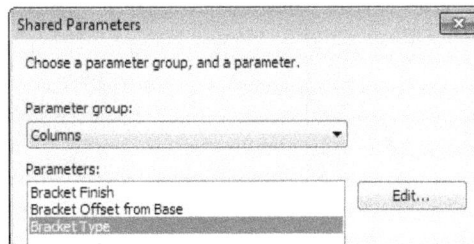

Figure 6–73

13. Click **OK** until you reach the Edit Label dialog box.

14. Select **Bracket Type** and click ⬆ (Add parameter(s) to label).

15. Repeat with the **Bracket Offset from Base** and **Bracket Finish** parameters. In the *Break* column, select the option for the first two parameters, as shown in Figure 6–74. This forces each parameter to be on a separate line.

	Parameter Name	Spaces	Prefix	Sample Value	Suffix	Break
1	Bracket Type	1		Bracket Type		☑
2	Bracket Offset from Base	1		Bracket Offset fro		☑
3	Bracket Finish	1		Bracket Finish		☐

Figure 6–74

16. Click **OK** to insert the label into the family.

17. Click ⌖ (Modify) and select the new label. Resize the outline of the text box so that it fits inside the box, and move the label so that it is top-centered in the box, as shown in Figure 6–75.

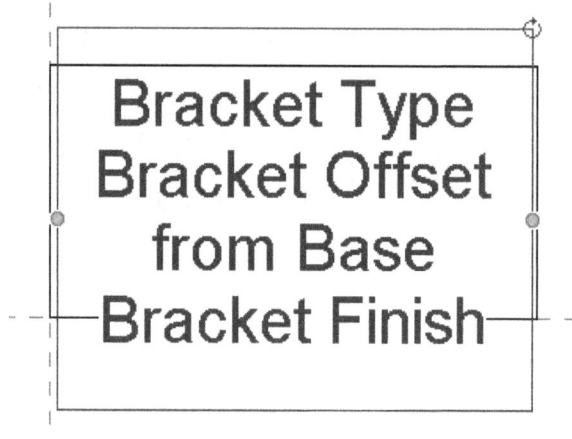

Bracket Type
Bracket Offset
from Base
Bracket Finish

Figure 6–75

18. Save the new family with the name **Column-Bracket-Tag.rfa**.

19. Load the family into the project **Events-Plaza.rvt**.

20. The **Tag** command is automatically started. Tag one of the columns.

21. The tag is empty as shown in Figure 6–76, because no values have been added to the parameters.

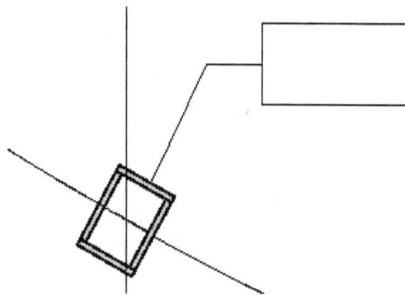

Figure 6–76

22. Save the project.

Task 3 - Add Tags and modify information.

1. In the *Annotate* tab>Tag panel, click (Tag All).

2. In the Tag All Not Tagged dialog box, select the *Category* **Structural Column Tags** with the *Loaded Tags* set to **Column-Bracket-Tag**. Select **Leader** and click **OK**.

   - All of the columns are tagged. The tags are blank but display question marks when selected, as shown in Figure 6–77. This is because the corresponding information has not been entered into the properties.

Figure 6–77

3. Select a column.

4. In Properties, scroll down to the *Other* area. The **Bracket Finish**, **Bracket Type**, and **Bracket Offset from base** parameters are available but have no information stored in them yet, as shown in Figure 6–78.

Figure 6–78

5. Right-click on the column and select **Select All Instances> Visible in View**.

   - In this case, you will set the default values for all columns once. Individual columns can be changed later.

6. In Properties, set the *Bracket Offset from Base* to **12'-0"**, set the *Bracket Type* to **Banner**, and set the *Bracket Finish* to **Metal**.

7. Select two or three individual columns, and in Properties change the *Bracket Type* to **Sculptural** and the *Bracket Offset from Base* to **15'-0"**. The tags update only for those columns, as shown in Figure 6–79.

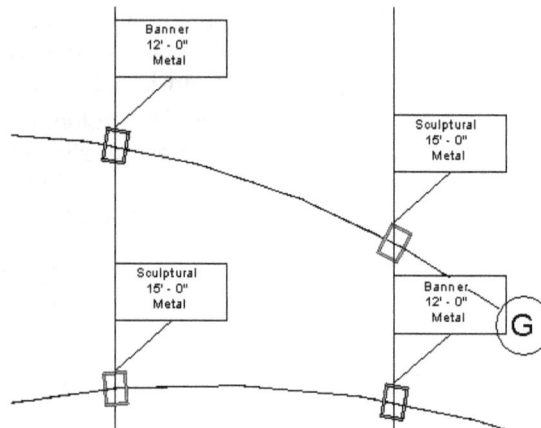

Figure 6–79

8. Save the project.

Task 4 - Create a Structural Column schedule.

---

1. Create a new building component schedule for structural columns.

2. In the Schedule Properties dialog box, in the *Fields* tab, add the **Column Location Mark** parameter and then add **Mark**, **Bracket Type**, **Bracket Offset from Base**, and **Bracket Finish**, as shown in Figure 6–80.

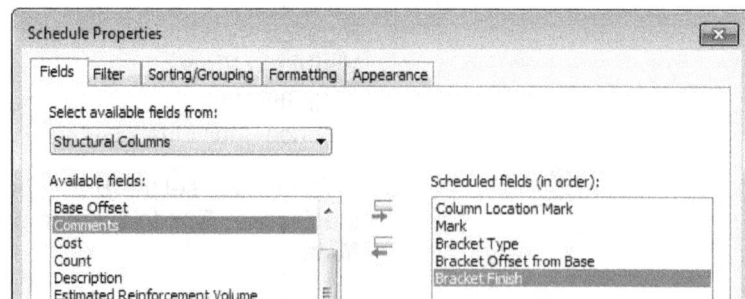

Figure 6–80

3. Sort by the Column Location Mark and modify the other schedule properties as required. Click **OK** when finished. The schedule should display the information you entered in the column's properties, as shown in Figure 6–81.

<Structural Column Schedule>				
A	B	C	D	E
Column Location M	Mark	Bracket Type	Bracket Offset fro	Bracket Finish
A-1	1	Banner	12' - 0"	Metal
A-2	2	Sculptural	15' - 0"	Metal
A-3	3	Banner	12' - 0"	Metal
A-4	4	Sculptural	15' - 0"	Metal
A-5	5	Banner	12' - 0"	Metal
A-6	6	Sculptural	15' - 0"	Metal
A-7	7	Banner	12' - 0"	Metal

Figure 6–81

4. Save the project.

Chapter Review Questions

1. An in-place family is created whenever you need a custom family that is:

   a. Not available in your library.

   b. Built using profiles.

   c. Directly connected to elements in the project.

   d. Requires shared parameters.

2. Which of the following are examples of elements for which you can create profiles? (Select all that apply.)

   a. Wall reveals

   b. The top rail of railings

   c. In-place Sweeps

   d. Curtain Wall mullions

3. At what size should you create the tag family elements, as shown in Figure 6–82?

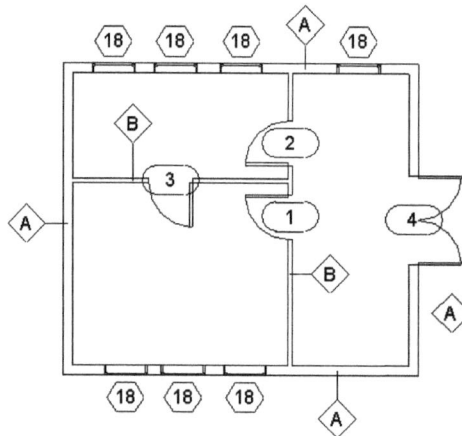

Figure 6–82

   a. Full scale to match the size of the tagged element in the project.

   b. Full scale to match the size of the annotation on the sheet.

   c. One size for each scale.

   d. It varies according to the type of annotation.

4. Where are shared parameters (access shown in Figure 6–83) stored?

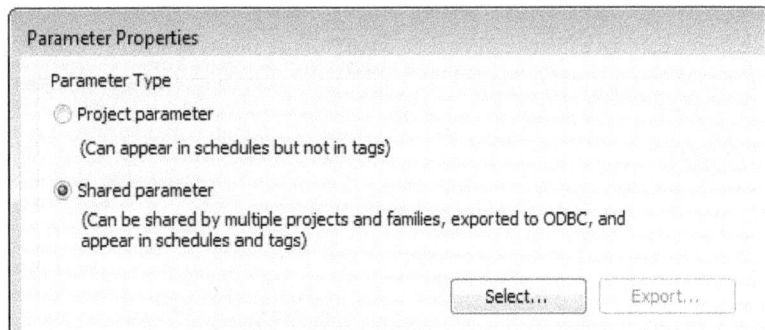

Parameter Properties

Parameter Type

○ Project parameter

(Can appear in schedules but not in tags)

◉ Shared parameter

(Can be shared by multiple projects and families, exported to ODBC, and appear in schedules and tags)

Select...   Export...

Figure 6–83

a. In a text file.

b. In the current project.

c. In a shared project.

d. In the family file.

Command Summary

Button	Command	Location
	Annotation Symbol	• **File** tab>expand New
	Model In-Place	• **Ribbon:** *Architecture* tab>Build panel> expand Component • **Ribbon:** *Structure* tab>Model panel> expand Component • **Ribbon:** *Systems* tab>Model panel> expand Component
	Project Parameters	• **Ribbon:** *Manage* tab>Project Settings panel
	Shared Parameters	• **Ribbon:** *Manage* tab>Project Settings panel

Creating Architectural Specific Families

Architectural families include elements that are created using standard component family methods (such as doors and windows). There are also ways to create other elements that use profiles and are best created directly in the project as in-place families (such as angled cornices and coping). Another important family is railings. These families are put together using other families, including rails, balusters, posts and panels.

Learning Objectives in this Chapter

- Create custom door and window families from existing families and templates.
- Use in-place families to create angled cornices, fascias, and copings.
- Create railing types, including the rails, balusters, posts, and panels.

7.1 Creating Custom Doors and Windows

You can create custom doors and windows by copying and modifying an existing family, enabling you to use all of the existing detailed elements and parameters. For example, in Figure 7–1 the full panel door family on the left can be transformed into the square panel on the right.

Figure 7–1

When you use a template, only the most basic elements are included. For example, in the Window with Trim template (shown in Figure 7–2), only the opening for the window, basic trim, and parameters are included. Everything else must be added.

Figure 7–2

Practice 7a

Create Custom Doors

Estimated time for completion: 20 minutes

Practice Objectives

- Create a custom family based on an existing family.
- Add reference planes and dimensions.
- Set formulas for parameters.

In this practice, you will create new door family based on an existing door family. You will modify a nested door grill family so that it is square. Your will then insert the new square grill into the door and modify dimensions and labels so that the grill, glass, and panel all work together at different sizes, as shown in a project in Figure 7–3.

Figure 7–3

Task 1 - Create door types,

1. In the Autodesk Revit Library's *Doors>Residential* folder, open **Door-Interior-Single-Full Glass-Wood.rfa**.
   - The family is also available in the practice files *Architectural* folder.

2. Save the file in the practice files folder with the name **Door-Single-Glass-Square.rfa**.

3. Create three Family Types. Modify the *Width* and *Height* values to match the name.
   - **32" x 80"**
   - **36" x 80"**
   - **36" x 84"**

4. Use the new types to flex the parameters.

5. Select the **Doors: Door Grill: Door Grill**, as shown in Figure 7–4. In the Type Selector, note that this is a nested family, along with the Door Swing and Handle families, as shown in Figure 7–5.

Figure 7–4

Figure 7–5

6. With the Door Grill family selected, in the *Modify | Doors* tab> Mode panel, click ▣ (Edit Family). Note that it might take some time for this to open.

7. Once you are in the family editor, save the file as **Door Grill-Square.rfa** in the practice folder.

Task 2 - Modify the door grill.

---

1. Working in the **Door Grill-Square.rfa** family, open the **Elevations: Front** view. This is where the primary parameters display.

2. Delete the reference planes and associated elements shown in Figure 7–6, as well as the center vertical sweep and line (do not delete the center reference plane).

Figure 7–6

3. Select the dimension on the right that controls the placement of the remaining grids and click the **Toggle Dimension Equality** control. The muntin grids are spaced out equally again.

4. Open the Family Types dialog box.

5. Under the *Dimensions* heading, change the formula for the *Glazing Height* to **Glazing Width** and click **OK**.

6. Save the family.

Task 3 - Load and place the square grill in the door.

1. Load the square grill family into the door family and then click **Modify**.

2. Open the interior elevation of the door family. Select the existing grill and, in the Type Selector, change it to **Door Grill-Square**.

   - The existing grill is placed in the correct location in the door panel.

3. Align and lock the bottom of the square grill to the reference plane associated with the Bottom Rail, as shown in Figure 7–7.

Figure 7–7

4. Delete the Bottom Rail dimension, but not the reference plane.

5. Create a new dimension from the Top Rail reference plane to the former Bottom Rail reference plane. Label it **Glass Height** (a **Type** parameter in the *Dimensions* category), as shown in Figure 7–8.

Figure 7–8

6. Select the square door grill. In Properties, click **Edit Type**.

7. Under the *Dimensions* heading, beside the *Width* parameter, click the **Associate Family Parameter** button, as shown in Figure 7–9.

8. In the Associate Family Parameter dialog box, select **Width**, as shown in Figure 7–10, and click **OK**. Remain in the Type Properties dialog box.

Figure 7–9

Figure 7–10

9. Repeat the process and associate the **Height** parameters.

10. Associate the **Muntin Material** with the **Trim Material** and then click **OK** to close the Type Properties dialog box.

11. Open the Family Types dialog box and set the formula for the *Glass Height* to **Width - (Stiles *2)**, as shown in Figure 7–11.

Dimensions			≫
Glass Height	22 1/2"	= Width - (Stiles * 2)	☑
Width	32"	=	☑
Height	80"	=	☑
Rough Width	34"	= Width + 2"	☑
Rough Height	81"	= Height + 1"	☑
Thickness	1 3/8"	=	☑
Stiles	4 3/4"	=	☑
Top Rail	4 11/16"	=	☑

Figure 7–11

12. Click **Apply**. The grill should move to the top of the window. The panel and glass move up as well because they were locked to the former Bottom Rail reference plane.

13. Use the family types to flex the parameters and ensure that the square grill is working with th different door sizes.

14. Click **OK**.

15. Save the family.

Task 4 - Set the exterior grill placement.

1. Open the **Elevations: Exterior** view and select the grill. Note that it is still the full sized grill.

2. Change the grill to **Door Grill-Square**.

3. Change the *Visual Style* to **Wireframe** so you can see the square grill.

4. Align and lock the bottom of the grill to the reference plane, as shown in Figure 7–12.

Align to this reference plane

Figure 7–12

5. Flex the family to ensure that the grill is working correctly.

6. Return the *Visual Style* to **Hidden Line**.

7. Save the family.

8. Load and test the new door type in a project.

Practice 7b

Create Custom Windows

Practice Objectives

- Create a custom family based on a template.
- Add trim and glass to the window.

Estimated time for completion: 20 minutes

In this practice, you will create a new window family based on a family template. You will modify the existing opening, trim it, and add materials and glass to the window, as shown in Figure 7–13.

Figure 7–13

Task 1 - Create a custom window family.

1. Create a new family based on the **Window with Trim.rft** template found in the Autodesk Revit Library.
   - The family is also available in the practice files *Architectural* folder.

2. Save the family to the practice files folder as **Arched Window with Trim.rfa**.

3. Open the **Elevations: Exterior** view.

4. Edit the sketch of the **Opening Cut** element and lock the tangency locks, as shown in Figure 7–14. Delete the extra horizontal sketch line.

Figure 7–14

5. Click ✓ (Finish Edit Mode).

6. Add a dimension to the arc and label it **Radius** (a **Type** parameter in the *Dimensions* category).

7. Edit the **Trim: Extrusion** element and modify the sketch so that it matches the new arc opening, as shown in Figure 7–15.

Trim Width C

Figure 7–15

8. Click ✓ (Finish Edit Mode).

9. Open the Family Types dialog box and modify the **Radius** parameter to use the formula **Width/2**. Flex the model by trying different widths.

10. Set the final *Width* to **3'-0"** and click **OK**

11. Save the family.

12. Click 🔲 (Load into Project) and test it in the same project as the door you just created.

Task 2 - Add a material to the window trim.

1. View the project with the door(s) and window(s) in a 3D view.

2. Set the *Visual Style* to ☐ (Shaded). The door has glass in the windows and materials applied to it, but the window does not have glass or materials, as shown in Figure 7–16.

Figure 7–16

3. Select one of the windows. In the *Modify | Windows* tab> Mode panel, click ☐ (Edit Family).

4. In the Family Editor, open the **Elevations**: **Exterior** view.

5. Set the *Visual Style* to ☐ (Shaded).

6. Select the **Trim Projection : Extrusion**.

7. In Properties, next to the **Materials** parameter, select **<By Category>**. Click ☐ (Browse) at the end of the row.

8. In the Materials Browser, under *Autodesk Materials*, select **Wood** and click ☐ (Add material to document), as shown in Figure 7–17.

Click here if the Autodesk Materials library pane does not display

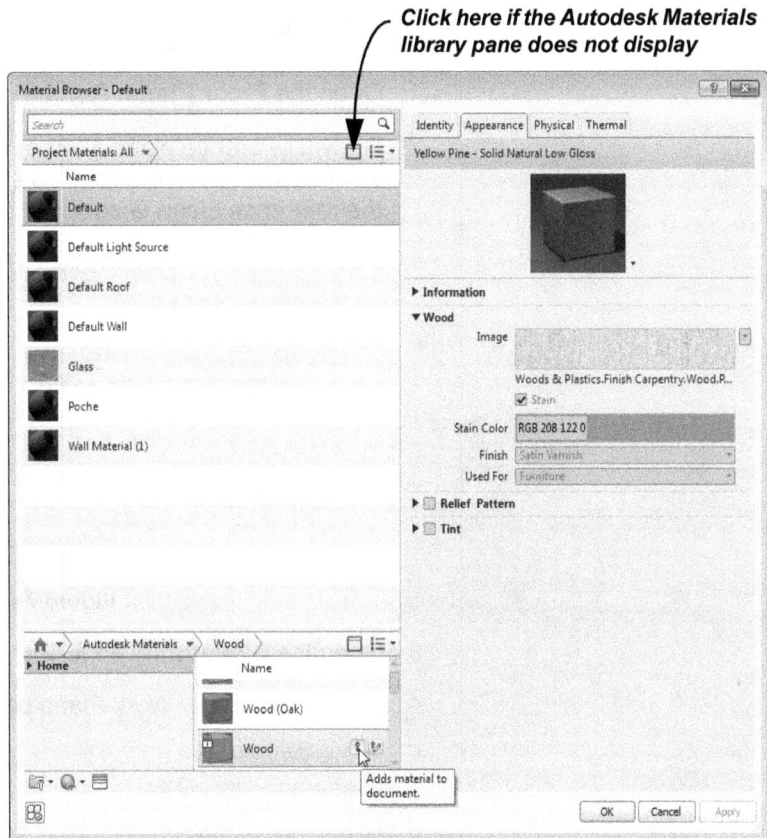

Figure 7–17

9. Select the new material. In the *Graphics* tab, in the *Shading* area, select **Use Render Appearance**, as shown in Figure 7–18.

By default this material only displays when the Visual Style is set to Realistic. By using the Render Appearance, the color displays when the Visual Style is set to Shaded or Consistent Colors.

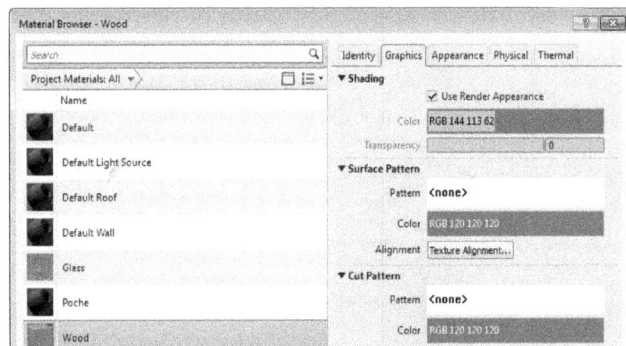

Figure 7–18

10. Close the Material Browser.

11. Save the window family file.

Task 3 - Add glass to the window.

1. Open the **Floor Plans: Ref. Level** view.

2. Draw a reference plane **1"** from the exterior face of the window and lock it in place, as shown in Figure 7–19. Name the reference plane **Glass**.

Figure 7–19

3. Open the **Elevations: Exterior** view.

4. In the *Create* tab>Work Plane panel, click ▦ (Set).

5. In the Work Plane dialog box, select the new reference plane **Glass** and click **OK**.

6. In the *Create* tab>Form panel, click ⬚ (Extrusion).

7. Sketch the outline of the glass inside the window.

8. In Properties, set the *Extrusion End* to **1/2"**.

9. In the Material Browser, open the *AEC Materials* library and select the *Glass* category.Select **Glass, Clear Glazing** and click 🔼 (Add material to document), as shown in Figure 7–20.

Figure 7–20

10. In the *Project Materials* list, select the **Glass, Clear Glazing** material and, in the *Graphics* tab, select **Use Render Appearance**.

11. Close the Material Browser.

12. Click ✔ (Finish Edit Mode). The glass material displays.

13. Save the family file.

14. Click 📥 (Load into Project) and select **Overwrite the existing version and its parameter values**. The new glass and trim material display in the project.

7.2 Creating Angled Cornices and Copings

You might have tried to add a wall sweep to a wall at an angle, and found that it does not work. The **Wall Sweep** command only works horizontally or vertically. For example, to add a cornice to the top of a wall following the angled profile, as shown in Figure 7–21, you need to use a workaround, such as an in-place family using a solid sweep. A solid sweep can also be used to create a coping on the top of a short wall running beside steps.

Attempting to place a wall sweep   In-place solid sweep family

Figure 7–21

Creating Fascias

Another way to create profiles along an angle is to use a workaround to create a roof fascia on a model line, as shown in Figure 7–22. Typically, a fascia is applied to a roof edge but it can also be applied to a model line placed anywhere in a project.

Figure 7–22

How To: Create a Fascia Type

The process is similar for creating new Gutter types.

1. Load the profile for the fascia.
   - Many options are available in the Autodesk Revit library *Profiles>*Roofs folder.

2. In the *Architecture* tab>Build panel, expand ⬛ (Roof) and click ⬛ (Roof: Fascia).

3. In Properties, click ⬛ (Edit Type).
4. In the Type Properties dialog box, click **Duplicate**.
5. In the Name dialog box, type a name and click **OK**.
6. In the Type Properties dialog box, select the appropriate profile, as shown in Figure 7–23.

Figure 7–23

7. Click **OK** and the new fascia type is ready to be used.

How To: Add a Fascia Using Model Lines

1. In the *Architecture* tab>Work Plane panel, click ⬛ (Set) and select the appropriate work plane.

2. In the *Architecture* tab>Model panel, click ⬛ (Model Line). Draw the model lines on the face of the wall where you want to add a fascia.
   - Check the height of the fascia profile first so that you know where to put the model lines.

3. In the *Architecture* tab>Build panel, expand ⬛ (Roof) and click ⬛ (Roof: Fascia).
4. Select the model lines.

Hint: Object Style Subcategories

When creating an in-place family, you might want the family member to be modified in Visibility/Graphic Overrides separately from the main component. For example, if you are creating a cornice or coping for a wall and want to be able to toggle it off separately from the wall, you can create an Object Style subcategory.

1. In the *Manage* tab>Settings panel, click ⊞ (Object Styles).
2. In the *Modify Subcategories* area, click **New**.
3. In the New Subcategory dialog box, type a *Name* and select the category it is going to be a *Subcategory of*, as shown in Figure 7–24.

Figure 7–24

4. Click **OK** twice to finish the command.
5. The object style is now available in Visibility/Graphic Overrides, as shown in Figure 7–25.

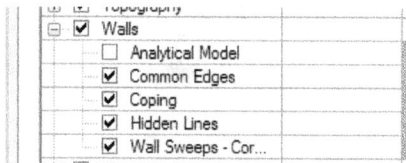

Figure 7–25

6. In the in-place family, select the object you want to add to the new subcategory. In Properties, under the *Identity Data* heading, select a *Subcategory* from the list (as shown in Figure 7–26), and then click **OK**.

Figure 7–26

Practice 7c

Create Angled Cornices and Copings

Estimated time for completion: 15 minutes

Practice Objectives

- Create a coping using an in-place family.
- Use Model Lines and Roof Fascia to add a Profile to a Sloped Wall.

In this practice, you will create a coping using an in-place family with a solid sweep. You will then add a profile to a sloped wall using the **Roof: Fascia** command and a model line, as shown in Figure 7–27.

Figure 7–27

Task 1 - Create a coping using an in-place family.

1. In the practice files *Architectural* folder, open **Plaza.rvt**. This is the beginning of a site design consisting of two slabs with retaining walls connected by a stair.

2. Open the **Floor Plans: Site** view. This project has three sections to help you draw additional elements.

3. Open the **Sections: East-West Site Section** view and zoom in on the lower wall, where you are going to add a stone coping to the top of the wall.

4. In the *Architecture* tab>Build panel, expand (Component) and click (Model In-Place).

5. In the Family Category and Parameters dialog box, select **Walls** and click **OK**.

6. Name the family **Coping**.

You are placed in the Family Editor with the corresponding tabs in the ribbon

7. In the *Create* tab>Forms panel, click (Sweep).

8. In the *Modify | Sweep* tab>Sweep panel, click (Sketch Path).

9. In the Work Plane dialog box, select **Pick a plane** and click **OK**. Select the face of the concrete retaining wall.

10. Draw the path, as shown in Figure 7–28.

Figure 7–28

11. Click (Finish Edit Mode).

12. In the Sweep panel, click (Edit Profile).

13. In the Go To View dialog box, select **Section: Wall Section** and click **Open View**.

14. Zoom in and draw the profile, as shown in Figure 7–29.

Figure 7–29

15. Finish the profile, sweep, and model.

16. Switch to a 3D view to see the coping in place.

Task 2 - Use Model Lines and Roof Fascia to add a profile to a Sloped Wall.

---

1. Open the **Sections: East-West Site Section** view and zoom in on the upper plaza.

2. In the *Insert* tab>Load from Library panel, click (Load Family). Navigate to the practice files *Architectural* folder and load the **Wall-Profile.rfa.**

3. In the *Architecture* tab>Model panel, click (Model Line).

4. In the Work Plane dialog box, select **Pick a Plane** and click **OK** and select the face of the concrete retaining wall.

5. Draw a model line from the left to the right, **7"** down from the top of the retaining wall.

If you use Pick Lines or draw from the right to the left, the fascia faces the wrong direction when it is applied.

6. In the *Architecture* tab>Model panel, expand 📄 (Roof) and click ⌄ (Roof: Fascia).

7. In Properties, click **Edit Type**.

8. In the Type Properties dialog box, create a new fascia type named **Wall Sweep** using the profile you loaded earlier, and set the *Material* to **Masonry-Stone**, as shown in Figure 7–30.

Type Parameters

Parameter	Value
Construction	☆
Profile	Wall-Design-Profile : Wall-Design
Materials and Finishes	☆
Material	Masonry - Stone

Figure 7–30

9. Once you have finished creating the **Roof Fascia** type, select the model line to place it in the project, as shown in Figure 7–31.

If you do not see the fascia, switch to a plan view, select it and click the Flip control.

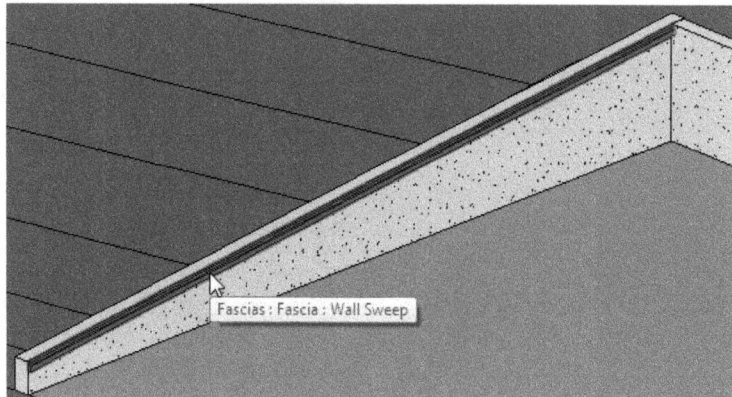

Figure 7–31

10. Save the project.

7.3 Creating Custom Railings

Creating a railing is more complex than creating a standard component family, as railings consist of several preset families for the rails, balusters, posts, and panels, as shown in Figure 7–32. Once you have the collection of families ready, you can create a Railing type.

Figure 7–32

- It helps to create all of the components for a Railing type (e.g., rails, handrails, top rails, posts, balusters, and panels) before creating the type.

Creating Rail Profiles

Top Rails, Handrails, and rails within a railing structure are all based on a rail profile. The rail profile is made of 2D elements that are swept along the railing lines, as shown in Figure 7–33.

Top Rails : Top Rail Type : Fancy

Figure 7–33

- Existing profiles for rails are found in the Autodesk Revit library in the *Profiles>Railings* folders.

- The **Profile-Rail.rft** template is specifically created for railings. The template indicates where to start drawing the outline, as shown in Figure 7–34.

Rail Centerline

Rail Top

Figure 7–34

- Rail profiles must be closed shapes.

- Once you have created a rail profile, you can apply it to a Top Rail or Handrail system family type.

Creating Baluster, Post, and Panel Families

Balusters and posts are created from solid elements made with extrusions and revolves. Having the correct reference planes is important for flexibility. Standard balusters also require void elements to cut the angle on stair railings.

There are three baluster templates for standard balusters, posts, and panels. The example in Figure 7–35 shows a custom baluster modified from an existing baluster family supplied with the Autodesk Revit software.

When you are creating a family, see if you can modify an existing one to suit your needs. This is much faster than creating a new family from scratch and helps you learn how to construct the specific family.

Original Baluster   *Modified Baluster*

Figure 7–35

The templates for these families include reference planes for the slope angles, as shown for a baluster panel in Figure 7–36. For stair railings, you can lock the solid elements to these angles so that they respond to the slope of the stair.

Baluster Panel Elevation

Figure 7–36

- Component families are found in the *Railings* folder, with subfolders for *Balusters*, *Supports*, and *Terminations*.

- To create elements from scratch, use the following family templates:
  - **Baluster.rft**
  - **Baluster-Panel.rft**
  - **Baluster-Post.rft**
  - **Railing Support.rft**
  - **Railing Termination.rft**

Hint: Adding Custom Posts

Posts are the point at which railings join. In many cases, this is the area in which railings need to change pitch and extend into adjacent railings, creating an integral, non-interrupted system. When designing a post, it is important to have a good grasp of creating custom families and to want to experiment. An example is shown in Figure 7–37.

Figure 7–37

- If you create a post as a post family, you cannot insert it as an independent component in the model. However, if you create a post as a generic model, you cannot use it in the Baluster dialog box and add it to a rail system. For this reason, it is recommended that you create the post family as an actual post, and then save a copy as a generic model. This gives you the option of using the post in any situation.

Creating Railing Types

To create a railing type, select an existing railing, duplicate it, and modify the Type properties, as shown in Figure 7–38. Click **Preview** to display a thumbnail of the railing.

Figure 7–38

- When editing a type, any changes that you make to one type impacts all instances of the railing type, as shown in Figure 7–39. Make duplicate copies of the top rail and railing type before making changes so that you can have one without extensions, as shown in Figure 7–40.

Figure 7–39   **Figure 7–40**

How To: Set the Rail Structure (Non-Continuous)

1. In the Type Properties dialog box, next to the **Rail Structure (Non-Continuous)** parameter, click **Edit...**.
2. In the Edit Rails (Non-Continuous) dialog box, click **Insert** to add a new rail to the list. You can have a single rail or multiple rails in a Railing type, as shown in Figure 7–41.

   - If there are no other horizontal members, this dialog box remains empty.

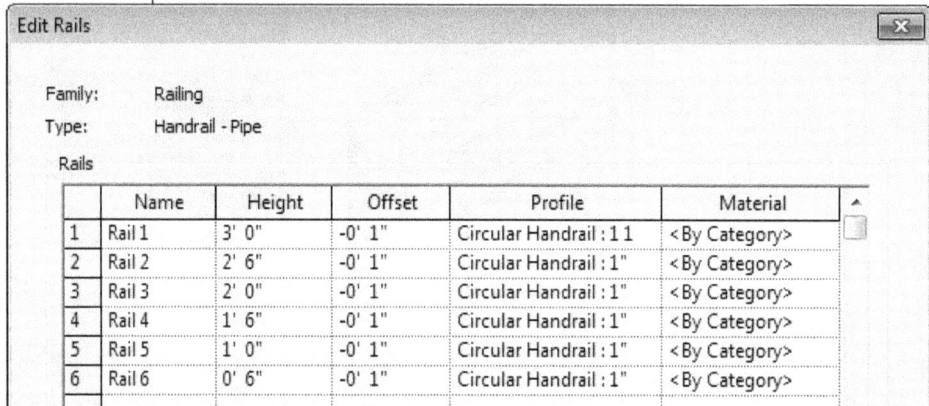

Edit Rails   [X]

Family: Railing

Type: Handrail - Pipe

Rails

	Name	Height	Offset	Profile	Material
1	Rail 1	3' 0"	-0' 1"	Circular Handrail : 1 1	<By Category>
2	Rail 2	2' 6"	-0' 1"	Circular Handrail : 1"	<By Category>
3	Rail 3	2' 0"	-0' 1"	Circular Handrail : 1"	<By Category>
4	Rail 4	1' 6"	-0' 1"	Circular Handrail : 1"	<By Category>
5	Rail 5	1' 0"	-0' 1"	Circular Handrail : 1"	<By Category>
6	Rail 6	0' 6"	-0' 1"	Circular Handrail : 1"	<By Category>

Figure 7–41

3. Fill out the information about the rails as required:

Name	The name of the individual railing component. Select the name to modify it.
Height	The height for each rail from the base height.
Offset	The distance from the rail sketch line.
Profile	Select a profile in the drop-down list. You need to have the profile loaded before you can use it. (This is just a profile family, not a rail type as is required when you specify the top rails and handrails.)
Material	Specify a material for the rail. This is the only place where you can apply the material for rails.

4. Click **Up** and **Down** to move the rail to the correct location in the group.
5. Click **OK** to finish the command.

How To: Edit the Baluster Placement

1. In the Type Properties dialog box, next to the **Baluster Placement** parameter, click **Edit...**. The Edit Baluster Placement dialog box has two main areas: *Main pattern* and *Posts*, as shown in Figure 7–42.

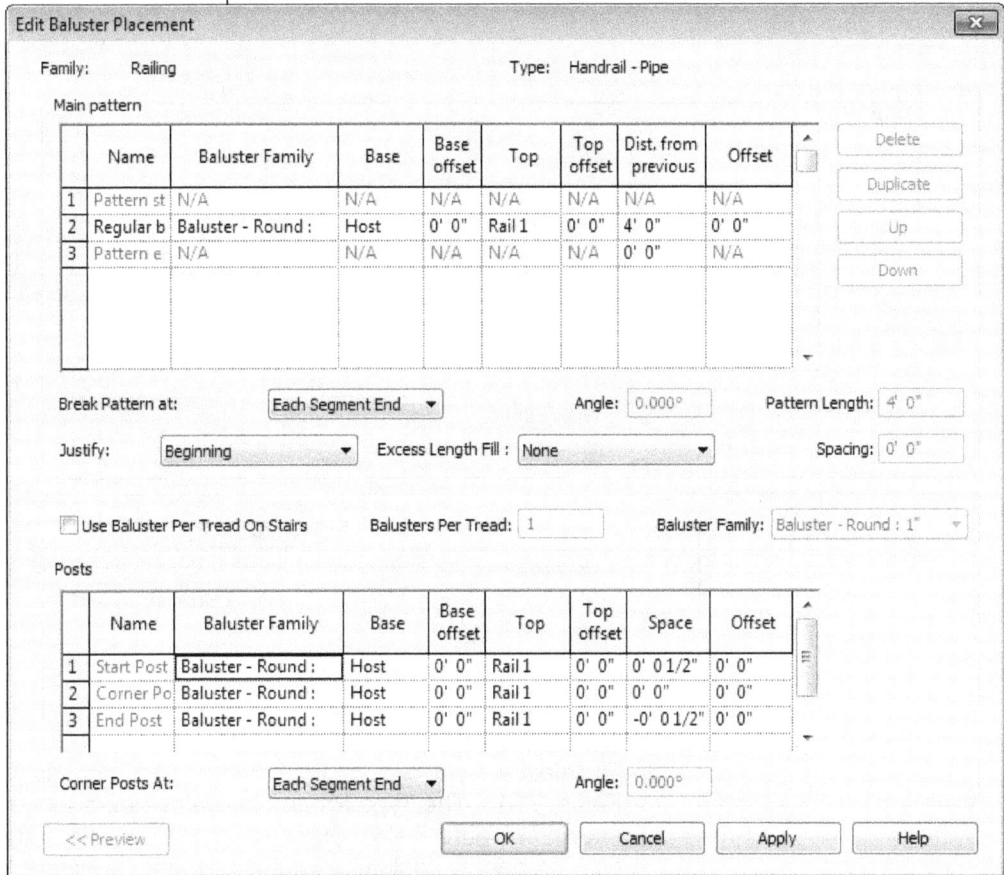

Figure 7–42

2. In the *Main pattern* area, add the baluster family and its sizes, such as the distance from the previous baluster. You can also add panels in this area.
3. If you are using a baluster on stairs and want a specific number per tread, select **Use Baluster Per Tread On Stairs** and specify the number per tread.
4. In the *Posts* area, specify the profiles for the *Start*, *Corner*, and *End* posts, and then specify their dimensions and locations.

How To: Set the Top Rail and Handrail

1. In the Type Properties dialog box, set up the information for *Top Rail, Handrail 1*, and *Handrail 2*, as shown in Figure 7–43.

The Top Rail is either the top of a guardrail (specify the handrail separately) or the top of the handrail (no separate handrail type needed).

Type Properties		×
Family:	System Family: Railing	Load...
Type:	Guardrail - Pipe	Duplicate...
		Rename...

Type Parameters

Parameter	Value	=
Top Rail		»
Use Top Rail	Yes	
Height	3' 6"	
Type	Circular - 1 1/2"	
Handrail 1		»
Lateral Offset	0' 3"	
Height	3' 0"	
Position	Left	
Type	Circular - 1 1/2" ...	
Handrail 2		»
Lateral Offset	*Browse*	
Height		
Position	None	
Type	<None>	

Figure 7–43

Enhanced in 2018

2. To select a *Type*, click on the Browse (...) button, as shown in Figure 7–44. The Type Properties dialog box displays (as shown in Figure 7–44), where you can duplicate and modify type properties (including Extensions and Terminations).

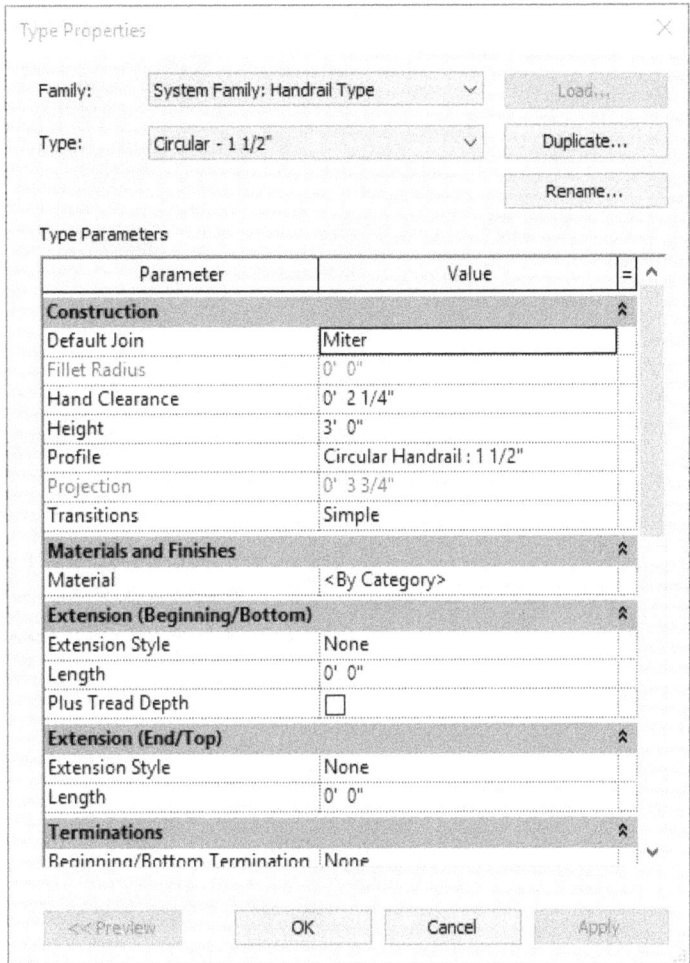

Figure 7–44

- In the *Extension (Beginning/Bottom)* area, set the *Extension Style*. The properties are **None**, **Wall**, **Floor**, and **Post**, as shown in Figure 7–45.

Wall

Floor

Post

Figure 7–45

- A Termination can be added if required. The default rectangular termination works best with the Floor Extension Style, but you can also create custom ones.
- For Handrail types, you can also specify *Supports*, as shown in Figure 7–46. These are typically used if you are creating a wall-based railing type.

Supports	
Family	Support - Metal - Circular
Layout	Align With Posts
Spacing	None
Justification	Fixed Distance
Number	Align With Posts
	Fixed Number
Identity Data	Maximum Spacing
Keynote	Minimum Spacing

Figure 7–46

3. If you are creating a guardrail, you also need to specify the *Type* and *Position* of the handrail. The handrail can be set to **Left**, **Right**, or **Left and Right** of the main railing as shown in Figure 7–47. The **Lateral Offset** and **Height** are read-only parameters.

Handrail 1	
Lateral Offset	0' 3"
Height	3' 0"
Position	Left
Type	None
Handrail 2	Left
Lateral Offset	Right
Height	Left and Right
Position	None
Type	None

Figure 7–47

- If you do not want to include a separate handrail in the railing type, set the *Type* to **None**.

Hint: Additional Clean up Options

When railings are not cleaning up as expected, ensure that the Stair Properties are correct. For example, *Rail Connections* can be set to **Trim** (as shown in Figure 7–48) or **Weld**. The **Weld** option forces a miter joint, rather than a butt joint.

Type Parameters	
Parameter	Value
Construction	
Railing Height	0' 0"
Rail Structure (Non-Continuous)	Edit...
Baluster Placement	Edit...
Baluster Offset	0' 0"
Use Landing Height Adjustment	No
Landing Height Adjustment	0' 0"
Angled Joins	Add Vertical/Horizontal Segments
Tangent Joins	Extend Rails to Meet
Rail Connections	Trim

Figure 7–48

When a straight rail joins an arc rail, the Autodesk Revit software tends to distort the geometry. To fix this, select the segment of a rail in the railing's Sketch mode and modify the *Height Correction* in the Options Bar, as shown in Figure 7–49.

Slope: By Host	Height Correction: By Type	0.0

Figure 7–49

Practice 7d	# Create Custom Railings

Practice Objectives

- Duplicate and modify existing baluster and baluster panel families.
- Create a custom railing type using the baluster and baluster panel families.

Estimated time for completion: 25 minutes

In this practice, you will make copies of existing baluster and baluster panel families and modify them slightly. You will also create new Top Rail and Handrail types. You will then use the various families and types to create a new Railing type, as shown in Figure 7–50.

Figure 7–50

Task 1 - Set the material of a baluster family.

1. In the practice files *Architectural* folder, open **Modern-Hotel-Railings.rvt**.

2. Open the **3D Views: Hall Balcony** view. This is the railing style you are going to use to create a new railing style.

3. Switch to the **Floor Plans: Floor 2** view. Families cannot be opened when you are in a 3D camera view.

4. In the *File* tab, expand 📂 (Open) and click 🖳 (Family).

5. In the Library, expand the *Railings>Balusters* folder and open **Baluster-Round.rfa**.

   • The family is also available in the practice files practice files *Architectural* folder.

6. Save the file as **Baluster-Round-Wood.rfa** in your practice files folder.

7. In the Baluster family file, in the *Manage* tab>Settings panel, click ⊚ (Materials). A short list of materials is available in the family and no wood materials are available.

8. In the Material Browser, expand *Autodesk Materials* and select **Wood**, as shown in Figure 7–51.

Figure 7–51

9. In the selection set next to **Birch**, select **Adds material to document**, as shown in Figure 7–52.

Figure 7–52

10. In the *Project Materials* area, select the **Birch** material and in the *Graphics* tab, select **Use Render Appearance**, as shown in Figure 7–53.

Figure 7–53

11. Click **OK**.

12. In the *Create* tab>Properties panel, click ⊞ (Family Types).

13. In the Family Types dialog box, change the current type to **2"**.

14. Beside the *Type name*, click ⬚ (New Type) and name the new type **2" - Birch**.

15. Set the *Baluster Material* to **Birch**, as shown in Figure 7–54.

The material for balusters cannot be set in the railing style, only in the family.

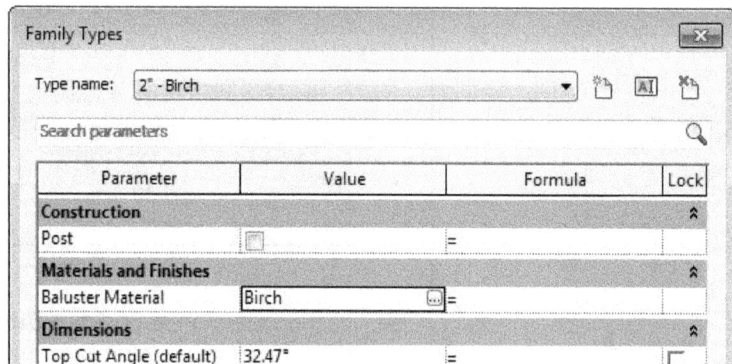

Figure 7–54

16. Click **OK**.

17. In the View Control Bar, set the *Visual Style* to ⬚ (Consistent Colors) and then to ⬚ (Realistic) to display the new wood shade.

18. Save the baluster family.

19. In the *Create* tab>Family Editor panel, click ⬆️ (Load into Project and Close).

20. If the Modern Hotel project is the only one you have open, the family automatically loads and switches to the project file. If you have others open, select the Modern Hotel project from the list and click **OK**.

Task 2 - Modify a baluster panel family.

---

1. In the Revit Library's *Railings>Balusters* subfolder, open the family file **Baluster Panel - Glass w Brackets.rfa.**

    • The family is also available in the practice files practice files *Architectural* folder.

2. Save it as **Baluster Panel - Glass with Open Brackets.rfa** in your practice files folder.

3. Open the **Elevations: Left** view.

4. Zoom in on one of the brackets and select it.

5. In the *Modify | Extrusion* tab>Mode panel, click 📝 (Edit Extrusion).

6. Sketch a **3/4"** radius circle inside the bracket, as shown in Figure 7–55. This creates a hole in the extrusion.

*To snap to the center of the arc, type the shortcut **SC** for Snap to Center.*

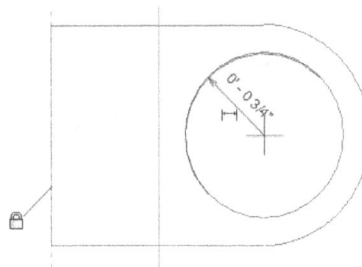

Figure 7–55

7. Click ✔ (Finish Edit Mode).

8. Repeat the process with the other three brackets.

9. Open the **3D Views: View 1** view and set the *Visual Style* to ◻ (Consistent Colors). The panel displays with the opening in the brackets, as shown in Figure 7–56.

Figure 7–56

10. In the *Modify* tab>Properties panel, click ▦ (Family Types).

11. Create a new family type named **36" w 1" Gap**.

12. In the Family Types dialog box, change the *Width* to **3'-0"**.

13. Click **Apply**. The panel updates, as shown in Figure 7–57. Click **OK**.

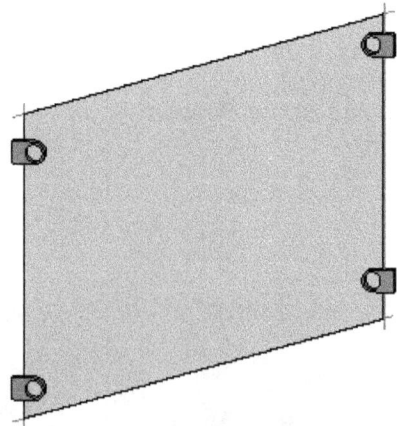

Figure 7–57

14. Save the baluster panel and load it into the Modern Hotel project.

Task 3 - Create Top Rail and Handrail types.

1. In the Modern Hotel project, in the Project Browser, expand **Families>Railings>Top Rail Type** node.

2. Right-click on **Circular - 1 1/2"** and select **Type Properties**.

3. In the Type Properties dialog box, duplicate the type, and name it **Circular - 1 1/2" - Birch**.

4. Change the *Material* to **Birch** and set the *Extension (Beginning/Bottom)* and *Extension (End/Top)* to **Wall**, as shown in Figure 7–58.

Figure 7–58

5. Click **OK**.

6. Repeat the process to create a new Birch Handrail type.

7. Save the project.

Task 4 - Create custom Railing types.

1. In the Modern Hotel project, open the **3D Views: Hall Balcony** view.

2. Select the railing.

3. In Properties, click 🔲 (Edit Type).

4. In the Type properties dialog box, click **Duplicate** and name the new railing type **Hotel Balcony Guardrail - Glass Panel**.

5. Next to the **Rail Structure (Non-Continuous)** parameter, click **Edit...**.

6. In the Edit Rails dialog box, delete all of the Rails and click **OK**.

7. Click **OK**. The new railing displays with wooden guardrail and handrail and existing posts, as shown in Figure 7–59.

Figure 7–59

8. Select the railing and edit the Railing type again.

9. Next to the **Baluster Placement** parameter, click **Edit...**.

10. In the *Main pattern* area, next to *Regular Baluster* (in the *Baluster Family* column), change the type to **Baluster-Round-Wood: 2"-Birch**, as shown in Figure 7–60.

Figure 7–60

11. Click **Duplicate**.

12. In row *2*, change the *Name* to **Panel** and the *Baluster Family* to **Baluster Panel-Glass w Open Brackets: 36" w 1" Gap**.

13. Click **OK** twice and view the railings. The panel displays, but it is not in the correct location in relation to the posts, as shown in Figure 7–61.

Figure 7–61

Distances between balusters is measured from center to center.

14. Edit the type again and open the Edit Baluster Placement dialog box. In the *Dist. from Previous* column, you can see that the settings are now **4'-0"** for both the baluster and the panel. Therefore, the baluster and panel placement is spread out.

15. Set the *Dist. from Previous* to **1'-7 1/8"** for both the baluster and panel.

16. Set *Justify* to **Beginning** and *Excess Length Fill* to **None**, as shown in Figure 7–62.

Main pattern

	Name	Baluster Family	Base	Base offset	Top	Top offset	Dist. from previous	Offset	
1	Pattern sta	N/A	N/A	N/A	N/A	N/A	N/A	N/A	Delete
2	Panel	Baluster Panel - Gla	Host	0' 0"	Top Rai	0' 0"	1' 7 1/8"	0' 0"	Duplicate
3	Regular ba	Baluster - Round -	Host	0' 0"	Top Rai	0' 0"	1' 7 1/8"	0' 0"	Up
4	Pattern en	N/A	N/A	N/A	N/A	N/A	0' 0"	N/A	Down

Break Pattern at: [Each Segment End ▼]   Angle: [0.000°]   Pattern Length: [3' 2 1/4"]

Justify: [Beginning ▼]   Excess Length Fill : [None ▼]   Spacing: [0' 0"]

Figure 7–62

17. While still in the Edit Baluster Placement dialog box, in the *Posts* area, change the *Baluster Family* for all of the posts to **Baluster - Round - Wood: 2" - Birch** and click **OK**.

18. In the Type Properties dialog box, change the *Top Rail Type* to the new **Circular - 1 1/2" - Birch** top rail type and *Handrail 1* to the new **Circular - 1 1/2" - Birch** handrail type.

19. Close the dialog boxes and view the new Railing type. This time, the baluster to panel fit is better, as shown in Figure 7–63.

Figure 7–63

20. Save the project.

Chapter Review Questions

1. The door family shown in Figure 7–64 does not exist in the default library. Which one of the following methods should you use to create the door family?

Figure 7–64

a. Start a new door family based on the default door template and build it from there.

b. Copy the existing **Single-Flush.rfa** family as the base and draw the panel outlines using detail lines.

c. Copy an existing panel-style family and modify the panel extrusions.

d. Start a new door family based on the **Single-Panel.rfa** template and modify the panel extrusions.

2. Based on the information in the Family Types dialog box (shown in Figure 7–65), if you changed the *Trim Projection Ext* value, would the *Trim Projection Int* also update?

Family Types

Type name: 36" x 48"

Search parameters

Parameter	Value	Formula	Lock
Dimensions			
Height	4' 0"	=	✓
Default Sill Height	3' 0"	=	✓
Trim Projection - Ext.	0' 0 1/2"	=	✓
Trim Projection - Int.	0' 0 3/4"	=	✓
Trim Width - Exterior	0' 3 1/2"	=	✓
Trim Width - Interior	0' 3 1/2"	=	✓
Width	3' 0"	=	✓
Window Inset	0' 0 3/4"	=	✓
Rough Width		=	✓
Rough Height		=	✓

Figure 7–65

   a. Yes

   b. No

3. Which of the following must be in place before you can add a fascia to an angled wall? (Select all that apply.)

   a. A profile

   b. A fascia type

   c. A wall sweep

   d. A model line

4. Which of the following parts of a railing type (shown in Figure 7–66) is created by a profile?

Figure 7–66

   a. Rail

   b. Post

   c. Baluster

   d. Baluster panel

5. What is the main difference between a Baluster family and a Post Family?

   a. A Baluster is created using a profile and a Post is created using solid forms.

   b. A Baluster has top and bottom angles programmed into the family, while a Post does not have any angles.

   c. Balusters can be placed on stair treads, but posts can only be placed on landings.

   d. Balusters are typically placed 4" apart, and Posts are placed 3'-0" apart.

Command Summary

Button	Command	Location
	Roof: Fascia	• **Ribbon:** *Architecture* tab>Build panel
	Object Styles	• **Ribbon:** *Manage* tab>Settings panel
	Model Line	• **Ribbon:** *Architecture* tab>Model panel

Creating MEP Specific Families

MEP families include elements such as plumbing fixtures, light fixtures, data devices, and pipe fittings. By working through practices, you can learn how to upgrade an architectural plumbing fixture to use connectors, create a custom light fixture, and create a data device with annotation options. For an advanced challenge you can also create a pipe fitting flange. Select the practices that you find most helpful and relevant to your work.

Learning Objectives in this Chapter

- Upgrade an architectural plumbing fixture with MEP connectors.
- Create a custom lighting fixture.
- Create a data device family that includes a tag in the family.
- Create a pipe fitting flange.

Practice 8a

Upgrade an Architectural Plumbing Fixture to MEP

Practice Objective

*   Upgrade an existing architectural toilet fixture with pipe sizes and connectors for use in a MEP project.

Estimated time for completion: 15 minutes

In this practice, you will upgrade an existing architectural toilet fixture to be used in an MEP project. You will create parameters for pipe sizes. You will also add connectors for cold water and Sanitary systems, as shown in Figure 8–1.

Figure 8–1

Task 1 - Create parameters for pipe sizes.

1. In the practice files *MEP* folder, open **Toilet-Commercial-Wall-3D.rfa**.

2. Save the family as **Toilet-Commercial-Wall-3D-MEP.rfa**.

3. In the Family Types dialog box, add the following Type parameters:

Name	Discipline	Type of Parameter	Group
Sanitary Radius	Piping	Pipe Size	Dimensions
Cold Water Radius	Piping	Pipe Size	Dimensions

4. Set *Sanitary Radius* to **2"** and *Cold Water Radius* to **1/2"**. Lock the parameters.

The related diameter parameters need to be Shared because they are often used in plumbing fixture schedules.

5. Add shared type parameters selected from the **MEP.txt** parameter file:
   - Sanitary Diameter
   - Cold Water Diameter

6. Create formulas for *Sanitary Diameter* and *Cold Water Diameter* based on the corresponding radius parameters, as shown in Figure 8–2.

Dimensions			☆
Sanitary Radius	2"	=	☑
Sanitary Diameter	4"	= Sanitary Radius * 2	☑
Cold Water Radius	1/2"	=	☑
Cold Water Diameter	1"	= Cold Water Radius * 2	☑
Mounting Height	1' 3"	=	☑

Figure 8–2

7. Click **OK**.

8. Save the family.

Task 2 - Add connectors.

1. Rotate the view so that the back of the toilet is displayed. (If the wall displays, hide it temporarily or set the *Visual Style* to **Wireframe** while you are adding connectors.)

2. In the *Create* tab>Connectors panel, click ⚙ (Pipe Connector).

3. In the Options Bar, select **Domestic Cold Water**.

4. Hover the cursor over the face of the pipe opening, as shown in Figure 8–3, and click to place the connector.

Figure 8–3

5. Click ⌖ (Modify) and select the Connector.

6. In Properties, set the following values for parameters:
   - *Flow Configuration*: **Fixture Units**
   - *Flow Direction:* **In**
   - Clear the **Allow Slope Adjustments** option.
   - *Fixture Units:* **2.5**

7. In the *Dimensions* area, and next to *Diameter*, click
   ⬚ (Associate Parameter).

8. In the Associate Family Parameter dialog box, select **Cold Water Diameter**, as shown in Figure 8–4, and click **OK**.

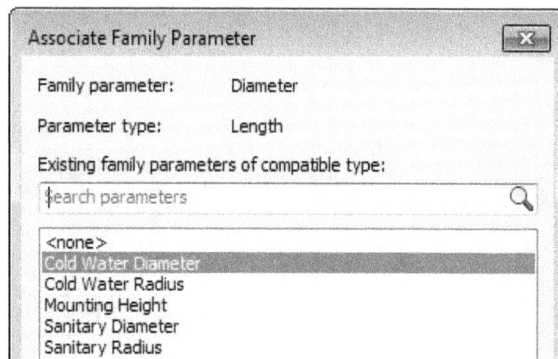

Figure 8–4

9. The connector resizes to fit the correct pipe size.

10. Add a Pipe Connector for a Sanitary system to the back of the fixture, as shown in Figure 8–5.

Figure 8–5

11. Select the connector and set the following properties.
    - *Diameter:* Associate with **Sanitary Diameter** parameter
    - *Flow Configuration:* **Fixture Units**
    - *Flow Direction:* **Out**
    - Select **Allow Slope Adjustments**.
    - *System Classification:* **Sanitary**
    - *Fixture Units:* **4**

12. Add any other parameters or values required to make this a more useful MEP fixture.

13. Save the family.

14. Test the fixture in a project.

Practice 8b

Upgrade an Architectural Lighting Fixture to MEP

Practice Objectives

- Modify the light source.
- Apply a power connector.
- Create family types with different materials for the pendant and glass shade.

Estimated time for completion: 10 minutes

In this practice, you will modify a lighting fixture family with a specific light source and connector, as shown in Figure 8–6. You will also create family types using different materials.

Figure 8–6

Task 1 - Set up a new light fixture family.

1. In the practice files *MEP* folder, open the family **Pendant-Light-Fixture.rfa**.

2. Open the **Elevations: Front** view. It includes reference planes for the Ceiling and Light Source, a ceiling element, the fixture elements, and the Ref. Level, as shown in Figure 8–7.

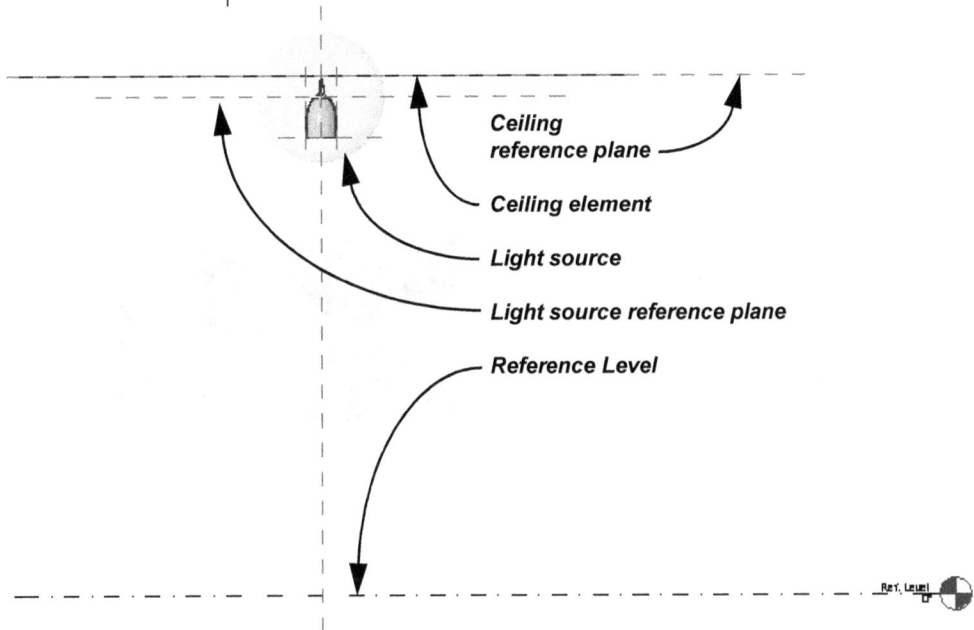

Ceiling reference plane

Ceiling element

Light source

Light source reference plane

Reference Level

Ref. Level

Figure 8–7

3. Select the light source. In the *Modify | Light Source* tab> Lighting panel, click (Light Source Definition).

4. In the Light Source Definition dialog box, change the Light distribution to ![icon] (Photometric Web), as shown in Figure 8–8 and click **OK**.

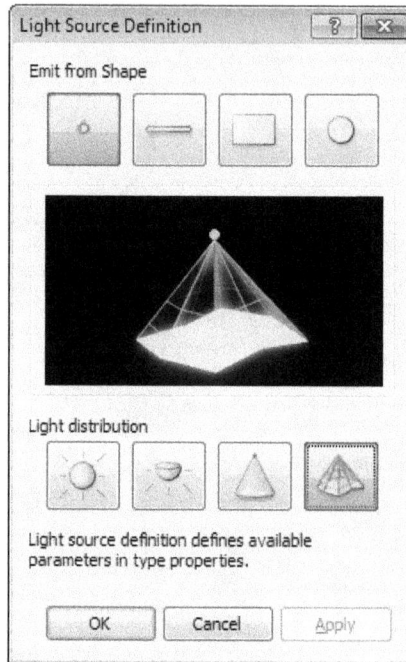

Figure 8–8

5. Open the Family Types dialog box and set the following values for the parameters:

   - *Lamp:* **CF42TRT**
   - *Apparent Load:* **44.21 VA**
   - *Tilt Angle:* **90**
   - *Photometric Web File:* Click ![...] and select **spot_ideal.ies**.
   - *Light Loss Factor:* **0.85**
   - *Initial Intensity:* **Luminous Flux, 3200**

6. Save the family.

Task 2 - Add a connector.

1. Open a 3D view and set the *Visual Style* to **Wireframe**.

2. In the *Create* tab>Connectors panel, click ![icon] (Electrical Connector).

3. In the Options Bar, select **Power - Balanced**.

4. Attach the connector to the face of the pendant at the point where the pendant touches the ceiling, as shown in Figure 8–9.

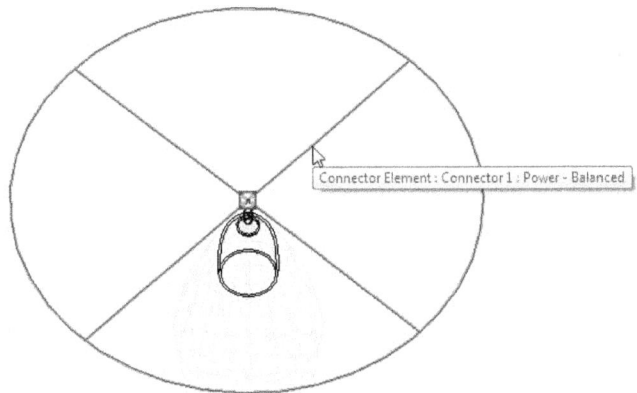

Connector Element : Connector 1 : Power - Balanced

Figure 8–9

5. Click (Modify) and select the connector.

6. In Properties specify the values for the following parameters:
   • *System Type:* **Power - Balanced (verify)**
   • *Load Classification:* **Lighting**
   • *Voltage:* **277**
   • *Power Factor:* **0.95**

7. While still in Properties, beside the *Apparent Load* parameter, click (Associate Family Parameter).

8. In the Associate Family Parameter dialog box, select **Apparent Load**. Click **OK**.

9. Save the family.

Task 3 - Create Family types.

1. In the *Create* tab>Properties panel, click ⬚ (Family Types).

2. In the Family Types dialog box, click 📄 (New Type).

3. In the Name dialog box, enter **Brass and Green Glass** as the name.

4. In the *Materials and Finishes* area, verify or set the following values for the parameters, as shown in Figure 8–10:

   - **Pendent Material:** Metal - Brass
   - **Glass Material:** Glass - Green

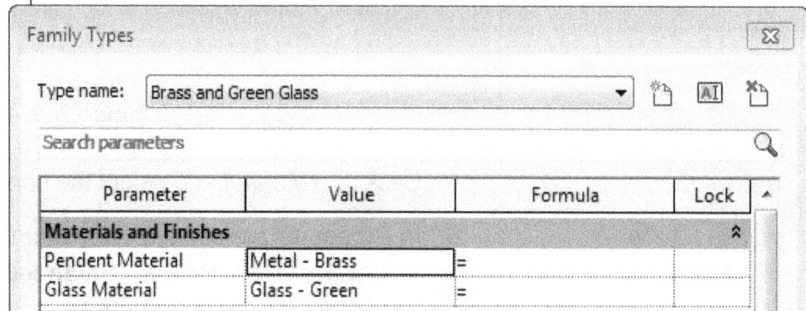

Figure 8–10

5. Click **Apply**.

6. Create several other Family Types that use different colors of glass and different pendent materials.Save the family.

Practice 8c

Create a Data Device with Annotation Parameters

Estimated time for completion: 20 minutes

Practice Objective

- Create a data device with both solid elements and annotation elements.

In this practice, you will create a data device using reference planes, extrusions, and connectors. You will then add an annotation symbol to the family with its related parameters, as shown in Figure 8–11. You will also test the family in a project.

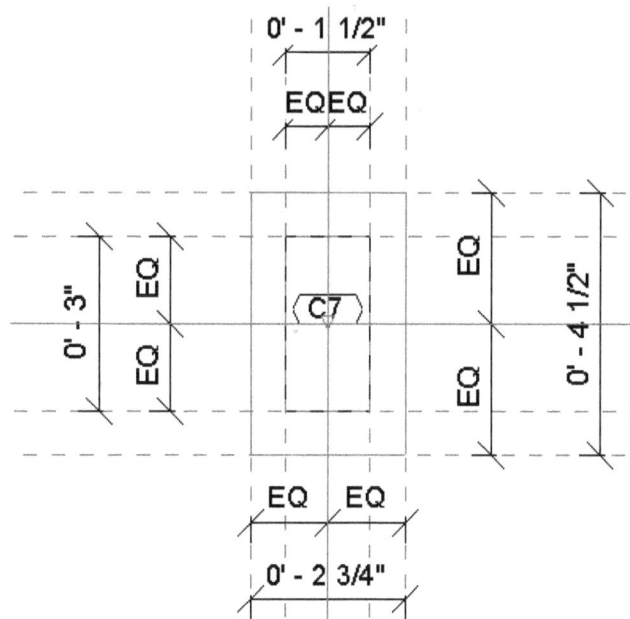

Figure 8–11

Task 1 - Set up reference planes.

1. Create a new family based on the **Data Device Hosted.rft** template found in the Autodesk Revit Library.

2. Save the family to your practice folder as **Data Receptacle Type C.rfa.**

3. Set the *Length* units to **Fractional Inches**.

4. In the **Floor Plans: Ref. Level** view, set the *View Scale* to **3"=1'-0"**.

5. Zoom in closer to the intersection of the reference planes.

6. Create and dimension the reference planes, as shown in Figure 8–12. You do not need to label these dimensions as all of the data receptacles are the same size.

Figure 8–12

7. Save the family.

Task 2 - Create the model extrusions.

---

1. Create the two extrusions shown in Figure 8–13. Set the *Depth* of the extrusions as follows:

   • Extrusion 1 = (negative) **-2 1/8"**
   • Extrusion 2 = **3/16"**

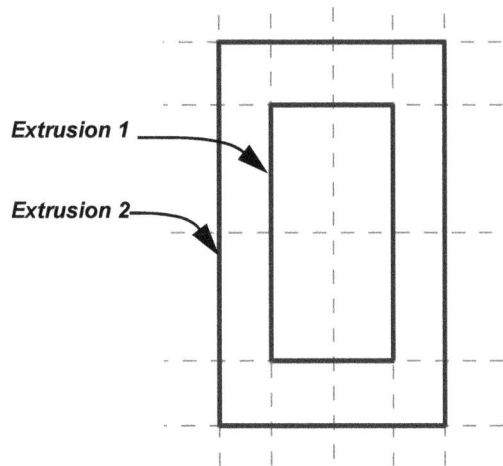

Figure 8–13

2. Open a 3D view and set the *Visual Style* to **Wireframe**. The finished view displays as shown in Figure 8–14.

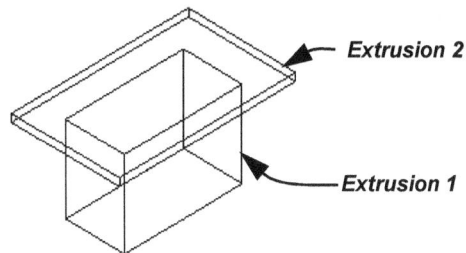

Figure 8–14

3. In the *Create* tab>Connectors panel, click 🖈 (Electrical Connector).

4. In the Options Bar, select **Data**.

5. Select the face of the top extrusion.

6. Click ⌕ (Modify) and select both extrusions.

7. In the *Modify | Extrusion* tab>Mode panel, click 🖿 (Visibility Settings).

8. In the Family Element Visibility Settings dialog box, clear **Front/Back**, **Coarse**, and **Medium**. Click **OK**.

   • This causes the 3D elements to display only at the Fine detail level where it is often used to coordinate the placement of items by their real dimensions. At the Coarse and Medium detail levels the tag is more useful.

9. Return to the **Ref. Level** view.

10. Save the family.

Task 3 - Create an Annotation symbol.

---

1. Create a new family based on the **Generic Annotation.rft** template found in the *Annotations* folder of the Autodesk Revit Library.

2. Save the family to your practice folder as **Data Device Annotation.rfa.**

3. Read and delete the red note. You will not modify the Family Category in this case because you need it to remain a generic annotation.

4. Draw the sketch as shown in Figure 8–15.

Do not add the dimensions, they are for information only.

Figure 8–15

5. In the *Create* tab>Text panel, click ![label icon] (Label).

6. Click inside the new symbol sketch.

7. In the Edit Label dialog box there are no parameters listed. Click ![add parameter icon] (Add Parameter).

Ensure that this is an instance parameter.

8. Create an Instance parameter named **Tag**, set *Type of Parameter* as **Text**, and set *Group parameter under* as **Identity Data**. Click **OK**.

9. Back in the Edit Label dialog box, add the parameter to the label, set the *Sample Value* to **A1**, as shown in Figure 8–16, and click **OK**.

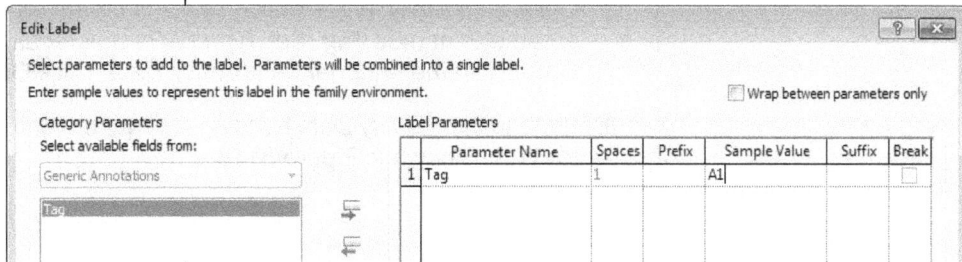

Figure 8–16

10. Select the new label and, in Properties, click 🖻 (Edit Type). In the Type Properties dialog box, set the *Background* to **Transparent** and click **OK**.

11. Relocate the label to fit inside the symbol sketch.

12. With nothing selected, in Properties, select **Rotate with component** and **Keep text readable.**

13. Save the annotation family and load it into the data receptacle family.

Task 4 - Add the Label Family to the Data Receptacle.

---

1. In the data receptacle family, place a copy of the Data Device Annotation family at the center of the elements, as shown in Figure 8–17.

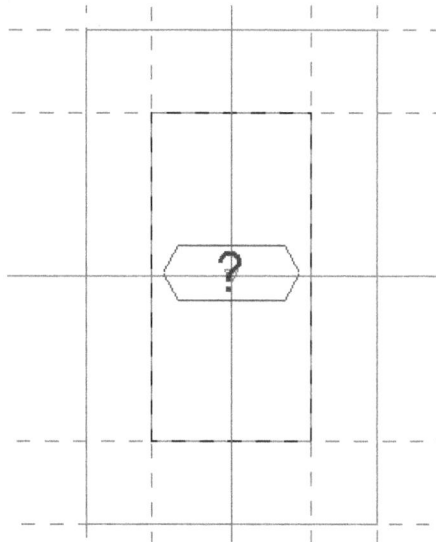

Figure 8–17

---

2. Open the Family Types dialog box and create an Instance parameter named **Tag**. Set *Type of Parameter* as **Text** and *Group parameter under* as **Identity Data**. Click **OK**.

3. Expand the *Identity Data* heading (if required) and set the *Tag* to **C7**, as shown in Figure 8–18.

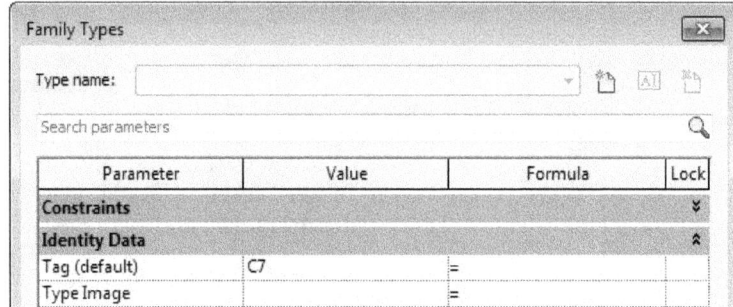

Family Types			
Type name:			
Search parameters			
Parameter	Value	Formula	Lock
Constraints			≫
Identity Data			≫
Tag (default)	C7	=	
Type Image		=	

Figure 8–18

4. Close the dialog box.

5. Select the Data Device Annotation element.

6. In Properties, under the *Identity Data* heading, beside the

    Tag parameter, click ⬚ (Associate Family Parameter).

7. In the Associate Family Parameter dialog box, select **Tag** and click **OK**.

8. When you finish, the parameters are associated together and the tag displays as **C7**, as shown in Figure 8–19.

Figure 8–19

9. If time permits, you can create Family Types for C1, C2, C3, C4, C5, C6, and C7. Change the value of the **Tag** parameter for each of these, as required.

10. Save the family.

Task 5 - Test the family.

1. Create a new project using the **Electrical-Default.rte** or **Systems-Default.rte** template.

2. Open the **Floor Plans: 1- Power** view and close the **1-Mech** view. (Data devices do not display in Mechanical views.)

3. Add a couple of walls.

4. Switch to the data receptacle family and load it into the project.

5. Add it several times using different types if you have created them.

6. Save the project and the family and close the files.

Practice 8d

Estimated time for completion: 90-120 minutes

Create a Pipe Fitting Flange (Advanced)

Practice Objectives

- Create reference planes, dimensions, and labels.
- Draw single-line representations for Coarse and Medium detail levels.
- Create solids for the Fine detail level.
- Create and apply Family Types.

In this practice, you will create a family file based on a template and add parameters, some of which include formulas. You will then add reference planes, dimensions, and labels and create family types to help you flex the framework. You will then create the flange components: a single-line representation for **Coarse** and **Medium** detail levels, and an extrusion and blend solid elements for **Fine** detail level, as shown in Figure 8–20. Finally, you will test the flanges in a project and draw pipe between them.

Figure 8–20

Task 1 - Open a family template.

1. Create a new family based on the **Plumbing Fixture.rft** template found in the Autodesk Revit Library.

2. Save the family to your practice folder as **Pipe Fitting Flange.rfa**.

3. In the *Create* tab>Properties panel, click ⬛ (Family Category and Parameters).

4. In the Family Category and parameters dialog box, set the *Filter list* to **Piping** and in the *Family Category* area, select **Pipe Fittings**.

5. In the *Family Parameters* area, set the following options:
   - Clear the **Work Plane-Based** option.
   - Select **Always Vertical**.
   - For the *Part Type*, select **Transition**.
   - Clear the **Shared** option.

6. Click **OK**.

7. Type **UN** to open the Project Units dialog box.

8. Change the format of *Length* to **Fractional inches**, and set it to the nearest **1/16"**.

9. Set the *Discipline* to **Piping** and change the format of *Pipe Size* to the nearest **1/16"**.

10. Click **OK**.

11. Set the *Scale* to **1" = 1'-0"**.

12. Save the family.

Task 2 - Create parameters.

---

1. In the *Create* tab>Properties panel, click (Family Types).

2. At the bottom of the Family Types dialog box, click (New Parameter).

3. In the Parameter Properties dialog box, in the *Parameter Type* area, select **Family Parameter** (if it is not already selected) and specify the following:
   - *Name:* **NomRad**
   - *Discipline:* **Piping**
   - *Type of Parameter:* **Pipe Size**
   - *Group Parameter Under:* **Dimensions**
   - Select **Type**.

4. Click **OK**.

5. Repeat the steps, creating instance parameters named **NomDia**, **FlgRad**, **FlgDia**, **PipeOD**, **PipeOR**, **RFD**, **RFR**, **RFT**, **FT**, **LTH**, **HT**, and **HubRad**. Define the parameters as follows:
   - *Parameter Type:* **Family Parameter**
   - *Discipline:* **Piping**
   - *Type:* **Pipe Size**
   - *Group Parameter Under:* **Dimensions**
   - Select **Instance**.

6. In the Family Types dialog box, specify the following values:
   - *FT:* **3/4"**
   - *FlgDia:* **9"**
   - *LTH:* **5"**
   - *NomRad:* **2"**
   - *PipeOD:* **4 1/2"**
   - *RFD:* **7"**
   - *RFT:* **1/16"**

By default, the parameters are listed in alphabetical order.

7. In the Family Types dialog box, enter the following formulas for the parameters:
   - *FlgRad:* **FlgDia / 2**
   - *HT:* **LTH - (FT + RFT)**
   - *HubRad:* **PipeOR * 1.5**
   - *NomDia:* **NomRad * 2**
   - *PipeOR:* **PipeOD / 2**
   - *RFD:* **FlgDia - 2"**
   - *RFR:* **RFD / 2**

The final information displays as shown in Figure 8–21.

Parameter	Value	Formula	Lock
Dimensions			⌃
FT (default)	3/4"	=	☐
FlgDia (default)	9"	=	☐
FlgRad (default)	4 1/2"	= FlgDia / 2	☐
HT (default)	4 3/16"	= LTH - (FT + RFT)	☐
HubRad (default)	3 3/8"	= PipeOR * 1.5	☐
LTH (default)	5"	=	☐
NomDia (default)	4"	= NomRad * 2	☐
NomRad	2"	=	☐
OffsetHeight (default)		=	
OffsetWidth (default)		=	
PipeOD (default)	4 1/2"	=	☐
PipeOR (default)	2 1/4"	= PipeOD / 2	☐
RFD (default)	7"	= FlgDia - 2"	☐
RFR (default)	3 1/2"	= RFD / 2	☐
RFT (default)	1/16"	=	☐

Figure 8–21

8. Click **OK**.

9. Save the family.

Task 3 - Create plan view reference planes.

1. Place three vertical reference planes 2" apart, with one to the left of the **Center (Left/Right)** reference plane, and two on the right, as shown in Figure 8–22.

2. Name the new reference planes, as shown in Figure 8–22, with the *Is Reference* parameter set to **Not a Reference**.

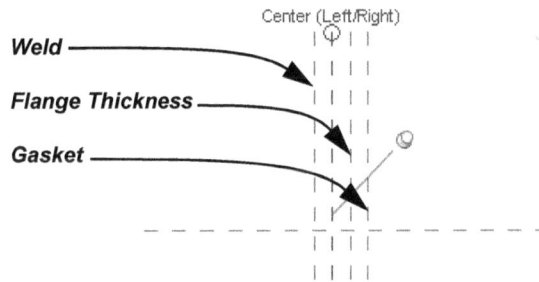

Figure 8–22

3. Dimension the reference planes, as shown in Figure 8–23. Apply the labels shown in Figure 8–24 to the dimensions.

Figure 8–23

Figure 8–24

4. Add horizontal reference planes, dimensions, and labels on either side of the **Center (Front/Back)** reference plane, as shown in Figure 8–25.

Figure 8–25

5. Save the family.

Task 4 - Create family types so that you can test the framework.

---

1. In the Properties panel, click ⊞ (Family Types).

2. In the Family Types dialog box, beside the *Type name*, click ▯ (New Type).

3. In the Name dialog box, type **4"** and click **OK**. Note that the existing values are applied to this type by default.

4. Click ▯ (New Type) again. In the Name dialog box, type **6"**.

5. In the *Dimensions* area, change the parameter values as follows:
   - *FT:* **15/16"**
   - *FlgDia:* **11"**
   - *LTH:* **3 1/2"**
   - *NomRad:* **3"**
   - *PipeOD:* **6 5/8"**

6. Move the Family Types dialog box so that the reference planes are displayed.

7. Click **Apply**. The reference plane locations change according to the new parameter values, as shown in Figure 8–26.

Family Types

Type name: 6"

Search parameters

Parameter	Value
Graphics	
Use Annotation Scale (d	☐
Dimensions	
FT (default)	15/16"
FlgDia (default)	11"
FlgRad (default)	5 1/2"
HT (default)	2 1/2"
HubRad (default)	4 31/32"
LTH (default)	3 1/2"
NomDia (default)	6"
NomRad	3"
OffsetHeight (default)	
OffsetWidth (default)	
PipeOD (default)	6 5/8"
PipeOR (default)	3 5/16"
RFD (default)	9"
RFR (default)	4 1/2"
RFT (default)	1/16"

LTH = 3 1/2"

FT = 15/16"

RFT = 1/16"

PipeOD = 6 5/8"

EQ EQ

EQ EQ

EQ

FlgDia = 11"

Figure 8–26

8. In the Type Name drop-down list, select **4"**.

9. Click **Apply**. Note that the flange returns to its original size.

10. Click **OK** to close the dialog box.

11. Save the family.

Task 5 - Create plan view graphics.

1. Continue working in the **Floor Plans: Rev. Level** view.

2. Open the Visibility Graphics dialog box. In the *Model Categories* tab, click **Object Styles**.

3. In the Object Styles dialog box, click **Select All**. Change the *Projection Line Weight* to **5** for all objects, as shown in Figure 8–27.

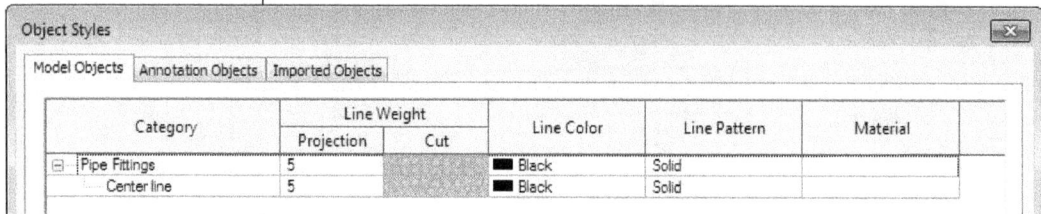

Category	Line Weight		Line Color	Line Pattern	Material
	Projection	Cut			
⊟ Pipe Fittings	5		■ Black	Solid	
Center line	5		■ Black	Solid	

Figure 8–27

4. Click **OK** twice to close the dialog boxes.

5. In the *Create* tab>Model panel, click ⌐ (Model Line).

6. Draw the lines shown in Figure 8–28. If you do not see the thickness, toggle ▤ (Thin Lines). Ensure that you draw from the intersections of the reference planes so that the lines will flex with the reference planes.

RFT = 1/16"

Draw this line on the vertical reference plane to the right

PipeOD = 4 1/2" EQEQ EQ EQ FlgDia = 9"

Figure 8–28

7. Open the Family Types dialog box. Use the new Types to verify that the lines work with the changes.

8. Reset the *Type Name* to **4"** and click **OK** to close the dialog box.

9. Select the three lines.

10. In the *Modify | Lines* tab>Visibility panel, click ⌐⊙¬ (Visibility Settings).

11. In the Family Element Visibility Settings dialog box, in the *Detail Levels* area, clear the **Fine** option. Leave all of the others selected, as shown in Figure 8–29.
    • This enables the selected elements to be visible only at the Coarse and Medium detail levels.

Figure 8–29

12. Click **OK**.

13. In the View Control Bar, select ⬚ (Preview Visibility On). Test the *Detail Levels*. When you select **Fine**, the line elements should disappear. End on **Medium.**

14. Save the family.

Task 6 - Create the Raised Face and Flange extrusions.

1. In the Project Browser, open the **Elevations: Left** view.

2. Select the model lines and temporarily hide the elements.

3. In the *Create* tab>Forms panel, click ⬚ (Extrusion).

4. In the *Modify | Create Extrusion* tab>Work Plane panel, click ⬚ (Set).

5. In the Work Plane dialog box, in the Name drop-down list, select **Reference Plane: Gasket** and click **OK**.

6. Draw a circle at the intersection of the **Ref Level** and **Center (Front/Back)** reference planes. Dimension and label it using the **RFR** parameter, as shown in Figure 8–30.

Figure 8–30

7. Click (Modify).

8. In Properties, in the *Extrusion End* row, click the **Associate Family Parameter** button.

9. In the Associate Family Parameter dialog box, select **RFT**, as shown in Figure 8–31, and click **OK**.

Figure 8–31

10. Click ✓ (Finish Edit Mode).

11. Click ▯ (Extrusion).

12. Set the Work Plane to **Reference Plane: Center (Left/Right)**.

13. Draw a larger circle at the same intersection.

14. Make the temporary dimension permanent and label it as **FlgRad**.

15. In Properties, in the *Extrusion End* row, click the **Associate Family Parameter** button. In the Associate Family Parameter dialog box, select **FT** and click **OK**. The new radius displays as shown in Figure 8–32.

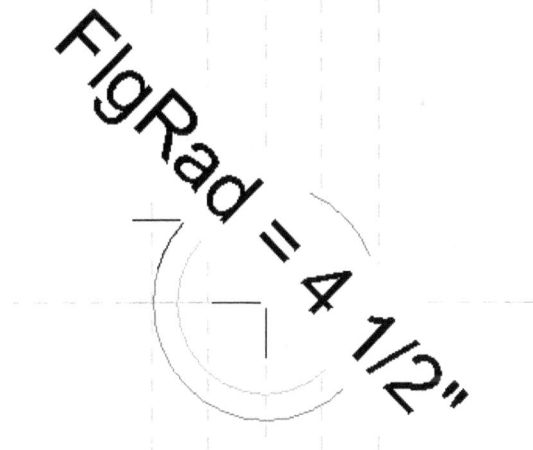

Figure 8–32

16. Click ✓ (Finish Edit Mode).

17. Open the **3D views: View 1** view. The two circular extrusions and the model lines should display. Shade and rotate the element as required, as shown in Figure 8–33. Flex it using the family types.

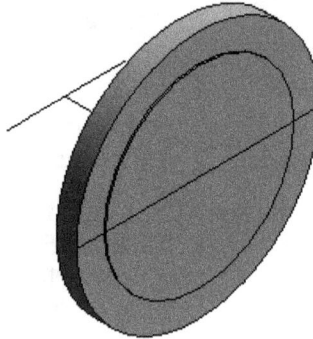

Figure 8–33

18. Save the family.

Task 7 - Create the pipe connection blend.

---

1. Return to the **Elevations: Left** view.

2. In the *Create* tab>Forms panel, click (Blend).

3. Draw a circle at the same intersection. Dimension and label it **HubRad**.

4. In the *Modify | Create Blend Base Boundary* tab>Mode panel, click (Edit Top).

5. Draw a smaller circle at the same intersection as the other element. Dimension and label it **PipeOR**.

6. In Properties, set the *Second End* to (negative) **-4"**.

7. Click (Finish Edit Mode).

8. Open the **Elevations: Front** view. Align and lock the small end of the blend to the Weld reference plane, as shown in Figure 8–34.

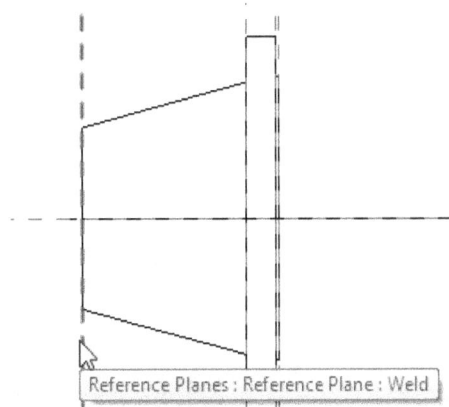

Reference Planes : Reference Plane : Weld

Figure 8–34

9. Open the **3D Views: View 1** view and flex the types to ensure that everything is working, as shown for two possible flexes in Figure 8–35 and Figure 8–36.

Figure 8–35   **Figure 8–36**

10. Temporarily hide the model lines.

11. Save the family.

Task 8 - Add connectors.

1. Continue working in the **3D Views: View 1** view.

2. In the *Create* tab>Connectors panel, click ⬦ (Pipe Connector).

3. In the *Modify | Place Pipe Connector* tab>Placement panel, verify that ⬦ (Face) is selected.

4. In the Options Bar, in the System type drop-down list, select **Hydronic Supply**.

5. In Properties, set the *Round Connector Dimension* parameter to **Use Radius**.

6. Rotate the view and press <Tab> as required to highlight the small face of the blend and click to add the connector.

7. The arrow of the connector should be pointing outward from the flange object, as shown in Figure 8–37. If the arrow is pointing inward, click the **Flip** control.

Figure 8–37

- The connector arrow does not indicate flow direction. Instead, it points in the direction from which the pipe is going to connect into it.

8. Spin the view so that the raised face is visible and apply another connector to that face, as shown in Figure 8–38.

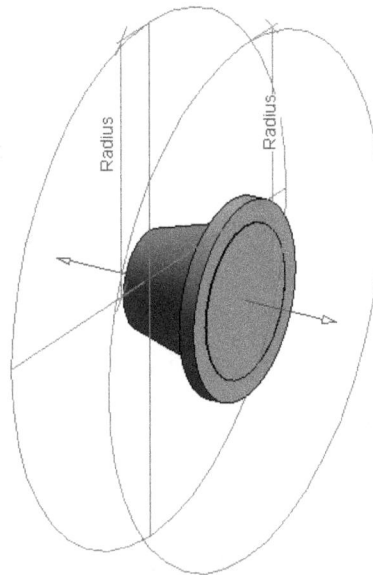

Figure 8–38

9. Select the first connector. In the *Modify | Connector Element* tab>Connector Links panel, click ⬭ (Link Connectors).

10. Click the second connector to link it to the first.

11. Select both connectors.

12. In Properties, for *Radius,* associate it with the **NomRad** parameter and click **OK**.

13. The connectors are resized as shown in Figure 8–39.

Figure 8–39

14. Save the family.

Task 9 - Test the flange in a project.

1. Start a new project and switch back to the family.

2. In the Family Editor panel, click ⬆ (Load into Project).

   - If you have one project open, the new family loads directly into it. If you have more than one project open, select the right one(s) in the dialog box.

3. You are returned to the project.

4. Place an instance of each type into the drawing area of the project.

   - If a command is not automatically started, in the *Systems* tab>Model panel, click ⬜ (Component).

5. Zoom in to display the plan view of the flanges at a **Coarse** detail level. Ensure that **Thin Lines** is toggled off so that the line weight is displayed, as shown in Figure 8–40.

6. With **Thin Lines** on, change the *Detail Level* to **Fine**. The flanges display in detail at full size, as shown in Figure 8–41.

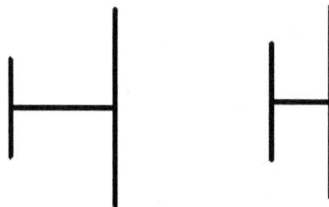

Figure 8–40   **Figure 8–41**

7. Ensure that the flanges are aligned with each other, and then draw pipe between them.

8. Open a 3D view.

9. Zoom in on the flanges and toggle on  (Thin Lines) as required.

10. Change the *Detail Level* to **Fine** and type to **SD** to shade the view.

11. Spin the view to examine the flanges from all sides.

12. Save the project file.

13. Close the project and family files. Save any changes you want to keep.

Chapter Review Questions

1. The architect has requested that you use a vanity design that is not designed to work with MEP systems, such as the one shown in Figure 8–42. What do you need to do to upgrade it?

Figure 8–42

a. Add pipes to the family where you want the project pipes to tie in.

b. Add connectors to the family where you want the project pipes to tie in.

c. Create a separate MEP specific vanity and use **Copy/Monitor** to add it to the project.

d. Import an existing sink designed to work with MEP systems into the family.

2. Which of the following Light Source Definition distribution options enables you to specify an IES file?

a. (Spherical)

b. (Hemispherical)

c. (Spot)

d. (Photometric Web)

3. If you want to include an annotation element, such as a label that references a parameter in a family, you can only do so by creating a separate annotation tag.

   a. True

   b. False

4. How do you have a family display different elements when you change the *Detail Level* from *Coarse* to **Fine**?

   a. In the project file, select the family and in Properties change the detail level.

   b. In the family file, select the elements and modify the *Visibility Settings*.

   c. In the family file, in the View Properties, set the detail level.

   d. In the project file, set the *Visibility Settings* for the view.

5. In the Family Types dialog box shown in Figure 8–43, if the *Pump Length* changed to **2'-0"**, what would the value of *Radius 2* be?

Parameter	Value	Formula	Lock
Pump Length	3' 1 1/4"	=	☑
Pump Height	3' 5 1/8"	=	☑
Panel Height	1' 8"	=	☑
Outlet Radius	3/16"	=	☑
Outlet Diameter	3/8"	= Outlet Radius * 2	☑
Inlet Radius	9/16"	=	☑
Inlet Diameter	1 1/8"	= Inlet Radius * 2	☑
Fan Radius	1' 1 205/256"	= Fan Diameter / 2	☑
Fan Diameter	2' 3 77/128"	=	☑
C2 Offset 2	0' 8 5/8"	=	☑
C2 Offset 1	0' 3 3/8"	=	☑
C1 Offset 2	0' 6"	=	☑
C1 Offset 1	0' 3 7/8"	=	☑
Other			☆
Radius 1	7' 9 1/8"	= 2.5 * Pump Length	☑
Radius 2	7' 8 1/8"	= Radius 1 - 0' 1"	☑

Figure 8–43

   a. 5'-0"

   b. 4'-0"

   c. 4'-11"

   d. 5'-1"

Chapter
9

Creating Structural Specific Families

Structural specific families include everything from column and beam design, to detail items such as gusset plates. By working through a series of practices, you learn about creating a parametric gusset plate, an in-place stiffener plate, an in-place slab depression, a built-up column, a tapered concrete column, a truss family, a precast hollow core slab and a tapered moment frame. Select the ones that are most helpful in your work.

Learning Objectives in this Chapter

- Create a gusset plate with parametric properties.
- Create an in-place column stiffener family.
- Create a floor-based family with a void that cuts out a depression in a floor when inserted in a project.
- Create a built-up column family made of steel plates.
- Create a tapered concrete column family.
- Create a truss family.
- Create a precast hollow core slab family that uses an imported CAD file for the profile.
- Create a tapered moment frame family that includes two columns with a connecting beam.

Practice 9a

Parametric Gusset Plate

Practice Objectives

- Create reference planes, dimensions, and parameters.
- Create solid geometry for the plates.
- Modify Visibility Settings and create Family Types.

Estimated time for completion: 30 minutes

In this practice, you will create a family file based on a template and create reference planes. You will then create gussets as a mass, create material parameters, and apply Family Types. Finally, you will toggle off the visibility of the gusset plate from the coarse detail to all views, as shown in Figure 9–1.

Figure 9–1

Task 1 - Start a new family using a template and add reference planes.

1. Create a new family based on the **Structural Stiffener.rft**. template found in the Autodesk® Revit® Library.

2. Save the family to your practice folder as **Parametric Gusset Plate.rfa**.

3. Open the Project Units dialog box. Change the *Length Format* to **Fractional inches**. This makes the dimensions easier to read.

4. Open the **Elevations: Left** view.

5. Create and dimension the new reference planes, as shown in Figure 9–2.

   • Ensure that the diagonal reference plane being added crosses the intersection of the **Center (Front/Back)** and **Ref. Level** reference planes.

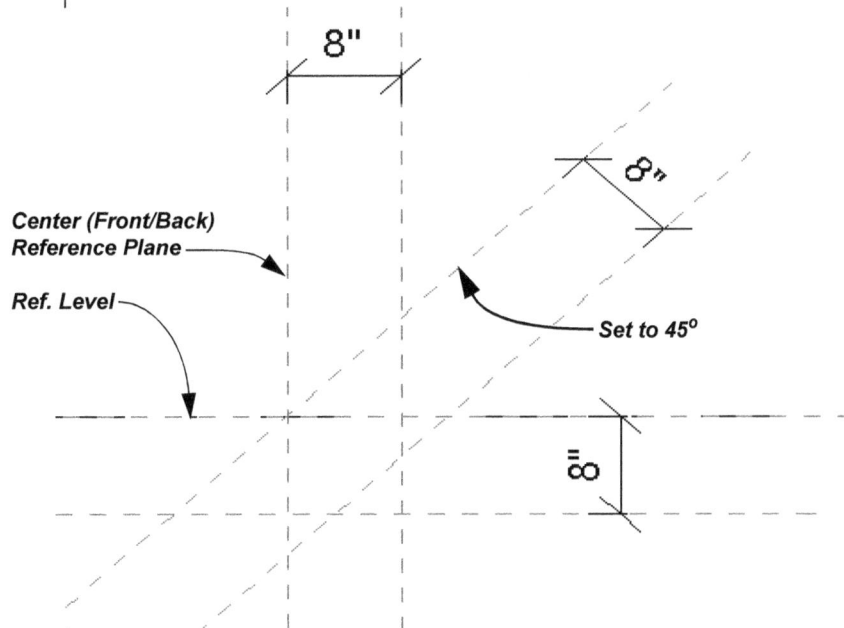

Figure 9–2

6. Label one of the dimensions with a new parameter named **Width**.

7. Select the other two dimensions and apply the same parameter to them.

8. Flex the parameter to test the stability of the framework.

9. Set the *Width* to **8"**.

10. Save the family.

Task 2 - Create Front View reference planes.

1. Switch to the **Elevations: Front** view and create two reference planes, **1/4"** on either side of the **Center (Left/Right)** reference plane and add dimensions. Label the overall dimension as **Thickness**, as shown in Figure 9–3.

Modify the scale so that the dimensions are clearly displayed.

Figure 9–3

2. Flex the parameter to test the stability of the framework.

3. Set the *Thickness* to **1/2"**.

4. Save the family.

Task 3 - Creating family geometry.

1. Switch to **Elevations: Left** view.

2. In the *Create* tab>Forms panel, click (Extrusion). In the Options Bar, set the *Depth* to **1/2"**.

3. Draw individual lines across the outside intersections of the reference planes, and lock all five lines to the reference planes, as shown in Figure 9–4.

*Use the **Align** command to help lock the lines to the reference plane.*

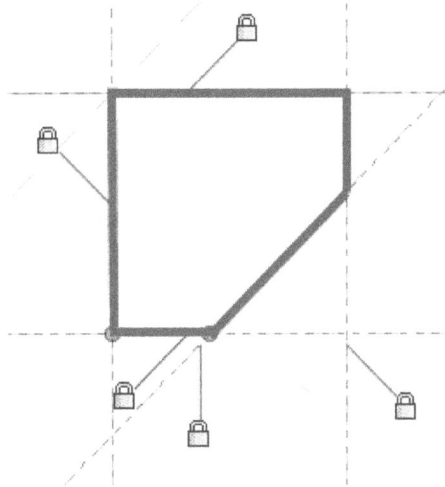

Figure 9–4

4. Click ✔ (Finish Edit Mode).

5. Switch to the **Elevations: Front** view. Align the left and right sides of the extrusion with the reference planes you created earlier and lock them.

6. Switch to a 3D view and shade the model.

7. In the *Create* tab>Properties panel, click ⬚ (Family Types) to flex the model to ensure that everything is working together. The model displays as shown in Figure 9–5.

Figure 9–5

8. Save the family.

Task 4 - Add material parameters.

1. Open the Family Types dialog box.

2. At the bottom of the dialog box, click (New Parameter).

3. Create an Instance parameter named **Material** and set the *Type of Parameter* to **Material**. The Group automatically updates to Materials and Finishes, as shown in Figure 9–6. Click **OK**.

*Setting the parameter as an **Instance** makes it easier to modify it in the project file.*

Figure 9–6

4. In the 3D view, select the plate.

5. In Properties, in the *Materials and Finishes* area, in *Material* row, click (Associate Family Parameter).

6. In the Associate Family Parameter dialog box, select **Material**, as shown in Figure 9–7, and click **OK**.

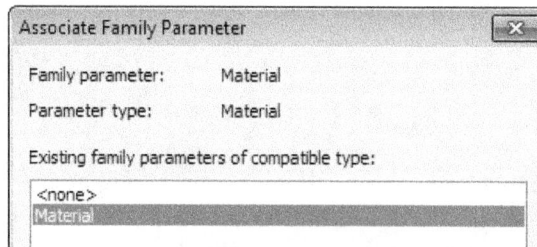

Figure 9–7

7. In Properties, the **Material** parameter is now marked with the = sign, as shown in Figure 9–8. Therefore, when the family is loaded into a project, you can control its material using Properties.

Materials and Finishes		≫
Material	<By Category>	
Identity Data		≫

Figure 9–8

Task 5 - Change the visibility settings in a family.

1. Select the extrusion.

2. In the *Modify | Extrusion* tab>Mode panel, click (Visibility Settings).

3. In the Family Element Visibility Settings dialog box, clear the **Coarse** option, as shown in Figure 9–9, so that the gusset plate does not display at a **Coarse** detail level.

Figure 9–9

4. Click **OK**.

5. In the View Control panel, select (Preview Visibility On).

6. Change the *Detail Level* to **Coarse**, **Medium**, and **Fine**. The outline of the Gusset Plate remains in the **Medium** and **Fine** detail levels but disappears in the **Coarse** detail level. This means that it will not display in a project when inserted in a view set to the **Coarse** detail level.

7. Save the family.

Task 6 - Create family types.

1. Open the Family Types dialog box.

2. Create three Family Types. Set the *Name* and the *Width* parameter of each as follows:
   - **8"**
   - **10"**
   - **12"**

3. Use the new types to flex the gusset plate family.

4. Save the family.

5. Ensure that you have a structural project open and then load the family into the project.

6. In the project, open a 3D View and set the *Detail Level* to **Medium**.

7. Insert one of each Plate type into the project.

8. Switch to a 3D view to see the differences.

9. Shade the view, using the shortcut **SD** as required.

10. Select one of the Plates. In Properties, apply a material to it. Repeat with the others using different materials.

11. Save the family and project.

Practice 9b

Estimated time for completion: 15 minutes

In-Place Column Stiffeners

Practice Objective

- Create an in-place family in a detail view

In this practice, you will create a stiffener plate to strengthen a column's flange, as shown in Figure 9–10.

Figure 9–10

Task 1 - Create an in-place family in a detail view.

1. In the practice files *Structural* folder, open **Column-Stiffeners.rvt**. The file opens in the **Structural Plans: Level 2** view.

2. In the Project Browser, open **Detail Views: Detail 0**. It displays a column supporting a beam and concrete on metal deck slab, as shown in Figure 9–11.

Figure 9–11

3. The column requires stiffeners to strengthen its flanges. In the *Structure* tab>Model panel, expand ⬛ (Component) and click ⬛ (Model In-Place).

4. In the Family Category and Parameters dialog box, set the *Filter list* to **Structure** and select **Structural Stiffeners**, as shown in Figure 9–12. Click **OK**.

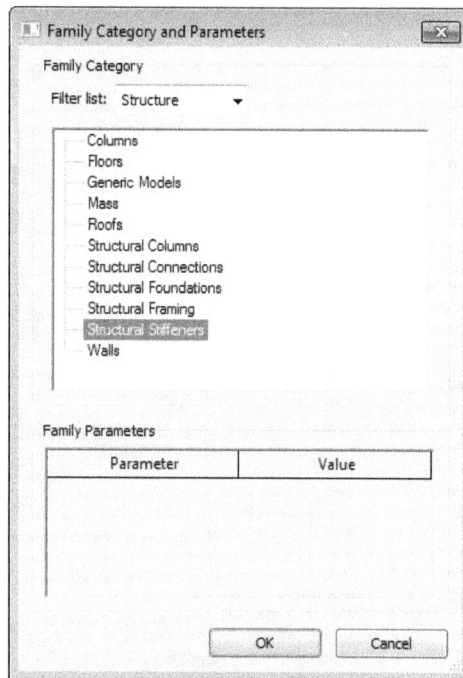

Figure 9–12

5. Enter a name for the stiffener plate, as shown in Figure 9–13.

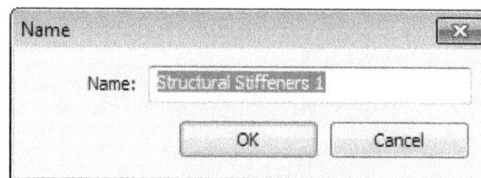

Figure 9–13

6. You are now in the In-Place Editor. In the **Detail 0** view, draw two horizontal reference planes and name them, as shown in Figure 9–14. These reference planes assist in locating the stiffener plates.

Top of Beam

Bottom of Beam

Figure 9–14

7. In the *Create* tab>Forms panel, click ⬚ (Extrusion).

8. In the Work Plane dialog box, in the drop-down list, select **Reference Plane: Top of Beam**, and then click **OK**.

9. In the Go To View dialog box, select **Structural Plan: Level 2**. This view is used to draw the stiffener plate.

10. Click **Open View**.

11. In the **Structural Plans: Level 2** view, zoom into the grid intersection **1/A**.

12. In the *Modify | Create Extrusion* tab>Draw panel, click

⬚ (Pick Lines). In the Options Bar, select **Lock**. This ensures that the stiffener edges adjust to any changes to the column size.

13. Select and trim the perimeter of the inside face of the column, as shown in Figure 9–15.

You might need to zoom in very close to display the faint background image.

Figure 9–15

14. In Properties, set the *Extrusion End* value to (negative) **-1"**, as shown in Figure 9–16.

Extrusion		▼	Edit Type
Constraints			
Extrusion End	-0' 1"		
Extrusion Start	0' 0"		
Work Plane	Level : Level 1		

Figure 9–16

15. Click ✓ (Finish Edit Mode).

16. Switch to the **Detail 0** view. Note that the stiffener plate is located under the **Top of Beam** reference planes.

17. Select the stiffener plate and click ⌖ (Copy). In the Options Bar, clear the **Constrain** option. Select the starting point as the bottom of the stiffener plate and copy it halfway down between the two reference planes.

18. Select the copied stiffener plate.

19. In the *Modify | Extrusion* tab>Work Plane panel, click **Edit Work Plane**.

20. In the Work Plane dialog box, select **Reference Plane: Bottom of Beam** and click **OK**. The plate moves into a new position.

21. The stiffener plate thickness must be adjusted upward. Select the new stiffener plate and change the *Extrusion End* to **1"**.

22. The new plates are now in place, as shown in Figure 9–17.

Figure 9–17

23. In the In-Place Editor panel, click ✓ (Finish Model).

24. In the project file, navigate through the different views to see the stiffener plates.

25. Save the project.

Practice 9c | In-Place Slab Depression

Practice Objectives

- Create a floor-based family by setting up the parametric framework.
- Create a void form for a depression in the floor.
- Apply the family in a project.

Estimated time for completion: 15 minutes.

Slab depression family is an important host-based family that you need to modify for your projects. In this practice, you will create a slab depression using a template file and apply it in a project, as shown in Figure 9–18.

Figure 9–18

Task 1 - Create a family and add reference planes, insertion points, and dimensions.

1. Create a new family based on the **Generic Model floor based.rft** template found in the Autodesk Revit Library.

2. Save the family to your practice folder as **Slab Depression Component.rfa**.

3. In the Create Tab>Properties panel, click 🔲 (Family Categories and Parameters).

4. In the Family Category and Parameters dialog box, select **Structural Foundations** and click **OK**.

5. In the *Create* tab>Datum panel, click ✏️ (Reference Plane).

6. Add the horizontal and vertical reference planes and dimensions, as shown in Figure 9–19.

Figure 9–19

7. Label the horizontal dimension as **Slab Depression Length** and the Vertical dimension as **Slab Depression Width**. In both cases set the parameter to **Instance**. The parameters display as shown in Figure 9–20.

*Ensure that you set these parameters and the one below to **Instance** parameters. This ensures that they can be set in the project.*

Figure 9–20

8. Open the **Elevations: Front** view where you create the depth of the depressed slab.

9. Add another reference plane **3"** down from the reference level. Add a dimension between the reference level and the new reference plane. Label the dimension as **Slab Depression Depth**, as shown in Figure 9–21.

Figure 9–21

10. Save the family.

Task 2 - Create the depressed area for the slab.

---

1. Now you will create the depressed area for the slab by creating a void form and locking it to the reference planes. Switch to the **Floor Plans: Ref. Level** view.

2. In the *Create* tab>Forms panel, expand (Void Forms) and click (Void Extrusion).

3. In the Draw panel, click (Rectangle).

4. Add the rectangle by clicking at the top left corner of the intersecting reference planes and then the bottom right corner. Click the lock controls to constrain the void form to the reference planes, as shown in Figure 9–22.

Figure 9–22

5. Click ✓ (Finish Edit Mode).

6. Open the **Elevations: Front** view.

7. In the *Modify* tab>Modify panel, click 🔲 (Align).

8. Select the lower reference plane first and then pick the bottom of the void form, as shown in Figure 9–23. Select the lock control to constrain the bottom of the void form to the reference plane.

Figure 9–23

9. Still in the **Align** command, select the reference level and pick the top of the void form. Select the lock control to constrain the top of the void form to the reference level.

10. In the *Modify* tab>Geometry panel, click 🔳 (Cut Geometry) and pick the void form and the slab object. (The order of the selection does not matter.)

11. Open a 3D view to see the depression in the slab object. Type **SD** to shade the view, as shown in Figure 9–24.

Figure 9–24

12. Use the Family Types dialog box to flex the depression.

13. Close the dialog box.

14. Save the Depressed Slab component family file. Do not close the family file.

Task 3 - Test the component family file.

1. Create a new project and save the file as **Depressed Slab Example.rvt**.

2. In the *Structure* tab>Foundation panel, click ⬭ (Structural Foundation: Slab). Create an **8" Foundation Slab** in the new project.

3. When the slab has been created in the project file, return to the **Slab Depression Component.rfa** family file.

4. In the Family Editor panel, click ⬛ (Load into Project).

5. If it is not automatically started, start the **Component** command.

6. Pick a location for the slab depression. The insertion is based on the origin in the family file. In the family file you based the insertion point at the center of the recessed slab.

7. Select different views to display the depression. Cut some sections through it.

8. To change the size of slab depression, return to the **Floor Plans: Level 2** view, and select the component.

9. In Properties, change the values to any required size, as shown in Figure 9–25.

Properties		✕
	Slab Depression Component	▾
Structural Foundations (1)		▾ 🔲 Edit Type
Constraints		�
Structural		�
Dimensions		⌃
Slab Depression Depth	0' 6"	
Slab Depression Length	4' 0"	
Slab Depression Width	2' 0"	

Figure 9–25

10. Return to the 3D view and Section view to see the new shape of the depressed slab.

11. Save and close the project and family files.

Practice 9d | Built-Up Column

Practice Objectives

- Set up the parametric framework for a column.
- Use extrusions to create the sides of the column.

Estimated time for completion: 15 minutes.

The Autodesk Revit Structure software has an extensive structural columns library to meet many standard types and sizes in the industry. However, there is still a need for built-up (custom) made columns. In this practice, you will create a built-up column from steel plates, as shown in Figure 9–26.

Analytical line

Figure 9–26

- The analytical line is already incorporated into the family in the structural system family template. Therefore, it is not required to be created in the new family.

Task 4 - Set up reference planes and dimensions.

1. Create a new family based on the **Structural Column.rft** template found in the Autodesk Revit Library.

2. Save the family to your practice folder as **Built-Up Column.rfa**.

3. In the **Structural Plans: Lower Ref. Level** view, add reference planes to the inside of the four exterior reference planes using ✎ (Pick Lines) with an *Offset* of **2"**, as shown in Figure 9–27.

Figure 9–27

4. Delete the vertical **EQ** dimensions to prevent over-constraining and re-insert new vertical EQ dimensions at the inner reference planes, as shown in Figure 9–28.

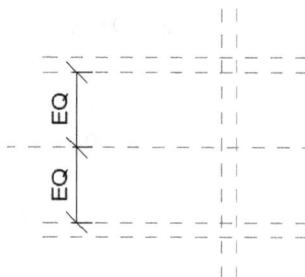

Figure 9–28

5. Place single dimensions horizontally and vertically above the EQ dimensions, as shown in Figure 9–29.

Figure 9–29

6. Select the horizontal dimension and label it. Set the *Name* to **Primary Plate Length** and select **Instance**, as shown in Figure 9–30.

*The **Instance** option enables the value to be modified per element.*

Figure 9–30

7. Follow the same procedures for the vertical dimension, naming it **Secondary Plate Length**.

8. Add four more dimensions, as shown in Figure 9–31. Set the parameters for these new dimensions to determine the thickness of the primary and secondary plates.

Figure 9–31

9. Flex the sizes to ensure that they are moving together.

10. Save the family.

Task 5 - Create the plates.

---

1. In the *Create* tab>Forms panel, click 🗋 (Extrusion) to create the plates. Only one plate can be created at a time because each extrusion must be a closed loop.

2. Sketch the rectangle, based on the start and end points shown in Figure 9–32.

   • Lock the lines to the reference planes.

   • Leave the **Extrusion Start** and **Extrusion End** parameters as default. The column height is adjusted later by aligning with other reference planes.

Figure 9–32

3. Click ✓ (Finish Edit Mode).

4. Select the primary plate created and mirror it using the center line as the axis of reflection.

5. Create the secondary plate (sketch shown in Figure 9–33) and mirror it to the other side.

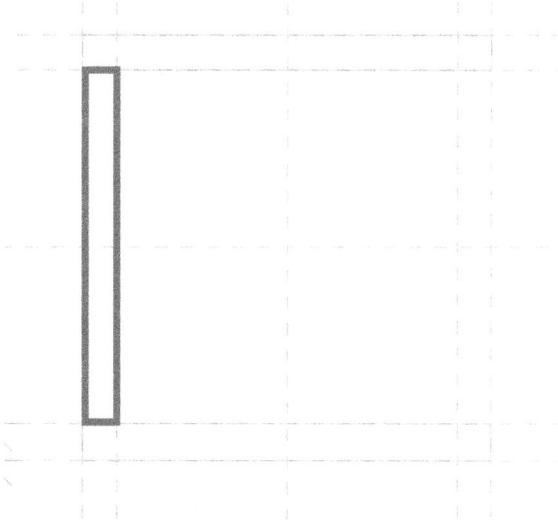

Figure 9–33

6. Flex the sizes to ensure that the extrusions move as expected.

7. Open the **Elevations: Front** view to establish the height of the column.

8. Use ⬜ (Align) to align the four plates to the **Upper Ref. Level.** Select the **Upper Ref. Level** and then the top of a plate and lock it in place. Repeat this procedure until all four plates are locked to the **Upper Ref. Level** and **Lower Ref. Level**, as shown in Figure 9–34.

Ensure that the view is in Wireframe mode to see all of the plates.

Figure 9–34

9. Set the *Visual Style* of the view to **Hidden Line**. Note that the secondary plates behind the primary plates disappear.

10. Use Symbolic Lines to display the secondary plates with hidden lines. In the *Annotate* tab>Detail panel, click

    ⬜ (Symbolic Line).

11. In the *Modify | Place Symbolic Lines* tab>Subcategory panel Type Selector, select **Hidden Lines (projection)**.

12. In the Options Bar, verify that the **Chain** option is cleared. Draw a line from the intersection of the **Upper Ref. Level** and the inside reference planes on both sides of the column, as shown in Figure 9–35. Lock these lines to both the **Upper** and **Lower Ref. Levels**.

Figure 9–35

13. Temporarily hide the reference plane category so you can see the new lines.

14. Flex the sizes and **Upper Ref. Level** height.

15. Save the family.

16. To test the Built-Up Column, open a new project and load the **Built-Up Column** family into the new project. Insert a column, as shown in Figure 9–36, and navigate from one view to another to see the new column. Add other columns and change the size and offset from the level.

Figure 9–36

Practice 9e

Tapered Concrete Column

Practice Objectives

- Create Reference Planes and Parameters as the framework of the column family.
- Create geometry using a solid blend.

Estimated time for completion: 15 minutes

In this practice, you will create a tapered concrete column using a column family template. You will create its geometry using a solid blend and add a taper parameter that can be modified as shown in Figure 9–37.

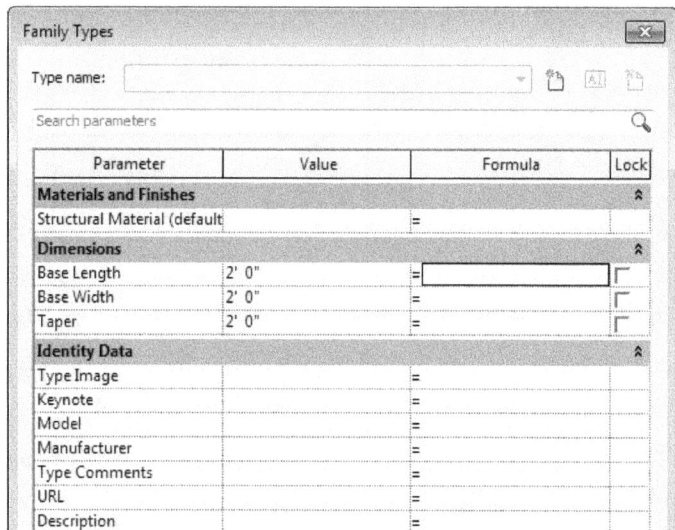

Figure 9–37

Task 1 - Create Reference Planes and Parameters.

1. Create a new family based on the **Structural Column.rft** template found in the Autodesk Revit Library.

2. Save the family to your practice folder as **Tapered-Concrete-Column.rfa**.

3. Add dimensions and labels for the **Base Width** and **Base Length**, as well as a reference plane named **Taper**. Dimension and label it, as shown in Figure 9–38.

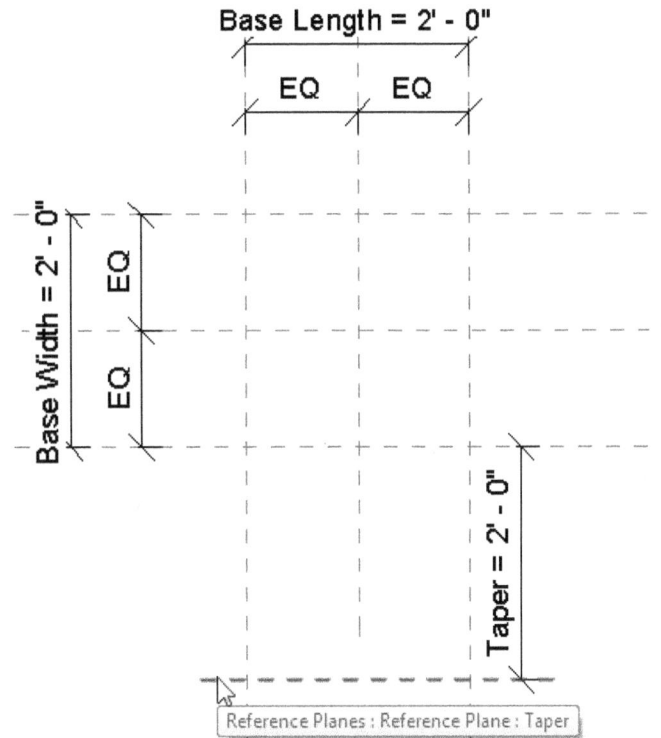

Figure 9–38

4. Flex the sizes to test the framework.

5. Save the family.

Task 2 - Create geometry.

1. In the *Create* tab>Forms panel, click ⬡ (Blend).

2. Sketch the base of the blend, as shown in Figure 9–39.

3. Click ⬡ (Edit Top) and sketch the top of the blend (the overhanging taper - it is larger than the base), as shown in Figure 9–40.

Figure 9–39

Figure 9–40

4. In the Mode panel, click ✔ (Finish Edit Mode).

5. Open the **Elevations: Front** view.

6. Align and lock the blend to the **Upper Ref. Level**, as shown in Figure 9–41.

7. Open the **3D Views: View 1** view and shade it. Rotate to display the taper side of the column, as shown in Figure 9–42.

Upper Ref. Level
9' - 0"

Lower Ref. Level
0' - 0"

Figure 9–41

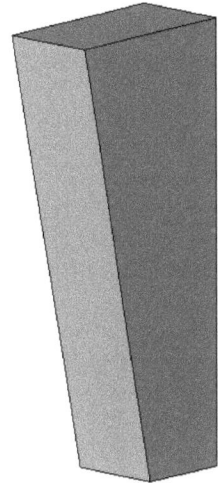

Figure 9–42

8. Use the Family Type dialog box to flex the column.

9. Reset the default values and close the Family Types dialog box.

10. Save the family.

11. If time permits, you can create Family Types using various dimensions and test them in a project.

Practice 9f | Truss Family

Practice Objectives

- Start a truss family and add reference planes and labels.
- Add Top Chord, Bottom Chord, and Web layout lines.

Estimated time for completion: 40 minutes

In this practice, you will create a truss using a truss family template. You will add reference planes, create parameters, and add chords and webs to form the structure of the trusses, as shown in Figure 9–43. You will then test it in a project.

Figure 9–43

Task 1 - Add reference planes and labels.

1. Create a new family based on the **Structural Trusses.rft** template found in the Autodesk Revit Library.

2. Save the family to your practice folder as **Custom Truss.rfa**.

3. Add the reference planes, dimensions, and labels (Instance parameters) shown in Figure 9–44.

Figure 9–44

4. Open the Family Types dialog box and scroll down to the *Dimensions* area. Add the formula *Top Chord Length* = **Truss Length / 3**, as shown in Figure 9–45.

If you forgot to set any of the labels as Instance parameters, you can edit it in the Family Types dialog box.

Dimensions			
End Height (Left) (default)	4' 0"	=	☐
End Height (Right) (default)	4' 0"	=	☐
Top Chord Length (default)	26' 8"	= Truss Length / 3	☑
Truss Length (default)	80' 0"	=	☑
Truss Height (default)	10' 0"	=	☑

Figure 9–45

5. Click **OK**.

Task 2 - Add the Top Chord, Bottom Chord, and Web layout lines.

---

1. In the *Create* tab>Detail panel, click ⬚ (Top Chord).

2. In the Options Bar, verify that the **Chain** option is cleared so that you can lock each line as it is created.

3. Starting from the left vertical reference plane, draw the top chord, locking each sketch before you draw the next, as shown in Figure 9–46.

Figure 9–46

Alternatively, in the Create tab>Detail panel,

click ⬛ *(Bottom Chord).*

4. In the *Modify | Top Chord* tab>Draw panel, click ⬛ (Bottom Chord).

5. Draw the bottom chord, across the bottom of the truss, as shown in Figure 9–47. Lock the bottom chord sketch line in place.

Figure 9–47

6. In the *Create* tab>Detail panel, click ⬛ (Web). In the Options Bar, verify that the **Chain** option is not selected.

7. Draw vertical web lines, as shown in Figure 9–48. Dimension and set them EQ in three different sets.

Figure 9–48

- Start at the far left reference plane and work over to the right.
- Ensure that you dimension to the vertical reference planes where available or the truss will not flex correctly.
- DO NOT mirror the Web lines as this might cause undesirable results or errors in the truss family.

8. Add diagonal web members to the left of the truss, from the top chord to the bottom chord. Start from the far left side working toward the center of the truss. Repeat the process from the other direction. The final outcome is shown in Figure 9–49.

Figure 9–49

- Snap to the intersections of elements. Type **SI** to force the snap points.
- DO NOT mirror the web lines, as this might cause errors when the truss is loaded into a project.

9. Flex the geometry.

10. Reset the values to the dimensions shown in Figure 9–49.

11. Save the family.

12. Load the truss into a project and test it.
   - Note that the default framing sizes might be too large. In the truss family (or in the truss type in the project), set appropriate framing members for the chords and webs.

13. Save and close the project and the family.

Practice 9g

Precast Hollow Core Slab

Practice Objectives

- Create a family using the Structural Framing - Beams and Braces template.
- Use a CAD file to modify the sketch of an extrusion.
- Assign a material to the extrusion.
- Set visibility settings for Medium and Fine detail levels along with simple geometry for the Coarse detail level.

Estimated time for completion: 20 minutes

In this practice, you will use the **Structural Framing - Beams and Braces.rft** file as the base of the hollow core slab. You will modify an existing extrusion and import a CAD drawing to assist in setting up the new profile. You will assign a material to the extrusion and establish the visibility settings for **Medium** and **Fine** detail levels. You will then draw a second extrusion with a simple rectangular profile, assign the material and set the visibility settings so that it only displays at a **Coarse** detail level as shown in Figure 9–50.

Detail Level: Coarse   *Detail Level: Medium and Fine*

Figure 9–50

Task 1 - Import a CAD file into a family template to create the hollow core geometry.

1. Create a new family based on the **Structural Framing - Beams and Braces.rft** template found in the Autodesk Revit Library.

2. Save the family to your practice folder as **Precast-Hollow-Core-Slab.rfa**.

3. Close any other projects or family files that you might have open.

4. Open and tile the following views:
    *   **Floor Plans: Ref Level**
    *   **Elevations: Front**
    *   **Elevations: Left**
    *   **3D Views: View 1**

5. In the **Elevations: Left** view, zoom in on the geometry.

6. Select the extrusion. In the *Modify | Extrusion* tab>Mode panel, click ⬛ (Edit Extrusion).

7. Select the outline geometry (as shown in Figure 9–51) and the reference planes that are part of the extrusion and delete them from the view.

Figure 9–51

In this example, a CAD drawing is used to create the geometry of the hollow core slab.

8. In the *Insert* tab>Import panel, click 🗔 (Import CAD).

9. In the Import CAD Formats dialog box, navigate to the practice files *Structural* folder. Select **Precast-Hollow-Core-Slab.dwg** and then and set the following options, as shown in Figure 9–52:
    *   Select **Current View Only**.
    *   *Colors:* **Black and White**
    *   *Layers:* **All**
    *   *Import units:* **Auto-Detect**
    *   *Positioning:* **Auto - Center to Center**

Figure 9–52

10. Click **Open**.

11. A message box opens prompting you about exploding import instances. Click **Yes** to continue. The family now includes the sketch lines from the AutoCAD drawing, as shown in Figure 9–53.

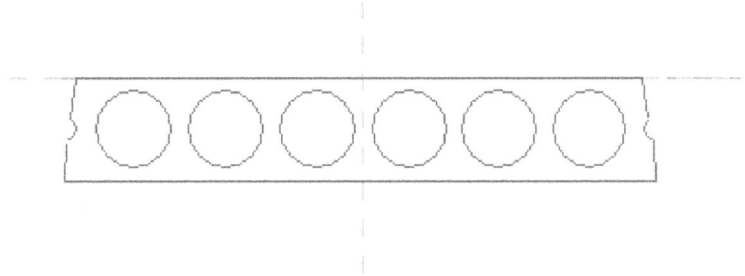

Figure 9–53

12. To select the material for the hollow core slab, in Properties, in the *Materials and Finishes* area, select **<By Category>**, and then click ⌐…⌐ (Browse).

13. In the Material Browser, select **Concrete-Precast Concrete**, as shown in Figure 9–54.

Figure 9–54

14. Click **OK** to close the dialog boxes. The Material is assigned.

15. Click ✓ (Finish Edit Mode).

16. Click in empty space to release the selection.

17. In the 3D view, zoom out as required to display the slab. Set the *Visual Style* to ⬛ (Shaded) to display the new slab with the concrete material applied, as shown in Figure 9–55.

Figure 9–55

18. Save the file.

Task 2 - Establish visibility settings.

1. Select the new extrusion.

2. In the *Modify | Extrusion* tab>Mode panel, click 📷 (Visibility Settings).

3. In the Family Element Visibility Settings dialog box, in the *Detail Levels* area, verify that **Coarse** is cleared, as shown in Figure 9–56.

Figure 9–56

4. Click **OK**.

5. In the View Control Bar, click 🖼 (Preview Visibility On).

6. Test the *Detail Levels*. In the **Coarse** detail level, the extrusion should not display.

7. Activate the **Elevations: Left** view.

8. In the *Create* tab>Forms panel, click ⬜ (Extrusion). In the Work Plane dialog box, select **Pick a plane** and click **OK**. Select the face of the existing extrusion.

9. Draw a rectangle around the perimeter of the hollow core slab and lock it in place.

   • Start the rectangle at the lower left corner.
   • To select the appropriate upper right corner, press <Tab> once to force the horizontal temporary dimension, as shown in Figure 9–57.

Figure 9–57

10. In Properties, set the *Extrusion End* to (negative) **-8'-0"** and the *Material* to **Concrete - Precast Concrete**.

11. Click ✓ (Finish Edit Mode).

12. Activate the **Floor Plans: Ref. Level** view.

13. Align and lock the new extrusion to the **Member Left** reference plane, as shown in Figure 9–58.

Figure 9–58

14. Align the other end to the **Member Right** reference plane.

15. Select the new simple rectangular extrusion.

16. In the *Modify | Extrusion* tab>Mode panel, click (Visibility Settings).

17. In the Family Element Visibility Settings dialog box, in the *Detail Levels* area, clear **Medium** and **Fine**, as shown in Figure 9–59.

Figure 9–59

18. Click **OK**.

19. Release the selection and preview the different *Detail Levels*.

Task 3 - Add hidden lines.

1. Activate the **Floor Plans: Ref. Level** view.

2. In the View Control Bar, set the *Visual Style* to (Wireframe).

3. In the *Annotate* tab>Detail panel, click (Symbolic Line).

4. In the *Modify | Place Symbolic Lines* tab>Subcategory panel, set *Subcategory* to **Hidden Lines [projection]**.

5. In the *Modify | Place Symbolic Lines* tab>Draw panel, click (Line). In the Options Bar, clear the **Chain** option.

6. Draw hidden lines horizontally along the edges, as shown in Figure 9–60. You cannot see them as you draw because they are in the same location as the elements displayed through the wireframe view.

Figure 9–60

7. In the View Control Bar, set the *Visual Style* to ▱ (Hidden Line). The hidden lines should be displayed.

8. Select the 12 hidden lines that you just created.

9. In the *Modify | Lines* tab>Visibility panel, click ▱ (Visibility Settings).

10. Set the visibility of only the lines to the **Medium** and **Fine** detail levels.

11. Save the family.

12. Load the family into a project.

13. Using ▱ (Beam) draw a beam using the new **Precast-Hollow-Core-Slab** family.

14. Test the visibility settings in the plan and elevation views.

15. Close but do not save the project.

16. Save and close the family.

Practice 9h

Estimated time for completion: 40 minutes

Tapered Moment Frame

Practice Objectives

- Set up reference planes, reference lines, and parameters as the framework of the family.
- Create geometry for the columns and beams of the family.

In this practice, you will use the family template file **Structural Column.rft** as the basis of the Tapered Moment Frame. You will create reference planes, reference lines, and parameters and then create the geometry for the columns and tapered beam using both solid sweeps and extrusions, as shown in Figure 9–61.

Figure 9–61

Task 1 - Set up the reference planes and parameters.

1. Create a new family based on the **Structural Column.rft** template found in the Autodesk Revit Library.

2. Save the family to your practice folder as **Tapered-Moment-Frame.rfa**.

3. Add dimensions and labels for **Overall Length** and **Column Width** to the existing reference planes, as shown in Figure 9–62. Create them as **Type** parameters.

Figure 9–62

4. Open the Family Types dialog box

5. In the Family Types dialog box, change the values of *Overall Length* to **26'-0"** and *Column Width* to **1'-0"**, as shown in Figure 9–63. Click **OK**.

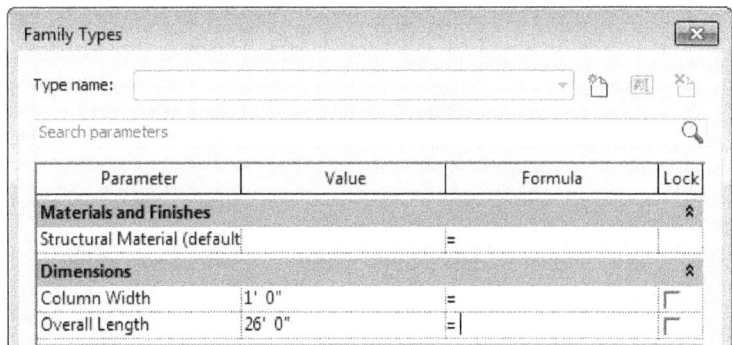

Figure 9–63

6. Zoom out and extend the horizontal reference planes beyond the new vertical reference planes, as shown in Figure 9–64.

   • Unpin the **Front/Back** reference plane to lengthen it. Click on the **Pin** icon to pin the reference plane back in place so that it will not move when you add dimensions and labels.

Figure 9–64

7. Add two new horizontal reference planes with associated dimensions and label (type parameter) to represent the **Beam Width**, as shown in Figure 9–65.

   • **Hint:** Use **Pick Lines** with an *Offset* of **2"** and place them inside the existing outer reference planes.

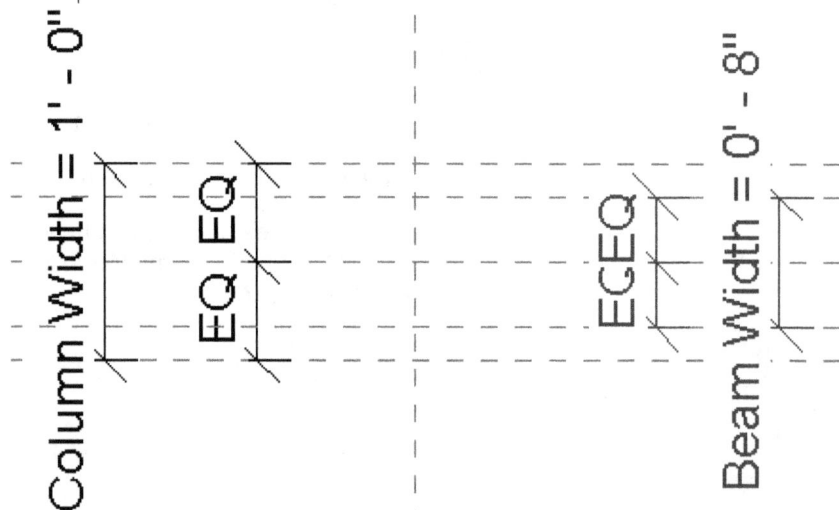

Figure 9–65

8. Open the **Elevations: Front** view.

9. Change the *elevation* of the **Upper Ref. Level** to **13'-0"**.

10. Extend the reference planes and levels so that they all overlap.

11. Add a reference plane on top of the **Upper Ref. Level**, as shown in Figure 9–66, and lock it into the level.

12. Add reference planes and labels (type parameters), as shown in Figure 9–66.

Column Top = 2' - 0"

Reference plane on top of Upper Ref. Level.

Beam Middle Height = 12' - 0"

Knee Height = 10' - 0"

Column Base = 1' - 0"

Figure 9–66

13. Add **Column Base** and **Column Top** reference planes and labels on the other end of the frame. (Do not use Mirror.)

14. Temporarily hide the **Upper Ref. Level**, but not the associated reference plane.

15. Draw two reference lines from the intersection of the top and outside reference planes to the center vertical reference plane, as shown in Figure 9–67. Lock the reference lines to the related reference planes.

Column Top = 2' - 0"   Column Top = 2' - 0"

: 12' - 0"

Figure 9–67

16. Reset **Temporary Hide/Isolate**.

17. Flex the framework. End with the **Upper Ref. Level** height of **13'-0"** and **Beam Middle** height of **12'-0"**.

18. Save the family file.

Task 2 - Create the geometry for the Tapered Columns.

---

1. In the *Create* tab>Forms panel, click 🦑 (Sweep).

2. In the *Create* tab>Work Plane panel, click ⊞ (Set).

3. In the Work Plane dialog box, select **Reference Plane: Center (Front/Back)**, as shown in Figure 9–68. Click **OK**.

Work Plane

Current Work Plane
Name:
Reference Plane : Center (Front/Back)

Show   Dissociate

Specify a new Work Plane
◉ Name   Reference Plane : Center (Front/Back) ▼
○ Pick a plane
○ Pick a line and use the work plane it was sketched in

OK   Cancel   Help

Figure 9–68

4. In the *Modify | Sweep* tab>Sweep panel, click ✐ (Sketch Path).

5. In the Draw panel, ✐ (Line) is selected by default. In the Options Bar, verify that the **Chain** option is selected.

6. Sketch the path for the column of the moment frame. Align the two vertical sketch lines to their parallel reference planes.

7. Align and lock the angular sketch line to the reference line, as shown in Figure 9–69.

Draw the left vertical sketch first. The profile is drawn in this plane.

Column Top = 2' - 0"

Beam Middle Height = 12' - 0"

Knee Height = 10' - 0"

Column Base = 1' - 0"

Figure 9–69

8. In the Mode panel, click ✔ (Finish Edit Mode).

9. In the *Modify | Sweep* tab>Sweep panel, click ✐ (Edit Profile).

10. When the Go To View dialog box opens, select **Floor Plan: Lower Ref. Level**. Click **Open View**.

11. If you have not already done so, zoom out to see the full framework and expand the Reference lines to the ends.

12. Zoom in on the Profile target and draw a rectangle **3/4" x 1'-0"**. Lock it to the reference planes, as shown in Figure 9–70.

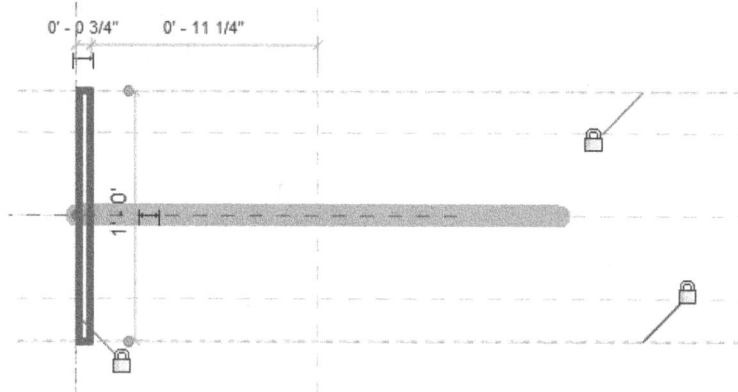

Figure 9–70

13. Click ✔ (Finish Edit Mode) twice to finish the Profile and the Sweep.

14. Open the **3D Views: View 1** view. Rotate and shade it to display the column up to this point, as shown in Figure 9–71.

Figure 9–71

15. Return to the **Elevations: Front** view.

16. Click ⬜ (Extrusion) and set the *Work Plane* to **Reference Plane: Center (Front/Back)**.

17. In the *Modify | Create Extrusion* tab>Draw panel, click

    ⤸ (Pick Lines). In the Options Bar, select **Lock**.

18. Zoom into the sweep that was created earlier and select all of the interior lines, as shown in Figure 9–72.

*The lines are automatically locked to the selected lines because you selected the **Lock** option.*

Figure 9–72

19. In Properties, set the values of the *Extrusion End* to **3/8"** and *Extrusion Start* to (negative) **-3/8"**, as shown in Figure 9–73.

Figure 9–73

20. Click ✓ (Finish Edit Mode)

21. Display the column profile in a shaded 3D View and return to the **Elevations: Front** view. (**Hint:** Press <Ctrl>+<Tab>.)

22. Mirror the new tapered column (both extrusion and sweep) along the center vertical reference plane, as shown in Figure 9–74.

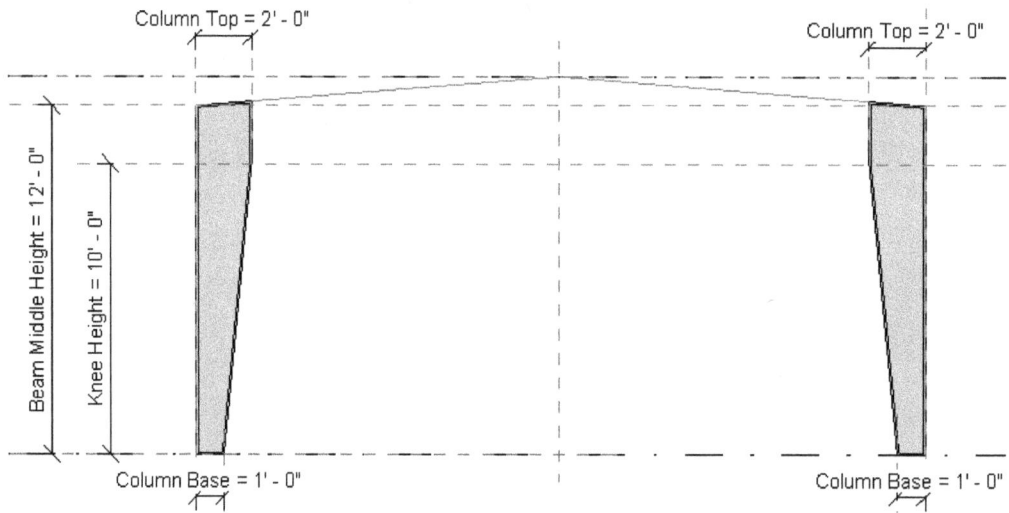

Figure 9–74

23. Edit the path sketch of the mirrored sweep and align and lock the sketch to the reference line.

24. Flex the framework to ensure that everything is working as expected.

25. Save the family file.

Task 3 - Create the geometry for the Tapered Beam.

1. Start the **Sweep** command and add a path, as shown in Figure 9–75. Use **Pick Lines** with the **Lock** option on and select the angled reference lines.

Figure 9–75

2. Click ✓ (Finish Edit Mode).

3. In the *Modify | Sweep* tab>Sweep panel, click 🗁 (Load Profile).

4. In the Load Family dialog box, navigate to the practice files *Structural* folder. Select **Tapered-Frame-Profile.rfa** and click **Open**.

5. In the *Profile:* drop-down list, select **Tapered-Frame-Profile**, as shown in Figure 9–76.

Figure 9–76

6. Click ✓ (Finish Edit Mode).

7. Display the top plate of the beam profile in a 3D View, as shown in Figure 9–77.

Figure 9–77

8. Return to the **Elevations: Front** view and create another sweep for the beam's bottom flange using the sketch for the path shown in Figure 9–78 and the same profile family.

Hint: You can temporarily hide existing solid elements so that you can attach the sketch to the reference planes.

Figure 9–78

9. The final 3D view should display, as shown in Figure 9–79.

Figure 9–79

10. Return to the **Elevations: Front** view and add an extrusion using the interior of the previously created sweeps, as shown in Figure 9–80. Set the *Extrusion End* to **3/8"** and *Extrusion Start* to (negative) **-3/8"**.

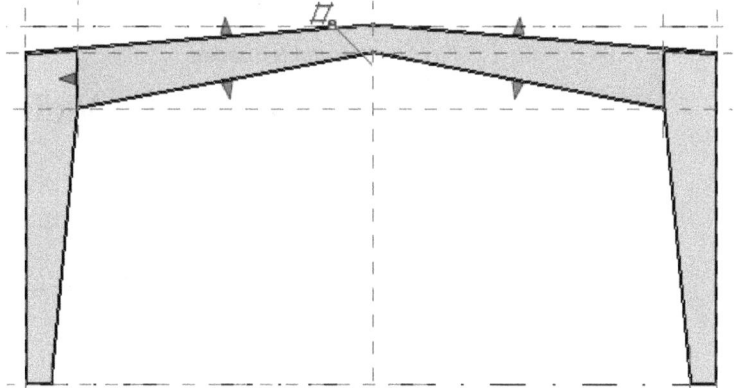

Figure 9–80

11. Open the 3D view and move it to one side. Open the Family Types dialog box and flex the geometry of the **Tapered Moment Frame** parameters, as shown in Figure 9–81.

Figure 9–81

12. Save the family file.

13. Create a new structural project, load the family, and test it.

Chapter Review Questions

1. How do you change a standard dimension to a parameter-based dimension, as shown in Figure 9–82?

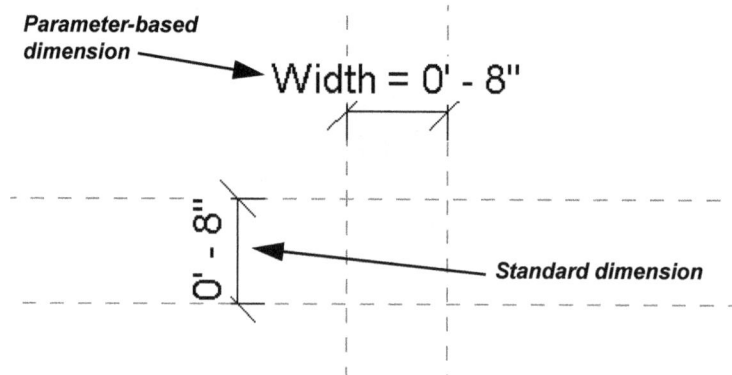

Figure 9–82

   a. In the Type Selector, select a parameter-based type.

   b. In Properties, change the *Value*.

   c. In the ribbon, click **Create Parameter**.

   d. In the Family Types dialog box, in the *Parameters* area, click **Add**.

2. Why would you create an in-place family rather than a component family?

   a. An in-place family can be used several times in the current project only.

   b. An in-place family is used once in the current project for a specific location and size.

   c. A component family cannot be modified to fit the specific location.

   d. A component family cannot be joined to other elements in the project.

3. Which of the following Generic Model family templates would you use to create a slab depression?

   a. **Generic Model wall based.rft**

   b. **Generic Model face based.rft**

   c. **Generic Model line based.rft**

   d. **Generic Model floor based.rft**

4. In a truss family, is the highlighted element shown in Figure 9–83 a Chord or a Web?

Figure 9–83

a. Chord

b. Web

5. When assigning material to a solid form you can select the **Associate Family Parameter** option. The option to select the material is grayed out, as shown in Figure 9–84. Where do you assign the material?

Figure 9–84

a. In the Family Types dialog box, select the associated parameter and select the material.

b. In the *Manage* tab>Settings panel, click ⬡ (Materials) and select the material.

c. In the *Modify* tab>Geometry panel, click 🖌 (Paint).

d. In the Family Category and Parameters dialog box, specify the material in the *Family Parameters* area.

Additional Management Tools

There are many tools available in the Autodesk® Revit® software that you can use when creating and using templates and projects. This appendix provides details about several additional tools and commands that are related to those covered in this learning guide.

Learning Objectives in this Appendix

- Set up units, snaps, temporary dimensions, and arrowheads.
- Create object styles for components that include line weight, color, pattern, and material.
- Create patterns used in the Filled Region command and for cut and surface patterns in materials.
- Create materials and material libraries that can be used in multiple projects.
- Review mechanical settings (for ducts and pipes) and electrical settings (for wiring, cable trays, and conduits).
- Review structural specific settings.
- Create sheet list schedules
- Modify the keyboard shortcuts and double-click function of the mouse.
- Create new Project Browser organization layouts for views and sheets.

A.1 General Settings

A variety of settings are available to help you customize the projects you create and keep everything consistent with your office's standards. Other settings can make the process of working in Autodesk Revit more productive.

Specifying Units

Although you select Imperial or Metric units when you create the project template, you can set up the Project Units with specific formats and options. For example, if you are working on a Civil project where everything is set up in feet, you specify **Decimal Feet** as the Length Format. For an international metric project, you can specify the length units as Meters, Centimeters, or Millimeters.

How To: Set Up Project Units

1. In the *Manage* tab>Settings panel, click 🖫 (Project Units) or type **UN**.
2. In the Project Units dialog box, in the *Format* column, click the button next to the unit type that you want to modify, as shown in Figure A–1. The related Format dialog box opens, as shown in Figure A–2.

Figure A–1

Figure A–2

3. Set the *Units*, *Rounding*, and other options as required.
4. In the Project Units dialog box, you can also select the *Discipline* (**Common** by default) and change the Unit format for each discipline. The other options are **Structural**, **HVAC**, **Electrical**, **Piping**, and **Energy**. The options vary according to the discipline-specific software in use.
5. Click **OK** to close each dialog box.

Format Options

Each unit has specific formatting options. The option is grayed out if it is not applicable to that unit type.

Units	Select the type of units in the Units drop-down list. Units: `Feet and fractional inches` ▼ Decimal feet Feet and fractional inches Rounding: Decimal inches Fractional inches `To the nearest 1/32"` Meters Centimeters Unit symbol: Millimeters Meters and centimeters
Rounding	Specify how precisely you want the dimensions to be rounded. The options depend on the *Units* you selected.
Unit Symbol	If you are using metric units, you can select a unit symbol, such as **cm** for centimeters or **None**.
Suppress trailing 0's	(For decimal-based units) If selected, this option removes any trailing 0s. For example, it displays 1.5 instead of 1.50 if you are using two decimal places.
Suppress 0 feet	(Imperial Units only) If selected, this option removes the 0 in front of a dimension in inches only. For example, the dimension displays as 0'-4", rather than 4".
Use digit grouping	If selected, the unit uses the Decimal symbol/digit grouping specified in the Project Units dialog box. Decimal symbol/digit grouping: `123,456,789.00` ▼ 123,456,789.00 123.456.789,00 123 456 789,00 123'456'789.00 12,34,56,789.00 12.34.56.789,00 12 34 56 789,00 12'34'56'789.00
Suppress spaces	(Imperial Units only) If selected, this option removes the spaces between the feet and inches, so that a dimension reads 1'-2", rather than 1' - 2".

- The **Use project settings** and **Show + for positive values** options are grayed out when setting units for the project. This dialog box is used when creating dimension styles or specifying label formats when the options are available.

Snap Settings

The Snaps dialog box controls *Dimension Snaps,* which are the increments you see in temporary dimensions, and *Object Snaps,* which are the points on elements that you can select. In the *Manage* tab>Settings panel, click 🧲 (Snaps) to open the dialog box, as shown in Figure A–3.

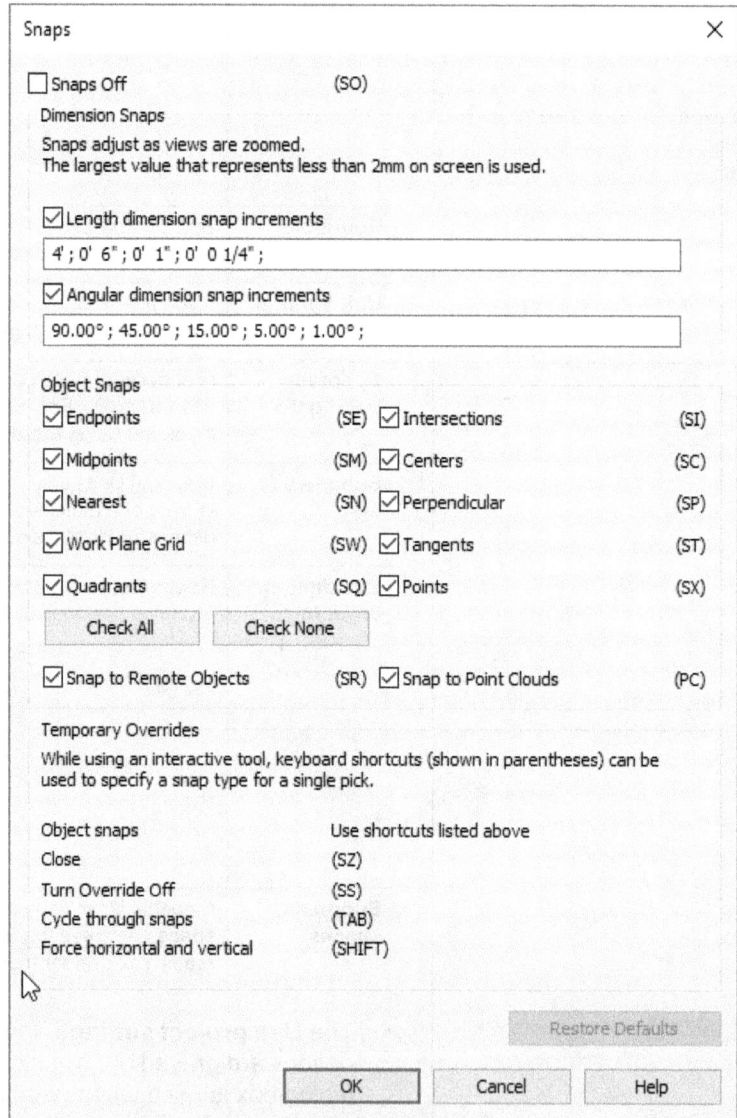

Snaps			✕
☐ Snaps Off	(SO)		

Dimension Snaps

Snaps adjust as views are zoomed.
The largest value that represents less than 2mm on screen is used.

☑ Length dimension snap increments

4' ; 0' 6" ; 0' 1" ; 0' 0 1/4" ;

☑ Angular dimension snap increments

90.00° ; 45.00° ; 15.00° ; 5.00° ; 1.00° ;

Object Snaps

☑ Endpoints	(SE)	☑ Intersections	(SI)
☑ Midpoints	(SM)	☑ Centers	(SC)
☑ Nearest	(SN)	☑ Perpendicular	(SP)
☑ Work Plane Grid	(SW)	☑ Tangents	(ST)
☑ Quadrants	(SQ)	☑ Points	(SX)

Check All	Check None

☑ Snap to Remote Objects	(SR)	☑ Snap to Point Clouds	(PC)

Temporary Overrides

While using an interactive tool, keyboard shortcuts (shown in parentheses) can be used to specify a snap type for a single pick.

Object snaps	Use shortcuts listed above
Close	(SZ)
Turn Override Off	(SS)
Cycle through snaps	(TAB)
Force horizontal and vertical	(SHIFT)

		Restore Defaults
OK	Cancel	Help

Figure A–3

- Snap overrides are listed as keyboard shortcuts in parentheses, next to the corresponding snap. When a snap override is used, the cursor finds that specified snap type in your view until something is selected.

- Snap overrides can be used while inside a command by right-clicking and selecting **Snap Overrides** and then selecting the one that you want to use from the list.

Temporary Dimension Settings

Temporary dimensions display when you draw or edit building elements in the software. By default, they measure from the center lines of walls to the center lines of openings, as shown in Figure A–4.

Figure A–4

- When you move a witness line to another element or part of an element, the location is remembered in the current session of program.

You can control where temporary dimensions are placed by default. In the *Manage* tab>Settings panel, expand

(Additional Settings) and click (Temporary Dimensions) to open the Temporary Dimension Properties dialog box, as shown in Figure A–5.

Figure A–5

- You can set up these properties in the project template file or modify them at any time. They do not affect existing elements in your project.

- You can control the size of the temporary dimension text in the Options dialog box in the *Graphics* area.

Setting Up Arrowheads

A variety of arrowhead types are supplied with the Autodesk Revit software, including open and filled arrow styles, tick marks, and dots. You can also create custom styles by duplicating an existing style and defining the parameters, such as the *Arrow Style* shown in Figure A–6. In the *Manage* tab>Settings panel, expand ✎ (Additional Settings) and click ⇄ (Arrowheads) to open the dialog box.

Type Parameters

Parameter	Value
Graphics	☆
Arrow Style	Arrow
Fill Tick	☐
Arrow Width Angle	30.000°
Tick Size	1/8"
Heavy End Pen Weight	7

Figure A–6

- Arrowheads are used by both text (with a leader) and dimensions.

- The templates include loop leaders, typically used in MEP projects, that can be set as *Tick Mark* for dimensions and *Leader Arrowhead* for text, as shown in Figure A–7. You can also create an Arrow Style using Loop in the Arrowhead settings.

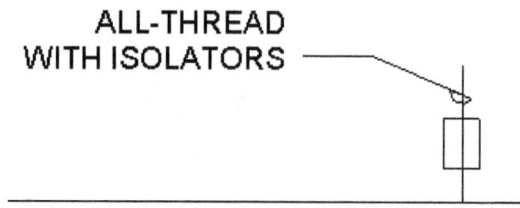

ALL-THREAD WITH ISOLATORS

Figure A–7

A.2 Creating Object Styles

Every element in the Autodesk Revit software contains object styles that control how its components display in various views. For example, the *Doors* element includes the *Elevation Swing*, *Frame/Mullion*, *Glass*, *Hidden Lines*, *Opening*, *Panel*, and *Plan Swing* as components, as shown in Figure A–8. The *Elevation Swing* is set to a light line weight, displayed in black with a dashed line pattern. It does not have any material attached to it, but the *Glass* component does.

Object Styles

Model Objects   Annotation Objects   Analytical Model Objects   Imported Objects

Filter list: Architecture

Category	Line Weight		Line Color	Line Pattern	Material
	Projection	Cut			
⊞ Casework	1	3	■ Black	Solid	
⊞ Ceilings	2	5	■ Black	Solid	
⊞ Columns	1	4	■ Black	Solid	
⊞ Curtain Panels	1	2	■ Black	Solid	
⊞ Curtain Systems	2	2	▨ RGB 000-127-000	Solid	
⊞ Curtain Wall Mullions	1	3	■ Black	Solid	
⊞ Detail Items	1		■ Black	Solid	
⊟ Doors	2	2	■ Black	Solid	
Elevation Swing	1	1	■ Black	Dash 1/16"	
Frame/Mullion	1	3	■ Black	Solid	
Glass	1	4	■ Black	Solid	Glass
Hidden Lines	2	2	▨ Blue	Dash	
Opening	1	3	■ Black	Solid	
Panel	1	3	■ Black	Solid	
Plan Swing	1	1	■ Black	Solid	
⊞ Electrical Equipment	1		■ Black	Solid	
⊞ Electrical Fixtures	1		■ Black	Solid	

Select All   Select None   Invert

Modify Subcategories

New   Delete   Rename

OK   Cancel   Apply   Help

Figure A–8

- In the *Manage* tab>Settings panel, click 🗗 (Object Styles) to open the Object Styles dialog box.

- To modify an object style, select the element to change and then select an option in the appropriate column in the drop-down list or dialog box.

- Most categories enable you to create subcategories. For example, you can create subcategories for reference planes that can be toggled off while leaving other reference planes visible in a view.

Line Weights

Line weights for model elements can be set for a **Projection** (in elevations) or **Cut** (in section and plan). For example, a wall displays a heavy line weight while the door and window cuts are lighter, as shown in Figure A–9.

Figure A–9

- Annotation elements are only set for projection.

Hint: Setting Line Weights

In the *Manage* tab>Settings panel, expand ✎ (Additional Settings) and click ☰ (Line Weights) to open the Line Weights dialog box, as shown in Figure A–10. It contains three tabs: *Model Line Weights* (vary by scale), *Perspective Line Weights* (control elements like walls and windows in perspective views), and *Annotation Line Weights* (not dependent on the scale).

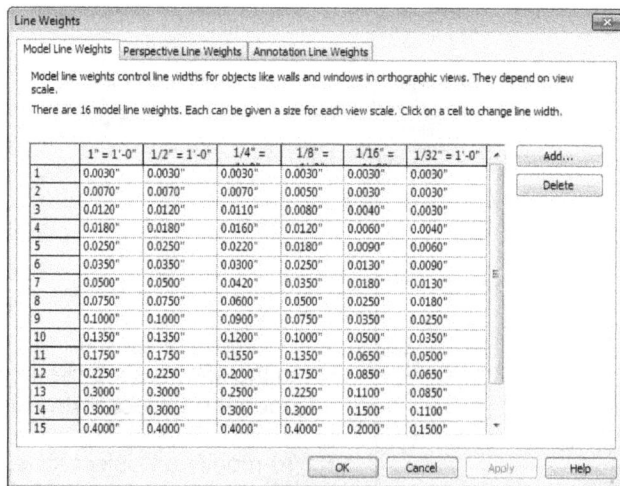

Figure A–10

You can customize the line weights in each tab and add scales as required for the model line weights.

Line Color

When you select **Line Color** in Object Styles or elsewhere, the Color dialog box opens, as shown in Figure A–11.

Figure A–11

You can select from thousands of colors, including options from the Pantone color system, as shown in Figure A–12. Typically, most elements in the Autodesk Revit software are black for printing purposes. When you shade and render, the elements take on the color of the assigned material. Therefore, these dialog boxes are opened when you create materials.

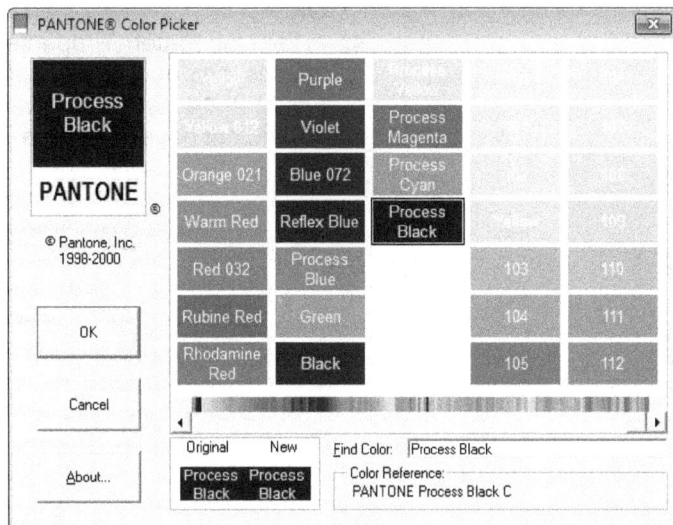

Figure A–12

Line Patterns

Line Patterns can be specified for various components in the Object Styles dialog box. In the example shown in Figure A–13, the line pattern **Dash** is used for the elevation door swing and the line pattern **Dash dot** is used for the callout bubble.

Figure A–13

How To: Create Line Patterns

A wide variety of patterns are supplied with the Autodesk Revit software and you can create your own with a series of dashes, spaces, and dots.

1. In the *Manage* tab>Settings panel, expand ✐ (Additional Settings) and click ⋯ (Line Patterns) to open the Line Patterns dialog box.
2. In the Line Patterns dialog box, click **New**.
3. In the Name dialog box, type a name for the pattern and click **OK**.
4. In the Line Pattern Properties dialog box, add a list of dashes, spaces, and/or dots and specify their values, as shown in Figure A–14. *Space* is always the option after a dash or dot. You do not have to enter a value for dots.

Figure A–14

Line Styles

Line styles are a specific type of object style used with the sketching tools. They are not part of the Object Styles dialog box, but are created in a similar way.

In the *Manage* tab>Settings panel, expand 🔧 (Additional Settings) and click ≣ (Line Styles). In the Line Styles dialog box (shown in Figure A–15), specify the *Line Weight*, *Line Color*, and *Line Pattern* for each line style.

Line Styles ✕

Line Styles

Category	Line Weight Projection	Line Color	Line Pattern
⊟ Lines	1	RGB 000-166-000	Solid
<Area Boundary>	6	RGB 128-000-255	Solid
<Beyond>	1	Black	Solid
<Centerline>	1	Black	Center 1/4"
<Demolished>	1	Black	Demolished 3/16"
<Fabric Envelope>	1	RGB 127-127-127	Dash
<Fabric Sheets>	1	RGB 064-064-064	Solid
<Hidden>	1	Black	Hidden 1/8"
<Overhead>	1	Black	Overhead 1/16"
<Room Separation>	1	Black	Solid
<Sketch>	3	RGB 225-000-255	Solid
<Space Separation>	1	Black	
Axis of Rotation	6	Blue	Center 1/4"
Hidden Lines	1	RGB 000-166-000	Dash
Insulation Batting Lines	1	Black	Solid
Lines	1	RGB 000-166-000	Solid
Medium Lines	3	Black	Solid

Modify Subcategories

Select All   Select None   Invert   New   Delete   Rename

OK   Cancel   Apply   Help

Figure A–15

A.3 Creating Fill Patterns

Fill patterns are used by the various **Filled Region** commands and material specifications. In the *Manage* tab>Settings panel, expand ✎ (Additional Settings) and click ▦ (Fill Patterns). Select from two types: **Drafting** and **Model**.

- Fill Patterns can also be created while you are working in the Visibility/Graphics dialog box. When you select a Fill Pattern override, the dialog box displays ⸬ (Browse), which opens the Fill Patterns dialog box.

Drafting patterns are symbolic. The view scale controls the size of the pattern. Basic patterns include hatching and cross-hatching, as well as designs that display material (such as aluminum or concrete), as shown on the left in Figure A–16. These are used in details and in plan or section cuts.

Model patterns are full scale to the actual elements they represent. They do not change if the view scale changes. You can select brick, various sizes of tile, lines that are a specific distance apart, roof shakes, etc., as shown on the right in Figure A–16. These patterns are primarily used in elevation and plan views.

Drafting Fill Patterns   **Model Fill Patterns**

Figure A–16

How To: Create a New Simple Fill Pattern

1. In the *Manage* tab>Settings panel, expand 🔧 (Additional Settings) and click ▨ (Fill Patterns).
2. In the New Pattern dialog box, select the type of pattern you want to create: **Drafting** or **Model**.
3. Click **New**.
4. In the New Pattern dialog box, specify the required **Orientation in Host Layers** option and select the *Simple* pattern style, as shown in Figure A–17.

Figure A–17

5. Type a name for the new pattern.
6. Type values for the *Line angle* and *Line spacing*, and select **Parallel lines** or **Crosshatch**.
7. Click **OK** to finish. The pattern can now be used to create a filled region type or used in a material.

- Filled regions can have either **Opaque** or **Transparent** backgrounds. This is set up in the Type Properties of the filled region.

How To: Create a New Custom Fill Pattern

1. In the *Manage* tab>Settings panel, expand ✐ (Additional Settings) and click ▨ (Fill Patterns).
2. In the Fill Patterns dialog box, select the type of pattern you want to create: **Drafting** or **Model**.
3. Click **New**.
4. In the New Pattern dialog box, select **Custom**, as shown in Figure A–18.

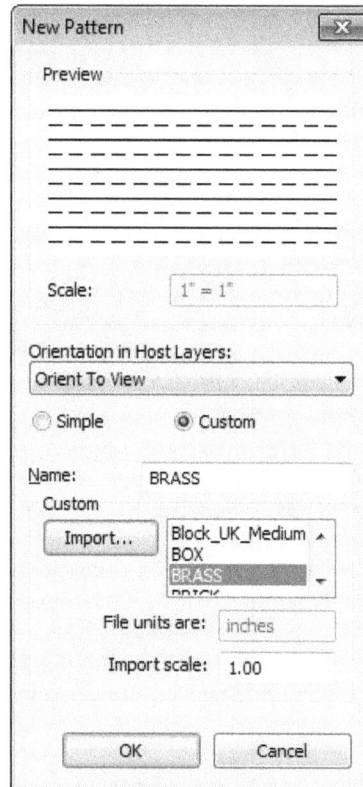

Figure A–18

5. Click **Import...** and select a PAT file. This file can be created specifically for the Autodesk Revit software or it can be based on an AutoCAD® PAT file.
6. Once the file is imported, a list of available patterns is displayed. Select the pattern. The name is automatically assigned. You can change the name after it has been selected.
7. Set the *Import Scale* as required.
8. Click **OK** to finish.

Importing Patterns from AutoCAD

Pattern files (PAT) can be imported from the AutoCAD software, such as the Escher pattern shown in Figure A–19.

Figure A–19

One change must be made in the pattern file for it to be usable in the Autodesk Revit software. Open the PAT file and add the following line after the title of a custom hatch, as shown in Figure A–20.

```
*AR-HBONE, Standard brick herringbone pattern @ 45 degrees
;%TYPE=MODEL
45,          0,0,        4,4,                  12,-4
135,      2.828427125,2.828427125,  4,-4,      12,-4
```

Figure A–20

- A line with a semicolon in front it is ignored by the AutoCAD software, while the type is specified for the Autodesk Revit software.

- Any pattern in the **Acad.pat** file can be automatically brought in as a drafting pattern. However, you must add the string above to specify model patterns.

A.4 Creating Materials

When you shade or render Autodesk Revit models, their appearance depends on the materials that have been associated with the elements, as shown in a shaded view in Figure A–21. Materials also include information that can be used in material takeoff schedules and in energy and structural analysis. You can use materials supplied with the Autodesk Revit software or create custom materials.

Figure A–21

- Materials can be assigned in several ways: using ⬚ (Paint) on faces, setting it in the layers of system families (such as walls and floors), and in object styles. You also assign materials when you create other component families, such as doors and furniture.

- Materials consist of 2D graphic settings for shading, surface, and cut patterns and the 3D rendering appearance, as well as physical and thermal properties. You can also include identity data, such as manufacturer, model, and keynotes.

Material Libraries

Materials are stored in libraries, which can be shared between Autodesk Revit projects and the AutoCAD, Autodesk® Inventor®, Showcase and Autodesk® 3ds Max® software. Before creating custom materials it is recommended that you create a custom library. Materials can be copied between the current project and the library.

*   You can also use Transfer Project Standards to bring in all the materials from another project into the current project.

How To: Create a Material Library

1. In the *Manage* tab>Settings panel, click 🌐 (Materials).

2. At the bottom of the Material Browser, expand 📑 (Creates, opens and edits user-defined libraries) and select **Create New Library** as shown in Figure A–22.

Figure A–22

3. In the Select File dialog box, navigate to the appropriate folder, type a *File name* and save the library. The Material Library displays in the Library list without any materials displayed.

4. Create new materials as required in the current project. Then drag and drop both new and existing materials from the project materials into the new library as shown in Figure A–23.

Libraries that come with the Autodesk Revit software are locked. You can copy materials from them but cannot add or change materials in them.

Figure A–23

How To: Create a Material

1. In the *Manage* tab>Settings panel, click ⊚ (Materials).

2. In the Material Editor, expand 🔾 (Creates or duplicates a material), and select either **Create New Material** or **Duplicate Material** as shown in Figure A–24. If you are duplicating a material, select an existing material similar to what you want to use first.

*You can also right-click on an existing material in the Material Browser and select **Duplicate**.*

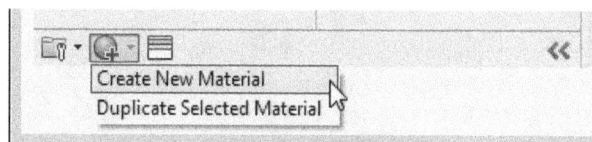

Figure A–24

3. A new material is added to the current project. Modify the name of the material or right-click on the Material name in the Material Browser and select **Rename**.

   - Duplicated materials include all of the properties of the existing material as shown for a new Aluminum material in Figure A–25.

Figure A–25

4. Fill out the information on each of the tabs.
5. Click **Apply** and add additional materials as required.
6. Click **OK** when you are finished.

Identity Tab

In the *Identity* tab, you set up the *Descriptive Information*, *Product Information*, and *Revit Annotation Information* for the material, as shown in Figure A–26. This information can be used in material takeoff schedules.

Identity	Graphics	Appearance	Physical	Thermal

Name: Brick, Common

Descriptive Information
Description: Common brick
Class: Masonry
Comments:
Keywords:

Product Information
Manufacturer:
Model:
Cost:
URL:

Revit Annotation Information
Keynote:
Mark:

Figure A–26

Graphics Tab

In the *Graphics* tab (shown in Figure A–27), you set how a material displays in shaded or hidden line mode.

Identity	Graphics	Appearance	Physical	Thermal

▼ **Shading**
  ☐ Use Render Appearance
  Color: RGB 170 98 104
  Transparency: 0

▼ **Surface Pattern**
  Pattern: **Brick**
  Color: RGB 0 0 0
  Alignment: Texture Alignment...

▼ **Cut Pattern**
  Pattern: **Diagonal up**
  Color: RGB 0 0 0

Figure A–27

- The *Shading* area controls how the material displays when an element is shaded. If you want the shaded view to resemble the rendered view, select **Use Render Appearance**. The color and other options are modified to match the Render Appearance selection. Alternatively, you can set up a color and transparency ratio. Only use this if the render appearance would be too dark or otherwise not suit the use.

- The *Surface Pattern* and *Cut Pattern* areas enable you to select a fill pattern and color to display on a surface or in a section cut. Surface patterns stay true to size. Cut patterns are drafting patterns, which change size according to the view scale.

Appearance Tab

In the *Appearance* tab, you can set different aspects of a rendered material, including **Information**, the type of material (in this example Masonry is selected as shown in Figure A–28) and other parameters depending on the type of material you are working with. Note that changing the asset changes all of the information, so check if that is an option first.

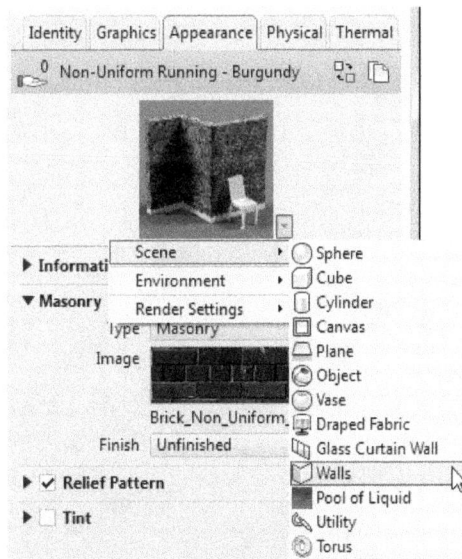

Figure A–28

- You can select how to display the preview of the material by expanding the Scene list next to the graphic, as shown in Figure A–28, above.

- You can modify the *Render Settings* of the preview to either **Draft Quality** or **Production Quality**.

- If you duplicate a material and then change asset-related information (such as the Image or Color) the original material also updates. To prevent this from happening, duplicate or change the asset before making changes.

Physical Tab

In the *Physical* tab, you can specify information about the physical properties of the material. The options vary by material type, as shown in Figure A–29.

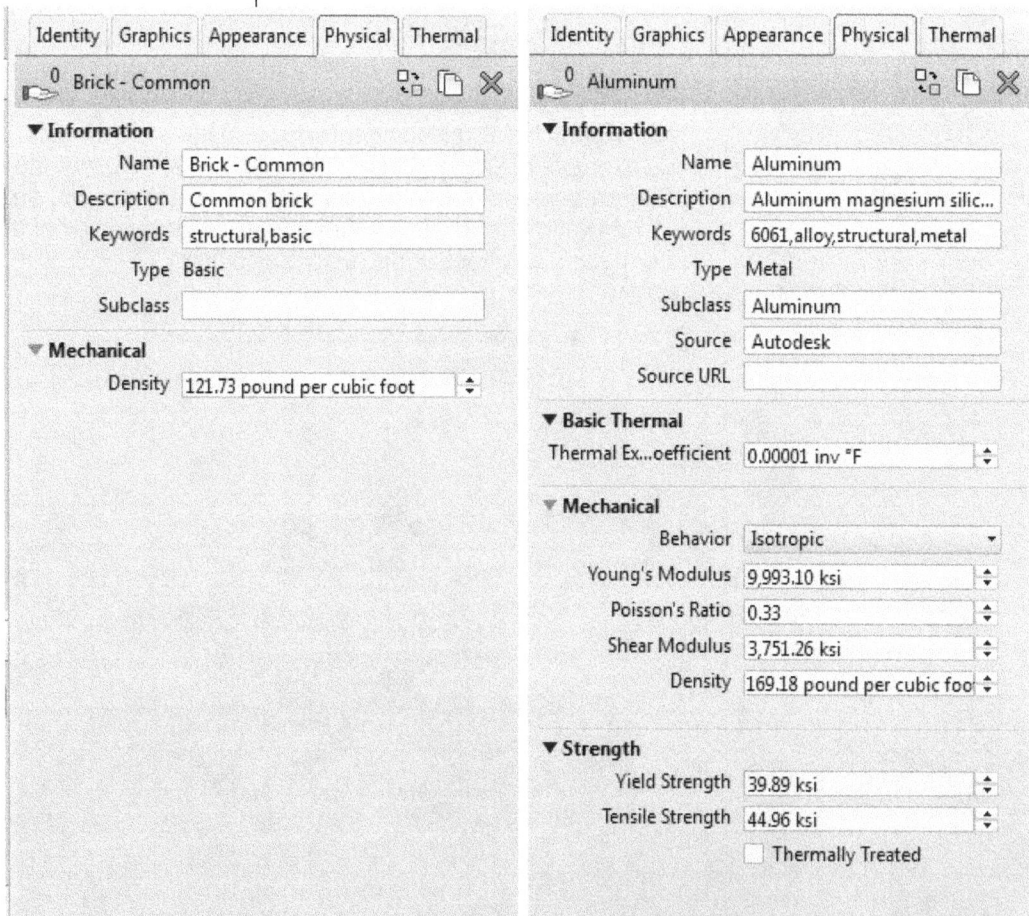

Figure A–29

- Some materials, such as **EPDM Membrane** or **Vapor Retarder**, do not have physical properties, but do have thermal properties.

- Analytical surface and Default materials do not have physical or thermal properties.

- As changing the asset changes all of the information, you should check to see if that is an option first.

Working with Assets

Physical Assets contain preset parameters for materials. These assets are available in the *Appearance*, *Physical* and *Thermal* tabs. Autodesk provides an extensive library of assets that are divided by material type as shown in Figure A–30. You can modify and add assets to materials depending on the variables required in the project.

Figure A–30

How To: Replace an Asset for a Material

1. In the Material Browser, select the material that you want to modify.
2. In the *Appearance*, *Physical*, or *Thermal* tab, click

   (Replaces this asset).
3. In the Asset Browser, hover the cursor over the required

   asset and click (Replaces the current asset in the editor with this asset), as shown in Figure A–30.
4. Close the Asset Browser.

- The assets are filtered by type. Therefore, you need to modify the Appearance asset by clicking through the *Appearance* tab, etc.

- You can create new assets by duplicating an existing one and then modifying the parameters.

A.5 Settings for Mechanical and Electrical Projects

In addition to the standard settings common to all Autodesk Revit projects, the Autodesk Revit MEP software also has specific Mechanical and Electrical settings that can be used in a template or a project.

- In the *Manage* tab>Settings panel, expand ⚏ (MEP Settings) and click ⚏ (Mechanical Settings) or ⚏ (Electrical Settings).

- Additional types of settings include Load Classifications, Demand Factors, and Building/Space Type Settings.

- You can also access the settings in the *Systems* tab by clicking on the related panel, as shown in Figure A–31.

Figure A–31

Mechanical Settings

Mechanical settings enable you to preset many items relating to duct and pipe sizes, conversion settings, and other key defaults, as shown in Figure A–32.

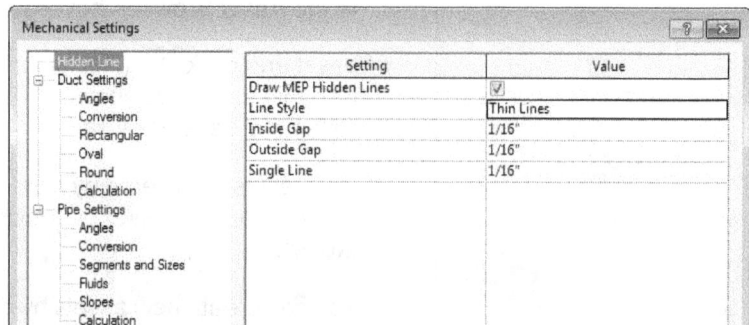

Figure A–32

Hidden Line

If the **Draw MEP Hidden Lines** option is selected, hidden lines are displayed to indicate pipes and ducts that are below other pipes and ducts, as shown in Figure A–33.

Figure A–33

The **Line Style**, **Inside Gap**, and **Outside Gap** options enable you to specify how the hidden lines are displayed.

Angles

In the *Angles* category you can specify the limits on the angles that can be used as ducts or pipes are being drawn, as shown in Figure A–34. This is most often used with piping.

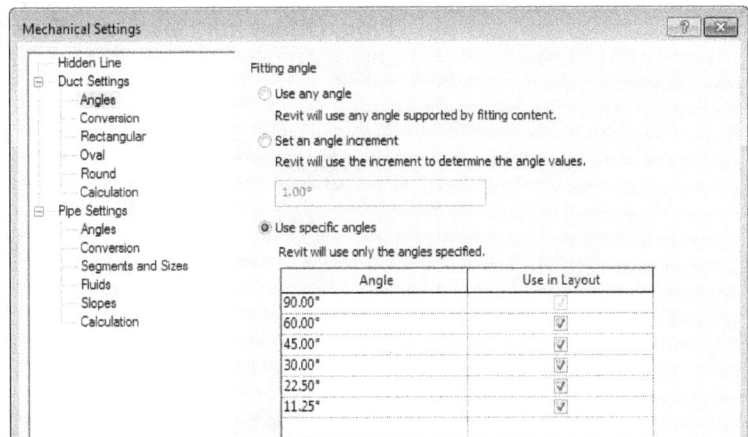

Figure A–34

- The **Duct Settings>Angles** options also include **Set an angle increment** for determining the angle values.

Duct Settings

For the **Single Line Fittings** option, the first two settings relate to how fittings are displayed in a single line view, as shown in Figure A–35. If the **Use Annot. Scale for Single Line Fittings** option is selected, the single line fittings are displayed at the same size on every sheet, regardless of the view scale. The **Duct Fitting Annotation Size** option enables you to specify the size at which the fittings should be displayed.

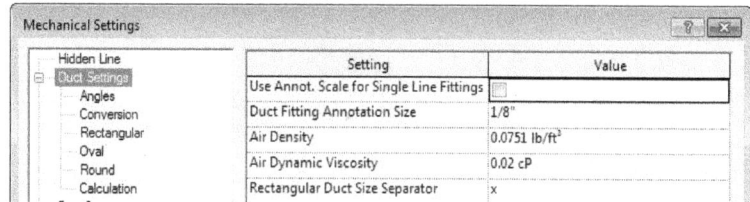

Figure A–35

The **Air Density** and **Air Viscosity** options (not shown) are used when sizing the ducts. The remaining options set the separators and suffixes that are used for duct objects.

Conversion

The *Conversion* area is used to set the routing solutions for ductwork. The settings for the **Main** and **Branch** options can be set separately for each system type. You can specify the **Duct Type**, **Offset** from level, and **Flex Duct Type** settings (this is only applicable to branches), as shown in Figure A–36.

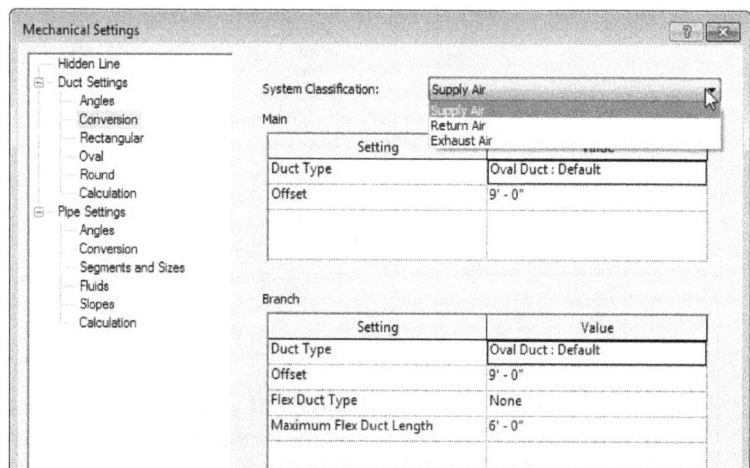

Figure A–36

Rectangular, Oval, and Round

The **Rectangular, Oval,** and **Round** options enable you to adjust the sizing tables. The *Size* column lists all of the sizes. You can click **New Size...** to add a size to the list and **Delete Size** to remove sizes from the list.

In addition, you can specify whether a size is displayed in the size lists (to be available when you place a new duct or select existing ducts) or if the size is used by the sizing routine (automatic sizing of duct branches and systems), as shown in Figure A–37.

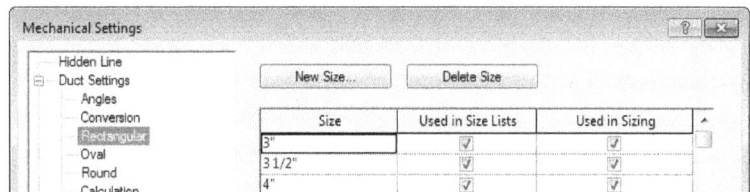

Figure A–37

- For example, if you do not want the sizing routine to use any odd numbered sizes, clear the **Used in Sizing** option for all odd-numbered sizes.

Pipe Settings

Most of the options in the *Pipe Settings* area are identical to or similar to those in the *Duct Settings* area.

Pipe Segments and Sizes

Pipe segment and size settings are more complex due to the many different materials and connections available. Each material has its own roughness, connection types, schedule/types, and sizes that correspond to each combination, as shown in Figure A–38.

Figure A–38

The actual size lists are identical in function to those for ducts, except for the inclusion of the **ID** (inside diameter) and **OD** (outside diameter) parameters.

- Click (Create New Pipe Segment) to open the New Segment dialog box (as shown in Figure A–39), where you specify new Material, and/or Schedule/Type for the segment.

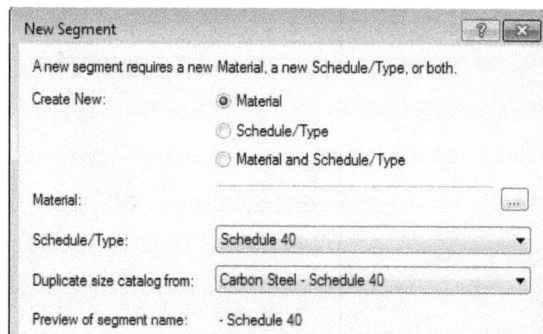

Figure A–39

- To delete a segment, click (Delete Pipe Segment).

Fluids

The *Fluids* area enables you to specify the viscosity and density of fluids at different temperatures, as shown in Figure A–40. You can add or delete fluid types, and for each type, add or delete temperatures.

Figure A–40

Slopes

In the *Slopes* area, you can add or delete typical slopes used in a project, as shown in Figure A–41.

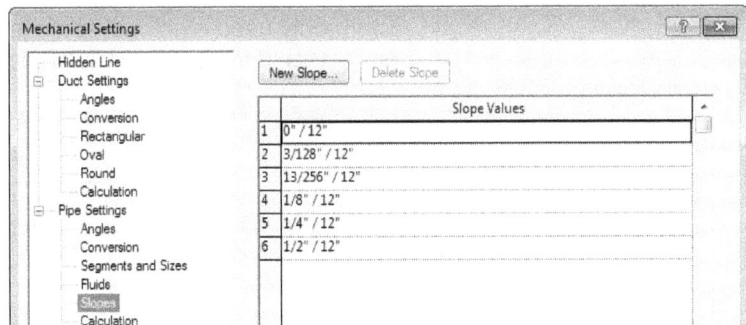

Figure A–41

Calculation

Both Duct and Pipe settings include methods for Pressure Drop that are specific to their needs, as shown for Pipe Settings in Figure A–42. For pipes, the calculation method for converting fixture units to flow for plumbing fixtures is also included.

Figure A–42

Electrical Settings

In the Electrical Settings dialog box, you can preset many options relating to wiring, voltage, cable trays and conduits as well as Load Calculations and Panel Schedules, as shown in Figure A–43. Setting these up in the template for all of the commonly used electrical settings, saves time for individual projects and increases consistency.

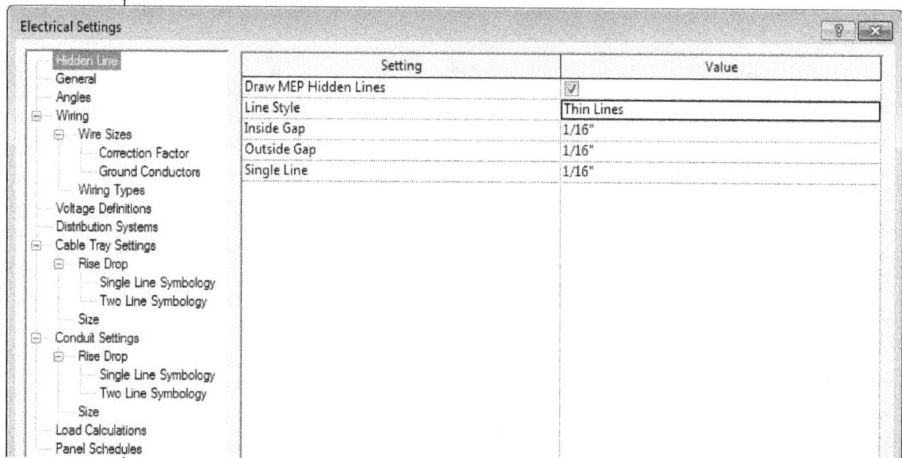

Figure A–43

General

The parameters in the *General* area affect the display of electrical information. The **Electrical Data Style** option sets how the power information is displayed in the **Electrical Data** parameter in the Instance Properties of the electrical component. The **Circuit Description** option sets the formatting of the circuit description.

Wiring

The *Wiring* area enables you to specify the ambient temperature for wiring and some annotation settings related to wiring. The **Tick Mark** families need to be preloaded into the template so that they can be selected in this area, as shown in Figure A–44.

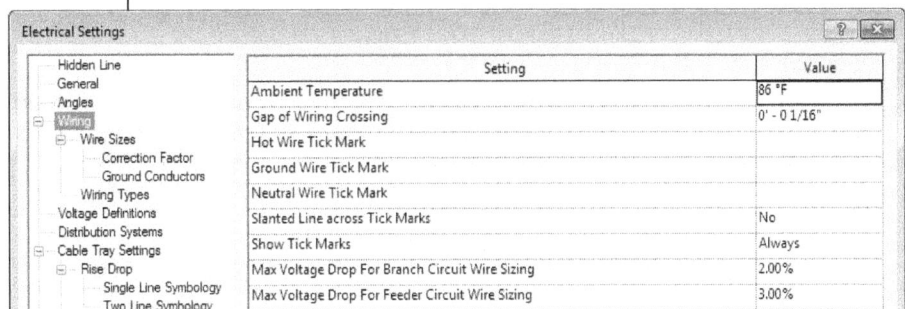

Electrical Settings		
Hidden Line	Setting	Value
General	Ambient Temperature	86 °F
Angles	Gap of Wiring Crossing	0' - 0 1/16"
Wiring	Hot Wire Tick Mark	
Wire Sizes	Ground Wire Tick Mark	
Correction Factor	Neutral Wire Tick Mark	
Ground Conductors	Slanted Line across Tick Marks	No
Wiring Types	Show Tick Marks	Always
Voltage Definitions	Max Voltage Drop For Branch Circuit Wire Sizing	2.00%
Distribution Systems	Max Voltage Drop For Feeder Circuit Wire Sizing	3.00%
Cable Tray Settings		
Rise Drop		
Single Line Symbology		
Two Line Symbology		

Figure A–44

Wire Sizes

The Wire Size settings enable you to create new wire materials, temperature ratings, and insulation types. You can then specify the ampacity, size, diameter, and if the size is used by the wire sizing tools.

• The functionality in the *Wire Sizes* area is similar to that in the *Pipe Sizes* and *Fluids* areas.

Correction Factor

The *Correction Factor* area enables you to specify the correction factors for different temperatures and for each wire type, as shown in Figure A–45.

Figure A–45

Ground Conductors

The Autodesk Revit software sizes ground conductors according to their circuit rating. The *Ground Conductors* area enables you to customize the sizes it uses for each wire material and ampacity, as shown in Figure A–46.

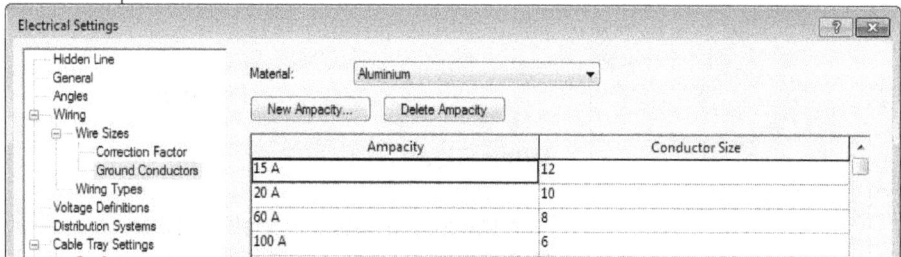

Figure A–46

Wiring Types

The *Wiring Types* area enables you to create wiring types by clicking **Add** and to delete them by clicking **Delete**. You can also specify their properties.

Voltage Definitions

In the *Voltage Definitions* area, you can specify the minimum and maximum voltages of devices that can be added to the distribution systems of a specified voltage. For example, the Autodesk Revit software permits devices ranging from 110V to 130V on a 120V distribution system, as shown in Figure A–47. You can also add or delete definitions.

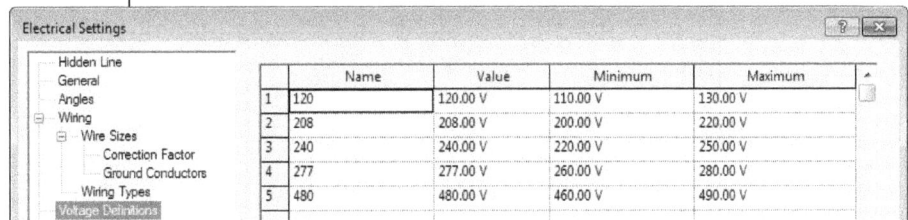

Electrical Settings

	Name	Value	Minimum	Maximum	
1	120	120.00 V	110.00 V	130.00 V	
2	208	208.00 V	200.00 V	220.00 V	
3	240	240.00 V	220.00 V	250.00 V	
4	277	277.00 V	260.00 V	280.00 V	
5	480	480.00 V	460.00 V	490.00 V	

Figure A–47

Distribution Systems

The *Distribution Systems* area sets the distribution systems that are available in your project, as shown in Figure A–48. You can edit the names by selecting them. The options for *Phase* are preset and affect the options that are available in the *Configuration* and *Wires* columns and whether L-L Voltage is available. You can add more systems and delete existing systems if they are not assigned to devices in the current project.

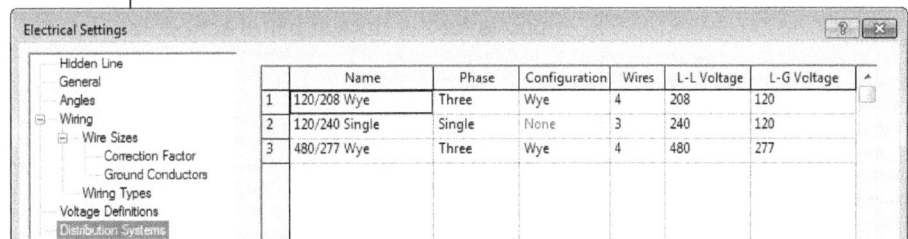

Electrical Settings

	Name	Phase	Configuration	Wires	L-L Voltage	L-G Voltage	
1	120/208 Wye	Three	Wye	4	208	120	
2	120/240 Single	Single	None	3	240	120	
3	480/277 Wye	Three	Wye	4	480	277	

Figure A–48

Cable Tray and Conduit Settings

Cable Trays and Conduits settings include annotation, Rise Drop Symbology, and sizing, as shown in Figure A–49.

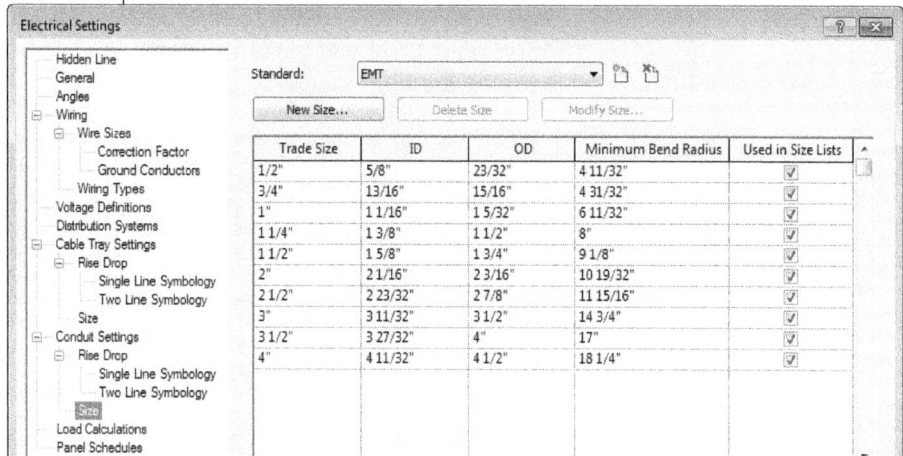

Figure A–49

Load Calculations and Panel Schedules

The *Load Calculations* area gives you access to additional dialog boxes where you can set Load Classifications and Demand Factors.

The *Panel Schedules* area enables you set up labels and other options for the default panel schedule.

A.6 Settings for Structural Projects

In addition to the standard settings common to all aspects of the Autodesk Revit software, there are structural settings that need to be customized.

- In the *Manage* tab>Settings panel, expand Structural Settings and click ⬚ (Structural Settings), or click the arrow in the *Structure* tab>Structure panel title.

- If you are preparing the model for a higher level of detail and have access to the subscription feature, in the *Manage* tab> Settings panel, expand **Structural Settings** and click ⬚ (Connection Settings) to specify these connections.

Symbolic Representation

There are several tabs at the top of the Structural Settings dialog box, as shown in Figure A–50. The first tab, *Symbolic Representation Settings*, contains options that are mainly used for the graphical model and the common defaults.

Figure A–50

The **Symbolic Cutback Distance** setting represents the distance that cuts a framing member back from a column or into another framing member. This cutback distance is symbolic and does not affect the 3D view. For example, in plan, beams do not extend into the column and there is a gap between them, as shown in Figure A–51. The same connection in 3D displays the beams back from the column, which is more consistent with a real-world situation.

Figure A–51

The *Brace Symbols* and *Connection Symbols* areas enable you to specify the kinds of symbols that are shown for the braces in plan, and for frame and shear connections. For many of these items, only one symbol is loaded into the default template.

Load Cases and Load Combinations

Two tabs are related to setting up Load Cases and Load Combinations. These vary by project and by region and typically requires the input of a company's engineer.

* See the *Autodesk Revit Structure Fundamentals* learning guide by ASCENT for additional information about creating Load Cases and Load Combinations.

Analytical Model Settings

The process of modeling a building simultaneously creates a digital model and its corresponding analytical model. As this is done, the software can check for consistency between these two models. The *Analytical Model Settings* tab contains settings for automatic checks, tolerances, and checks, as shown in Figure A–52.

Figure A–52

It is a best practice not to enable **Automatic Checks** in the template, as in the early stages of design there might be many elements that are not supported, causing many warning boxes to open. Automatic Checks are very useful when most of the structure has been modeled and should be enabled at that time.

The values in the *Tolerances* area informs the kind of tolerance that is permitted for supports, differences between the analytical and physical distance, adjusting, and auto-detects. For example, when the **Analytical Model** parameters for a wall are set to auto-detect, the software adjusts the analytical lines, provided it can do so within the specified tolerances.

The *Analytical/Physical Model Consistency Check* area enables you to specify the kinds of consistencies to be checked for.

Boundary Condition Settings

In the last tab, you can select the family symbols used for boundary conditions, as shown in Figure A–53 (from left to right: **Fixed**, **Pinned**, **Roller**, and **User**).

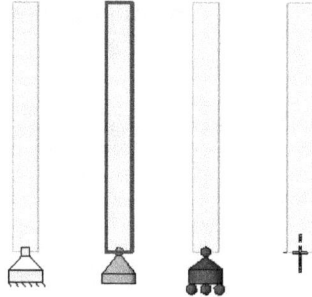

Figure A–53

The structural templates typically include four boundary condition families: **Fixed**, **Pinned**, **Roller**, and **Variable**. They are assigned to the corresponding boundary conditions, as shown in Figure A–54.

Figure A–54

- You can create new boundary condition families, load them into the template, and select them from the drop-down lists as required.

A.7 Sheet List Schedules

Sheet List schedules are used to keep track of all of the sheets in a project and any list sheets that could be added. Sheet lists are often used by architects to display all of the sheets in a building project. This includes any consultant sheets that are not in the architectural project file, as they would only be in the Sheet List schedule and not created as actual sheets.

How To: Create a Sheet List Schedule

1. Open a project template file (or a project).
2. In the *View* tab>Create panel, expand ▦ (Schedules) and click ▥ (Sheet List).
3. In the Sheet List Properties dialog box, in the *Fields* tab, select the **Sheet Number** and **Sheet Name** and add them to the *Scheduled fields* list, as shown in Figure A–55.

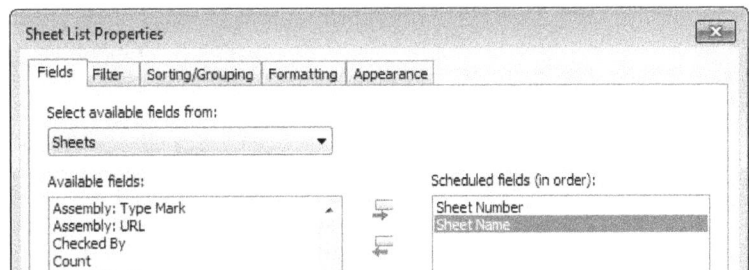

Figure A–55

4. Depending on the complexity of your sheet naming scheme, you can also modify items on the *Filter* and *Sorting/Grouping* tabs.
5. Click **OK** when you are finished.
6. You are placed in the schedule view with the two parameters displayed. Stretch out the columns as shown in Figure A–56.

Figure A–56

If sheets are already in the project, they display here.

7. In the *Modify Schedule/Quantities* tab>Rows panel, click

   ▦ (Insert Data Row).

8. A new row is added below the schedule names. If no sheets are in the project, it comes in automatically as **A101** and **Unnamed**.

9. Add as many rows as you have sheets. If you are using a numbering scheme such as A1xx for site plans, A2xx for Floor Plans, A3xx for Detail plans, etc., then you should rename the sheet number for the first row of a set before creating more rows so that they increment automatically.

10. Enter the name of each sheet. Once you have added a new name, it is available in the drop-down list, as shown in Figure A–57.

	<Sheet List>	
A	**B**	
Sheet Number	Sheet Name	
CS000	Cover Sheet	
A201	First Floor Plan	
A202	Second Floor Plan	
A203	Fifth Floor Plan	
A204	First Floor Plan	
A205	Fouth Floor Plan	
A206	Second Floor Plan	
A101	Site Plan	
	Sixth Floor Plan	
	Third Floor Plan	

Figure A–57

How To: Use Sheet List Tables

1. Create a new sheet. In the Sheet List Schedule view, in the

   Modify Schedule/Quantities tab>Create panel, click 🗋 (New Sheet), You can also access the command on the *View* tab or right-click on *Sheets* in the Project Browser.

2. In the New Sheet dialog box, select the placeholder sheets you want to use, as shown in Figure A–58. To select more than one, hold <Ctrl> or <Shift> as you select.

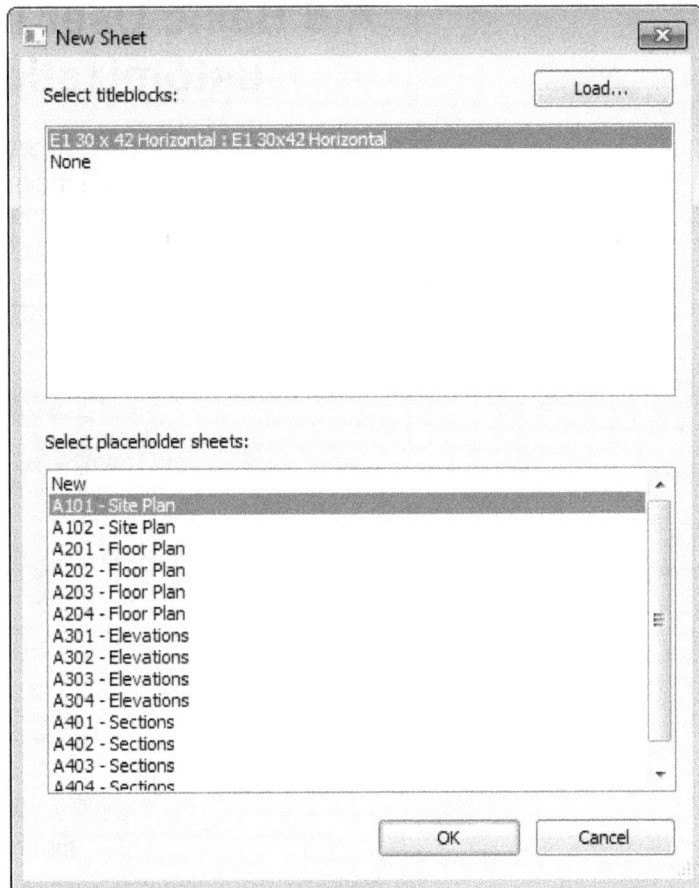

Figure A–58

3. Click **OK**. The new sheets are created in the project.

- This sheet list is available in all projects based on the project template where it was created.

- You can import the sheet list schedule into another project, but it does not import the associated sheets. That is because they are part of the project, not the schedule view.

A.8 Basic User Interface Customization

The Revit User Interface has a variety of features that can be customized. From moving ribbon panels around by dragging and dropping them to a new location, to the activation and location of palettes, and items that display on the status bar. For example, if you do not use Design Options you can clean up the Status Bar by clearing **Status Bar - Design Options**, as shown in Figure A–59.

Figure A–59

You can also customize other parts of the Autodesk Revit software, including which tabs are displayed in the ribbon, customizing keyboard shortcuts, specifying how the double-click functions work and setting up the Project Browser organization.

Configuring the Ribbon

The Autodesk® Revit® software is used by many different disciplines including Architecture, Structure, Mechanical, Electrical, and Plumbing. All of these tools are setup to display in the ribbon by default. Most users only need access to a specific set of tools and the interface can be customized to suit those needs.

How To: Configure the Ribbon to Suit Your Needs

1. In the *File* tab, click **Options**.
2. In the Options dialog box, in the left pane, select **User Interface**.
3. In the *Configure* area, under *Tools and analyses* (as shown in Figure A–60), clear all of options that you do not want to use.

You are not deleting these tools, just removing them from the current user interface.

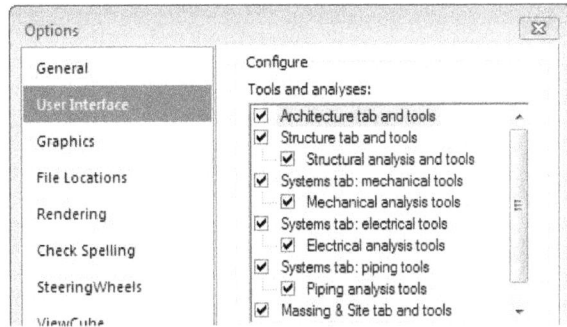

Figure A–60

Customizing Shortcuts

A helpful customization is to set up the keyboard shortcuts for frequently used commands. These are not saved by project, but on each computer. To display the shortcuts that are already available, hover the cursor over a tool, such as **Wall**, to display the tooltip that displays the associated shortcut, as shown in Figure A–61.

When you type keyboard shortcuts, you do not need to press <Enter> or the <Spacebar>.

Figure A–61

How To: Customize the Keyboard Shortcuts

1. In the *View* tab>Windows panel, expand ⬚ (User Interface), and click ⬚ (Keyboard Shortcuts) or, in the Application Menu, click **Options**. In the Options dialog box, in the *User Interface* pane, in the *Configure* area, next to *Keyboard shortcuts:* click **Customize...**.

2. In the Keyboard Shortcuts dialog box, use **Search** or **Filter** to narrow the search, as shown in Figure A–62.

Figure A–62

3. Select the command that you want to add or modify.
4. In the Press new keys edit box, type the shortcut that you want to use, as shown in Figure A–63, and click **Assign**.

If a shortcut has already been assigned, you can still use it. Press the <Spacebar> to cycle through the options.

Figure A–63

5. Click **OK** when you have finished.

• To remove shortcuts, select the shortcut, and click **Remove**.

• You can import or export the shortcut file to be used in other stations of the Autodesk Revit software than the one on which they were created. When you export to XML, all of the commands are exported. You can then add the required shortcuts to the XML file and import them into your program.

Customizing Double-click Settings

When you double-click on elements, you can specify what you want this to do. For example, by default, double-clicking on a family, such as a chair, column, or plumbing fixture, opens the element in the Family Editor. In most cases that is not something you want to do, editing the type would be better. You can change this in the Customize Double-click Settings dialog box, as shown in Figure A–64.

Figure A–64

How To: Customize Double-Click Settings

1. In the *File* tab, click **Options**.
2. In the Options dialog box, in the *User Interface* pane, in the *Configure* area, next to *Double-click Options:* click **Customize...**.
3. Select the method that you want to use for each of the element types.

Customizing the Browser Organization

The name of the current organization type is in parentheses.

The Project Browser is the heart of the Autodesk Revit software. It is where you access all of the different views, sheets, family types, etc. When working with complex projects, it can help to organize the views and sheets so that it is most useful to the methods used in your firm. It is easy to switch between different organizations and you can create custom ones to suit your work.

- To switch between existing organization types, in the Project Browser, select the **Views** node at the top of the palette, and in the Type Selector, select the type that you want to use, as shown in Figure A–65.

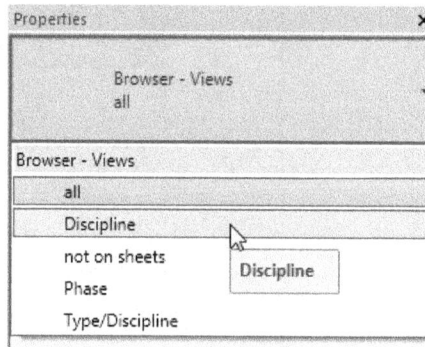

Figure A–65

- You can also switch sheet organizations by selecting the *Sheets* node and changing the type in the Type Selector.

How To: Customize the Browser Organization

1. In the *View* tab>Windows panel, expand (User Interface), and click (Browser Organization) or, in the Project Browser, right-click on the *Views* or *Sheets* node and select **Browser Organization**.
2. In the Browser Organization dialog box, select the *Views* or *Sheets* tab, and click **New**.
3. Name the new browser organization and click **OK**.
4. In the Browser Organization Properties dialog box, in the *Filtering* tab, specify the filtering rules, as required.
5. In the *Grouping and Sorting* tab, assign the various groups as required. The example shown in Figure A–66 is by discipline, an organization that is used most often in the MEP templates.

Figure A–66

6. Click **OK** to finish the property changes.
7. In the Browser Organization dialog box, you can continue to create the new organization and then select the current organization. Click **Apply** between sets if you are creating multiple organizations. Click **OK** when you have finished.

• In the Options dialog box, in the *General* tab, in the *View Options* area, you can set the *Default view discipline* that is used when you create new views, such as sections, callouts, and elevations, as shown in Figure A–67.

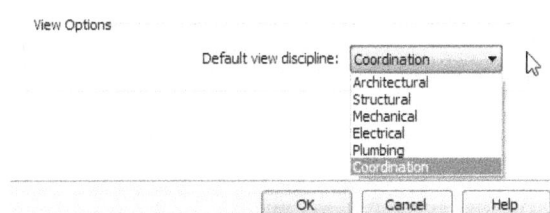

Figure A–67

• When you duplicate a view, it automatically assumes the discipline and other view properties of the original view.

Command Summary

Button	Command	Location
	Arrowheads	• **Ribbon:** *Manage* tab>Settings panel> expand Additional Settings
	Browser Organization	• **Ribbon:** *View* tab>Windows panel> expand User Interface • **Application Menu:** Options>*User Interface* tab
	Electrical Settings	• **Autodesk Revit MEP** • **Ribbon:** *Manage* tab>Settings panel> expand MEP Settings
	Fill Patterns	• **Ribbon**: *Manage* tab>Settings panel> expand Additional Settings
	Keyboard Shortcuts	• **Ribbon:** *View* tab>Windows panel> expand User Interface • **Application Menu:** Options>*User Interface* tab
	Line Patterns	• **Ribbon:** *Manage* tab>Settings panel> expand Additional Settings
	Line Styles	• **Ribbon:** *Manage* tab>Settings panel> expand Additional Settings
	Line Weights	• **Ribbon:** *Manage* tab>Settings panel> expand Additional Settings
	Materials	• **Ribbon**: *Manage* tab>Settings panel
	Mechanical Settings	• **Autodesk Revit MEP** • **Ribbon:** *Manage* tab>Settings panel> expand MEP Settings
	Object Styles	• **Ribbon:** *Manage* tab>Settings panel
Options	**Options**	• **Application Menu**
	Structural Settings	• **Autodesk Revit Structure** • **Ribbon:** *Manage* tab>Settings panel
	Temporary Dimensions	• **Ribbon:** *Manage* tab>Settings panel> expand Additional Settings

Autodesk Revit Architecture Certification Exam Objectives

The following table will help you to locate the exam objectives in the chapters of the Autodesk® Revit® learning guides to help you prepare for the Autodesk Revit Architecture Certified Professional exam.

Exam Topic	Exam Objective	Learning Guide	Chapter & Section(s)
Collaboration			
	Copy and monitor elements in a linked file	• Revit Collaboration Tools	• 2.3
	Use worksharing	• Revit Collaboration Tools	• 4.1, 4.2, 4.3
	Import DWG and image files	• Revit Architecture Fundamentals	• 3.4
		• Revit Collaboration Tools	• 3.1, 3.2, 3.3
	Use Worksharing Visualization	• Revit Collaboration Tools	• 4.4
	Assess review warnings in Revit	• Revit Architecture Fundamentals	• 12.1

Exam Topic	Exam Objective	Learning Guide	Chapter & Section(s)
Documentation			
	Create and modify filled regions	• Revit Architecture Fundamentals	• 16.3
	Place detail components and repeating details	• Revit Architecture Fundamentals	• 16.2
	Tag elements (doors, windows, etc.) by category	• Revit Architecture Fundamentals	• 15.1
	Use dimension strings	• Revit Architecture Fundamentals	• 14.1
	Set the colors used in a color scheme legend	• Revit Architecture: Conceptual Design and Visualization	• 2.3
	Work with phases	• Revit Collaboration Tools	• 1.1
Elements and Families			
	Change elements within a curtain wall (grids, panels, mullions	• Revit Architecture Fundamentals	• 6.2, 6.3, 6.4
	Create compound walls	• Revit BIM Management	• 3.1
	Create a stacked wall	• Revit BIM Management	• 3.3
	Differentiate system and component families	• Revit BIM Management	• 3.1 • 4.1
	Work with family parameters	• Revit BIM Management	• 4.2
	Create a new family type	• Revit Architecture Fundamentals	• 5.3
		• Revit BIM Management	• 4.4
	Use family creation procedures	• Revit BIM Management	• 4.1 to 4.4

Exam Topic	Exam Objective	Learning Guide	Chapter & Section(s)
Modeling			
	Create a building pad	• Revit Architecture: Site and Structure	• 1.2
	Define floor for a mass	• Revit Architecture: Conceptual Design and Visualization	• 1.7
	Create a stair with a landing	• Revit Architecture Fundamentals	• 12.1
	Create elements such as floors, ceilings, or roofs	• Revit Architecture Fundamentals	• 9.1 • 10.1 • 11.2, 11.4
	Generate a toposurface	• Revit Architecture: Site and Structure	• 1.1
	Model railings	• Revit Architecture Fundamentals	• 12.3
	Edit a model element's material (door, window, furniture)	• Revit Architecture Fundamentals	• 5.3 • B.4
	Change a generic floor / ceiling / roof to a specific type	• Revit Architecture Fundamentals	• 9.1 • 10.1 • 11.2
	Attach walls to a roof or ceiling	• Revit Architecture Fundamentals	• 11.2
	Edit room-aware families	• Revit BIM Management	• 5.1
Views			
	Define element properties in a schedule	• Revit Architecture Fundamentals	• 15.3
	Control visibility	• Revit Architecture Fundamentals	• 7.1
	Use levels	• Revit Architecture Fundamentals	• 3.1
	Create a duplicate view for a plan, section, elevation, drafting view, etc.	• Revit Architecture Fundamentals	• 7.2
	Create and manage legends	• Revit Architecture Fundamentals	• 14.4
	Manage view position on sheets	• Revit Architecture Fundamentals	• 13.2
	Organize and sort items in a schedule	• Revit Architecture Fundamentals	• B.10
		• Revit BIM Management	• 2.2

Appendix
C

Autodesk Revit MEP Electrical Certification Exam Objectives

The following table will help you to locate the exam objectives in the chapters of the Autodesk® Revit® learning guides to help you prepare for the Autodesk Revit MEP Electrical Certified Professional exam.

Exam Topic	Exam Objective	Learning Guide	Chapter & Section(s)
Collaboration	Import AutoCAD files into Revit	• Revit Collaboration Tools	• 3.1
	Link Revit models	• Revit MEP Fundamentals	• 4.1
	Copy levels and setup monitoring	• Revit MEP Fundamentals	• 4.2 & 4.3
	Create floor plans	• Revit MEP Fundamentals	• 4.2
	Use Worksets	• Revit Collaboration Tools	• 4.1 to 4.3
	Resolve Coordination Review Errors	• Revit MEP Fundamentals	• 4.5
Documentation	Electrical: Tag components	• Revit MEP Fundamentals	• 14.1
	Create sheets	• Revit MEP Fundamentals	• 12.1
	Electrical: Create panel schedules	• Revit MEP Fundamentals	• 11.4
	Add and modify text	• Revit MEP Fundamentals	• 13.2
	Add and modify dimensions	• Revit MEP Fundamentals	• 13.1
Elements	Differentiate system and component families	• Revit BIM Management	• 3.1 • 4.1
	Edit Family Connectors	• Revit BIM Management	• 5.1
	Create a new family type	• Revit BIM Management	• 4.4

Exam Topic	Exam Objective	Learning Guide	Chapter & Section(s)
Modeling	Electrical: Add and modify receptacles	• Revit MEP Fundamentals	• 11.2
	Electrical: Add and modify panels	• Revit MEP Fundamentals	• 11.2
	Electrical: Create and modify circuits	• Revit MEP Fundamentals	• 11.3
	Electrical: Add and modify lighting fixtures	• Revit MEP Fundamentals	• 11.2
	Electrical: Add and modify switches	• Revit MEP Fundamentals	• 11.2
	Electrical: Create and modify lighting circuits	• Revit MEP Fundamentals	• 11.3
	Electrical: Create and modify switching circuits	• Revit MEP Fundamentals	• 11.3
	Electrical: Add and modify conduit	• Revit MEP Fundamentals	• 11.5
	Electrical: Use cable trays	• Revit MEP Fundamentals	• 11.5
	Electrical: Add and modify switch systems	• Revit MEP Fundamentals	• 11.3
	Electrical: Create Distribution System	• Revit MEP Fundamentals	• 11.1
	Electrical: Add and modify security devices	• Revit MEP Fundamentals	• 11.2
	Electrical: Add and modify wiring	• Revit MEP Fundamentals	• 11.3
	Electrical: Generate automatic wire layouts	• Revit MEP Fundamentals	• 11.3
	Electrical: Check circuits and disconnects	• Revit MEP Fundamentals	• 11.6
	Perform interference check	• Revit Collaboration Tools	• 2.4
	Electrical: Work with Spaces	• Revit MEP Fundamentals	• 6.1 to 6.3
	Electrical: Perform a Lighting Analysis	• Revit MEP Fundamentals	• 11.6
	Electrical: Work with Fire Alarm Devices	• Revit MEP Fundamentals	• 11.2
	Electrical: Work with Site Lighting	• Revit MEP Fundamentals	• 11.2
Views	View models	• Revit MEP Fundamentals	• 1.4
	Apply view templates	• Revit MEP Fundamentals	• 6.1
	Create detail views	• Revit MEP Fundamentals	• 15.1
	Electrical: Create and label wiring plans	• Revit MEP Fundamentals	• 5.2 • 11.3 • 13.1 to 13.3 • 14.1

Autodesk Revit MEP Mechanical Certification Exam Objectives

The following table will help you to locate the exam objectives in the chapters of the Autodesk® Revit® learning guides to help you prepare for the Autodesk Revit MEP Mechanical Certified Professional exam.

Exam Topic	Exam Objective	Learning Guide	Chapter & Section(s)
Collaboration	Import AutoCAD files into Revit	• Revit Collaboration Tools	• 3.1
	Link Revit models	• Revit MEP Fundamentals	• 4.1
	Copy levels and setup monitoring	• Revit MEP Fundamentals	• 4.2 & 4.3
	Create floor plans	• Revit MEP Fundamentals	• 4.2
	Use Worksets	• Revit Collaboration Tools	• 4.1 to 4.3
	Resolve Coordination Review Errors	• Revit MEP Fundamentals	• 4.5
Documentation	Mechanical: Tag ducts and piping	• Revit MEP Fundamentals	• 14.1
	Create sheets	• Revit MEP Fundamentals	• 12.1
	Add and modify text	• Revit MEP Fundamentals	• 13.2
	Add and modify dimensions	• Revit MEP Fundamentals	• 13.1
	Mechanical: Create duct/pipe legends	• Revit MEP Fundamentals	• B.3

Exam Topic	Exam Objective	Learning Guide	Chapter & Section(s)
Elements	Differentiate system and component families	• Revit BIM Management	• 3.1 • 4.1
	Edit Family Connectors	• Revit BIM Management	• 5.1
	Create a new family type	• Revit BIM Management	• 4.4
Modeling	Mechanical: Add and use mechanical equipment	• Revit MEP Fundamentals	• 8.1
	Mechanical: Add and modify air terminals	• Revit MEP Fundamentals	• 8.1
	Mechanical: Add and modify ducts	• Revit MEP Fundamentals	• 8.2 & 8.3
	Mechanical: Add and modify return ducts	• Revit MEP Fundamentals	• 8.2 & 8.3
	Mechanical: Add and modify duct accessories and fittings	• Revit MEP Fundamentals	• 8.3
	Mechanical: Work with heating and cooling zones	• Revit MEP Fundamentals	• 7.1
	Plumbing: Add and modify fixtures	• Revit MEP Fundamentals	• 9.1
	Plumbing: Add and modify piping	• Revit MEP Fundamentals	• 9.2
	Plumbing: Add and use plumbing equipment	• Revit MEP Fundamentals	• 9.1
	Plumbing: Create a plumbing system	• Revit MEP Fundamentals	• 10.1
	Plumbing: Add and modify pipe accessories	• Revit MEP Fundamentals	• 9.3
	Mechanical: Add and modify placeholder duct	• Revit MEP Fundamentals	• 8.2
	Mechanical: Define a duct system	• Revit MEP Fundamentals	• 10.1
	Mechanical: Add and modify placeholder duct	• Revit MEP Fundamentals	• 8.2 & 8.3
	Mechanical: Define a duct system	• Revit MEP Fundamentals	• 10.1
	Mechanical: Work with spaces	• Revit MEP Fundamentals	• 6.1 to 6.3
	Plumbing: Add and modify placeholder pipe	• Revit MEP Fundamentals	• 9.2
	Size duct and pipe systems	• Revit MEP Fundamentals	• 8.3
	Perform interference check	• Revit Collaboration Tools	• 2.4
	Check duct and pipe systems and disconnects	• Revit MEP Fundamentals	• 10.3

Exam Topic	Exam Objective	Learning Guide	Chapter & Section(s)
Views	View models	• Revit MEP Fundamentals	• 1.4
	Apply view templates	• Revit MEP Fundamentals	• 6.1
	Create detail views	• Revit MEP Fundamentals	• 15.1
	Mechanical: Create and label HVAC plans	• Revit MEP Fundamentals	• 5.2 • 13.1 to 13.3 • 14.1
	Plumbing: Create a plumbing view	• Revit MEP Fundamentals	• 5.1
	Plumbing: Create and label plumbing plans	• Revit MEP Fundamentals	• 5.2 • 13.1 to 13.3 • 14.1

Autodesk Revit Structure Certification Exam Objectives

The following table will help you to locate the exam objectives within the chapters of the Autodesk® Revit® learning guides to help you prepare for the Autodesk Revit Structure Certified Professional exam.

Exam Topic	Exam Objective	Learning Guide	Chapter & Section(s)
Collaboration	Create and modify levels	• Revit Structure Fundamentals	• 3.3
	Create and modify structural grids	• Revit Structure Fundamentals	• 5.1
	Import AutoCAD files into Revit	• Revit Structure Fundamentals	• 3.1
		• Revit Collaboration Tools	• 3.1
	Link Revit models	• Revit Structure Fundamentals	• 3.2
		• Revit Collaboration Tools	• 2.1
	Control the visibility for linked objects	• Revit Collaboration Tools	• 2.2
Documentation	Using temporary dimensions	• Revit Structure Fundamentals	• 2.1
	Annotate beams	• Revit Structure Fundamentals	• 13.3
	Add and modify text annotations	• Revit Structure Fundamentals	• 13.2
	Add and use dimensions and dimension labels	• Revit Structure Fundamentals	• 13.1
	Use detail components	• Revit Structure Fundamentals	• 14.2
	Create and modify column schedules	• Revit Structure Fundamentals	• 15.2

Exam Topic	Exam Objective	Learning Guide	Chapter & Section(s)
Documentation *(continued)*	Create and modify footing schedules	• Revit Structure Fundamentals	• 15.3 • B.8
		• Revit BIM Management	• 2.2
	Create and modify standard sheets	• Revit Structure Fundamentals	• 12.1, 12.2
Modeling	Place and modify structural columns	• Revit Structure Fundamentals	• 5.2
	Place and modify walls	• Revit Structure Fundamentals	• 6.1
	Create custom wall types	• Revit BIM Management	• 3.1
	Place footings	• Revit Structure Fundamentals	• 6.2, 6.4
	Create concrete slabs and/or floors	• Revit Structure Fundamentals	• 8.1
	Create and modify stepped walls in foundations	• Revit Structure Fundamentals	• 6.2
	Place rebar	• Revit Structure Fundamentals	• 9.2
	Add beams	• Revit Structure Fundamentals	• 7.1
	Add beam systems	• Revit Structure Fundamentals	• 7.1
	Add joists	• Revit Structure Fundamentals	• 7.1
	Add cross bracing to joists	• Revit Structure Fundamentals	• 7.1
	Create and use trusses	• Revit Structure Fundamentals	• 7.3
	Create and modify floors	• Revit Structure Fundamentals	• 8.1
	Create and modify custom floors	• Revit BIM Management	• 3.1
	Create and modify sloped floors	• Revit Architecture Fundamentals	• 9.3
	Add floor openings for stairs	• Revit Structure Fundamentals	• 8.2
	Create and modify stairs	• Revit Architecture Fundamentals	• 12.1
	Create and modify ramps	• Revit Architecture Fundamentals	• 12.5
	Model and use roofs	• Revit Structure Fundamentals	• 8.1
		• Revit Architecture Fundamentals	• 11.2, 11.4
Views	Create section views	• Revit Structure Fundamentals	• 4.4
	Create framing elevations	• Revit Structure Fundamentals	• 4.4
	Use callout views	• Revit Structure Fundamentals	• 4.3

Index

V

W